I0356192

The Tamil Auxiliary Verb System

The Tamil Auxiliary Verb System introduces the syntactic process of auxiliary formation and applies it to the grammatical analysis of the indicative, or non-modal, auxiliary verbs of Modern Tamil. Data from the spoken and written registers, gathered over several years, form the basis of this synchronic study, which focuses on the semantic and syntactic properties of twenty-four auxiliary verbs.

This book demonstrates for the first time the systematic nature of auxiliary verb phenomena and how they are integrated into the grammar of the language. Discoveries are presented at several levels of Tamil grammar: morphology, syntax, semantics and pragmatics, new constructions, verbal categories and tenses are all analysed. This book will have further implications for historical and typological linguistics, particularly as they bear on the formation of the compound verbs as an isogloss feature of the South Asian linguistic area.

The Tamil Auxiliary Verb System will be of interest to linguists, Dravidian scholars and students of Tamil.

Sanford B. Steever holds three degrees in linguistics and a diploma in Tamil. The author of four books and fifty articles on Historical Linguistics, Syntax, Dravidian Linguistics and Tamil, he spent three years of study and fieldwork in India. He is the editor of *The Dravidian Language* (1997).

Routledge Asian Linguistics Series

Editor-in-Chief:
Walter Bisang, Mainz University
Associate Editors:
R. V. Dhongde, Deccan College, Pune and Masayoshi Shibatani, Rice University, Texas

Asia is the world's largest continent, comprising an enormous wealth of languages, both in its present as well as in its eventful past. The series contributes to the understanding of this linguistic variety by publishing books from different theoretical backgrounds and different methodological approaches, dealing with at least one Asian language. By adopting a maximally integrative policy, the editors of the series hope to promote theoretical discussions whose solutions may, in turn, help to overcome the theoretical lean towards West European languages and thus provide a deeper understanding of Asian linguistic structures and of human language in general.

VIETNAMESE-ENGLISH BILINGUALISM
Patterns of code-switching
Ho-Dac Tuc

LINGUISTIC EPIDEMIOLOGY
Semantics and grammar of language contact in mainland Southeast Asia
Nick J. Enfield

A GRAMMAR OF MANGGHUER
A Mongolic language of China's Qinghai-Gansu Sprachbund
Keith W. Slater

FUNCTIONAL STRUCTURE(S), FORM AND INTERPRETATION
Perspectives from East Asian languages
Edited by Yen-hui Audrey Li and Andrew Simpson

FOCUS AND BACKGROUND MARKING IN MANDARIN CHINESE
System and theory behind ***cai***, ***jiu***, ***dou*** and ***ye***
Daniel Hole

GRAMMATICALIZATION AND LANGUAGE CHANGE IN CHINESE
A formal view
Xiu-Zhi Zoe Wu

TAMIL AUXILIARY VERB SYSTEM
Sanford B. Steever

The Tamil Auxiliary Verb System

Sanford B. Steever

Routledge
Taylor & Francis Group
LONDON AND NEW YORK

First published 2005 by Routledge

2 Park Square, Milton Park, Abingdon, Oxon OX14 4RN
711 Third Avenue, New York, NY 10017, USA

Routledge is an imprint of the Taylor & Francis Group, an informa business

First issued in paperback 2016

Typeset in New Times Roman and Transindic Transliterator by SBS

British Library Cataloguing in Publication Data
A catalogue record for this book is available from the British Library

Library of Congress Cataloguing in Publication Data
A catalog record for this book has been requested

ISBN 978-1-138-99673-1 (pbk)
ISBN 978-0-415-34672-6 (hbk)

To the memory of:

James D. McCawley (1938-1999)

K. Paramasivam (1933-1993)

A.K. Ramanujan (1929-1993)

Contents

Contents *vii*
Preface *ix*
Acknowledgement *xii*
Abbreviations and conventions *xiv*
List of figures and tables *xvi*

1 Auxiliary Formation 1

2 The Tamil background 31

3 Tamil verb morphology 53

4 The internal syntax of the Tamil indicative AVC 88

5 The external syntax of the Tamil indicative AVC 144

6 The major indicative auxiliary verbs of Tamil 167

7 The minor indicative auxiliary verbs of Tamil 209

8 Auxiliaries of attitude and abuse 239

9 Conclusion 290

Bibliography 303
Index 310

Preface

How does a book—an entire book—come to be written on the Tamil auxiliary verb system? My interest in the topic dates back thirty years when I began to study the language. Almost from the beginning, it became clear that I would not be able to navigate a sentence of the language, much less hold a conversation, without coming to grips with auxiliary verbs. That these phenomena came to loom so large in my consciousness now seems to me to be due to two facets of Tamil grammar. First, the language distinguishes just two major parts of speech, noun and verb. Second, and cognizant of the need to describe languages *sui generis*, verbs in Tamil are from a cross-linguistic perspective endowed with relatively modest inflections. These two factors narrowed my attention until it came to rest on one of the primary ways in which Tamil elaborates its system of basic verb forms: through the generation of numerous auxiliary verb constructions.

Studying Tamil was just one current in my linguistics education. As a graduate student at Chicago, I concentrated mainly on the trinity of syntax, semantics and pragmatics, although my eye would also wander to phonetics, morphology, typology and historical linguistics, particularly comparative Dravidian linguistics. After three years of course work in Chicago, I spent a year in Tamil Nadu to sharpen my Tamil language skills, and perhaps find myself a dissertation topic. In the end, four years of courses, including one year of intensive study, proved insufficient to answer all my questions about Tamil auxiliaries, and following examinations in Chicago, I returned to India on a research fellowship to carry out research on the syntax, semantics and pragmatics of the Tamil auxiliary verb system. The book now before you is a reworking of my doctoral dissertation, *A study in auxiliation: the grammar of the indicative auxiliary verb system of Tamil*, which was submitted to the Linguistics Department of the University of Chicago two decades ago.

In a field that evolves as rapidly as linguistics, publishing a work so long after its initial composition may entail a number of risks, not the least of which concerns its relevance to current linguistic issues. Nevertheless, several reasons may be cited for undertaking a revision of this work which seem to outweigh the risks that its publication might raise. They are noted here briefly starting with the more specific ones, of interest primarily to specialists in Tamil, and progressing to the more general, of concern to general linguists who might otherwise feel no need to consult a specialist study of the Tamil verb system.

First, apart from a scattering of articles, virtually nothing new has been published on the Tamil auxiliary verb system in the intervening twenty years, and—the fate of many a dissertation—those few that have made it into print do not take into account the findings originally presented in my dissertation. As a consequence, many of the conclusions drawn here, as well as the data and arguments on which they rest, are made explicit for the first time. The original contents have been supplemented with further material gathered during a third, postdoctoral year in India, as well as examples from my continued reading of modern linguistics and Tamil literature. Tamil grammatical phenomena in fields as diverse as morphology and semantics, syntax and pragmatics, are extensively described and analyzed here for the first time; in other instances, new interpretations are given to a number of phenomena obliquely noted in the literature, but barely touched upon. Given its breadth of coverage, then, this book may among its other uses serve as a reference work for Tamil verbal morphology and syntax.

Second, much of the material that is presented here was assumed in my previous book *Analysis to Synthesis*, a study in comparative Dravidian linguistics of some of the diachronic implications of a model that was originally proposed for the synchronic study of the Tamil auxiliary. Publishing this book now is, in effect, redeeming a promissory note that I issued to the readers of that earlier one.

Third, interest among linguists in auxiliary verbs has never abated because these phenomena have achieved a certain prominence in the development of generative grammar. Early on, Chomsky's 1957 analysis of English auxiliaries in *Syntactic Structures* attained the status of an exemplar in the paradigm of classical transformational grammar. And today, the study of auxiliaries still captures the imagination of linguists, particularly in studies of typology and grammaticalization. But the model that is used here, based on an article published by Benveniste 1965, is little known and has had virtually no impact on the practice of modern linguistics. Understandably, Chomsky's *Aspects of the Theory of Syntax*, published in the same year, overshadowed most everything else that linguists were reading then. Even so, as this book hopes to show, Benveniste's model for analyzing auxiliary verb phenomena remains worthwhile, and has enduring utility in the description and explanation of auxiliary verb phenomena.

In revising this work, I had to make two kinds of omission. First, and the more regrettable of the two, in order to shrink the original manuscript to a more manageable size, I had to leave out multiple attestations of certain Tamil phenomena so that in many places, two examples must now make do where formerly there were five or six. Second, and less crucial, I have omitted a several sections, notably comparisons with other models of linguistic analysis, that I now regard as either premature or no longer germane. In updating the text, no attempt has been made to recast the original analysis in later programs of linguistic analysis such as government and binding theory, GPSG, optimality theory, or principles and parameters. As will become clear, this book aims in the first instance to provide a case study of the Tamil auxiliary verb system, not to promote one particular theory over all others. Moreover, because of the relatively small linguistic literature on Tamil, I fear that such reformulations would at this stage of our knowledge amount to little more than notational exercises without shedding much light on either Tamil or linguistic theory. As explained in the text, the program of linguistic analysis assumed here retains its ability to pose interesting questions about language. Accordingly, while some readers may view the dialect of linguistics spoken here as somewhat archaic, I believe they will still find it intelligible and, perhaps, characterized by a broader vocabulary than might otherwise be found in any single model.

Readers are warned that the scope of linguistic phenomena treated in this book is actually narrower than its present title would suggest, treating in detail only what I call the indicative, or nonmodal, auxiliary verb subsystem while consciously setting aside consideration of the modal auxiliary subsystem. This omission should not be taken as meaning that modal auxiliaries are not deserving of linguists' attention. Far from it. But for reasons discussed in this book, primarily the unmarkedness of modal forms, the system of modal auxiliaries is not as easily circumscribed as that of indicative auxiliaries, so that the analysis of modal auxiliary verbs would need to address issues of modal logic and their application to Tamil long before we ever got to a single modal auxiliary. But no fraud is intended by shortening the title: what this study may lack in breadth, it attempts to make up for in depth of analysis. As our study of the indicative auxiliary verb system proceeds, we will explore issues of morphology, syntax, semantics and pragmatics, all of which take us well beyond the scope of a traditional analysis of auxiliary phenomena. If the intervening years have had an impact on how I now view the Tamil auxiliary verb system, I am convinced more strongly than ever of the strong, mutual interaction between morphology and syntax in the Tamil verbal system.

Finally, this book is offered in part as a tribute to three scholars who directly shaped the original dissertation. It is dedicated to the memory of three linguists, each of whom had a profound influence not only on the formation of this text, but on my entire pursuit of linguistics: James D. McCawley (1938-1999), A.K. Ramanujan (1929-1993) and K. Paramasivam (1933-1993). Jim's intellectual generosity and depth of insight are well known; it is my hope that as my dissertation advisor, he was able to infuse some measure of those qualities into this work, making it better than it would have been without his guidance. Raman gave me my first lessons in Tamil and Kannada, and showed me that approaches beyond the narrowly linguistic, including the cultural and poetic, can also enhance our understanding of language. K.P. taught me Tamil, old and new, in Chicago and Madurai, and gave unstintingly of his friendship as well as his knowledge of Tamil language, literature and grammatical tradition. Though not an official member of my dissertation committee, his judgments and wisdom inform much of this work.

New Canaan, Connecticut
Memorial Day 2005

Acknowledgements

Any project this long in the making naturally accrues many debts, and from many different quarters. The three scholars to whom this volume is dedicated had a profound influence on the contents of this book: James D. McCawley , K. Paramasivam and A.K. Ramanujan. My thanks also go to D. Srinivas Aiyengar, Bill J. Darden, Salim Firdouze, M. Israel, R. Kothandaraman, Bh. Krishnamurti, James Lindholm, M. Shanmugam Pillai, Rajasekharan, Richard Scherl, Sarasvati Venugopal, and Vijaya Venugopal.

The Department of Linguistics and the Committee on South Asian Studies at the University of Chicago provided me with many opportunities, and the financial resources, to pursue the research that ultimately led to this book. The American Institute of Indian Studies generously supported me with three separate fellowships to study in India: a Tamil language fellowship (1977-78), a dissertation research fellowship (1979-80) and a postdoctoral fellowship (1983-84).

I would like to thank three scholars who read through the original dissertation, offered comments on it and persuaded me to publish it. These are E. Annamalai, Thomas Lehmann and Peter Brown. Special mention must be made of Annamalai, whose involvement in this project has spanned nearly three decades. In the midst of my dissertation research, he lent me a prepublication typescript of his own book on this very topic; in the midst of preparing this manuscript for publication, he was still offering me helpful suggestions and commentary. These three scholars have done much to enhance what is contained herein; none of them should incur any blame for any deficiencies that remain.

Special thanks are due to Bernard Comrie, who has generously promoted my work and encouraged me to get this manuscript into shape. Thanks also go to Walter Bisang, editor of this series, who brought me on board and took a personal interest this project. I must also express my gratitude to Jonathan Price, formerly of Routledge, who took the risk of commissioning such a specialist work, and to Terry Clague and Tracy Morgan, who both helped bring it before the reading public. Finally, thanks are due to Sean P. Campbell who produced the graphics in Chapter 8.

Portions of the material covered in Chapter 5 appeared in the following two publications. "Direct and Indirect Discourse in Tamil." In T. Gueldeman and M. von

Roncador (eds.) *Reported Discourse: A Meeting Ground for Different Linguistic Domains.* 2002, pp. 91-108. Used with kind permission by Benjamins Publishing Company, Amsterdam/Philadelphia. *www.benjamins.com*. "A functional constraint on auxiliary verbs: the contrast of discourse vs. narrative." In R. Hendrick, C. Masek and M. Miller (eds.), *Papers from the Seventeenth Regional Meeting*, 1981, pp. 383-392. Used with kind permission of The Chicago Linguistic Society, Department of Linguistics, The University of Chicago.

The TransIndic® Transliterator font used to realize the language examples in this work is available from Linguist's Software, Inc. PO Box 580. Edmonds, WA 98020-0580 USA, *www.linguistsoftware.com*.

Abbreviations and conventions

The following abbreviations are used in the interlinear glosses of the example sentences in the text.

1	first person
2	second person
3	third person
ABL	ablative
ACC	accusative
ADN	adnominal verb
ADV	adverbial
AF	affective
BVB	bare verb base
CAUS	causative
CF	conjunctive form
CND	conditional verb
COMP	complementizer
DAT	dative
DUB	dubitative
ECHO	echo word
EF	effective
EMP	emphatic
EXG	exaggeration
F	feminine
FUT	future
GEN	genitive
H	honorific
HORT	hortative
IMP	imperative
IND	indicative
INF	infinitive
INT	interrogative
INST	instrumental
LOC	locative
M	masculine
N	neuter, noun
NEG	negative
NOM	nominative
onom	onomatopoeia
OPT	optative
P	plural
PCL	particle
PRES	present
PST	past
S	singular
SOC	sociative
SUP	supine
V	verb
VF	verb form
VN	verbal noun
VOC	vocative
we^{ex}	exclusive plural
we^{in}	inclusive plural

-	morpheme boundary
+	portmanteau morph
=	clitic boundary
X.V	V is a phonological adjustment to the following segment

Additional abbreviations and conventions used in the text and figures include the following:

AVC	auxiliary verb construction
CSC	coordinate structure constraint
NP	noun phrase
S	sentence
SVA	subject-verb agreement
V	verb
WFR	word-formation rule

[...]	constituent
$_X$[...]	constituent belonging to category X
φ	marks a deletion site

?X	X is of questionable grammaticality/acceptability
??X	X is of very questionable grammaticality/acceptability
*X	X is ungrammatical/unacceptable
**X	X is emphatically ungrammatical/unacceptable
*(X)Y	XY is ungrammatical/unacceptable if X is excluded
(*X)Y	XY is ungrammatical/unacceptable if X is included

A note on the transcription

The transcription system for Tamil that is used here substantially agrees with that used in the *Tamil Lexicon*, with the following alteration: in preference to the symbol *ḻ* used in the *Lexicon*, the symbol for the voiced retroflex approximant used here is *ẓ*. Thus, all retroflex consonants are marked by an underdot, rather than a mixture of underdots and underlines. Specific discussion of how examples are transcribed from written and from spoken sources is given in Chapter 2.

Figures and tables

Figures

1.1 Different analyses of two verbs in sequence. 3
1.2 The underlying structure of an auxiliary verb construction. 17
1.3 The surface structure of the AVC. 17
1.4 An ill-formed tree structure. 17
1.5 Proposed derivation of the AVC. 18
1.6 Underlying structure for ditransitive auxiliaries. 19
3.1 Basic structure of the Tamil verb. 55
3.2 The structure of the Tamil verb base. 55
4.1 Constituent structure of a matrix-complement sentence. 89
4.2 Constituent structure of a coordinate sentence. 90
4.3 Surface structure of a lexical compound verb. 90
4.4 Proposed derivation of the AVC. 91
4.5 The underlying structure of an auxiliary verb construction. 92
4.6 The surface structure of the AVC. 94
4.7 Constituent structure of a matrix-complement clause. 113
4.8 Derivation of a nested AVC. 135
5.1 Unmarked order among multiple indicative auxiliaries. 165
8.1 Graphic representation of the perfect and antiperfect tense series. 255
8.2 Branching futures of perfect and antiperfect tense-forms. 259

Tables

2.1 Sample declension of Tamil nouns 34
2.2 Finite forms of *kalaikka* 'disperse' 35
2.3 Nonfinite forms of *kalaikka* 'disperse' 36
2.4 Some auxiliaries in the anthology *naṟṟiṇai* 41
3.1 The morphophonemic classification of Tamil verbs 56
3.2 Personal endings of finite verbs 66
4.1 Insertion of clitic particles between auxiliate and auxiliary 133
5.1 Direct and indirect discourse in Tamil 155
8.1 Displacement of tense and time reference in the antiperfect series 254

1 Auxiliary Formation

INTRODUCTION

Grammars of Tamil may give casual readers the impression that the language has a simple verbal system, a characterization which appears to be justified at every level of grammar. Tamil's transparent word structure, for example, permits the ready segmentation of a verb into a lexical base and at most two suffixes. Compared with many other languages, it has relatively few verbal inflections so that no single verb has over 60 different forms. The seven morphophonemically distinct conjugations noted in the standard handbooks of the language may on closer inspection be reduced to an even smaller figure. Lexically, the set of verbs is closed: unlike English with its ability to coin new verbs spontaneously, all verbal bases of Tamil may be enumerated in a finite list. Syntactically, a distinction is strictly drawn between finite and nonfinite forms limiting the more complex finite forms to one token per sentence. Additional grammatical observations serve only to reinforce our initial impression of the Tamil verb as a simple, virtually self-evident element of the language.

Despite its reputation for formal simplicity, the Tamil verb has proven remarkably resistant to grammatical analysis. In assuming verbs have a self-evident structure, analysts have generally confined themselves to listing basic forms without addressing the underlying grammatical principles that organize them. Uncritical application of alien labels and categories, such as participle, has further impeded our understanding of the Tamil verbal system. Even when restricted to just the nonfinite forms, some descriptions seem to imply that such commonplace forms as the infinitive and conjunctive are interchangeable, and that their appearance in one context or another reflects a speaker's personal preferences, not the operation of grammatical rules. Employing vocabulary more esthetic than grammatical, researchers have portrayed the Tamil verb in terms of style (Dale 1975: 415), balance (Dale 1975: 415), metaphor (Schiffman 1999b), nuance (Fedson 1981: xii), and even as colorful (Fedson 1993: 74). In its apparent simplicity, then, the Tamil verb has frustrated attempts at analysis, leaving in its wake conflicting and often confusing descriptions with scant linguistic content.

No single facet of the Tamil verb has defied analysis more stubbornly than the auxiliary verb system. Because they take simple verb forms as their building blocks, auxiliary verb structures naturally inherit the problems, noted above, associated with the analysis of those basic forms. Moreover, since auxiliaries participate in a variety of morphological, syntactic, semantic and lexical processes in the language, each of these additional components holds the potential to complicate their analysis further. In fact, auxiliaries have proven so unwieldy that no two linguists can agree on the number of auxiliary verbs in Tamil (see Krishnamurti 2003: 377), the criteria for identifying them or what structural properties they actually possess.

Failure to produce a satisfactory account should not be blamed on a quirk of Tamil grammar or a lack of scholarly effort but on the absence of a model that provides insightful explanations of its auxiliary phenomena. Lacking concepts and tools congenial to the study of Tamil auxiliaries, existing approaches have generally produced descriptions that are both reductionistic and formalistic. Reductionistic because they view auxiliaries as epiphenomena to be resolved into more substantial elements of linguistic structure, such as V, AUX, or INFL; formalistic because in the pursuit of this goal, they concentrate almost exclusively on the auxiliary's formal properties, while virtually ignoring the functions that auxiliary verbs serve in grammar.

A new paradigm for studying auxiliary phenomena is introduced, based on the process of Auxiliary Formation, which correlates their form and function, and is applied to the analysis of the indicative auxiliaries of Tamil. The synchronic process of Auxiliary Formation combines basic elements of the language, specifically its simple verb forms, to generate periphrastic verbs. It does so to create constructions that convey verbal categories which are not encoded in the verbal inflections of simple verbs. As a result, Auxiliary Formation establishes a grammatical opposition between unmarked simple verbs and marked periphrastic verbs. Thanks to the relationship forged between the two by markedness, linguistic solutions for the more marked periphrastic forms imply solutions for the unmarked simple forms, ultimately shedding light on both.

Application of Auxiliary Formation to Tamil auxiliary verbs reveals that the simple and periphrastic verb forms of the language constitute part of a well-articulated system, not a list of isolated curiosities. Among this book's discoveries are new auxiliary verbs, new verbal categories, new constructions and explicit arguments for their special status. And since auxiliaries interact with many levels of linguistic structure, new findings are also presented in Tamil morphology, syntax, semantics and pragmatics. While this analysis will not exhaust everything of interest that might be said about the Tamil auxiliary verb system, it will amply illustrate the insights that Auxiliary Formation brings to bear on the grammatical analysis of auxiliary verb phenomena.

Our model invites readers to reconsider how they approach and analyze auxiliary verb phenomena. Naturally, asking readers to shift their perceptions is a much simpler task than accomplishing it. As an ordinary working grammarian, I would rather let my exposition unfold through a series of favorite examples and select paradigms; however, the introduction of a novel model seems to demand a concise summary rather than piecemeal delivery. While this schematic introduction touches on many topics that in themselves are of interest to general linguists who would otherwise feel no urge to consult a study of Tamil, I would recommend suspending judgment on their utility until readers have had the opportunity to review their application to the analysis of the Tamil auxiliary system in the remainder of the book. Also, given the discursive tone of this chapter and the fact that it anticipates a number of results established only in later chapters, its contents may not be readily digested at one sitting. With this caveat in mind, readers may wish to read this chapter lightly, and return to it later.

Rules of thumb

Tamil examples are now introduced to illustrate what sorts of linguistic phenomena figure in this book; from them may be extracted some preliminary tests to identify auxiliaries in the language. Informal usage defines 'auxiliary verb' in contrast to 'main verb'; at the minimum, the presence of an auxiliary tends to imply the presence of a main verb elsewhere in a structure. However, the reverse need not hold, for many constructions have main verbs without auxiliaries. For present purposes, then, our search for auxiliaries concentrates on analyzing sequences of two or more verbs.[1] But not all sequences of two verbs in Tamil contain an auxiliary; the different ways they may be analyzed appear in Figure 1.1.

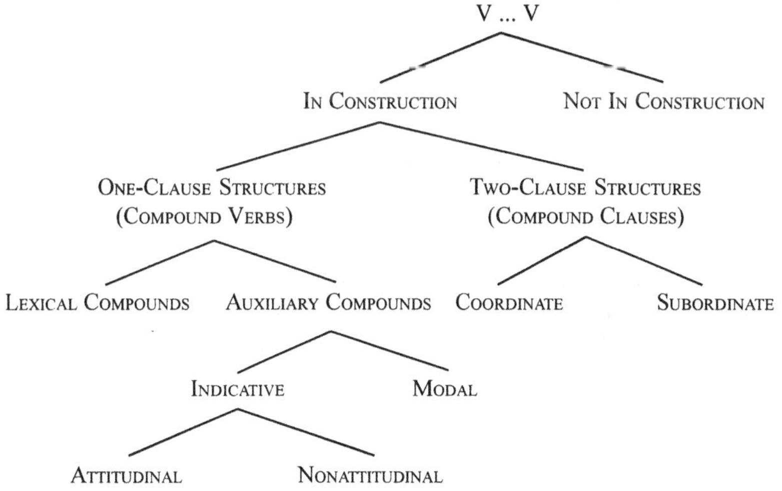

Figure 1.1 Different analyses of two verbs in sequence.

The first possibility is that the two verbs are not in construction at all but belong to independent structures. Consider the sequence of verbs in example (1a).

1 Sequences of three or more are treated as a series of nested binary constructions. In some contexts an auxiliary may occur alone, even though there is always an "understood" main verb.

(1) a *avaḷ vantu paṭittu.k koṇṭirunta maṉitaṉai.p pārttāḷ.*
she-NOM come-CF read-CF hold-CF.be-PST-ADN man-ACC see-PST-3FS
'She came and looked at the man who was reading.'

b $_{S0}$[$_{S1}$[*avaḷ vantu*] $_{S2}$[$_{NP}$[$_{S3}$[*paṭittu.k koṇṭirunta maṉitaṉai.p*] *pārttāḷ*]].

The string … *vantu* … *paṭittu* … in (1a), formed by juxtaposing *vantu* 'coming' and *paṭittu* 'reading', is not a constituent. The bracketing in (1b) shows that *vantu* belongs to the first conjunct (S_1) of a coordinate sentence (S_0), while *paṭittu* is part of a larger construction, *paṭittu.k koṇṭirunta* 'was reading', a relative clause that belongs to the second conjunct (S_2). Such sequences represent a limiting case and are ignored hereafter.

When two verbs do enter into construction, the sequence may be construed in two primary ways. First, it may be analyzed as consisting of two clauses: each verb in the sequence makes a separate predication and refers to a distinct situation. Figure 1.1 indicates that Tamil has two main kinds of compound clause, coordinate and subordinate. Sentence (2a) illustrates a coordinate structure where the

(2) a $_{S0}$[$_{S2}$[*paiyaṉ* $_{S1}$[*pāmpu kaṭittu.c*] *cettuppōṉāṉ*]].
boy-NOM snake-NOM bite-CF die-PST-3MS
'The snake bit the boy and he died.'

b $_{S0}$[$_{S1}$[*kamalā pāṭa*] $_{S2}$[*carōjā āṭiṉāḷ*]].
Kamala-NOM sing-INF Saroja-NOM dance-PST-3SF
'As Kamala sang, Saroja danced.'

(3) a $_{S0}$[*avaṉ* $_{S1}$[*nāṉ colli*] *kēṭka.v illai*].
he-NOM I-NOM say-CF listen-INF IND-NEG
'He didn't listen to what I told him.'

b $_{S0}$[$_{S1}$[*avaḷ pāṭa*] *nāṉ kēṭṭēṉ*].
she-NOM sing-INF I-NOM hear-PST-1S
'I heard her sing(ing).'

verb in the first conjunct, the conjunctive form *kaṭittu* 'biting', joins the two clauses.[2] In (2b) the verb in the first clause, the infinitive *pāṭa* 'sing', serves a similar function. Sentence (3a) illustrates a subordinate clause joined to its following matrix clause by the conjunctive form *colli* 'saying'. Sentence (3b) uses the infinitive *pāṭa* in a similar capacity.[3] Note that the two verbs in these sequences may be contiguous, as in (2a) and (3a), or not, as in (2b) and (3b).

2 This order illustrates a transformation of the basic sentence, given below, in order to juxtapose the two verbs. The basic order more transparently reflects its coordinate structure.

$_{S0}$[$_{S1}$[*pāmpu kaṭittu.p*] $_{S2}$[*paiyaṉ cettuppōṉāṉ*]].
snake-NOM bite-CF boy-NOM die-PST-3MS

3 Since both (2a) and (3a) use a conjunctive form to join two clauses, other criteria are required to distinguish coordinate from subordinate sentences. For example, backwards pronominalization is possible into a subordinate, but not a coordinate clause.

The next branch in Figure 1.1 leads to sequences of two verbs that constitute a compound verb. Here, the separate verbs combine to form a periphrastic verb which makes one predication and denotes a single situation. Between them, the two component verbs have only one subject, one set of modifiers and one complement; under the application of various grammatical rules, they function as a unit. Inspection of examples reveals that basic nonfinite forms such as the infinitive and conjunctive appear in compound verbs as well as compound clauses. While this flexibility illustrates the economy with which Tamil utilizes its basic verb forms, it also creates the possibility of structural ambiguity. So while nonfinite forms may link two structures syntactically, they do not necessarily represent a logical connection between two expressions referring to separate situations. We cannot thus automatically analyze a sequence as a compound clause or a compound verb just by identifying the nonfinite forms they contain.

Compound verbs subdivide into lexical and auxiliary compounds. As above, both divisions use the infinitive and conjunctive, necessitating additional criteria to distinguish them.[4] Lexical compound verbs[5] extend the basic lexical resources of the language by providing complex morphosyntactic vehicles for those configurations of lexical meanings not encoded in any single verb base of the language. As a rule of thumb, in lexical compounds the verb on the right, which denotes some basic activity, is "modified" by the verb on the left, which commonly adds a specification of direction, manner, etc. Apart from idiomatic combinations, the entire compound is essentially a hyponym of the verb on the right.

(4) a *avaḷ avaṉai nimirntu pārttāḷ.*
she-NOM he-ACC straighten-CF look.at-PST-3FS
'She looked up at him.'

b *avaṉ akala niṉṟāṉ.*
he-NOM widen-INF stand-PST-3MS
'He stood apart/aloof.'

In (4a) the conjunctive form *nimirntu* 'straighten' modifies the basic action denoted by the verb *pārttāḷ* '(she) looked at' with a specification of direction, viz. 'up'. Similarly, in (4b) the infinitive *akala* 'widen' adds a specification of manner, viz. 'apart', to the basic verb *niṉṟāṉ* '(he) stood'.

The auxiliary compound verb is a complex morphosyntactic vehicle that conveys those grammatical categories, or combinations of categories, which happen not to be encoded in any of the basic verbal inflections of the language. In such compounds, the verb on the left, the main verb, is modified by the verb on the right, the auxiliary.[6] Roughly speaking, the auxiliary compound expresses a se-

4 In fact, the occurrence of both forms in such a wide range of constructions may have led to the belief in their interchangeability.

5 These collocations may turn out not to be compound verbs as strictly understood (Chapter 4). But since nothing in our analysis of auxiliaries depends on this, the term is provisionally retained.

6 The distinction between lexical and auxiliary compounds broadly recalls Masica's (1976: 141) distinction between what he calls *CP ... V* sequences and explicator compound verbs.

mantically more specific verbal category than is conveyed by the basic inflections of the language. Closer scrutiny reveals that the compound's denotational and inflectional functions are distributed over both the main and the auxiliary verbs. The base of the main verb lexically identifies the whole compound, indicating what range of situations it denotes, while the auxiliary bears the verbal endings that the larger grammatical frame imposes on the entire compound. When these two elements are factored out, what remains are the grammatical inflection of the main verb and the lexical base of the auxiliary: it is the combination of these two remaining elements that conveys the verbal category which is associated with the particular auxiliary compound, e.g., perfect tense, passive voice.

Tamil further divides auxiliary compounds into modal and indicative subsets. In modal compounds, the main verb is inflected for the infinitive.

(5) *avaṉ* *ceṉṉaikku.c* *cella.p* *pōkiṟāṉ.*
he-NOM Madras-DAT go-INF go-PRS-3MS
'He is going to go to Madras.'

The modal compound *cella.p pōkiṟāṉ* '(he) is going to go' in (5) illustrates how the denotational and inflectional functions are distributed over its component parts. In keeping with its denotational function, the main verb, *cel.l-a* 'go', incorporates the verb base *cel-* 'go'. The auxiliary *pō-kiṟ-āṉ* 'he goes' bears the present tense marker *-kiṟ-* and the personal ending *-āṉ* imposed by the surrounding context. What remains, namely the infinitive marker *-a* of the main verb and the verb base *pō-* of the auxiliary, jointly signal prospective tense,[7] viz. 'is going to V', which when combined with the present tense on the auxiliary yields a present prospective tense form. Verbal categories in modal auxiliaries generally, though not invariably, involve modal concepts such as possibility and necessity.[8]

In indicative compounds—the primary focus of this book—the main verb inflects for the conjunctive. The verbal categories in such compounds generally characterize the internal composition of the situation named by the main verb.

(6) *avaḷ* *camaittu* *irukkiṟāḷ.*
she-NOM cook-CF be-PRS-3SF
'She has cooked.'

In the compound verb *camaittu irukkiṟāḷ* '(she) has cooked' in (6), the main verb incorporates the lexical root *camai-* 'cook' while the auxiliary verb bears inflec-

7 The prospective tense series is modal in that the (purported) event time follows the speech time so that the event of going is unrealized at the time the speaker uttered the sentence. See Chapter 3 for further discussion of modal versus nonmodal, or indicative, categories.

8 As argued in Chapter 3, the infinitive is the least marked verb form in the language, occurring in contexts of neutralization. To borrow terminology from another time, it occurs when a verb form is "transformationally inserted" into a construction rather than being "base-generated." Examples include the passive construction with auxiliary *paṭa* '(be)fall' and the emphatic construction with auxiliary *ceyya* 'do, make'.

tions for the present tense, *-(k)kiṟ-*, and the personal ending of the third person singular feminine, *-āḷ*, imposed by the surrounding context. The remaining elements, the conjunctive suffix *-(t)tu* of the main verb and the verb base *iru-* 'be' of the auxiliary, jointly secure the meaning of the perfect tense. The entire compound thus constitutes a present perfect tense form.[9]

A final, significant subdivision of indicative auxiliary compound verbs is made into those that express the speaker's attitude and those that do not. Example (6) above illustrates an auxiliary that does not mark attitude; these auxiliaries are analyzed in Chapters 6 and 7. The remaining indicative compounds, analyzed in Chapter 8, encode the category of attitude, introduced here by example.

(7) *contakkāraṉ vantu tolaintāṉ.*
relative-NOM come-CF lose-PST-3SM
'My relative arrived, damn it!'

The sequence *vantu tolaintāṉ* 'he arrived, damn it' in (7) exhibits the same basic properties as in (6), viz., each compound, no matter how internally complex, has but one set of modifiers, complements, etc. Here *vantu* 'coming' incorporates the lexical base *va-* 'come' fulfilling the compound's denotational function. The auxiliary *tolaintāṉ*, lit., 'he got lost', bears the past tense marker *-nt-* and the agreement marker *-āṉ* imposed on the compound by the surrounding context. The main verb's conjunctive suffix *-ntu* and the auxiliary's lexical base *tolai-* jointly convey the speaker's antipathy toward that event, roughly translated by the epithet 'damn it'. All attitudinal auxiliaries characterize the speaker's subjective evaluation of the narrated event; it is usually—though not invariably—a negative one. Their impact resembles that of the highlighted English verbs in *Bill* ***went*** *and told the IRS*, *they* ***upped*** *and left the concert*, *Mary* ***got*** *her cell phone stolen* and *he* ***come*** *telling me how fine I was* (Spear 1982). Evidence in Chapter 4 shows that while the grammar of attitudinal and nonattitudinal auxiliaries largely coincides, small, predictable differences remain. Chapter 5 studies further how different contexts influence the distribution of attitudinal and nonattitudinal auxiliaries.

Four primary diagnostic tests may be extrapolated from this discussion which allow us to identify the indicative auxiliary compound verb; note that their hierarchical organization reflects the various branchings in Figure 1.1.[10] Any sequence of verbs in Tamil that satisfies the first four criteria in (8) belongs to the set of indicative auxiliary compounds; those that additionally satisfy the fifth criterion belong to the subset of attitudinal compounds.

9 Evidence from Chapter 6 will show that this example is in fact general between a present perfect and a present progressive reading.

10 Annamalai (1982) provides a set of valuable heuristics that permit us to preliminarily identify these auxiliaries. These heuristic tests are broadly reminiscent of the kinds of tests that scholars have used to pinpoint English auxiliaries, such as the ability to undergo the transformation of Subject-Auxiliary Inversion.

(8) a *Two independent verbs enter into construction with each other.*
b *The two verbs form a periphrastic (compound) verb.*
c *The compound verb serves a grammatical, not a lexical function, conveying verbal categories.*
d *The main verb inflects for the conjunctive form, not the infinitive.*
e *Attitudinal auxiliaries express the speaker's subjective evaluation of the narrated event.*

Helpful as these heuristics are, they must be treated as provisional because they anticipate conclusions established only later, mainly in Chapter 4. Moreover, as currently formulated, they fail to address several important issues. First, they are language-specific: criteria (8b and d), for example, assume Tamil morphological and syntactic structures just as surely as Subject-Auxiliary Inversion, a diagnostic for English auxiliaries without any counterpart in Tamil, assumes English structures. Second, they account for only a fraction of the grammatical behavior that Tamil auxiliary compounds typically display. Third, their relation to more general linguistic concerns, such as defining the concept of "possible auxiliary verb," is not immediately evident at this juncture. Without a more explicit model of these phenomena, it would seem rash to apply the terms auxiliary or auxiliary verb to structures in Tamil or, indeed, other languages.

New perceptions and paradigms

Embarking on a new paradigm may require us to radically modify, or abandon wholesale, certain assumptions that are rooted in older ways of tackling linguistic problems. Common as the terms auxiliary and auxiliary verb are in current linguistics, they originated in traditional grammar and passed through successive programs of linguistic analysis to reach the present. Along the way, they have acquired some accretions which may impede our study of auxiliary phenomena, two of which are addressed here. The first stumbling block is the tendency, frequently assumed in discussions on grammaticalization,[11] to view auxiliaries as an intermediate stage in a diachronic process from word to clitic. After all, the terms auxiliary and auxiliary verb date from a time before the diachronic and synchronic dimensions of linguistic analysis were clearly distinguished. However, this tacit diachronic orientation tends to divert attention from providing an explicit synchronic analysis of auxiliary verb phenomena.

The second tendency is the traditional practice of viewing individual words as the locus of linguistic generalization, one which appears to have been reincarnated in modern debates over whether auxiliaries constitute a distinct category of their own or are just ordinary verbs. The terms auxiliary and auxiliary verb, as well as the lexical bias that informs them, come from a time before an epochal paradigm

11 See the discussion in Chapter 9 on two competing treatments of the grammaticalization of auxiliary phenomena in the literature.

shift took place in grammatical analysis: whereas the basic ingredients of language were once catalogued as a taxonomy of words, in modern linguistics they are analyzed as elements functioning within a structured system and generated by its rules. Thus, while more familiar approaches concentrate on the auxiliary's lexical dimension, ours will emphasize its morphological and its syntactic functions. This statement may strike some as particularly brazen since standard analyses of auxiliary phenomena generally purport to be syntactic; however, this claim appears to pertain more to the nature of the formal devices used in analyzing auxiliary phenomena and less to the phenomena themselves. Studies of auxiliary phenomena routinely invoke several levels of linguistic structure, but generally avoid correlating them, seeking instead to reduce them a single level privileged in a particular theory.[12] Their nearly exclusive concern with formalism concentrates on which notational devices best reconstruct the concept of auxiliary. Accordingly, in bringing these terms up to date, we shall also want to examine what sorts of functions auxiliary verbs serve within a grammatical system.

AUXILIATION

Benveniste (1965, 1974) provides an analysis of auxiliary verbs that remedies the diachronic and lexical biases of traditional grammar. Bringing the techniques of structural linguistics to bear on the study of auxiliaries leads him to conclude their analysis is fundamentally a matter of synchrony and syntax. While it stems from European structural linguistics and is applied to auxiliaries in the Romance languages, his model is sufficiently robust to be adapted to generative linguistics and the analysis of a broader range of languages.

Two components are central to Benveniste's model, a family of constructions and the linguistic process that characterizes them. First, Benveniste (1974: 177) defines a construction which he did not name but which we call the Auxiliary Verb Construction, or AVC:

> Il s'agit d'une forme linguistique unitaire qui se réalise, à travers des paradigmes entiers, en deux éléments, dont chacun assume une partie des fonctions grammaticales, et qui sont à la fois liés et autonomes, distincts et complémentaires.[13]

Extrapolating from this definition reveals that members of the set of AVCs must satisfy two criteria, one syntactic, the other semantic. First, the AVC is a periphrastic verb form consisting of two lexically independent parts. Second, it serves to

12 Early generative studies of English, for example, commonly assimilated morphology to syntax so that Chomsky (1957) placed the inflectional affixes associated with auxiliary verbs, not by independent morphological principles, but by low-level syntactic rules such as Affix-Hopping.

13 'What is at stake is a unitary linguistic form that is realized across all paradigms in two elements, each one of which assumes a part of the grammatical functions, and which are simultaneously linked and autonomous, distinct and complementary [translation SBS].'

convey those verbal categories (or combinations of categories) not already encoded in the inflections of any simple verb form of the language.[14]

Benveniste (1974: 179) introduces the term Auxiliation to define the syntactic process that generates the AVC.

> Nous traiterons d'un procès linguistique, l'*auxiliation*, qui consiste en la jonction syntagmatique d'une *forme auxiliante* et d'une *forme auxiliée*, ou plus brièvement, d'un *auxiliant* et d'un *auxilié*.[15]

Auxiliation embraces two functions: it combines two independent forms into a syntactically complex structure which functions as a verb, and simultaneously casts one of the forms in the role of *auxiliant* (translated as 'auxiliary' in Benveniste 1968) and the other in the role of *auxilié* ('auxiliate' in Benveniste 1968). These two roles faintly echo the traditional terms auxiliary and main verb, but differ from them in crucial respects. Perhaps the most important difference is that auxiliary and auxiliate are defined solely by reference to the roles they play within the AVC. In short, an auxiliary is that which combines with an auxiliate to form an AVC while an auxiliate is that which combines with an auxiliary to form an AVC: both definitions presuppose a syntactic constituent, the AVC. One major consequence of viewing the AVC as a syntactic object in its own right is that we may talk about its general syntactic and semantic properties without constant reference to the specific forms that serve as auxiliary or auxiliate.

Benveniste's definition of the AVC indicates that its syntactic and semantic functions are distributed over its two components. He segments the AVC into its component parts, leading him to propose the following division of labor (Benveniste 1974: 184).

> L'auxiliant … a en propre la *fonction de flexion*: il porte en quelque sorte les désinences et indique la personne, le nombre, le mode, la voix … L'auxilié … a en propre la *fonction de dénotation*: il identifie lexicalement le verbe, dont it porte en quelque sorte le radical.[16]

The verb base of the auxiliate lexically identifies the AVC, indicating what sort of situation the entire construction denotes. It specifies which arguments, complements and modifiers—collectively, the satellites—may accompany the entire AVC.

14 This second criterion, not explicit in this passage, comes from how Benveniste applies the concept, and from what he says elsewhere (Benveniste 1968: 85): "We define categories as those form classes which are distinctively characterized and capable of grammatical function." Further, this second criterion has an understood morphological element, so we can talk about inflections on words (the phrase *liés et autonomes* talks about syntax, *distincts et complémentaires* semantics).

15 'We will characterize a linguistic process, auxiliation, which consists of the syntactic union of an auxiliating form and an auxiliated form, or more briefly, an auxiliary and an auxiliate [SBS].'

16 'The auxiliary has as its defining characteristic an inflectional function: it bears in one way or other the endings that signal person, number, mood, voice ... The auxiliate has a denotational function: it lexically identifies the verb, whose root it incorporates in one way or other [SBS].'

Cooccurrence arguments (pp. 91-102) show that the AVC's satellites are exactly those that accompany a simple, nonauxiliated counterpart with the same verb base as the auxiliate. The auxiliary is the head of the AVC and bears those inflections which any verb in that frame, simple or periphrastic, would have to bear; it does not influence the selection restrictions between the lexical base of the auxiliate and the AVC's satellites.

Once these elements are factored out, what remains are the auxiliary's lexical base and the auxiliate's inflections. Benveniste (1974: 184) insists that both components, taken together, are necessary to establish the characteristic meaning of the AVC.

> Mais seule la somme de l'auxiliant et de l'auxilié, associant le *sens* spécifique de l'*auxiliant* à la *forme* spécifique de l'*auxilié*, assure la *fonction de temporalité* et produit la valuer de parfait.[17]

Since both elements contribute to the AVC's characteristic meaning, the auxiliate's form cannot be considered merely as a semantically empty, mechanical adjustment triggered by the auxiliary, as has often been assumed in the generative literature on auxiliaries. Benveniste's (1974: 183) analysis of the French perfect tense series elaborates his argument for treating the AVC's characteristic meaning as a function of the meanings of its two component parts.

> Assurément *il a*-, auxiliant de *il a chanté*, indique la personne et le nombre, accessoirement le genre de la personne, grâce au pronom. Peut-on dire qu'il énonce lc temps? Il détiendrait alors, en effet, la totalité des fonctions verbales, moins les sens. Mais cette postulation admise partout nous semble insoutenable. *Il a* n'indique par lui-même qu'un temps: le présent. Mais en tant qu'auxiliant, il forme le parfait. C'est une vraie mutation. Comment cette mutation est-elle concevable si toutes les fonctions morphologiques sont concentrées, ainsi qu'on l'enseigne, dans le seul auxiliant? Par quelle magie la proximité de l'auxilié, s'il n'est que sémentème, transforme-t-elle le présent en parfait. Là est la vraie question, qui n'a été ni discutée ni même, semble-t-il, aperçue.[18]

17 'But it is only the sum of the auxiliary and auxiliate, associating the specific meaning of the auxiliary with the specific form of the auxiliate, that ensures the function of tense and produces the value of the perfect [SBS].' This passage appears in Benveniste's (1965) analysis of the French perfect tense series; remarks there and in Benveniste (1968) permit us to replace the specific term *fonction de temporalité* 'function of tense' with the more general term 'verbal category'.

18 'To be sure, *il a* [he has], the auxiliary of *il a chanté* [he has sung], signals person, number and, additionally, gender, with the help of the pronoun. But can we also say that it signals tense? If so, it would exhaust all of the grammatical functions, except for the [lexical] meaning. But this proposition, admitted everywhere, seems untenable to us. *il a* signals just one tense, the present. But as an auxiliary, it signals the perfect tense. That is a true mutation. How is such a mutation possible if, as we have been taught, all of the morphological functions are solely concentrated in the auxiliary? By what magic is the auxiliate able, if it is only a bearer of [lexical] meaning, to transform the present tense into the perfect tense? That is the real question, one which has neither been debated nor, it would seem, even perceived [SBS].'

Benveniste thus rejects the traditional assumption that only the auxiliary contributes to the AVC's characteristic meaning, arguing in effect that such analyses rest on an erroneous segmentation of the AVC, one that ignores what the auxiliate's form can contribute to the AVC's meaning.

A brief comparison of two English AVCs informally illustrates how this model may be used. In *he is giving a party*, the progressive AVC *is giving* combines the auxiliary *is* with the auxiliate *giving*. The auxiliate incorporates the base */give/* which lexically identifies the entire AVC, telling us for example that it is ditransitive. The auxiliary bears inflections for present tense and agreement with a third person singular subject, exactly those its nonauxiliated counterpart, *gives*, would bear in the same context. What remains—and what conveys the meaning of progressive tense of this AVC—is not just the auxiliary, but the auxiliary's lexical root *be* and the auxiliate's present participle suffix *-ing*. This analysis reflects the proper segmentation because *be* also serves as an auxiliary in the passive AVC *he is given* (*a party*), where the auxiliate *given* incorporates the past participle suffix *-en*. The auxiliary's lexical base *be* and the auxiliate's past participle inflection jointly convey the meaning of passive voice. The minimal contrast between the two AVCs thus resides precisely in the difference in the auxiliate's form: a present participle in the progressive, a past participle in the passive. Although one might claim English has two auxiliaries *be*, a position not unknown in the literature, one for progressive and one for passive, this feint ignores the morphological segmentation of the AVC, begging the question of what the meanings of the present and past participles contribute to the meanings of their respective AVCs.

Even as it incorporates two independent forms, the AVC functions as a single verb in the grammatical context; so regardless of formal differences, simple and periphrastic verbs both belong to the class of expressions that make a single predication. Benveniste (1974: 179) distinguishes them by a grammatical opposition of two terms: "La forme créée par auxiliation s'oppose, en tant que marquée, à une forme verbale simple, non auxiliée."[19] The opposition between unmarked simple verbs and marked periphrastic verbs serves to underscore the suppletive nature of this relation, viz., AVCs supplete the set of simple verb forms.

As seen below, the use of an opposition to define AVCs in contrast to simple verbs permits us to exclude excessive amounts of language-specific detail from the formulation of Auxiliation. Benveniste's model recognizes that since the set of simple verb forms, as well as the criteria that define them, varies from one language to the next, the set of AVCs, the basic forms they utilize and the linguistic process that generate them will also vary. This model is schematic and designed to encompass the wide range of auxiliaries encountered both within individual languages and across languages. As our discussion of Auxiliation progresses, we will have occasion to refer to it by the slightly less Gallic term Auxiliary Formation.[20]

19 'The form generated by auxiliation is opposed, and marked with respect to, a simple, nonauxiliated verb form [SBS].'

20 This term stresses the synchronic nature of the process. Much of the literature (e.g. Heine 1993) views auxiliation primarily as a historical process. See Chapter 9.

THE FUNCTIONS OF AUXILIARY FORMATION

Auxiliary Formation's primary function is to create a linguistic expression, generating a complex morphosyntactic vehicle to convey verbal categories not encoded in the basic verbal inflections of the language. This expressive function subsumes a number of subsidiary functions which may be distinguished according as they apply within the AVC, or outside it.

Auxiliary Formation has two internal functions, one syntactic, the other semantic. Its syntactic function generates a periphrastic verb form and is analyzed below; its semantic function, discussed here, associates a characteristic meaning to that periphrastic form. We may approach this semantic function by comparing it with the semantic functions associated with other kinds of expressions in the language. In contrast to complex clauses, which denote as many distinct situations as there are clauses, a compound verb's semantic function involves a single situation. Reflecting the morphological distinction between a lexical base and an inflection, the meaning of a compound verb is partitioned between its denotational and inflectional functions. In contrast to lexical compounds, the AVC does not elaborate the basic verb's denotational function; its characteristic meaning is instead consistent with the kinds of meanings that are ordinarily conveyed by verbal inflections, in short, by verbal categories. On the hypothesis that the meaning of a linguistic expression is a function of the meanings of its components, the well-known principle of compositionality, the AVC inherits the categories that are already associated with the inflection of the simple verb forms it incorporates. The subsequent combination of this meaning with the meaning of the remaining material, namely the auxiliary's lexical base, establishes a verbal category that is uniquely characteristic of the whole AVC. In the process, Auxiliary Formation creates a grammatical opposition between the two kinds of expressions that convey verbal categories, contrasting unmarked simple verbal inflections with marked periphrastic AVCs.

One of Auxiliary Formation's external functions is to increase the set of morphosyntactic devices that convey verbal categories: in effect, it suppletes the stock of simple verbal inflections with periphrastic verb forms.[21] For example, Tamil, English and Modern French, but not Latin, lack simple verb forms for either the perfect tense or passive voice. Since creating new word-formation rules would exact relatively expensive costs on the grammar, some means other than simple inflection are needed to convey these additional categories, if, of course, they are to be conveyed at all. In such circumstances, Auxiliary Formation is an obvious choice.[22] One of Auxiliary Formation's external functions may also be viewed as

21 While suppletion is traditionally treated as a relation between two words in a paradigm, e.g., *went* suppletes *go* in certain English paradigms, with the structuralist insight that paradigms are systematically related by oppositions of grammatical categories, suppletion can be naturally extended to the formal relation between entire paradigms.

22 In fact, Latin lacks a simple passive perfect form (Clackson 2004: 803) and uses a periphrastic form to express the combination of perfect tense and passive that basic verbal morphology implies but does not supply a simple form for. Auxiliary Formation in this case suppletes the simple verb forms which imply, but do not happen to provide, a perfective passive series.

economic in nature. To create periphrastic forms, it recycles the linguistic materials at hand, namely the existing morphological, syntactic and lexical resources of the language; in doing so, it extends the range of environments in which simple verbs appear to include a new construction, the AVC.

The opposition between unmarked simple verbs and marked AVCs cascades through the different levels of linguistic structure.[23] Morphologically, the periphrastic forms utilize, and therefore presuppose the existence of, simple forms. Syntactically, periphrastic verbs are more marked since, although periphrastic forms typically occur in the same syntactic structures as simple forms do, in contexts of neutralization simple verbs prevail. Semantically, periphrastic verbs are more marked because they express the meanings of their component simple forms as well as the characteristic meaning of the whole AVC. Pragmatically, periphrastic verbs are more marked because simple verbs occur in a wider variety of linguistically defined contexts.[24] Markedness relations thus serve as the ligaments that bind together the various levels of structure involved in auxiliary verb phenomena, allowing us to see how their formal and functional aspects are correlated.

SYNTACTIC FUNCTION—DERIVING THE AVC

Since Benveniste's model is more a way of looking at linguistic phenomena and less a theory-bound construct, it should survive translation into other programs of linguistic analysis without severe distortion. Throughout this book, appeal is made to various programs of linguistic analysis, including European structuralism, generative grammar, traditional Tamil grammar, localistic semantics and Gricean pragmatics. Despite such a heterogenous approach, generative grammar is the preferred paradigm, particularly in terms of the questions it asks. Even so, this analysis seeks to provide a case study of the Tamil auxiliary verb system, not an argument for preferring one school of grammar over another. A point-by-point comparison of Benveniste's model with other models of auxiliary verb phenomena, however desirable, must await separate treatment.[25]

Two facets of Benveniste's program permit us to reconstruct Auxiliary Formation in generative grammar and identify the AVC with a set of derivations that encapsulates its syntactic properties. The first is relevant to the AVC's underlying structure, the second to its surface structure; a set of rules is then proposed to economically relate the two. This reconstruction analyzes a linguistic expression, such as a sentence, in terms of a mapping between an underlying and a surface structure, intended to correlate the expression's meaning and form. Deep structure

23 The concept of markedness used here reflects Jakobsonian practice. For a recent discussion of different conceptions of markedness, see Croft (2003).

24 See Chapter 5. Also consult Herring (1991: 86-88) who notes that in three out of the four narrative genres she treats in Tamil, the unmarked simple forms are statistically more frequent than the marked complex forms.

25 See McCawley (1988), Scholten (1988) and Heine (1993) for summaries of various treatments of the auxiliary in generative grammar.

formation rules (McCawley 1988) characterize the set of well-formed underlying structures, which provide enough information about an expression's meaning and logical form to interpret it in model-theoretic semantics. Surface structure formation rules characterize well-formed surface structures of the language; they include the gross combinatoric restrictions usually described by phrase structure rules, telling us for example that determiners precede nouns in English but follow in Sinhala. Both sets of formation rules describe constituent structure trees, rather than linear strings. Transformations describe how one tree may differ from another, and in doing so, allow us to capture certain linguistic generalizations.

Generative grammar embraces a wide range of models, permitting great theoretical and practical latitude in syntactic analysis; although much of what appears here is familiar, some positions diverge from classical generative grammar, agreeing more with McCawley's (1981, 1982, 1988) proposals.[26] First, not all combinatoric restrictions are defined at a single level of linguistic structure, e.g. deep structure. What McCawley (1982) calls petty combinatoric restrictions are defined at the level of underlying structure and include selection restrictions and strict subcategorization rules. Gross combinatoric restrictions, principles that govern the overall shape constituents may take, pertain to surface structure. Second, syntactic categories are taken to be informal abbreviations of several kinds of information, e.g., the lexical category of a head, the logical category a node corresponds to, dependency relations and topological information such as c-command. Third, no principled distinction is made among transformations, rules of semantic interpretation or global rules.

Fourth, lexical decomposition is admitted, and indeed required by the rich, agglutinating morphology of Tamil.[27] Fifth, Lexical Insertion, which converts the semantic elements of underlying structure into the lexical elements of a language, need not take place at a single stage of derivation. While many lexemes correspond to a semantic element, some occur to satisfy requirements of surface structure. In Tamil, certain words which do not correspond to a semantic element in

26 Since the primary goal of this work is descriptive, no attempt has been made to update the analysis to the most recent paradigms or notational conventions. But although the dialect of syntax used here may have a slightly archaic flavor, it should be comprehensible to most working syntacticians. There are also reasons for maintaining the original framework. First, McCawley's approach to morphosyntactic phenomena, the kinds of questions it asks and the varieties of argumentation used to answer those questions remain substantially valid for many syntactic purposes. Second, my own review of the treatment of auxiliaries in other versions of generative grammar suggests that they largely follow the reductionist trends noted above, tending to reduce one level of structure to another rather than correlating them. Third, much of the generative literature on Tamil syntax over the past 30 years has been written by students of McCawley's approach, so the version used here may in some sense be considered "normative" for generative analyses of Tamil. There is no significant, coherent body of literature in alternative models, and to introduce them here would needlessly lengthen the present book.

27 For the purposes of this study, lexical decomposition is interpreted modestly as the necessity of segmenting polymorphemic words into bases and suffixes. Further, Chapter 3 shows that Tamil verb forms incorporate syntactic information their closest English counterparts do not. A Tamil word typically encodes several morphemes, some of which perform a syntactic rather than a purely lexical function.

underlying structure may be syncategorematically introduced into a derivation, such as the complementizer *āka* 'become' (Steever 1988), the emphatic auxiliary *ceyya* 'do' or the passive auxiliary *paṭa* 'befall'.

Sixth, underlying structure is morphologically indeterminate; consequently, at least some morphology is introduced in the course of a derivation. Further, some morphological processes may operate within the lexicon along with Lexical Insertion, while others, particularly the assignment of default values, may appear at the end of a derivation. Syntactic arguments for the AVC (pp. 123-27) even reveal an intermediate level of structure, one not deep enough to be model-theoretically interpreted, nor shallow enough to be pronounced. The petty combinatoric restrictions of the AVC range over the satellites and the verb base of auxiliate, not the fully inflected form it comes to have in surface structure; thus a verb's strict subcategorization is unlikely to vary, changing, say, from intransitive to transitive, with a change of tense marking. The robust interaction between morphology and syntax in Tamil makes it unlikely that all morphological processes in Tamil can be either constrained to one specific stage of a derivation, or reduced to a simple interpretation of syntactic structures.

Thanks to its denotational function, the auxiliate's lexical base determines the selection restrictions and strict subcategorization features between the AVC and its satellites. As selection restrictions are conventionally defined over constituents (Zwicky 1978), a derivational stage is implied in which the AVC's satellites and the auxiliate—specifically, its lexical base—form a constituent that excludes the auxiliary. That stage, representing an underlying structure, is given in Figure 1.2.

In Figure 1.2, V_1 dominates the auxiliate and V_0 the auxiliary. The auxiliate subcategorizes NP_1 and NP_2, two satellites that accompany the entire AVC in surface structure. S_1 is interpolated here because a verb and its satellites conventionally combine to form a sentence, the constituent over which the petty combinatoric restrictions are held to range. Note that Figure 1.2 segregates the auxiliary (V_0) and auxiliate (V_1) into two separate clauses. Support for this generative interpretation comes from Benveniste's (1974: 180) recognition that the different combinatoric properties of auxiliate and auxiliary impact their logical representation.

> On pourrait alors construire un modèle logique de cette rélation, à l'instar des fonctions propositionelles, et parler d'une fonction auxilationelle. Dans *il a frappé*, on considérerait *frappé* comme une « chose » dont *il a* serait « la propriété »: en effet *frappé* admet un grande nombre de substitutions possibles, dont chacun cré e une situation différente, tandis que *il a* demeure constant. On pourra dire alors que dans *il a frappé*, l'auxilié *frappé* réprésente l'« argument » et l'auxiliant *il a* la « fonction ».[28]

28 'We might then construct a logical model of this relation on the basis of propositional functions, and speak of an auxiliating function. In *il a frappé*, *frappé* may be considered to be an object of which *il a* is a property. In effect, while *il a* remains constant, *frappé* allows a great number of possible substitutions, with each one giving rise to a different state of affairs. We could then say that the auxiliate *frappé* represents the argument and the auxiliary *il a* the function [SBS].'

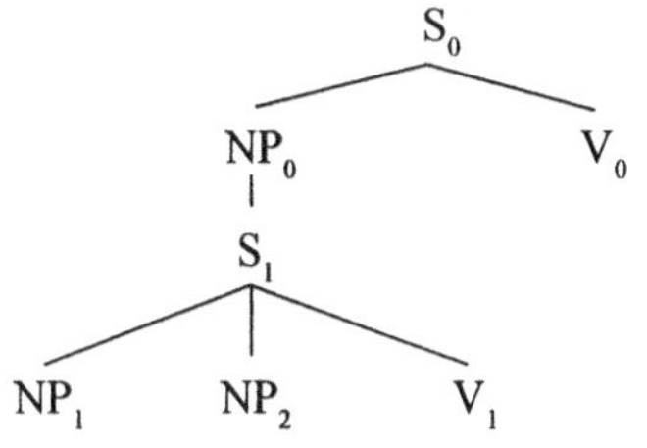

Figure 1.2 The underlying structure of an auxiliary verb construction.

Note the auxiliary verb V_0 in Figure 1.2 is in a position to impose selection restrictions on the sentential subject, $[NP_0[S_1]]$, it combines with. Such restrictions may involve global properties of that constituent and are discussed below.

A second aspect of Benveniste's theory bears on the AVC's surface structure. His initial definition states that two independent forms combine to form a single form, namely a periphrastic verb. The output of Auxiliary Formation thus implies a constituent structure as in Figure 1.3.

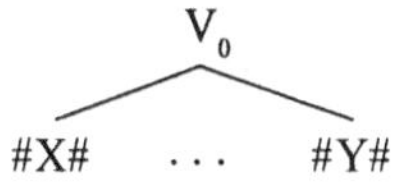

Figure 1.3 The surface structure of the AVC.

In Figure 1.3 the AVC itself is identified with V_0; its two daughters, the auxiliate and auxiliary, are represented by the nodes X and Y, each flanked by word boundaries (#). At this point, we need not commit X or Y to membership in any particular lexical class or syntactic category, nor even specify the relative linear order of auxiliate and auxiliary (see below).

Evidence in Chapter 4 indicates the need for both structures; S-Deletion treats the auxiliate and its satellites as a unit excluding the auxiliary, consistent with Figure 1.2, while Clefting and Right Dislocation treat the AVC as a single verb, consistent with Figure 1.3. The phenomena supporting Figure 1.2 are primarily semantic; those supporting Figure 1.3, syntactic. Both must be accommodated to adequately represent the full range of behavior the AVC exhibits. Under accepted conventions for tree structures, no single well-formed tree can baldly combine the structures in Figures 1.2 and 1.3: the result in Figure 1.4 is ill-formed because it includes a node (V_1) with multiple mothers. Therefore, a derivation, illustrated in Figure 1.5, is proposed to link the two structures as different stages in a derivation.

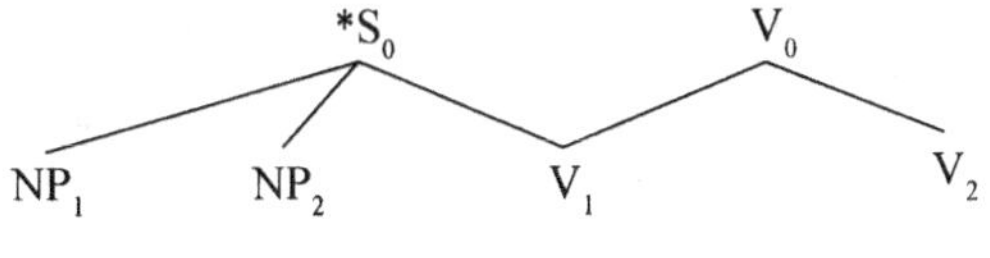

Figure 1.4 An ill-formed tree structure.

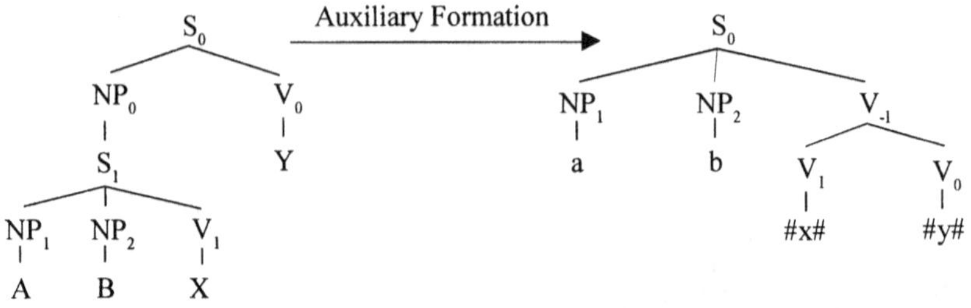

Figure 1.5 Proposed derivation of the AVC.

Rather than being associated with any single constituent structure, then, the AVC is identified with a derivation.

This derivation conflates three discrete steps. First, a rule such as Predicate Raising Chomsky-adjoins V_1 to V_0, creating the new node V_{-1}: this is the step most closely identified with Auxiliary Formation since it gives rise to a constituent, V_{-1}, that wholly includes the auxiliary and auxiliate.[29] Second, Tree Pruning conventions eliminate the now extraneous nodes NP_0 and S_1 bringing the transformed structures into conformity with permissible configurations for Tamil tree structures. Third, Lexical Insertion replaces the semantic primes, represented by capitals, with lexemes and morphemes of the language, represented by lower case letters. As applied here, it must ensure that V_0 and V_1 come to dominate phonological words in satisfaction of the condition that the AVC's two parts are independent. In one sense, Lexical Insertion serves to distinguish simple inflected verbs from compound verbs.[30] As before, V_0 dominates the auxiliary; V_1, the auxiliate. Specific arguments from Tamil structures presented in Chapter 4 lead inductively to the derivation in Figure 1.5 that is inferred here by deductive means from the initial definitions of Auxiliation and the AVC.

Transitivity of the auxiliary and the AVC

The structure in Figure 1.2 assumes that the auxiliary is an intransitive predicate that subcategorizes a sentential subject. If, as Auxiliary Formation implies, an auxiliary and its homophonous "main" verb counterpart are just two specialized uses of a single lexeme, it should be possible for auxiliary verbs to vary in transitivity just as main verbs do. Among the Tamil indicative auxiliaries, twelve are intransitive: *irukka* 'be', *āka* 'become', *kiṭakka* 'lie', *vara* 'come', *tolaiya* 'get lost', *oẓiya*

29 Chomsky Adjunction, the operation at the heart of Predicate Raising, is the least marked transformational operation available among the kinds of rules in classical versions of generative grammar: it preserves the constituency of the host node and introduces no new node label into the derivation.

30 Another output is possible at this point in which the semantic primes representing the "main" and "auxiliary" verbs are replaced by a single lexeme of the language. Such polycategorial attachment, as Gruber (1976) calls it, occurs when the verb morphology provides a single morphological form for the configuration of verb base and verbal category. Polycategorial attachment thus bleeds the set of AVCs.

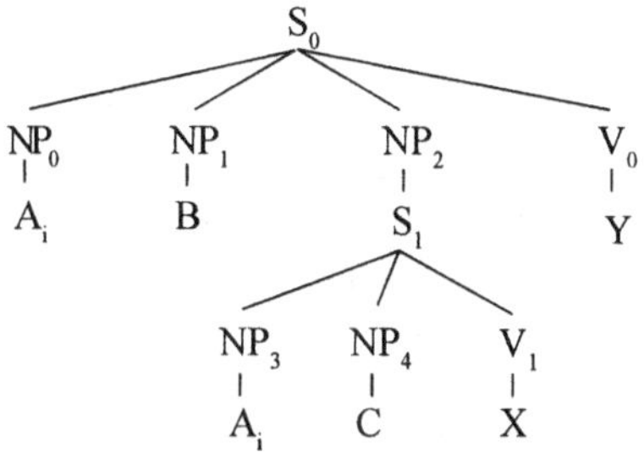

Figure 1.6 Underlying structure for ditransitive auxiliaries.

'be purged', *kiẓiya* 'get torn', *aẓa* 'cry', *vaẓiya* 'drip', *pōka* 'go', *aruḷa* 'be gracious', *muṭiya* 'finish'; ten are transitive: *koḷḷa* 'hold', *viṭa* 'leave', *vaikka* 'place', *pārkka* 'look at', *tolaikka* 'lose', *kiẓikka* 'tear', *pōṭa* 'put', *tīrkka* 'settle, exhaust', *taḷḷa* 'push', *muṭikka* 'finish'; and three are ditransitive: *koṭukka* 'give', *tara* 'give to you or me', *kāṭṭa* 'show'. To accommodate transitive and ditransitive auxiliaries, the structure in Figure 1.2 needs further elaboration. Figure 1.6 presents an underlying structure for ditransitive auxiliaries: V_0 is the auxiliary, NP_0 the subject of the main clause, NP_1 its indirect object and NP_2 a sentential object complement. Arguments in Chapter 4, for example, indicate the benefactive auxiliaries *koṭukka* 'give' and *tara* 'give to you or me' subcategorize NP_1, the beneficiary of the action denoted by the auxiliate V_1, independently of what V_1 can itself subcategorize. The object complement S_1 includes *inter alia* the auxiliate V_1 and the subject NP_3. The subjects of the upper and lower clauses, NP_0 and NP_3, respectively, are coreferential; Equi-NP Deletion deletes NP_3 under identity with NP_0. Due to this coreference, the petty combinatoric restrictions that hold between V_1 and NP_3 are projected to V_1 and NP_0 in surface structure. From this stage forward, the derivation proceeds as in Figure 1.5; however, Tree Pruning may have to apply more robustly to bring the constituents into line with the surface structure formation rules.

The underlying structure for transitive auxiliaries resembles that for ditransitives except that it lacks a node for beneficiary. Further, transitive auxiliaries, which are dominated by V_0 in Figure 1.6, may subcategorize two sentential arguments not just one, i.e., both NP_0 and NP_2 may dominate S nodes. This aptly represents auxiliaries that mark taxis,[31] expressing a relation between the action of the AVC and some other event or proposition, often implicit, whose content may be gathered from context (see Chapter 6). While three different underlying structures are postulated in which an indicative AVC may arise, one each for intransitive, transitive and ditransitive auxiliaries, all three must pass through the derivational steps in Figure 1.5; hence, that one is taken as representative of all of them.

31 The term taxis is preferred over relative tense because the latter term strongly suggests that the relation between two events must be temporal whereas the former term is neutral in that respect. As noted in subsequent chapters, some varieties of taxis may describe an epistemic relation between two events, a notion that may not be reduced to temporality.

Filling in the blanks

Our reconstruction leaves several features of the tree structures and their derivation unspecified. This is desirable for two reasons: a schematic presentation not only enables Auxiliary Formation to encompass many different kinds of auxiliary structures, but also relieves us of the need to include language-specific detail in its formulation which other, independently required principles may supply. The AVC's linear order in surface structure, for example, can be stipulated by reference to autonomous word-order rules needed elsewhere in the grammar. The left-to-right order of auxiliate and auxiliary in Tamil would then follow not from a condition inscribed directly into Auxiliary Formation, but from independent conventions governing the order of meaningful elements.[32] A language with different conventions, like English, naturally exhibits a different linear order.

Whether the surface constituent formed by the auxiliary and auxiliate is continuous or not is another example of variation among languages where independent parameters may be invoked to fill in the details. Whereas the two elements in a Tamil AVC may be interrupted only by the insertion of a particle (pp. 132-34), English and German are much freer, permitting auxiliary and auxiliate to be separated by adverbs, parentheticals and even subjects, e.g., *He has already gone*; *She has, I guess, left for good*; *Was hat er getan*? Such differences are attributed directly to the gross combinatoric restrictions that determine how tightly or loosely knit a constituent's elements may be.

The syntactic categories, as well as the material they dominate, are also subject to variation in a cross-linguistic perspective. Node V_1 in Figure 1.2, the auxiliate, may dominate a simple verb or another AVC; in fact, Auxiliary Formation proves to be a cyclic process capable of generating multiply nested AVCs (Chapter 5). Node V_{-1} in Figure 1.3 may represent a simple verb (V) or a verb-phrase (VP). As compelling evidence for a VP constituent is lacking in Tamil, the label V suffices for our purposes: two verbs may directly combine in surface structure as in Figure 1.3. When two verbs combine in English, however, they may do so through the intermediary of a VP; given its generality, Auxiliary Formation is sufficiently flexible to interact with the different categorial resources of the relevant language.

The terminal nodes X and Y in Figures 1.3 and 1.5 remain conspicuously unspecified. This reflects the fact that while the AVC functions as a verb, neither the auxiliary nor the auxiliate need actually manifest a full range of verbal properties to fulfill their respective roles. In its denotational role, the auxiliate, represented by node X, need only incorporate a verb base, a function that may be satisfied through use of a deverbal noun or adjective as well as a nonderived verb form.[33]

32 Tamil's robust SOV word order places the heads of constructions after their immediate constituents: matrix clauses follow their complements, nouns follow dependent genitives, head nouns follow relative clauses, and, relevant here, auxiliaries follow their auxiliates.

33 Friedin (1975) claims that the English progressive series, i.e., *I am running*, consists of the copula and a deverbal adjective, here *running*. Bolinger (1971) claims that *writing* in *I am writing* belongs to the category of nouns. Both proposals tacitly embody the claim that the AVC exploits an independently available English structure, an expansion of VP, *be* + *Adj* and *be* + *N*, respectively.

Tamil grammar permits two verbs to appear in construction in surface structure, but another language might not, requiring the auxiliate to assume some lexical category other than verb,[34] e.g., a deverbal noun, so that the AVC conforms to surface structure templates which stipulate, say, that N+V is well-formed, but V+V is not. Also relevant here is the fact that Tamil, like most Dravidian languages, distinguishes primarily between just two major parts of speech, verb and noun, so that categories such as adjectives, basic or deverbal, are simply unavailable. Further, what little noun to verb cross-categorial derivation there is in Tamil tends to alter the petty combinatoric restrictions of verbs so that deverbal nouns[35] are less suitable than full-fledged verbs as candidates for fulfilling the auxiliate's denotational function (see pp. 68-70).

To fulfill its inflectional role, the auxiliary is more likely to belong to a formally defined class of verbs, but even this stipulation admits some variation. Certain modal verbs in Tamil, as in English, lack the full range of verbal forms the language makes available,[36] yet still function as verbs and, therefore potentially, as auxiliaries. Though morphologically defective, they satisfy—albeit more weakly—an auxiliary's inflectional function because they occur where the syntactic rules of the language permit verbs to occur.[37]

The AVC's structure may vary in ways not wholly anticipated in Figure 1.3. The examples considered thus far involve combinations of a nonfinite auxiliate, e.g., the Tamil conjunctive, the English past participle, with an auxiliary which may or may not be finite according to context. Languages such as Old Tamil, however, permit serial verb constructions in which two or more formally finite verbs may enter directly into construction (Steever 1988, 2004); accordingly, some AVCs in Old Tamil, but not the modern language, appear as serial verbs (Chapter 2). The structure in Figure 1.3 appears to combine auxiliary and auxiliate through simple juxtaposition; another way in which languages may join two verbs in surface structure is through use of a conjunction. Although seldom encountered in the literature on auxiliaries,[38] such a conjunction strategy is in fact attested in several languages.

34 The Sanskrit periphrastic future (Renou 1938, Benveniste 1948), e.g. *dātāsmi* 'I am to give', consists of the agent noun *dātā* 'giving' and an inflected form of the copula *asmi* 'I am'. The noun is certainly deverbal; but a noun nonetheless. The sequence *N+V* is independently available in the language, and at one point became a target for the auxiliation of the periphrastic future.

35 For example, a deverbal noun takes a subject in the genitive, not the nominative. Further, deverbal nouns do not host past time adverbial expressions.

36 English modal auxiliaries, for example, lack the full range of verbal forms implied by English morphology, yet occur in contexts where other verbs occur. Importantly, they are suppleted in nonfinite positions by AVCs, e.g. *to have to* for **to must*.

37 Tamil permits both verbs and nouns to occur in predicate position. The distribution of finite and nonfinite predicates in a Tamil sentence is governed by a syntactic rule that is subsequently interpreted morphologically and reflected in the inflections of the predicate, be it noun or verb. Even though a predicate is formally a noun, a defective verb or full-fledged verb, it may meet the "inflectional" requirements of Auxiliary Formation simply by occupying predicate position and undergoing grammatical rules that apply to forms in that position. However, its lack of verbal morphology would tend to disqualify it from appearing in contexts requiring nonfinite verb forms.

38 Also see Kuteva (2001: 44) for examples from Danish, Norwegian, and Swedish.

Shopen (1971) and Carden and Pesetsky (1977), for example, describe a set of "fake" coordinate structures in English, i.e., structures coordinate in form but not in substance. Two English examples that appear to incorporate attitudinal auxiliaries include *Max* ***went*** *and lost my new CD*, and *Chris* ***upped*** *and left him*; these are unlike true coordinate structures in that they permit violation of the Coordinate Structure Constraint. As the surface structure templates of English permit two verbs to cooccur in coordinate structures, Auxiliary Formation opportunistically targets this structure to "patch" (Morgan 1972) these nascent AVCs into a fake coordinate structure.[39]

Even the transformations Auxiliary Formation deploys are subject to variation; perhaps reflecting differences in the stock of categories in each language, Tamil uses Predicate Raising[40] to adjoin the auxiliate to the auxiliary while English uses Raising to Subject Position and, perhaps, Conjunction for the same task.[41] What matters is that all these differences in category membership, lexical class, constituency, linear order and even transformational rules need not directly follow from—or encumber the formulation of—Auxiliary Formation but may be ascribed to independent principles of individual languages.

SEMANTIC FUNCTION

The AVC's primary semantic function is to convey verbal categories. Simple as that may sound, some authors have despaired of characterizing all indicative auxiliaries in Tamil in terms of a single category such as aspect. They appear to have concluded that verbal categories are only incidental to the AVC's analysis and have largely abandoned further semantic analysis of the categories that AVCs might encode, retreating to a simple listing of exemplars.

Jakobson's (1971) system of grammatical categories is utilized in the semantic analysis of Tamil AVCs. His model is used here to establish the basic oppositions that organize the verbal system of Tamil, and to provide general points of reference for preliminary definitions of various verbal categories. While there is much more that could be said concerning such categories as tense, aspect or evidentiality, particularly from a cross-linguistic perspective, this model will serve as our starting point. On Jakobson's theory, every utterance has four components: the speech event E^s, the narrated event E^n, the participants in the speech event P^s and the participants in the narrated event P^n. These four components, singly or in combination, define grammatical categories. A designator is a category that consists of just

39 English relies on this new strategy because the set of verbs that govern the past or present participle appears to be closed to all but a small set of verbs, e.g., *be*, *have*, *get*. Such a strategy is not open to Tamil first, because there is no separate word class of conjunctions, and second, because the clitic *=um* 'all, and', which has a conjoining function, may not attach to finite verbs.

40 Or Verb Raising, depending on how different underlying and surface structures are held to be.

41 Consonant with Benveniste's perspective, these devices are transformations that generate constituents, not word-formation rules that characterize words; their output is a syntactic object.

one of the four elements, and characterizes the quantitative or qualitative features of the element in question. For example, the familiar category of number is analyzed as the quantifier of P^n: it characterizes the number of participants in the narrated event without reference to any other element of the utterance, and includes such oppositions as plural vs. singular, mass vs. count, etc. Gender is the qualifier of P^n: it characterizes qualities, inherent or ascribed, natural or social, that the participants in the narrated event display, and includes such distinctions such as animate vs. inanimate, masculine vs. feminine, honorific vs. nonhonorific, as well as noun classifier systems.

A connector is a category that consists of two or more elements, and characterizes the relation between those elements. Voice, represented by P^nE^n, characterizes the roles the participants in the narrated event play in that event, and includes such oppositions as active vs. passive voice, reflexive vs. nonreflexive, etc. Taxis, known also as relative tense[42] and symbolized by E^nE^n, characterizes the relation between two narrated events. Any connector that refers to the speech event or its participants is called a shifter, i.e., its meaning "shifts" with the speaker. Person, P^n/P^s, for example, characterizes the relation of the participants in the narrated event with respect to the participants in the speech event. If a participant in the narrated event is identified with the speaker, it is marked for first person; with the hearer, second person; and with neither, third person. Tense, E^n/E^s, characterizes the temporal relation of the narrated event with respect to the speech event. If the time reference of the narrated event precedes the time reference of the speech event, it is marked for past tense; if it coincides, present tense; if it follows, future tense.

Certain details of this system require modification for Tamil. First, the concept of connector is broadened to capture certain generalizations about Tamil auxiliaries. At least two auxiliaries, *viṭa* 'leave' and *koḷḷa* 'hold' (see Chapter 6), must be treated as generalized connectors in the following sense. They appear general between the categories of taxis (E^nE^n), voice (P^nE^n) and status (E^sE^n), so that they are special cases of a more general category, symbolized by XE^n, where X ranges over P^n, E^s and E^n.[43] Second, the Tamil data require a new verbal category, attitude, which is symbolized as P^s/E^n and is distinct from what Jakobson calls status.[44] Attitude is a shifter that characterizes the speaker's (P^s) subjective evaluation of the narrated event (E^n); it conveys the speaker's subjective opinion about the content of the narrated event including, perhaps, its participants. Expressions that mark attitude may signal the speaker's disapproval of, or admiration for, the situation or

42 The term taxis is preferred over relative tense because as the Tamil evidence shows, the relation between two narrated events need not be temporal, but may be epistemic, logical, etc.

43 Our innovation amounts to allowing a fifth element, the variable X, to appear in the formulation of grammatical categories, where X is constrained to range over the four other elements, X^n over the narrated event and its participants, X^s over the speech event and its participants. Traditional Tamil grammar provides us with an example in which two related categories kept separate in the Western tradition are joined: *pāl* refers to number-gender, that is, to both the qualifier and the quantifier of P^n.

44 I am aware that since I first proposed it as a term of art in the early 1980s, 'attitude' has acquired certain overtones in popular culture. There should be little danger of confusing the two here.

its participants, but expressions that signal pejorative attitude are more frequent than those that do not. The overall behavior of attitudinal auxiliaries in Tamil places them squarely within the set of indicative auxiliaries, but certain grammatical behavior, predictable from their categorial analysis, sets them apart as a distinct subset (Chapter 8).

Verbal categories then are those grammatical categories, one element of which characterizes the narrated event E^n.[45] The semantic analysis of an AVC thus concentrates on specifying the exact content of the verbal category it conveys. The empirical methods used to elicit its meaning are familiar: determining the petty combinatorics of a given AVC; substituting one auxiliary for another in the same syntactic frame; and contrasting an AVC with its simple, nonauxiliated counterparts. These methods approach the AVC's semantics from the outside; our model permits us to triangulate its meaning from within. Since an AVC's characteristic meaning is by hypothesis a function of the auxiliate's form and the auxiliary's lexical base, we may ask how that meaning is distributed over the various components. Each element may be analyzed independently of the other to determine what it contributes to the content of the verbal category associated with an AVC. Analysis of Tamil AVCs will show that the auxiliate establishes the broad range of verbal categories within which the AVC's characteristic meaning falls, while the lexical base of the auxiliary further specifies and differentiates it from other AVCs.

The question of what the auxiliate's inflection contributes to an AVC's overall meaning has two parts. First, which inflections may the auxiliate bear, and which, if any, must it exclude? Second, once a range of acceptable inflections is established, what impact does the choice of one over another have on the AVC's meaning? As above, the answers to both questions ultimately require empirical study, but preliminary considerations can help establish some guidelines. First, mood and aspect are the most likely candidates to be expressed in the auxiliate's inflection. Mood, the qualifier of E^n, characterizes the ontological status of the narrated event as real or not (Aronson 1978). Aspect, the quantifier of E^n, characterizes the internal structure of the narrated event with such oppositions as punctual vs. durative, perfective vs. imperfective (Holisky 1981). They are the most basic verbal categories in Jakobson's system; of the two, mood is the more basic because, unlike aspect, it does not presuppose the division of the narrated event into parts, such as an onset, body and coda, over which aspectual distinctions such as perfectivity vs. imperfectivity may be realized.

A preliminary upper limit may also be placed on the categories for which an auxiliate can inflect; specifically, it should not inflect for taxis (E^n/E^n). Taxis presupposes the existence of two distinct narrated events, between which a particular relation is purported to hold; its appearance on the auxiliate would defeat the definition of an AVC as a periphrastic form that refers to a single situation. An auxiliate marked for taxis would force the auxiliate and auxiliary to have separate denotational functions, in direct contravention of the AVC's characterization which invests its denotational function solely in the auxiliate's verb base. In practical terms, this

45 As Jakobson (1971:133) succinctly observes, "Any verb is concerned with a narrated event."

stricture prohibits Tamil auxiliates from bearing the conditional suffix, e.g. *vant-āl* 'if (one) comes'; the conditional marks a species of taxis, linking one situation in a protasis to another in an apodosis.[46] What the auxiliate's inflection contributes to an AVC's characteristic meaning is analyzed in Chapter 3; arguments show that mood, represented by the opposition of modal vs. indicative, is the primary category that informs and organizes the entire Tamil verbal system, including AVCs.[47]

Our model also treats as a limiting case those AVCs in which the meaning associated with the auxiliate's inflection is so negligible as to contribute little or nothing to the overall meaning of the AVC. Recall that an AVC consists of two independent forms each of which is flanked by word boundaries; however, independence here may be construed weakly or strongly. The weak interpretation holds that the two forms are independent words; the strong interpretation adds that they occur in syntactic contexts outside the AVC. Tamil auxiliaries generally illustrate the strong interpretation: the auxiliate's inflection has an invariant meaning it contributes to the AVC's overall meaning. However, the weak interpretation is available cross-linguistically to describe AVCs in which the auxiliate's form has lost so much of its distributional freedom—and consequently its meaning—that its inflection now appears to be unilaterally governed by an auxiliary. In such situations the auxiliate's form does not occur outside an AVC; though an independent word on phonological and morphological grounds, it lacks syntactic freedom. The complex tense form in Macedonian (Friedman 1977: 13) *sum pravel* 'I am doing' appears to illustrate this possibility: it consists of an inflected form of the copula *sum* 'I am' and the verbal l-form (*glagolska l-forma*) *pravel* 'doing', which was once a resultative participle, but now occurs only inside an AVC. While the word-formation rules of the language continue to motivate a word boundary between the copula and the verbal l-form,[48] that form is now an automatic adjustment of the auxiliate's verb base in this AVC. Such a loss of distributional freedom tends to compromise the transparency and stability of an AVC, and may precipitate a diachronic change in which the auxiliate and auxiliary fuse to form a new conjugation (see Steever 1993). However, to take the weak interpretation as paradigmatic of Auxiliary Formation, which appears to be the stance in many analyses, would tend to deny the possibility that AVCs could be analyzed compositionally.

Localism

What the auxiliary's lexical base contributes to the meaning of the AVC is primarily an empirical matter. Our model assumes that, all things being equal, the meaning it contributes to the AVC should be the same meaning it contributes to other structures. For example, Benveniste's (1974) analysis of the perfect tense auxilia-

46 However, see Chapter 3 for a possible counterexample.

47 From these arguments also emanate the rule of thumb, discussed above, that whenever the auxiliate inflects for the infinitive, it is a modal AVC; for the conjunctive form, an indicative AVC.

48 Except in the third person singular where there is no explicit copula.

ries in French, *avoir* 'have' and *être* 'be', clearly indicates that he considers them the same lexemes *avoir* and *être* that function as main verbs. His approach seeks to establish invariant meanings for them, general between their use as simple, nonauxiliated verbs and as auxiliaries. Given the AVC's segmentation into four discrete components, this is the approach that a synchronic analysis of AVCs demands as a matter of course.[49]

Some observations may be made concerning the lexicography of verbs that serve as auxiliaries. Though some indeterminacy lingers over the exact choice of lexeme, certain trends emerge. First, when choosing among several verbs with similar meanings, the one with the least specific lexical content tends to serve as an auxiliary; in other words, a hypernym is chosen more often than a hyponym, explaining why *give* serves more readily as an auxiliary of benefactive voice than such hyponyms as *offer*, *donate*, *bestow*, etc.[50] Second, verbs of motion frequently serve as auxiliaries, apparently because they coordinate dimensions of space and time. When used as main verbs, i.e., as auxiliates in an AVC or simple, nonauxiliated verbs, they express motion or transition through a concrete domain such as space; when used as auxiliaries, the transition is through abstract domains such as time or knowledge. The spatial and temporal uses of words, as well as their interaction, have been studied under the rubric of localism (e.g. Anderson 1973, Bennett 1975, Lyons 1977), a model which contends that an expression's spatial use precedes its temporal use, both logically and in history. This view tends to privilege the nominal, spatial, concrete use of a word over its verbal, temporal, abstract use. The synchronic orientation of this book compels us to take the agnostic stance that at a given stage of a language, a form exhibits both spatial and temporal uses, without necessarily specifying which takes precedence.

The motive hypothesis proposes that verbs of motion, which correlate dimensions of space and time, are apt candidates for auxiliaries. It covers a broader range of verbs than the localistic hypothesis; in fact, a locative expression may be viewed as a special case of a motive expression, one whose spatial coordinates remain the same while its temporal coordinates change.[51] The Tamil auxiliaries do include several verbs of motion. The lexicography of attitudinal auxiliaries, however, requires yet further elaboration. Many are verbs of motion, but ones that additionally express an indeterminate manner of motion, e.g., *vaẓiya* 'ooze, drip', or an unspecified goal, e.g., *tolaiya* 'get lost'. Such verbs emphasize the liminal nature of the motion they denote, a hypothesis developed in Chapter 8.

49 Since languages do contain historical residue at any given point in time, the pristine functions and interactions of the auxiliate and auxiliary may be obscured to one degree or other.

50 The more specific petty combinatorics of the hyponym makes it less likely to subcategorize a sentential subject.

51 Verbs of motion ordinarily signal a transition from a starting point along a path to an endpoint. A verbal category is typically represented by a grammatical opposition of at least two terms; the information associated with these values qualifies the narrated event in some respect. Figuratively speaking, verbs of motion act as pointers that select one of these values from the specific range established by the opposition; the starting point and endpoint of the motion can serve to represent two different information-states, e.g. modal vs. nonmodal.

The localist, motive and liminal hypotheses have their limitations. They imply a congruence between a lexeme and a verbal category that should permit the substitution of a synonymous lexeme in an AVC without distorting the category. The history of Tamil (Steever 1993) does present instances of such interchangeability: in the medieval language, three auxiliaries *niṟka* 'stand', *irukka* 'be located' and *kiṭakka* 'lie' could all combine with an auxiliate to form a present progressive tense form.[52] Even the English passive auxiliary *be* appears to allow some degree of substitution, as in *we **stand** rebuked.*[53] However, the counterexamples where such substitution fails appear to outweigh these cases; one cannot replace the auxiliary *have* in *I have gone* with a verb such as *own, possess, enjoy* or *suffer* without creating word salad. Nor is it methodologically sound to retreat behind the claim that true synonyms are extremely rare as a means of resolving this problem. One final failing of these hypotheses is that they fail to explain the presence of certain words that do serve as of indicative auxiliants, e.g., *aẓa* 'cry' (Chapter 8).

The relation between Auxiliary Formation and these three lexical hypotheses, however provisional it may be, admits of several interpretations which may be used to describe different AVCs in different languages. The auxiliary is treated as a free form to distinguish it from a bound form, such as a verbal inflection. A strong interpretation defines this freedom as the ability to occur in grammatical contexts other than the AVC; such an interpretation implies that the meaning of the lexical item which occurs in an AVC is univocal throughout all its uses. An intermediate interpretation holds that the lexeme, as an auxiliary, is weakly related to homophonous forms outside the AVC; both represent different specializations of what may once have been a single form at some earlier stage of the language. This position is familiar to most linguists, in large part because it reflects the fact that at any given point in a language's history, a synchronic grammar often contains diachronic residue. A third, weak interpretation is that no synchronic connection remains between the lexeme that occurs as an auxiliant and a homophonous form that occurs elsewhere. The second and third interpretations, when they are reached, often signal a potential diachronic change. In medieval Tamil, for example, the auxiliary verb *kil-/kiṟ-* 'be able' came ultimately to occur only in an AVC then fused with its preceding auxiliate to form a new synthetic form, the present tense of Modern Tamil; the old auxiliary exists as an independent word only in the related language Toda (Steever 1993).

The second and third interpretations are generally to be avoided as long as possible, given that the forms in question often exhibit the same phonology and morphology inside the AVC and out, which would then have to be treated as accidental. As a matter of methodology, then, homophonous forms are assumed to have a

52 However, in the transition to Modern Tamil only the latter two auxiliaries survived (Steever 1993), but in different functional niches. See Chapter 6 for *irukka* and Chapter 7 for *kiṭakka*.

53 From one perspective, the English passive with *get* is a counterexample to this hypothesis of substitutability of synonyms; since it is not a clear synonym of *be*, it shouldn't occur as an auxiliary. However, its choice may also be motivated by the fact that it encodes attitude as well as voice. See also the German 'addressee' passive with auxiliary *kriegen* 'get' (Kuteva 2001: 38).

single meaning, valid in all contexts, until contrary evidence emerges. Whatever interpretation of the auxiliary's independence is taken, so long as the language motivates an AVC, not a synthetic, bound form, the AVC's lexical and syntactic dimensions are distinct and capable of independent analysis.

EXTERNAL FUNCTIONS

Our outline of Auxiliary Formation concludes with a brief discussion of its external functions. We have already noted that instead of conjuring up new conjugations or word-formation rules out of thin air, a language may utilize Auxiliary Formation to generate new forms, viz. AVCs. This process takes as its raw materials the existing morphological, lexical and syntactic resources of the language, and combines these basic elements to fashion periphrastic compound verbs. In doing so, Auxiliary Formation enlarges the range of grammatical frames in which various basic elements of the language may appear. This "value-added" function thus tends to maximize the use of basic verbal elements in the language by extending their range of occurrence into AVCs. Earlier, Bloch (1946: 69) had already observed the use of syntactic means to supplement the allegedly limited morphological resources of the Dravidian languages.

> Réduit à ses éléments essentiels, le verb dravidien est une construction fruste et pauvre. Les diverses langues l'ont enrichi quelque peu par les combinaisons variées introduisant des nuances d'aspect et de temps, mais généralement sans aboutir à des systèmes complets.[54]

Auxiliary Formation, whose AVCs are surely included among Bloch's *combinaisons variées*, may from a certain perspective be viewed as a syntactic response to two limitations in Tamil. First, the language has only a limited number of verbal categories; viewed from the cross-linguistic platform from which Bloch was evidently speaking, the number and variety of categories for which a Tamil verb may be inflected are relatively modest. This motivates the application of Auxiliary Formation to generate AVCs that convey verbal categories above and beyond what the basic verbal inflections of the language offer its speakers.

Second and tentatively, Auxiliary Formation may also be a response to the paucity of parts of speech in Tamil. There are arguably only two major parts of speech, nominals and verbs; other putative categories, such as determiners, postpositions, adjectives, adverbs and the like, may generally be resolved into simple or compound nominals or verbals. Thus, to express what other languages express through the use of these other categories, Tamil must resort to its two major categories, nouns and verbs, simple and complex. Study of individual AVCs in Chapters 6

54 'Reduced to its basic elements, the Dravidian verb is an incomplete and simple form. The various languages have enriched it somewhat through different combinations introducing nuances of aspect and tense, but without generally leading to complete systems [SBS].'

through 8 suggests that Tamil elaborates AVCs, particularly in the categories of taxis and attitude, to express meanings that in other languages might well be expressed through distinct categories of conjunctions and adverbs.

Bloch (1946: 50) had already noted the use of AVCs in the Dravidian languages to supplement the lack of such basic parts of speech; for example, the majority of Dravidian languages generally lack a primitive category of adverbs, and so lack negative adverbs such as English *not*; to surmount this, they generate a separate negative conjugation of the verb.

> Il ne manque pas en dravidien de mots exprimant la négation. Mais sont le cas d'emprunt ou d'imitation de l'aryen... ce ne sont pas des adverbes—il n'y a pas d'adverbes en dravidien.[55]

Since creating new conjugations and word-formation rules for each new meaning would exact a relatively high linguistic cost on speakers and, ultimately, grammars, it would therefore seem less expensive for Auxiliary Formation to create a novel form, an AVC, to convey the desired meaning. (Less expensive, but by the same token less tidy because this can give rise to structural ambiguities.) These limitations on the parts of speech and on verbal categories would thus appear to correlate with and support an elaborate auxiliary verb system in Tamil with as many as 50 distinct AVCs. With so many AVCs Tamil may provide an excellent proving ground for the theory of Auxiliary Formation.[56]

Such external functions and their possible underpinnings may not be readily discernable within the synchronic grammar of a language but are best elicited in comparisons with other grammars, either historical or typological. However, before attempting these or the many other comparisons that the material in this chapter invites, readers may wish first to turn their attention to the ways in which Auxiliary Formation operates within the grammar of a single language, Tamil. Since much of what has been introduced here is programmatic in nature, our model can prove itself as a worthwhile addition to linguistic analysis only after its application to concrete problems in a concrete language.

Chapter 2 provides a brief introduction to Tamil, including a critical synopsis of the literature on the Tamil auxiliary verb system, which will enable the reader to follow the gist of the grammatical arguments made in this book. Chapter 3 offers a morphological analysis of the Tamil verb to discover the system of grammatical categories that informs both simple and complex verb forms in the language. Chapter 4 analyzes the internal syntactic properties of the constructions in which Tamil

55 'It's not that Dravidian lacks words expressing negation. But they are cases of borrowing or imitation of Indo-Aryan...they are not adverbs, there are no adverbs in Dravidian [SBS].'

56 The correlation between a small number of parts of speech and an elaborate auxiliary verb system is proposed only in Tamil and, more tentatively, for Dravidian. Further typological study would help us determine whether this functional aspect is due to some feature of Dravidian or to some other general linguistic tendency.

auxiliaries occur. Chapter 5 analyzes their external syntax, including the relative ordering among multiple auxiliaries, as well as their pragmatics. Turning to lexical semantics, Chapters 6-8 study the semantic properties of twenty-five individual auxiliaries in the language. Chapter 9 offers some concluding remarks on the usefulness of Auxiliary Formation in the linguistic analysis of Tamil and other languages. If in some places we revert to the more familiar terms main verb and auxiliary verb in place of auxiliate and auxiliary, there should be no cause for misunderstanding so long as it is remembered that they are defined by reference to the syntactic and semantic roles they play in the AVC.

2 The Tamil background

A SKETCH OF TAMIL

This chapter provides readers with a sketch of Tamil grammar to enable them to follow our examples and arguments. Embedded within this sketch is a discussion of the methods used to gather and transcribe the primary data. Rounding off the discussion is a critical synopsis of the scholarly literature on Tamil auxiliaries to provide a context for our analysis.

Tamil (*tamiẓ*) is a Southern Dravidian language (see Steever 1987, Lehmann 1989, Annamalai and Steever 1998) that has been spoken in southern Indian and northern Sri Lanka from prehistoric times. Its closest relatives are Malayalam, spoken in Kerala, and Irula, a tribal language spoken in the Nilgiri Mountains. With over 50 million speakers, Tamil is a national language in India, Sri Lanka, Malaysia and Singapore; communities of speakers also live in Myanmar, South Africa, Fiji and around the Caribbean. It is the first official language of the Indian state of Tamil Nadu.

The earliest records of Tamil date to c. 250 BCE; these and subsequent records reveal three stages: Old Tamil (300 BCE–700 CE), Middle Tamil (700 CE–1600 CE) and Modern Tamil (1600 CE–the present). Besides these historical stages, Tamil varies along three other dimensions. The modern language embraces several geographic dialects, but distinguishes primarily between the conservative dialect of Sri Lanka and the innovating ones of India. Dialects also vary according to caste groupings, with the major distinction between Brahmin and non-Brahmin dialects. Finally, Tamil exhibits robust diglossia (see Britto 1986, Steever 1988), with a "high" variety (*centamiẓ*) used in formal settings and a "low" variety (*koṭuntamiẓ*) used in all face-to-face communication (see Asher 1985). This diglossic distinction overlaps, but does not entirely coincide, with the distinction between written and spoken Tamil (see Schiffman 1999a, Steever 2002a).

The varieties spoken by high non-Brahmin castes in Madurai, Tanjore and Tiruchirappalli appear to be converging as the modern spoken standard; this standard supplied the basic data for this book. Different sexes, age groups, literacy levels, castes and religious affiliations are represented; however, no attempt has been made to correlate the data with these indices, partly because only a small number of respondents were polled in any one group and partly because the actual responses were largely uniform over these groups.[1] Such differences, where they matter, are noted in the text. Crucial data, particularly so-called negative data, were gathered from speakers living in and around Madurai over the course of a year.[2] Primary data were elicited through interviews in Tamil and English, as well as observation of spontaneous speech. Sample sentences were constructed and submitted to native speakers for their judgments; the primary datum is therefore a pair consisting of an expression of Tamil, usually a sentence, and a grammaticality/acceptability judgment.[3] In order to get an insider's view of Tamil, many of the data were discussed in detail with native speakers who are professional linguists. Literary sources such as short stories, magazine articles and novels yielded supplemental material, frequently providing contexts to help focus the point under study.

Modern Tamil phonology has a native core and a borrowed periphery. The core has 12 vowel and 16 consonant phonemes. Five simple vowel qualities, *a, i, u, e, o*, occur short or long; the two diphthongs, *ai* and *au*, are treated as unit phonemes. The periphery contains such vowels as *æ*, usually in words borrowed from English. The core contains sixteen consonants in three groups: stops: *k, c, ṭ, t, p*; nasals: *ñ, ṇ, n, m*; and liquids: *y, r, l, v, ṟ, ẓ, ḷ*. The traditional Tamil alphabet also includes symbols for letters occurring mainly in Sanskritic loans, *ś, ṣ, h*, as well as symbols that are graphemically, but not phonemically distinct, *ṅ, ṉ, ṟ* (these latter two are distinguished from *n* and *r*, respectively, according to their morphophonemics). The periphery includes the additional consonants *b, d, ḍ, j, g, s, f*. In rapid, unguarded speech, sounds of the periphery, both vowels and consonants, are commonly assimilated to their nearest corresponding sound in the core, e.g., *f* is commonly assimilated to *p*. Syllable structure is relatively simple; the metrical structure of words is governed by quantitative length, not qualitative stress. When morphemes combine, a number of phonological processes may occur, such as the deletion of a final consonant or the insertion of a glide between the two. To preserve transparency in morphemic identity, we adopt Lehmann's convention of placing a period before a segment that automatically results from such processes, e.g., in *anta.p peṭṭi.y-ai.t tūkku* 'lift that box', the *.p* at the end of the demonstrative *anta* 'that' is triggered by the initial stop of the following word; the *.y* in *peṭṭi.y-ai* is automatically inserted between the final vowel of *peṭṭi* 'box' and the initial vowel of the accusative case marker *-ai*; the *.t* in *peṭṭi.y-ai.t* is triggered by the following voiceless stop of *tūkku* 'lift'.

Over the years phonology has received less scholarly attention than morphology

1 As a matter of methodology, the general grammatical properties of the phenomena that are said to vary should at least be provisionally established before studying its variation.

2 Additional data was gathered during a subsequent yearlong stay in India.

3 During a lecture reporting on this research, Fedson criticized the use of constructed examples, preferring only examples that occurred in texts. This philological method cannot yield negative data, i.e., the information that such and such a modifier is ungrammatical. While some examples may have been constructed, the grammaticality judgments were not. Furthermore, construction of examples offers a distinct advantage in the compact presentation of data, as will be seen in the section on the auxiliary *kiẓiya* 'be torn' and *kiẓikka* 'tear' (Chapter 8).

or syntax (but see Christdas 1988, Keane 2001). This has led many (Paramasivam 1979) to adopt the strategy of taking the transcription of the written language as the underlying phonological representation—simultaneously the output of the syntactic component and the input to the phonological component—and the corresponding spoken form as the surface representation. The rules that convert the one into the other are then considered to represent the content of Tamil phonology. While unsatisfactory in certain respects, this practice offers a tolerable view of Tamil phonology because the transparent, agglutinating morphology of the language tends to inhibit the development of complex morphophonemic patterns.

This book adopts the common practice of presenting examples from spoken Tamil using the conventions of written Tamil. The differences between the spoken and written varieties do not generally affect the analysis of morphology or syntax, but where phonological or phonetic issues are relevant, they are noted in the text.[4] This policy pertains to examples elicited from speakers; examples from written sources are not normalized but simply transliterated from the Tamil writing system (Steever 1996).

Tamil morphology distinguishes primarily between words, which are free forms, and clitics, which are not. The language has an agglutinative morphology; words transparently consist of a lexical root and a series of suffixes. Boundary markers for words, suffixes and morphemes are inserted where they help clarify morphemic identity; when not germane, they are omitted. Accordingly, the verb *cettuppōṉāṉ* 'he died', which may be analyzed into the compound verb *#ce-t.tu.p# #pō-ṉ-āṉ#* lit. 'having died, he went', is transcribed as a single verb unless its internal structure is at stake.

The language has two major parts of speech, noun and verb, both of which are identified by their inflectional patterns. Little consensus exists concerning minor parts of speech, e.g., some view adjectives expansively as an independent part of speech while others treat them restrictively as defective nouns. The language lacks basic determiners, adverbs and conjunctions; the functions normally associated with them are assumed by other morphosyntactic devices, including compounding, nonfinite verb forms and clitics. Tamil possesses a small but significant set of postclitic particles: when combined with individual words, they form a single phonological word; however, they semantically modify entire phrases or sentences. Members of this set include quantifiers, such as *=ō* 'any, or', *=um* 'any, every', and emphatic particles, such as *=tāṉ* 'indeed', *=ē* 'even'. Their presence is indicated in this work by the boundary marker =.

Nominals are inflected for gender, number, case and person; they include common nouns, proper names, pronouns, numerals and some so-called adjectives. Gender is based on natural, not grammatical classes: the basic opposition is between animate vs. inanimate, largely coinciding with human vs. nonhuman. Animates are further classified as masculine, feminine and honorific. Gender determines such properties as the choice between the inanimate locative suffix *-il* and

4 This policy does not materially differ from that adopted by syntacticians working on well-known languages such as English or French where examples are generally presented in their written forms.

Table 2.1 Sample declension of Tamil nouns

	maṉitaṉ 'man'	*paẓam* 'fruit'
Singular		
Oblique stem	*maṉitaṉ-*	*paẓatt-*
Nom.	*maṉitaṉ*	*paẓam*
Acc.	*maṉitaṉ-ai*	*paẓatt-ai*
Dat.	*maṉitaṉ-ukku*	*paẓatt-ukku*
Soc.	*maṉitaṉ-ōṭu*	*paẓatt-ōṭu*
Gen.	*maṉitaṉ-uṭaiya*	*paẓatt-uṭaiya*
Instr.	*maṉitaṉ-āl*	*paẓatt-āl*
Loc.	*maṉitaṉ-iṭam*	*paẓatt-il*
Abl.	*maṉitaṉ-iṭamiruntu*	*paẓatt-iliruntu*
Plural		
Nom.	*maṉitar-kaḷ*	*paẓaṅ-kaḷ*
Acc.	*maṉitar-kaḷ-ai*	*paẓaṅ-kaḷ-ai*
Dat.	*maṉitar-kaḷ-ukku*	*paẓaṅ-kaḷ-ukku*
Soc.	*maṉitar-kaḷ-ōṭu*	*paẓaṅ-kaḷ-ōṭu*
Gen.	*maṉitar-kaḷ-uṭiaya*	*paẓaṅ-kaḷ-uṭaiya*
Instr.	*maṉitar-kaḷ-āl*	*paẓaṅ-kaḷ-āl*
Loc.	*maṉitar-kaḷ-iṭam*	*paẓaṅ-kaḷ-il*
Abl.	*maṉitar-kaḷ-iṭamiruntu*	*paẓaṅ-kaḷ-iliruntu*

the animate locative marker *-iṭam*. Nouns inflect for two numbers, singular and plural, and for eight cases: nominative (zero), accusative (*-ai*), dative (*-k.ku*), genitive (*-uṭaiya, -iṉ*), sociative (*-ōṭa*), instrumental (*-āl*), locative (*-il, -iṭam*) and ablative (*-iliruntu, -iṭamiruntu*). Case markers are supplemented by postpositions which convey finer gradations of meaning (e.g., 'on account of', 'from within', etc.), e.g., *varai* 'up to, until' from the noun *varai* 'barrier'. There is, in effect, one declension: once the gender and the phonological shape of the noun are known, all subsequent forms can be predicted. The declension of animate *maṉitaṉ* 'man' and inanimate *paẓam* 'fruit' is illustrated in Table 2.1 above.

Tamil verbs are finite or nonfinite. Finite verbs generally mark both tense and subject-verb agreement, while nonfinite verbs do not. The marking for finite verbs may be overt or, as in the imperative, covert. There are seven morphophonemically distinct conjugations, one of which is illustrated below. Chapter 3 analyzes the verbal system in greater detail. Table 2.2 lists the finite forms of *kalaikka*[5] 'disperse' while Table 2.3 its nonfinite forms.

The basic word order in Tamil is Subject-Object-Verb;[6] in keeping with SOV word order, complement clauses precede matrix clauses, genitives precede their

5 Verbs are cited in their infinitive form, a departure from the practice of the *Tamil lexicon* (1982) which cites them in the deverbal noun in *–(t)tal*.

6 More precisely, Subject-Object-Predicate, where predicate includes both finite verbs and predicate nominals. However, verbs are far more common in this position.

Table 2.2 Finite forms of *kalaikka* 'disperse'

	Past	Present	Future	Future negative
1s	*kalai-t.t-ēṉ*	*kalai-k.kiṟ-ēṉ*	*kalai-p.p-ēṉ*	*kalaikka māṭṭ-ēṉ*
2s	*kalai-t.t-āy*	*kalai-k.kiṟ-āy*	*kalai-p.p-āy*	*kalaikka māṭṭ-āy*
3sm	*kalai-t.t-āṉ*	*kalai-k.kiṟ-āṉ*	*kalai-p.p-āṉ*	*kalaikka māṭṭ-āṉ*
3sf	*kalai-t.t-āḷ*	*kalai-k.kiṟ-āḷ*	*kalai-p.p-āḷ*	*kalaikka māṭṭ-āḷ*
3sh	*kalai-t.t-ār*	*kalai-k.kiṟ-ār*	*kalai-p.p-ār*	*kalaikka māṭṭ-ār*
3sn	*kalai-t.t-atu*	*kalai-k.kiṟ-atu*	*kalai-k.k-um*	*kalai-k.k-ātu*
1p	*kalai-t.t-ōm*	*kalai-k.kiṟ-ōm*	*kalai-p.p-ōm*	*kalaikka māṭṭ-ōm*
2p	*kalai-t.t-īrkaḷ*	*kalai-k.kiṟ-īrkaḷ*	*kalai-p.p-īrkaḷ*	*kalaikka māṭṭ-īrkaḷ*
3p	*kalai-t.t-ārkaḷ*	*kalai-k.kiṟ-ārkaḷ*	*kalai-p.p-ārkaḷ*	*kalaikka māṭṭ-ārkaḷ*
3pn	*kalai-t.t-aṉa*	*kalai-k.kiṟ-aṉa*	*kalai-k.k-um*	*kalai-k.k-ātu*

Nonfuture negative *kalaikka.v illai* (all persons, numbers, genders)

	Imperative	Negative imperative	Optative
s	*kalai*	*kalai-k.k-ātē*	*kalai.k-kuka*
p	*kalai.y-uṅkaḷ*	*kalai-k.kātīrkaḷ*	*kalai.k-kuka*

head nouns and auxiliates precede auxiliaries. The basic sentence consists of a subject and a predicate. The subject generally appears in the nominative case (9a and b), but a small set of predicates of cognition and possession select a subject in the dative case (9c and d). The predicate is generally a finite verb (9a and c), one that bears inflections for tense and agreement; in certain instances, however, the predicate may be a predicate nominal (9b and d). Combining the different kinds of subjects with the various kinds of predicates yields four basic sentence types. In the simple sentence, predicate nominals have the same distribution as finite verbs.

(9) a *avaṉ* *va.n-tāṉ.*
that.man-NOM come-PST-3SM
'He came.'

b *avaṉ* *nalla* *maṉitaṉ.*
that.man-NOM good man-NOM
'He is a good man.'

c *avaṉ-ukku* *caṅkītam* *piṭikkum.*
that.man-DAT music-NOM like-fut-3SN
'He likes music.'

d *avaṉ-ukku* *oru* *makaṉ.*
that.man-DAT one son-NOM
'He has a son.'

Complex sentences, coordinate and subordinate, consist of two or more clauses. Examples (2) and (3) in Chapter 1 have already shown that nonfinite verb forms such as the infinitive and conjunctive are commonly used to join together the vari-

Table 2.3 Nonfinite forms of *kalaikka* 'disperse'

	Past	Present	Future	Negative
Adnominal	*kalai-t.t-a*	*kalai-k.kiṟ-a*	*kalai-k.k-um*	*kalai-k.kāta*
Verbal noun	*kalai-t.t-atu*	*kalai-k.kiṟ-atu*	*kalai-p.p-atu*	*kalai-k.kātatu*
Infinitive	*kalai-k.ka*			
Conjunctive	*kalai-t.tu*			
Negative conjunctive	*kalai-k.kāmal, kalai-k.kātu*			
Conditional	*kalai-t.tāl*			
Negative conditional	*kalai-k.kāviṭṭāl*			
Deverbal noun	*kalai-k.kal, kalai-t.tal, kalai-p.pu, kalai-k.kai*			

ous clauses in complex sentences. So vigorously do they serve in this capacity, that the distribution of finite verbs is strictly limited, as a first approximation, to one finite verb per sentence. However, the identical distribution of predicate nominals and finite verbs in example (9a-d) demonstrates that finiteness in Tamil must be treated not as a morphological property of verbs, but as a syntactic property of sentences (Steever 1988). Hence, a Tamil sentence may have only one finite predicate: it occurs highest in the sentence's tree structure and c-commands all other predicates. With the head-final characteristics of Tamil, that means that the unmarked position for the lone finite predicate falls at the end of the sentence; all remaining predicates within the sentence must assume nonfinite forms. Two problems arise from this constraint. First, it allows no obvious way to form direct discourse; if sentences such as (9a or c), which have finite verb forms, were embedded under a verb of speech, they would have to change shape to a nonfinite form. Second, the constraint makes it impossible to embed sentences such as (9b or d), which have predicate nominals: as nouns, they lack verbal morphology altogether. In common with other Dravidian languages, however, Tamil has two sets of morphosyntactic devices that permit the embedding of finite predicates. First, forms of two verbs *eṉa* 'say' and *āka* 'become' frequently embed finite predicates. Example (10a) embeds a sentence with the predicate nominal *nallavaṉ* 'good man' in a complement clause under the conjunctive form of *eṉa*; (10b) embeds the finite verb *vantāṉ* 'he came' under the conditional form of *āka*.

(10) a [$_{S0}$ *nāṉ* [$_{S1}$ *avaṉ nallavaṉ*] *eṉṟu niṉaikkiṟēṉ*].
I-NOM he-NOM good.man-NOM say-CF think-PRS-1S
'I think that he is a good man.'

b [$_{S0}$ [$_{S1}$ *avaṉ vantāṉ*] *āṉāl nāṉ avanai.p pārkkavillai*].
he-NOM come-PST-3SM become-CND I-NOM he-ACC see-IND-NEG
'Although he came, I didn't see him.'

Second, Tamil also uses certain clitics, such as the quantifier *=ō* 'or, any', to embed finite predicates.

(11) $_{S0}[_{S1}[$*avaḷ* *pāṭukiṟāḷ*]=*ō* [*eṉakku.t* *teriyavillai*].
she-NOM sing-PRS-3SF=OR I-DAT know-IND-NEG
'I don't know whether she is singing.'

The number and position of finite predicates in the Tamil sentence can thus be seen to vary directly with the number and position of these two sets of devices (Steever 1988: 111-12).

PRIOR STUDIES OF THE TAMIL AUXILIARY

Several studies of the Tamil auxiliary are reviewed here; where one of them is pertinent to a specific point in our later analysis, it will be discussed at the appropriate place in the text. Tamil grammatical analysis includes three broad phases, reflecting different traditions and programs of analysis. The first phase, the indigenous grammatical tradition, begins in the first century BCE and continues to the present; it is represented by several grammars and supplemented by an extensive commentatorial tradition. The second phase begins with the European introduction of traditional Western grammatical analysis to Indian languages. Although its practitioners have included civil servants, clerics and entrepreneurs, it is called the missionary grammatical tradition, after the various missionaries to India who wrote grammars and handbooks of Tamil. It too continues to be practiced to the present. The third phase is the modern period, which begins with the comparative and historical analysis of the Dravidian languages in the nineteenth century and continues to the present along a continuous chain of linguistic studies, exemplified most recently by generative grammar.

Indigenous grammatical tradition

Two texts form the core of traditional Tamil grammar, the ancient grammar *tolkāppiyam* 'Ancient composition', c. first century BCE, and the medieval grammar *naṉṉūl* 'Good book', c. eleventh century CE. While others are known and studied, e.g. *viracōḻiyam*, these two anchor the tradition. Written in dense, aphoristic verse, they are now read only with difficulty; accordingly, an impressive commentatorial tradition has arisen to interpret them. There are, for example, six extant commentaries for the second book of the *tolkāppiyam*, the *collatikāram* 'On words' (see Cheveillard 1996). Both grammars figure actively in contemporary linguistic debate in Tamil.

tolkāppiyam and *naṉṉūl* describe the ancient and medieval stages of Tamil, respectively; as such, they are not directly relevant to our study, which focuses on the modern language. Accordingly, while we present some probable AVCs from Old Tamil, we cannot support them with the kinds of explicit arguments in Chapters 3-5. Earlier studies of the auxiliary have raised two interrelated questions about auxiliary verbs in Old Tamil. First, does the language have AVCs? Second, if it does, what do *tolkāppiyam* and *naṉṉūl* say about them? The silence of these grammars on the issue of auxiliary verbs has been interpreted to mean that Old Tamil lacked an auxiliary verb system. Dale (1975:47), for example, drew the following conclusion:

> In the traditional Tamil grammars, auxiliary verbs as such are never mentioned ... The reason that auxiliaries are not mentioned is doubtless that these works are concerned with the highly formalized Tamil of the classical literature in which auxiliary verbs occur only rarely or not at all.

This statement, which rests on an *argumentum ex silencio*, is best remedied by studying the pertinent texts. First, it is possible that *tolkāppiyam, collatikāram* 252, which is concerned with analysis of the *iṭaiccol ma<u>n</u>*, may be interpreted as discussing an auxiliary that signals perfect tense (see Steever 1993). Second, even a cursory reading of the classical anthologies reveals a robust auxiliary verb system. The silence over auxiliary verbs in Tamil grammatical tradition appears to follow from a general, often tacit presupposition of pan-Indic indigenous grammatical practice: matters of syntax are seldom treated because these grammars do not purport to generate well-formed sentences but, as we might now say, well-formed words. No attempt is made to describe phrasal categories or to define syntactic concepts such as construction or constituent; syntax, when treated at all, is analyzed obliquely in terms of words or word-classes.[7] Case, for example, is viewed as an exponent of the word-class of nouns rather than of noun phrases; tense is analyzed only when it is realized as a bound morph on a simple verb. If, as argued in Chapter 1, Auxiliary Formation is a syntactic rather than a lexical process, a word-based grammar would most likely fail to treat auxiliary phenomena.

Old Tamil AVCs based on the conjunctive

Old Tamil texts provide the best antidote to the claim that the language lacks auxiliaries, presenting several distinct AVCs and, for each AVC, several auxiliary verbs. The first kind of AVC combines the auxiliary with the conjunctive form of the auxiliate. The auxiliaries include *irukka* 'be' (progressive tense), *paṭa* 'befall' (passive voice), *vara* 'come' (durative), *aruḷa* 'grace' (benedictive voice), *iṭa* 'strike' (disjunctive taxis), *o<u>l</u>iya* 'purge' (pejorative attitude), *koḷḷa* 'hold' and *il* 'not be' (negative). The last two are illustrated in (12a and b). This AVC appears to be the forerunner of the indicative AVC in the modern language.

(12) a *nemiṭi* *koṇṭu* ... (*na<u>r</u><u>r</u>iṇai* 22.4).
scoop-CF hold-CF
'While (someone) was scooping up (something)...'

b *vant(u)* *illē<u>n</u>*.
come-CF be-IND-NEG-1s
'I do/did not come.'

7 Syntax is more likely to be treated in logical treatises of the *nyāya* philosophical school.

Old Tamil AVCs based on the bare verb base

The second kind of AVC combines the auxiliary with the auxiliate's bare verb base. In Old and Early Middle Tamil, but not later stages of the language, the bare verb base functioned as a free form. The auxiliaries include *tara* 'give to you or me' (benefactive voice), *vara* 'come' (durative aspect), *al* 'not become' (negative), and, in the early medieval period, *kil* 'be able'.

(13) a *iḻi* *tarum* ... (*naṟṟiṇai* 7.5).
descend-BVB give.to.you.or.me-FUT-3SN
'It will descend to us.'

b *acai* *vara* ... (*naṟṟiṇai* 20.4).
move-BVB come-INF
'As X keeps moving...'

This AVC disappeared during the medieval period; some of the auxiliaries that appeared in it have migrated into other AVCs; auxiliary *kil* contracted to become the present tense marker (see Steever 1993).[8]

Old Tamil AVCs based on muṟṟeccam

The third kind of AVC combines the auxiliary with a form of the auxiliate called *muṟṟeccam* in the commentatorial literature. A *muṟṟeccam* is formally finite, inflecting for tense and subject-verb agreement, but like a nonfinite form, it combines with another verb. The resulting structures are what have been called serial verbs (see Steever 1988). The two verb forms in (14a), *celvēm* 'we will go' and *allēm* 'we do not become', both formally finite, combine here to form an AVC that expresses negation. Example (14b), also a serial verb, is an AVC with the auxiliary *viṭa* 'leave'.

While the full range of the serial verb construction is not established, enough is known to see that it functioned in a variety of constructions. This kind of AVC disappears in the transition from Old to Middle Tamil; remarkably, the cognate of

8 Although Fedson (1981: 230) recognizes the unproductivity of the bare verb base in the modern language, also called the stem, she claims that it is an alternant of the infinitive: "The infinitive also occurs with *aTi* [= our *aṭikka*] 'beat' in a causative construction." Her example 459 is reproduced here as example (i).

(i) *toṇṭai taṇṇīrai vaṟṟ-aṭikkiṟa toḻil* ...
throat water-ACC dry-BVB-beat-PRES-ADN occupation
'An occupation that parches the throat...'

The form *vaṟṟaṭikka* 'parch' is a collocation of the bare verb base *vaṟṟu-*, not the infinitive which would have the shape *vaṟṟa*, and an inflected form of *aṭikka* 'beat'. If *aṭikka* truly governed the infinitive of the main verb, the combination of the two would, according to Tamil phonology, yield **vaṟṟa.v-aṭikka*, instead of *vaṟṟaṭikka*. This latter must be considered an idiomatic, nonsegmentable form, to be listed as such in the lexicon of Tamil.

(14a) construction survives in Muria Gondi, giving us independent verification of the auxiliary status of the Old Tamil construction (see Steever 1998).

(14) a *celvēm allēm* (*puṟanāṉūṟu* 31.11).
go-FUT-1P become-NEG-1P
'We will not go.'
b *nalkiṉam viṭṭatu* (*naṟṟiṇai* 176.2).
give-PST-1P leave-PST-VN
'That we did give ...'

Old Tamil AVCs based on verbal noun in -al

The fourth kind of AVC combines the auxiliary with the verbal noun in *-al* of the auxiliate, e.g. *var-al vēṇṭum* 'coming is necessary (i.e., someone has to come)'. Although this AVC appears in some modern belletristic prose, particularly with the auxiliaries *āka* 'become' and *vēṇṭum* 'be necessary', it is considered archaic, and no longer functions productively in the modern spoken language.

As Old Tamil verb morphology and syntax have only just begun to be satisfactorily analyzed (Lehmann 1991, 1998), we cannot yet say what factors motivate the choice of one AVC over another. We cannot project backwards directly from the modern language; the transition from Old to Modern Tamil is not one of simple merger, but of split and merger, in which the basic verb forms appear to have been revalorized. In Old Tamil the auxiliaries *paṭa* 'befall' and *il* 'not be' combined with the conjunctive form, but in latter stages with the infinitive; *tara* 'give to you or me' and *vara* 'come' combined with the bare verb base, but now with the conjunctive form. While *irukka* 'be' combines with the conjunctive form in both stages of the language, in Old Tamil it signals progressive tense and in Modern Tamil perfect tense. Table 2.4, compiled by the late K. Paramasivam in a separate project and presented opposite, is a partial catalogue of the AVCs and auxiliary verbs in the classical anthology *naṟṟiṇai*, showing how common they were in Old Tamil.

Missionary grammar and comparative philology

Missionaries to India, trained in Latin, Greek and Hebrew, wrote handbooks of many Indian languages, including Tamil, to translate the Bible and preach the gospel. Alongside them were civil servants and merchants who wrote (or had written) grammars for practical purposes in their respective administrative and mercantile pursuits. These grammars introduced a new tradition of grammatical analysis to India, one deriving from Western tradition. Along with them arrived philologists who took an interest in the origins and affiliations of the Indo-Aryan and Dravidian languages. They wrote descriptive grammars of individual languages, then comparative grammars of entire families. It is in this phase of grammatical study that we first encounter explicit mention of auxiliary verbs.

Missionary grammarians identified a number of auxiliary verbs. As their ends were largely practical, they provided lists and examples of auxiliary verbs, not the

Table 2.4 Some auxiliaries in the anthology *naṟṟiṇai*

Poem	Line	Auxiliate	Auxiliate's Form	Auxiliary
1	7	*nayantu* 'love'	conjunctive	*aruḷa* 'grace'
7	5	*iẓi* 'descend'	bare verb base	*tara* 'give to you or me'
20	4	*acai* 'move'	bare verb base	*vara* 'come'
22	4	*nemiṭi* 'scoop'	conjunctive	*koḷḷa* 'hold'
37	10	*tiri* 'wander'	bare verb base	*tara* 'give to you or me'
54	10	*tai* 'adorn'	bare verb base	*vara* 'come'
68	2	*iṟcerintu* 'be kept at home'	conjunctive	*irukka* 'be'
72	5	*aẓi* 'grieve'	bare verb base	*taka* 'be worthy'
84	9	*vīṟṟu* 'excel'	conjunctive	*irukka* 'be'
107	2	*piḷa* 'be broken hearted'	conjunctive	*iṭa* 'strike'
112	5	*aẓuntu* 'press'	conjunctive	*paṭa* 'befall'
149	10	*cumantu* 'bear'	conjunctive	*oẓiya* 'purge'
153	10	*kāttu* 'wait'	conjunctive	*irukka* 'be'
164	1	*turantu* 'neglect'	conjunctive	*irukka* 'be'
165	9	*olkāṇṭu* 'agree'	negative conjunctive	*oẓiya* 'purge'
176	2	*nalkiṉam* 'give'	*muṟṟeccam*	*viṭa* 'leave'
182	5	*eṭuttu* 'take'	conjunctive	*koḷḷa* 'hold'
189	1	*nayantu* 'love'	conjunctive	*aruḷa* 'grace'
202	7	*kāṇ* 'see'	bare verb base	*vara* 'come'
256	4	*vīṟṟu* 'excel'	conjunctive	*irukka* 'be'
293	8	*koṇṭu* 'hold'	conjunctive	*pōka* 'go'
308	8	*aṭai* 'reach'	bare verb base	*tara* 'give to you or me'
312	5	*kaḷaintu* 'soften the heart'	conjunctive	*aruḷa* 'grace'
316	7	*vāyttu* 'prosper'	conjunctive	*aruḷa* 'grace'
344	1	*vaḷarntu* 'grow'	conjunctive	*vara* 'come'
390	7	*celīiyar* 'go'	conjunctive	*vēṇṭum* 'be necessary'

necessary and sufficient conditions that a modern linguist would seek. Fabricius and Breithaupt (1789: 30ff.) list nine auxiliaries; eight combine with the conjunctive form of the main verb, one with the infinitive. Typical of nineteenth-century grammars is Pope (1855), who lists nine auxiliaries that govern the conjunctive form of the main verb. Comparative grammars of the Dravidian languages also mention auxiliary verbs. The first major work is Caldwell (1856); Bloch (1946) continues this line of inquiry, dedicating one section of his comparative grammar to an analysis of auxiliaries. Reference grammars were also written in support of the teaching and comparative grammars. Dupuis (1863: 285) treats auxiliary verbs in a section entitled "Des verbes composés." Vinson (1943) analyzes them in two sections, "Composés périphrastiques" and "Composés explétifs." Many of the constructions that have been catalogued under these headings would not meet our tests for AVCs; they even include noun-verb compounds (see Steever 1981). Conversely, certain AVCs, primarily those that convey attitude, are not treated. Dale (1975) and Fedson (1981) have compiled useful lists of these earlier grammars and their treatments of auxiliary verb phenomena.

Generative grammar

The analysis of Tamil auxiliary verbs continues into the period of generative grammar.[9] Several treatments have been proposed, including Bright and Lindenfeld (1968), Ramanujan and Annamalai (1969), Schiffman (1969), Dale (1975), Fedson (1981), Annamalai (1979, 1982), Steever (1983) and Herring (1991). Analyses of the Tamil auxiliary system exhibit virtually the same theoretical range as found in analyses of the English auxiliary system. Some, notably Agesthialingom (1963), Bright and Lindenfeld (1968) and Schiffman (1969), take the position that Tamil auxiliaries derive from an underlying phrasal category of AUX. Others, including Lindholm (1975), Dale (1975) and Fedson (1981), pursue a more traditional and lexically oriented approach. Annamalai (1982) takes the middle path of viewing auxiliaries as a subset of verbs that appear in syntactically specified contexts.

The use of labels in place of syntactic argument figures prominently in several analyses. Schiffman (1969) proposes a semantic feature [+MALEVOLENT] to explain the meaning of the auxiliary *tolaikka* 'lose'. This is fundamentally an ad hoc feature which performs no work in the grammar of Tamil. Similarly, Fedson (1981) applies the term 'perfect' to no less than four different auxiliaries, without indicating whether tense or aspect is involved, let alone how the four are to be distinguished. The function of auxiliaries in Tamil is sparsely described. Ramanujan and Annamalai (1968), Schiffman (1969) and Fedson (1981) all mention Jakobson's theory of verbal categories, but none claims that verbal categories necessarily figure in the definition of auxiliary verbs or puts Jakobson's theory to any meaningful use. Herring (1991) pursues a functionalist approach, studying the function of certain verb forms, among them auxiliaries, in oral narrative.

Another common shortcoming is neglect of the role that context plays in the analysis of Tamil auxiliary verbs. Annamalai (1982: 25) criticizes Dale because many of the sentences Dale deems unacceptable are normal when framed in the proper setting. Studies also differ as to what constitutes appropriate data. Some concentrate only on what speakers say (or write), not on what they can and cannot say or write. Schiffman (1969) extracts an invariant meaning from auxiliary *taḷḷa* 'push' on the basis of just three example sentences; problematically, none of them tests its limits through the use of negative data. Fedson (1981) largely limits her data to written texts, supplemented by her intuitions; she even calls into question the use of sentences constructed to test acceptability and grammaticality. Herring (1991) argues that certain Tamil verb forms, including auxiliaries, can be understood only by reference to their function within connected narrative, rather than in isolated sentences; however, she does not treat their use in conversation. The use of more examples, particularly of negative data, might have led to a fuller descrip-

9 In fairness it should be noted that not all the authors included in this section would consider themselves generative grammarians or their analyses generative studies. Dale (1975) and Fedson (1981), for example, eschew much of generative grammar. However, since these studies were written during a period in which generative grammar had become the dominant paradigm of grammatical analysis, they have been included here for convenience.

tion in several instances. Five analyses are reviewed here: Schiffman (1969), Dale (1975), Fedson (1981), Annamalai (1982) and Herring (1991).

Schiffman (1969)

Schiffman (1969) claims that the Tamil aspectual system, when compared with other languages, provides an argument to reject Chomsky's (1965) level of deep structure. Chomsky had argued that deep structure is where all Lexical Insertion takes place, before any transformations apply. He also required that wherever possible, deep structure should reflect what is universal in syntactic structure. Briefly, Schiffman argues the first criterion forces us to establish deep structures for Tamil radically different from those for English, in violation of the second criterion. He claims that on Chomsky's theory, languages which convey aspectual distinctions through affixation would have a radically different deep structure from those that specify aspect by auxiliary verbs. Schiffman attempts to retain the second criterion and dispense with the first, so that the difference between affixes and auxiliaries is attributed not to deep structure, but to differences in the application of Lexical Insertion. Unfortunately, Schiffman's (1969: 20) claim that aspectual distinctions in Tamil and English "probably have quite different underlying structures" tends to thwart this argument.

Schiffman's use of generative grammar, as then practiced, stumbles on the Tamil data. He claims, for example, that aspect in Tamil and English likely derive from separate sources.[10] He accepts Hoffman's (1966) claim that English aspect, as realized in the perfect auxiliary *have*, derives from underlying tense, presumably as an optional expansion of the AUX node. He then reasons that tense cannot be the source of aspect in Tamil because it is already the source of modals. But if tense is already the underlying source for both surface modals and surface tense in Tamil (Schiffman 1969: 14), nothing in principle precludes aspect from originating as another optional expansion of tense. Morever, Schiffman's implicit claim that since both tense and modals derive from underlying AUX, they should be in complementary distribution, is not borne out by observation. The modal auxiliary *muṭi-* 'be able' regularly inflects for tense, e.g. past *muṭintatu*, present *muṭikiṟatu* and tense *muṭiyum*, which should not be possible if, on his claim, two surface categories cannot both derive from the same source.

In any event, these general linguistic concerns have little impact on Schiffman's analysis of the Tamil auxiliary system. He questions whether all nonmodal auxiliaries can be brought under the semantic heading of aspect since the pejorative meaning of auxiliary *tolaikka* 'lose' does not conform to his idea of aspect. To overcome this, he proposes a redundancy rule: the feature [+MALEVOLENT] implies the feature [+ASPECT], but it is little more than a notational feint to assure taxonomic conformity among all auxiliaries, not because *tolaikka* 'lose' marks the category of as-

10 Kachru (1993: 127) observes that Schiffman's (1969) proposed derivation, the first generative treatment of Tamil auxiliaries, lacks explicit rules and argumentation.

pect. He further argues that Jakobson's theory of grammatical categories is not equal to the task of describing the semantic properties of individual auxiliaries in Tamil or the semantic properties they all share in common.[11] After rejecting Jakobson's theory of grammatical categories, he adopts Jespersen's (1965) procedure of listing a variety of grammatical phenomena which seem to involve aspect, directly or not. This approach, coupled with a paucity of empirical data, offers us no compelling explanation as to why all the items should appear together under a common heading.

Schiffman's analysis does not fully exploit the methods of research in generative grammar available at the time it was conceived. Surface and underlying structures for Tamil were proposed with no syntactic argumentation; there are, for example, no cooccurrence arguments of the kind in use since Lees' (1960) study of English nominalizations. Nor is such a criticism anachronistic since for centuries before generative linguistics, studying what kinds of expression can modify what other kinds of expressions has been part and parcel of the grammarian's work. His analysis forms the basis of subsequent descriptions (e.g., Schiffman 1999a) of auxiliary phenomena in spoken Tamil (see Steever 2002a).

Dale (1975)

Dale (1975) is concerned with the proper methods for collecting data on the Tamil auxiliary system and with how to draw conclusions from that data. His results are mainly statistical generalizations from the response sentences elicited through questionnaires. Grammatical theory was consciously avoided as prejudicial to this endeavor. Dale relies on such terms as content, style and delicacy to frame his results; while suggestive of Firthian functional grammar, without further elaboration, they appear to belong more to esthetics than grammar. The meaning of an auxiliary is claimed to be determined, "... for reasons of style, rather than content (Dale 1975: 415)." In discussing the role of auxiliaries in Tamil verb phrases, it is said that "... a great part of its flexibility and delicacy of implication is conveyed by the use of auxiliary verbs (Dale 1975: 21)." In studying the distribution of the auxiliary in the Tamil sentence, Dale (1975: 15) proposes the term auxiliary balance, the concept that "... the presence of an auxiliary verb in one clause tends to encourage an auxiliary in the other as well." Numerous examples here fail to exhibit this concept of auxiliary balance without leading to unidiomatic or unacceptable sentences; for now, the examples in (15) will suffice. In (15a) the first clause contains an AVC, *vantu viṭṭu* 'after X came'; the second clause, a simple verb, *tūṅkiṉāṉ* 'he slept'. In (15b) the reverse obtains: the first clause contains a simple verb, *pōy* 'going'; the second clause, an AVC, *āki viṭṭatu* 'it has been'.

11 He claims, for example, that it cannot include tense and aspect in the same subsystem "... since for Jakobson tense and aspect are unrelated ... (Schiffman 1969: 57)." However, in Jakobson's theory tense and aspect both make crucial reference to the narrated event, which is to say that both are verbal categories. As argued below, all Tamil indicative auxiliary verbs, even the attitudinal ones, refer to the narrated event.

(15) a $_{S0}$[*avaṉ* $_{S1}$[$_{AVC}$[$_{V1}$[*vantu*] $_{V2}$[*viṭṭu*]]] $_{S2}$[$_{V3}$[*tūṅkiṉāṉ*]].
he-NOM come-CF leave-CF sleep-PST-3MS
'He slept after he came home.'

b $_{S0}$[$_{S1}$[*avaṉ* *tamiḻnāṭṭukku.p* $_{V1}$[*pōy*]] $_{S2}$[*oru varuṣam*
he-NOM Tamilnadu-DAT go-CF one year-NOM
$_{AVC}$[$_{V2}$[*āki*] $_{V3}$[*viṭṭatu*]]]].
become-CF leave-PST-3N
'It's been a year since he went to Tamil Nadu.'

Dale lists seven criteria for defining auxiliary verbs. First, in the verb phrase, "... a great part of its flexibility and delicacy of implication is conveyed by the use of auxiliary verbs (Dale 1975: 21)." Second, "each auxiliary is ... identical in phonological shape to a main verb of the language, being differentiated from this on grounds of its syntactic behavior."[12] Third, auxiliary verbs have the same meaning as main verbs. Fourth, main verbs, but not auxiliaries, can occur alone following nominal arguments. Fifth, each conjoined main verb retains it capacity to occur with complements and form the nucleus of an independent clause. Sixth, auxiliary verbs cannot occur alone in a verbal phrase and are found following main verbs and auxiliary verbs. Seventh, when an auxiliary verb is added to another verb, "it gives an aspectual or relational sense to the resulting compound, rather than contributing a lexical sense (Dale 1975: 19-20)." The first condition is vague and of little practical use. The distinction between "lexical" and "grammatical" meaning, underscored in the fourth and seventh conditions is vitiated by the third condition, which claims no distinction in meaning between main and auxiliary verbs. The fourth condition does not apply to the entire range of auxiliaries in Tamil: under certain circumstances the indicative auxiliaries *āka* 'become' and *kiḻikka* 'tear', as well as most modal auxiliaries, can occur without a main verb, although one is generally recoverable from context.

Dale gathered his data in interviews where he presented speakers of Tamil with a stimulus sentence and an instruction to alter that sentence. The stimulus contained an auxiliary, and the instruction manipulated some parameter of the sentence thought to correlate with the auxiliary, e.g. tense. Each pair of stimulus sentence and instruction was presented to twenty-five speakers representing different social communities.

Some limitations of this method emerge in Dale's study of the cooccurrence restrictions of auxiliary *viṭa* 'leave'. He devised a stimulus-instruction pair designed to discover whether the auxiliary could occur in all three tenses. The stimulus included auxiliary *viṭa* inflected for past tense and the time expression *nēṟṟu* 'yesterday'. His informants were instructed to replace *nēṟṟu* with the future time expression *nāḷaikku* 'tomorrow' to determine whether the substitution would trigger a shift in the auxiliary's tense marking. His informants did replace the time expression as instructed, but failed to change the auxiliary's tense marking; the

12 This is not a necessary criterion. As noted in Chapter 1, an auxiliary verb could be an independent word which nevertheless occurs in no other context than the AVC in the language.

responses thus contained an auxiliary verb inflected for past tense and a future time expression. This perplexed Dale (1975: 152), prompting him to comment:

> If the response sounded suspiciously literary or contained some obvious performance error, such as using the past tense with naaLekki [= our *nāḷaikku*] 'tomorrow', the investigator might have brought this to the attention of the subject and tried to elicit a more natural response.

This done, however, the subjects did not alter their responses, leading Dale to conclude that auxiliary *viṭa* 'leave' could not cooccur with the future tense marker (see Chapter 6). The crux of the problem is that Dale lacked a grammatical standard according to which he could judge a sentence as 'natural' or as a 'performance error'. In fact, he seems unaware that the past tense form in Tamil regularly occurs with future time expressions, as in (16). Andronov (1969: 168-71) provides many such examples and, in doing so, only follows what Tamil grammarians have observed for two millennia.[13]

(16) *nāṉ* *itō* $[_{V0}$ $[_{V1}$ *vantu*] *viṭṭēṉ*]].
I-NOM next come-CF leave-PST-1S
'I'll come right away (you can count on it).'

Use of the past tense to signal the speaker's determination to carry out an act is a conventional device of Tamil grammar (see Chapter 3). But since Dale did not control for this convention, he drew the erroneous conclusion that his subjects' responses were unnatural or ungrammatical.

Dale advances another argument in support of his claim that auxiliary *viṭa* 'leave' is incompatible with the future tense. He presented sentence (17)—his 141—to subjects for manipulation.

(17) *nēṟṟē* *vivicayi* *anta* *nilattukku* *varappukkaḷ* $[_{V0}$ $[_{V1}$ *kāṭṭi*] *viṭṭār*].
yesterday farmers-NOM that land-DAT dikes build-CF leave-PST-3P
'The farmers did build dikes for the land yesterday.'

13 The use of one tense form to convey the time reference usually associated with another was already described in sutra 241 of *tolkāppiyam, collatikāram,* which licenses use of the past tense to denote immediate future time reference.

vārā *kālatum* *nikaẓum* *kālattum*
come-ANP time=AND occur-ANP time=AND
ōraṅku *varūum* *viṉaiccoṟ* *kiḷavi*
certain places come-ANP verb expression
iṟanta *kālattu.k* *kuṟippoṭu* *kiḷattal*
past times mark-SOC express-VN
viraiṇta *poruḷ* *eṉmaṉār* *pulavar.*
hurried meaning say-3P scholars-NOM
'Scholars say that any verbal act which occurs in future or present time, when it occurs with past tense inflections denotes a rushing/hurriedness.'

The subjects were asked to replace the time expression *nēṟṟu* 'yesterday' with *nāḷaikku* 'tomorrow' to induce a change in the tense marking of the auxiliary *viṭa*. In their responses, the subjects carried out the substitution of the time expressions. Twenty-five percent retained the AVC, with the auxiliary inflected for future tense, *kāṭṭi viṭuvār* 'they will build', while the remainder replaced the AVC altogether with the simple verb *kāṭṭuvār* 'they will build', inflected for future tense. On the basis of these responses, Dale concluded the auxiliary *viṭa* and future tense marking were incompatible without explaining either why this should be so, or why one subject in four ignored this constraint.

Chapter 6 provides an explanation why three-quarters of Dale's subjects omitted *viṭa* 'leave'. This auxiliary signals disjunctive taxis: it indicates that the activity denoted by the auxiliate contrasts with something else in the context. The presence of *viṭa* in the stimulus sentence (17) thus indicates that the activity "the farmers build/t dikes for the land (yesterday)" contrasts with some other proposition, e.g., "the farmers hired oxen." The very presentation of (17), with *viṭa* embedded in it, tells the subjects to revise the set of propositions in the context and substitute the new information for the old. Once that is done, further revision is unnecessary so that use of *viṭa* in their response sentences would be superfluous, indeed contrary to the rules of a well-ordered Tamil discourse. The response Dale sought would assert the proposition "the farmers build/t dikes for the land (yesterday)," which in view of the stimulus sentence is no longer new information. Most of his informants thus appear to have contextualized the stimulus and response sentences and, in doing so, were following rules for the orderly use of *viṭa*. Alternatively, the subjects might not have found enough information in the stimulus sentence or the context of a formal setting to justify the use of the auxiliary and would have omitted it from their responses altogether. Even Dale's principle of auxiliary balance could not guarantee the presence of the auxiliary in both the stimulus and response. The procedure did not control for this contextualization and permitted the erroneous conclusion that tense governed the use of this auxiliary.

Dale's use of questionnaires and interviews tended to establish a formal situation. Both he and his assistant projected higher social and educational status than his respondents, who largely came from so-called backward communities. That formality could have suppressed the use of attitudinal auxiliaries, which the respondents might have considered inappropriate to the setting. Dale consequently elicits only the attitudinal auxiliary *tolaikka* 'lose', already treated by Schiffman, but no others. In fact, he analyzes fewer auxiliaries than Schiffman.

Fedson (1981)

Fedson (1981) studies the lexical semantics of nearly 50 auxiliary verbs in Tamil, far more than in any previous analysis. Though many observations are subtle, the grammatical analysis appears as an afterthought. Fedson conflates three different constructions under the heading of compound verb: (1) those in which the main verb is an infinitive, (2) those in which it is a conjunctive form and (3) those in which it is a negative conjunctive form. However, a single lexeme such as *irukka* 'be' may appear in all three contexts (Chapter 6). If all three constructions have the same grammatical properties, they must then be distinguished solely by their auxiliaries. Following such a line of reasoning would require Fedson to posit three different verbs *irukka* 'be' which, quite by accident, have the same phonological and morphological properties.[14]

Fedson assumes that the three kinds of constructions have the same grammatical properties, with only insignificant differences among them. She claims (Fedson 1981: 301) that a distinction between AVCs with infinitives and those with conjunctive forms is unwarranted because they occur in similar clauses and because traditional Tamil grammar classifies the infinitive and conjunctive form under the heading of *viṉaiyeccam* 'verbs that combine with other verbs'.[15] While the infinitive and conjunctive do belong to the same morphological class, they have distinct syntax and semantics, as argued in the next two chapters.

Although compound verbs are morphosyntactic objects, little is said here about the syntax of these forms. Fedson (1981: xii) says that in a sequence of two verbs, "the non-finite form makes a predication, and the second, finite verb, contributes a specifying, modulating nuance, or ... the sequence as a whole forms a complex predicate." The use of a disjunction undermines her definition of compound verb. The syntactic tests for treating a sequence of two verbs as a compound verb are as follows (Fedson 1981: xiv): "Adverb scope, negative scope with *illai*, emphatic scope and relativization affect the sequences as a whole, except in the causative and 'allow to verb' serial sequences which have different semantic subjects for the two verbs in a sequence." The syntactic criteria are met by most, but not all compound verbs. The test of negative scope fails for the third kind of AVC, whose main verb is a negative conjunctive. Relativization does not distinguish AVCs from many matrix-complement structures (see p. 120ff.). Adverb scope can affect coordinate structures as a unit, as well. Emphatic scope is not defined. Most problematic, these tests do not even hint at the distinctions between AVCs and lexical compounds. Two additional tests, borrowed from Annamalai (1982), are presented to make the distinction.[16] Although the first verb in most lexical compound verbs may be postposed to the right of the second, the main verb in an AVC may not be postposed to the right of the auxiliary. The first verb of a lexical compound may be reduplicated, but only in a few AVCs may the main verb be reduplicated (Chapter 4). Her second test is not sufficient to sort out the two sets of compounds.

14 Curiously, Fedson's list of auxiliary verbs omits the two most common modal auxiliaries in the language, *muṭiyum* 'be able' and *vēṇṭum* 'must'. While both have defective morphology, auxiliary *āka* 'become', which Fedson does treat, is also defective. Also, she treats the periphrastic causatives in *ceyya* 'do' as auxiliary verbs, even though they are more likely matrix-complement constructions (see Paramasivam 1979).

15 The conditional form also belongs to the set of *viṉaiyeccam* (Chapter 3), but this does not mean that it can be freely substituted for other members of this set without severe syntactic or semantic repercussions.

16 While in India, Annamalai lent me a prepublication copy of his 1982 book, which I subsequently made available to Fedson. Since she was at an advanced stage of writing, she apparently had little opportunity to integrate his results. While some of his tests are mentioned in her preface, none figures notably in the body or argumentation of her text.

Fedson relies heavily on taxonomy, but fails to define her terms decisively. Her use of the term perfect is plastic enough to apply to four distinct AVCs without distinguishing among them.[17] The term manner of action, redolent of *Aktionsart*, is defined in contrast to the category of voice. Manner of action is a connector, symbolized as E^nP^n, and is opposed to voice, symbolized as P^nE^n. It is a label that unites a group of auxiliaries which Fedson thinks belong together; however, it appears to perform no work in the grammar in that no rule is shown to be sensitive to it. Nor is it clear whether, on a more general level, Jakobson's theory of grammatical categories accommodates two distinct categories which are no more than notationally mirror images of each other; such an extension would require far more of a demonstration than Fedson has provided.

Despite her prior claim that they do not differ, Fedson (1981: 301-04) attempts briefly to distinguish the infinitive from the conjunctive. She claims the conjunctive serial verb "indicates an action which is realized or at least instigated" while the meaning of the infinitive is "to indicate unrealized action (Fedson 1981: 302-303)." These definitions are not anchored in the grammatical system, and admit of numerous exceptions (see Chapter 3). Fedson dismisses the passive, the negative conjugation and many modal AVCs as not using the infinitive as the main verb, citing Jottimuttu's (1956) claim that these infinitives historically derive from verbal nouns. Infinitives and verbal nouns have existed side by side throughout the history of Tamil, and there seems to be no invariant correspondence between the two. Even if Jottimuttu's historical claim were true, it would not relieve Fedson of the task of showing why in Modern Tamil the infinitive, and not some other form, took over from the verbal noun in these constructions.

Unlike other researchers, Fedson makes extensive, almost exclusive use of written texts, thereby filling in a gap in earlier work. But heavy reliance on these sources tends to obscure the interaction of certain auxiliaries with the context of utterance. Although the lexical properties of auxiliaries are forefront in Fedson's study, little use is made of negative data, cooccurrence restrictions or, indeed, grammaticality judgments to delineate the lexical semantics of individual auxiliaries, except in the most general way (see Fedson 1981: 318-19).

Annamalai (1982)

Annamalai (1982) continues a line of research begun in Annamalai (1979), resulting in the most satisfactory analysis of the Tamil auxiliary system yet published. It treats those AVCs whose auxiliates appear in the conjunctive, and is restricted to sequences that appear only in main clauses. Thus, the auxiliaries in his examples are always finite. A set of heuristic tests is provided to locate a sequence of two verbs within the set of AVCs; the underlying theoretical properties of AVCs which

17 Fedson (1993: 64) claims she is the first to observe that in translating the English perfect auxiliary 'have', one must chose among four Tamil auxiliaries. A translation, however, is not a linguistic analysis. This confusion seems to stem from her reliance on English as the metalanguage for describing Tamil.

make such heuristics possible are not the object of his investigation. While he does not characterize the semantic properties that unite all these AVCs into a single set, he does analyze the lexical semantics of the individual auxiliaries with great care and insight. Especially welcome is his use of grammaticality judgments and negative data.

Annamalai (1982: 38) offers ten tests for auxiliaryhood in Tamil. Each is applied to a sequence of two verbs, the first of which is inflected for the conjunctive. It is characteristic of such constructions that (1) there is only one subject for both verbs; (2) there is only one complement for both; (3) the first verb cannot reduplicate; (4) the first verb cannot be independently negated; (5) the second verb cannot be independently negated; (6) both occur in the scope of a single negative operator; (7) the auxiliary cannot be independently causativized; (8) the two components cannot be causativized independently of each other; (9) the second verb cannot occur alone and retain its "grammatical" meaning; and (10) the second verb may have an irregular phonological shape. Such a list recalls the enumeration of diagnostic tests, such as Subject-Auxiliary Inversion, used to identify English auxiliaries (Pullum and Wilson 1977).

Annamalai's approach to the analysis of auxiliaries shares in common with ours the position that auxiliaryhood is a property not of a single verb, but of a *sequence* of two or more verbs. The approach is therefore syntactic, not lexical. Some of his tests are less compelling than others. Number 10, the possibility of an irregular phonological shape, is neither sufficient nor necessary; as subsequent chapters show, most Tamil auxiliaries do not in fact have an irregular phonological shape, only those that undergo the independent process of contraction (see Steever 1993). On the other hand, examples of lexical compound verbs may be cited that have irregular phonological shapes, e.g., the lexical compound *koṇṭu vara* 'bring' is regularly contracted to *koṇṭara* 'id.'. Test 1, a single subject for both verbs, does not distinguish AVCs from lexical compound verbs or even from coordinate clauses in which each clause has the same subject.

What Annamalai hopes to show is that there is significant variation within the set of AVCs: not all of the auxiliaries behave the same way under the ten tests. Tabulating their behavior, Annamalai is able to establish a squish (Ross 1972) from the most to the least auxiliary-like verbs. At one end of the scale, auxiliaries like *irukka* 'be' and *viṭa* 'leave' exhibit the maximum number of tests for auxiliaryhood; at the other end, an auxiliary like *muṭikka* 'finish' exhibits far fewer signs of auxiliaryhood. The variation among the different auxiliaries points toward a core of invariant grammatical properties defining auxiliaryhood, against which individual AVCs are observed to vary.

The real merit of Annamalai's work lies in the sharp observations on the lexical semantics of individual auxiliaries. His remarks are more valuable than those in earlier works because he supports them with negative data and cooccurrence restrictions, permitting him to define the meaning of individual auxiliaries with greater clarity than before. Where our observations differ, it is usually in degree; there is rarely any disagreement in principle. Annamalai does not consider the behavior of the AVC in subordinate clause, which data prove crucial in establishing the category of attitude (see Chapter 5). He did not attempt a uniform characterization of the semantics of the indicative auxiliary system, though in earlier collaboration (Ramanujan and Annamalai 1968), he proposed the idea of using Jakobsonian verbal categories to circumscribe the set of AVCs.

Herring (1991)

Herring (1991) discusses the role that the verbal system of Tamil, including the auxiliary verb system, plays within the structure of narrative. She takes as the basic unit of analysis a continuous stretch of discourse which she classifies as a narrative and distinguishes from conversation. What is particularly welcome about her approach is that it observes the crucial role that grammatical elements—here the verb—play in structures larger than the sentence. Though Herring claims hers is the first study to note the relevance of discourse structures to the analysis of the Tamil verb, the *Urtext* of this book, Steever (1983), which appears in her bibliography, does discuss at length what impact the distinction between discursive and nondiscursive forms of speech have on the auxiliary verb system (Chapter 5).

One drawback this approach shares with Fedson's work is the almost complete lack of negative data.[18] Without incorporating such data into her analysis, so that she can say that a certain rule predicts a certain form's distribution, she undermines the predictive power of her analysis. She elicits texts, rather than forms such as isolated words, phrases or sentences. Not unsurprisingly, she fails to uncover many auxiliary verbs discussed in the literature or examples that illustrate, say, selection or subcategorization restrictions. Only three auxiliaries, *irukka* 'be', *viṭa* 'leave' and *koḷḷa* 'hold' are discussed in any detail. Believing that their analysis makes sense only by reference to the narratives in which they are embedded, she tends to discount sentence-level accounts of the syntax and semantics of these three auxiliaries. The inherent meanings of the various basic verb forms, including auxiliaries, are consequently ill-defined. As a result, her analysis is unable to say what it is about the auxiliary's inherent meaning that suits it to a particular use in a discourse genre.[19] Without a grammatical hypothesis to validate, she appears to expect that linguistic generalizations will obtrude from the data.

Her concentration on narrative to the exclusion of discourse, which she calls conversation, eliminates an important source of data for the semantic interpretation of verbs in general and auxiliaries in particular, namely the speech event and its participants. Many grammatical categories such as tense, person and attitude make crucial reference to the speech event; however, as noted in Chapter 5, narra-

18 Understandably, the concept of an ill-formed discourse seems much harder to capture than the concept of an ill-formed sentence. Accordingly, the judgments about ill-formed discourses would be that much harder to educe.

19 She clearly eschews the use of compositional semantic analysis (Herring 1991: 70-71) when she states that "... the meanings produced by the combinations [of auxiliaries with tenses] may differ from the sum of the meanings of the parts." Another conclusion is that the meanings that have been ascribed to the individual tenses and auxiliaries are descriptively inadequate.

tive tends to obliterate this reference, neutralizing and leveling a number of categories whose definition is dependent on the speech event. Tense distinctions, for example, are neutralized in favor of taxis or aspect. It is not possible, however, to recover from narrative genres what meanings the verb forms, including auxiliaries, would have in discursive speech such as conversation. This leads to a curiously incomplete analysis, one that omits direct reference to such basic grammatical categories as tense and person.

The general remarks discussed here do not exhaust these scholars' contributions to the study of the Tamil auxiliary. Their analyses of specific matters of Tamil grammar are interspersed throughout the text and are noted, as relevant.

3 Tamil verb morphology

INTRODUCTION

Auxiliary Formation accords the category of verb a leading role in the analysis of auxiliary structures. This process takes simple verb forms as its input and generates a periphrastic verb form, the AVC, as its output; it further associates to that AVC a verbal category which is not encoded in the basic verbal inflections of the language. A survey of basic verb morphology is undertaken here to discover what basic verbal inflections and categories Tamil grammar makes available to this process. Specifically, we will seek to determine which categories may be encoded in an auxiliate's inflection and subsequently projected to the entire AVC. In the course of this search, we will review material on verbal morphology and categories which is subsequently utilized in the analysis of specific auxiliaries.

The Tamil word consists of several morphemes, comprising a lexical base and a series of suffixes. Words are characterized by two kinds of rules: word-formation rules (WFR), on one hand, and inflection and derivation, on the other. WFRs characterize the overall well-formedness of words in isolation from other forms, describing their internal composition and structure. They function not only in the lexicon, where they generate words, but elsewhere in the grammar where they may serve as filters on wordlike expressions that may arise through such diverse operations as compounding, borrowing or contraction (Steever 1993). A general WFR for Tamil states that a word consists of a lexical base, an optional derivational suffix and an inflectional suffix, with the whole bracketed by word boundaries.

Inflectional and derivational processes characterize the structure of a word with respect to another word or a set of words in terms of oppositions, and so help to create paradigms (Stankiewicz 1962). Inflection differs from derivation in that the members of an inflectional opposition are mutually implicating so that, for example, the existence of a past tense form always implies the existence of (at least) a nonpast tense, and vice versa. Semantically, inflection tends not to alter the petty combinatoric restrictions of the lexical bases to which it applies. Derivation creates an opposition of terms, a base and a derived form, whose members are not necessarily mutually implicating: while a derived word always implies the existence of a base form, forms that might otherwise serve as bases forms need not imply a derived form. Semantically, derivation may alter the petty combinatorics of the base form to which it applies. In practical terms, our demonstrations below utilize such common morphological procedures as minimal pairs, mutual substitutability and complementary distribution to deduce the system of grammatical oppositions and hierarchy of categories that underlie the Tamil verbal system.

Chapter 1 observed that some principles governing the distribution of forms and categories within an AVC are language-independent, others language-specific. A good candidate for the former is that no auxiliate should bear an inflection that marks taxis while a language-specific constraint for Modern Tamil holds that no auxiliate may be inflected as a finite verb (even though Old Tamil admitted this possibility). Observation reveals two primary kinds of AVC in Tamil distinguished according to the auxiliate's form, one with the infinitive, one with the conjunctive. As two of the least marked verb forms of the language, both make attractive candidates for use in AVCs. Analysis shows the formal distinction between them corresponds to a semantic opposition between modal and nonmodal (or indicative) verbal categories. On the assumption that Auxiliary Formation respects semantic compositionality, it projects the meaning of the auxiliate's inflection to the whole AVC so that AVCs may also be classified as modal or indicative.

The category of mood is something of a Whorfian cryptotype in that it lacks an overt, dedicated morphological marking; it is established by an opposition between entire paradigms, not a contrast between members within an individual paradigm. Two other cryptotypes relevant to the classification of Tamil verbs are aspect and event type, discussed below. These two, however, pertain to the classification of Tamil verb bases, not inflectional verb morphology, reflecting the fact that some facets of a verb's meaning are attributed to the lexical meaning of its base and others to the inflectional oppositions it participates in. These latter two cryptotypes inhere in verb bases—or in verb bases and their satellites—not in the inflectional suffixes or verbal categories of the language. Nonetheless, they will prove relevant to the selection restrictions between an auxiliary and the underlying sentential subject it combines with, e.g., the interpretation of auxiliary *irukka* 'be' as progressive or perfective varies with the kinds of event type it combines with while auxiliary *kiẓikka* 'tear' cannot combine with such event types as accomplishments.[1]

BASIC VERB FORMS OF TAMIL

Our survey of Tamil verb forms synthesizes much of what appears in Annamalai (1969, 1997), Andronov (1969), Lindholm (1975), Kothandaraman (1977), Paramasivam (1979, 1983), Asher (1985), Lehmann (1989) and Annamalai and Steever (1998). Several findings are reinterpreted here in pursuit of the system of verbal categories that underlies and organizes the various forms in the language.

All Tamil verb forms may be segmented into two major halves, the verb base and the grammatical formatives suffixed to it, as illustrated in Figure 3.1.

1 Thus an auxiliary may select a sentential argument of a specific aspect or event type, but it may not alter that aspect or event type in virtue of the inflectional category it conveys.

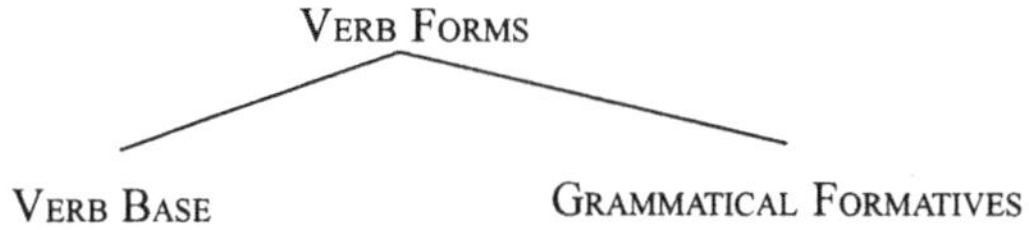

Figure 3.1 Basic structure of the Tamil verb.

Even though Tamil morphology is predominantly agglutinating, its verb morphology exhibits certain fusional tendencies so that seven conjugational patterns are distinguished according to the morphophonemic alternations that take place between the verb base and the grammatical formatives.[2] Table 3.1 overleaf, based on Fabricius (1972: vi-vii), presents these seven conjugations; their analysis belongs primarily to morphophonology, and is not pursued further here.[3] Indivudal verbs, including auxiliaries, will often be referred to by this classification.

VERB BASE

The verb base may consist of up to three parts: verb root, voice suffix and causative suffix (Figure 3.2). The root lexically identifies the verb base and is a necessary component of any stem. In common with many Dravidian languages, the set of roots is closed in Modern Tamil, and has been so ever since the medieval period, ending in the thirteenth or fourteenth century CE, which saw an influx of Sanskritic loans, e.g. Tamil *aṉupavikka* 'experience' was borrowed from Sanskrit *anubhava* 'experience'. Nonce formations such as *kāvuṇṭiṉēṉ* 'I counted', whose root *kāvuṇṭu-* is calqued on the English verb *count*, are viewed humorously and do not permanently enter the lexicon. This closure accounts for the extensive use of lexical compound verbs, as well as noun-verb compounds (Steever 1981: 109-28), to supplement the fixed set of verb roots.

The slot that immediately follows the verb root hosts two voice morphemes which mark the category of effectivity. The two are in minimal contrast, one marking affective, the other effective voice (Paramasivam 1979); their suffixation to the root creates the affective and effective stems, respectively. As we progress to the outmost layer of the verb base, a verb root, augmented for effectivity or not, may be followed by a causative suffix, giving rise to a causative stem.

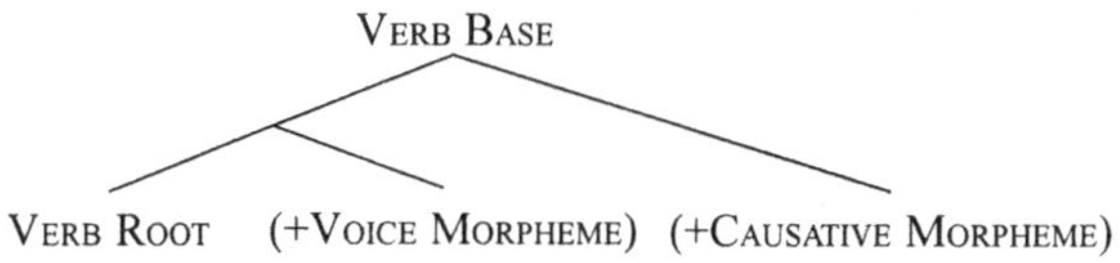

Figure 3.2 The structure of the Tamil verb base.

2 Asher (1966), for example, claims that in spoken Tamil there are but two classes.

3 However, this table does not factor out the contribution of the morphs for affective and effective voice on the shape of the verb classes. If this were done, the number of classes would likely decrease. The past, present and future finite forms cited are in the first person singular.

Table 3.1 The morphophonemic classification of Tamil verbs

Class	Base	Gloss	Present	Past	Future	Infinive	Conjunctive
I	*cey-*	'do'	*cey-kiṟ-ēṉ*	*cey-t-ēṉ*	*cey-v-ēṉ*	*cey-ya*	*cey-tu*
II	*aṟi-*	'know'	*aṟi-kiṟ-ēṉ*	*aṟi-nt-ēṉ*	*aṟi-v-ēṉ*	*aṟi-ya*	*aṟi-ntu*
III	*pēcu-*	'speak'	*pēcu-kiṟ-ēṉ*	*pēc-iṉ-ēṉ*	*pēcu-v-ēṉ*	*pēc-a*	*pēc-i*
IV	*naku-*	'laugh'	*naku-kiṟ-ēṉ*	*nak-k-ēṉ*	*naku-v-ēṉ*	*nak-a*	*nak-ku*
V	*kēḷ-*	'hear'	*kēṭ-kiṟ-ēṉ*	*kēṭ-ṭ-ēṉ*	*kēṭ-p-ēṉ*	*kēṭ-ka*	*kēṭ-ṭu*
VI	*tīr-*	'finish'	*tīr-kkiṟ-ēṉ*	*tīr-tt-ēṉ*	*tīr-pp-ēṉ*	*tīr-kka*	*tīr-ttu*
VII	*iru-*	'be'	*iru-kkiṟ-ēṉ*	*iru-nt-ēṉ*	*iru-pp-ēṉ*	*iru-kka*	*iru-ntu*

Verb root, aspect and event type

Inherent durativity of verb root

Paramasivam (1979: 50-51) observes that Tamil verb roots do not typically convey the notion of result of action, but an ongoing process: "It seems to me that markedness in English and the unmarkedness in Tamil for completion are not restricted to change of state verbs alone. It may be stated that a Tamil verb in general represents a process … [W]hereas English verbs generally represent actions, Tamil verbs represent processes." In aspectual terms, then, Tamil verb roots are inherently imperfective. As the quantifier of the narrated event, or E^n, aspect conveys information about the internal temporal divisions of the narrated event. Friedrich (cited in Holisky 1981: 128) defines aspect as that which "signals the relative duration or punctuality along a time line that may inhere in words or constructions." In general, imperfective is the unmarked and perfective the marked member of the opposition because the latter conveys more information than the former, namely, that the event is partitioned. Paramasivam (1979: 51) provides evidence of the root's imperfectivity in Tamil: in examples (18a and b) the past tense forms *vantēṉ* 'he came' and *paṭittēṉ* 'I read', despite their English translations, are understood by speakers to represent ongoing processes.

(18) a *avaṉ va.n-tāṉ. pātivaẓi.y-il oru peṇpuli avaṉai.t tākk-iṉ-atu.*
he-NOM come-PST-3SM halfway-LOC one tigress-NOM he-ACC attack-PST-3SN
'He {was coming. / *came.} Halfway along, a tigress attacked him.'

b *nāṉ nēṟṟu iravu oru nāval paṭi.t-t-ēṉ. pātiyil eṉakku.t*
I-NOM yesterday night one novel-NOM read-PST-1S path-LOC I-DAT
tūkkam va.n-t-atu. tūṅk-iṉ-ēṉ.
sleep-NOM come-PST-3SN sleep-PST-1S
'I {was reading / *read} a novel last night. I got sleepy midway and went to sleep.'

While evidence from the following chapters shows that certain AVCs may emphasize one reading or the other, the meaning of the simple verb form remains general between the two. As these and other examples suggest, the basic aspectual character of the Tamil verb root is best characterized by imperfectivity.

Event type

On Freed's (1976) model, an event may be partitioned into an onset, body and coda.[4] Depending on how these divisions combine, different event types, or "aspectual classes," are generated. The principal ones are states, activities, achievements and accomplishments, according to Vendler's (1967) celebrated taxonomy (see also Dowty 1979). Roughly speaking, states and achievements have homogenous bodies[5] whereas activities and accomplishments do not. Furthermore, achievements and accomplishments have codas that represent a change of state while states and activities do not. Several of the auxiliaries analyzed in Chapters 6, 7 and 8 are in fact constrained by the event type of the auxiliate with which they combine. This becomes particularly clear where a given lexical root is associated with two distinct senses, each corresponding to a different event type and where a particular auxiliary may cooccur with only one sense but not the other (see pp. 283-84 for *pōka* 'go'). Care must be exercised in such cases, however, because the auxiliate's exact event type is in some cases determined not simply by the verb base, but by the base and its accompanying satellites. Nonetheless, the expression over which an event type is defined excludes an auxiliate's inflections; event types therefore concern the base's denotational function, not the suffix's inflectional function.

Effective and affective voice

According to Figure 3.2, immediately following the verb root is the slot for members of the category which Paramasivam (1979) calls effectivity. Effectivity is a kind of voice (P^nE^n) that characterizes the subject's role in the narrated event, naming an opposition of two terms, affective versus effective.

Paramasivam estimated that, setting aside Sanskritic loans and those verbs that are derived from onomatopoeia,[6] approximately 60 percent of all verb roots in Tamil must be inflected for one of these two suffixes. In the following pairs, the verb in the first sentence is inflected for affective and the verb in the second for effective voice. In an instance of fusional morphology unusual for Tamil, the two voice markers typically combine with an adjacent morpheme to create a portmanteau morph, marked by +; in (19) and (20), they combine with the preceding verb root but in (21) they combine with the following tense marker.

4 The analysis of attitudinal auxiliary verbs in Chapter 8 shows further that the aspectual division of an event into an onset, body and coda may be paralleled by a tripartite division between separation, liminal and reincorporation phases.

5 Or, perhaps, they do not distinguish between onsets and bodies.

6 For example, the verb *muṇumuṇu-kka* 'mutter, mumble' is related to the onomatopoeic expression *muṇumuṇu-(v)eṉṟu* 'in a muttering manner'.

(19) a *avaṉ iṟaṅk-iṉ-āṉ.*
he-NOM descend+AF-PST-3M
'He descended.'

b *avaṉ cumai.y-ai iṟakk-iṉ-āṉ.*
he-NOM load-ACC descend+EF-PST-3SM
'He put his load down.'

(20) a *vaṇṭi pātai.y-ai vilak-iṉ-atu.*
cart-NOM path-ACC part+AF-PST-3SN
'The cart parted from/went off the road.'

b *avaṉ vaṇṭi.y-ai.p patai.y-iliruntu vilakk-iṉ-āṉ.*
he-NOM cart-ACC path-ABL part+EF-PST-3SM
'He parted/drove the cart from the path.'

(21) a *avaṉ maṉaivi.y-ai.p piri-nt-āṉ.*
he-NOM wife-ACC separate-AF+PST-3SM
'He separated/was separated from his wife.'

b *avaṉ manaivi.y-ai.p piri-tt-āṉ.*
he-NOM wife-ACC separate-EF+PST-3SM
'He separated his wife (from someone else).'

Paramasivam's analysis refutes two common misconceptions about such pairs. First, the affective-effective relation is not, as often portrayed (Schiffman 1999: 74-79), an intransitive-transitive relation. Though affective *iṟaṅkiṉāṉ* 'he descended' (19a) is intransitive, affective *vilakiṉatu* 'it parted' (20a) and *pirintāṉ* 'he separated' (21a) are transitive as the presence of direct objects in the accusative shows.

Second, this relation is not between noncausative and causative counterparts of a verb. Paramasivam (1979: 46-47) argues effective verbs are not semantically causative. He notes that while the most literal English translations of the sentences in (22) are ungrammatical, their Tamil originals are unremarkable and commonplace. If effectives were the causative counterparts of affectives, we would expect these Tamil sentences to be as unacceptable as their English translations because a form that means 'cause X to break' necessarily entails the proposition 'X broke'. He makes two arguments in support of these intuitive observations. He shows first that true causative constructions in Tamil, both morphological and periphrastic, do respect the anticipated causative entailments, and then that effective verbs, since they do not obey these entailments, cannot be considered causatives.

(22) a $[_{S0}[_{S1}$ *[aiyar tēṅkāy-ai uṭai-ttāl=um]* *atu uṭai.y-a.v illai*].
Brahmin-NOM coconut-ACC break-EF+CND=AND it-NOM break-AF+INF IND-NEG
?? 'Even though the Brahmin broke the coconut, it didn't break'.

b $[_{S0}[_{S1}$ *[nī niṟai-ttāl=um] inta.k kuṭam niṟai.y-ātu*].
you-NOM fill-EF+CND=AND this pot-NOM fill-AF+FUT-NEG-3SN
?? 'Even though you fill(ed) it up, the pot won't be filled up.'

c $[_{S0}[_{S1}$ *[avaṉ aṇai-ttāl=um] inta neruppu aṇai.y-ātu*].
he-NOM put.out-EF+CND=AND this fire-NOM put.out-AF+FUT-NEG-3SN
?? 'Even though he extinguishes it, the fire will not be extinguished.'

Paramasivam (1979: 20-21) characterizes an affective verb as "… one the subject of which undergoes the action (or state or change of state) described by the verb stem [= our verb root]." In example (19a) above the subject is presented as undergoing the process of descending; in (21a), as one whom the process of separation, emotional or physical, is said to impact; and in (23a), as being affected by the process of grazing, i.e., gaining nourishment. The subject of an affective verb is thus "affected" by the process the verb root denotes, but does not necessarily direct that process.

(23) a *māṭu pul.l-ai mēy-nt-atu.*
ox-NOM grass-ACC graze-AF+PST-3SN
'The ox grazed on the grass.'

b *avaṉ māṭ.ṭ-ai mēy-tt-āṉ.*
he-NOM ox-ACC graze-EF+PST-3SM
'He grazed the ox.'

By contrast, an effective verb is characterized as one whose subject directs the action or process named by the verb root. In (23b) the subject directs the ox to graze, in (20b) he directs the cart off the road and in (19b) he acts to remove a load from his shoulders. While the subject directs the process denoted by the verb stem, it does not necessarily undergo that process itself. Because effectivity describes the role of a participant in the narrated event, viz., the subject, in either undergoing (affective) or directing (effective) a process in the narrated event, it belongs to the category of voice P^nE^n.

Affective and effective voice are mutually implicating terms: if a root can occur with one, it can occur with the other. Moreover, no root ever occurs optionally with just effective or just affective voice.[7] There are thus no triplets where a root may be inflected for affective voice, effective voice or neither. So, morphologically, the two are mutually exclusive; semantically, mutually implicating. Effectivity thus marks an inflectional, not a derivational, relationship between the two members of the opposition.

The distinction between affective forms and their effective counterparts is signaled by a morphophonemic alternation between "weak" and "strong" clusters. In (23a), for example, affective voice is marked by the weak cluster *-nt-*, a portmanteau morph combining affective voice and past tense while in (23b) effective voice is marked by the strong cluster *-tt-*, another portmanteau morph combining voice and tense. The semantics of effectivity bears directly on the analysis of certain auxiliaries, e.g., *āka* 'become' (p. 211) combines only with affective verbs[8] while *pōṭa* 'put' (p. 274) combines only with effective verbs.

7 Rarely, a root may enter the set of verb roots that must be inflected for effectivity. The affective verb *poṭiya* 'be pulverized' is a recent back-formation from now effective form *poṭikka* 'pulverize'. Historically, the root *poṭi-* marked neither effective nor affective voice.

8 This makes an empirical difference. Some studies claim that this auxiliary occurs only with intransitive auxiliates; our data show it may combine with transitives as long as they are affective.

Morphological causatives

The causative suffix follows the slot for effectivity (Figure 3.2). Though once widespread in the medieval language, particularly in the language of *bhakti* literature, the formation of causative stems is lexically restricted in the modern language so that roots with a causative stem must now be marked as such in the lexicon (see Asher 1985: 153-54). The preferred and productive way to form a causative in Modern Tamil is through a matrix-complement periphrasis that combines a causative verb (e.g. *ceyya* 'do, make', *paṇṇa* 'make', or *vaikka* 'place') with the infinitive of the verb denoting the caused event.[9]

In morphological causatives, two allomorphs signal the presence of a causative stem: the weak form *-vi-* and the strong form *-(p.)pi-*, the choice between which is governed by the preceding morpheme.[10] All verbs with the causative marker are inflected as class VI verbs (Table 3.1). Morphological causatives form the basis of an argument for the derivation of AVCs (p. 106ff.). Many of the lexemes that function as auxiliaries, e.g., *vara* 'come', have morphological counterparts, e.g., *varu-vi-k.ka* 'cause to come'; however, none of these causatives can function as auxiliaries, for reasons discussed there. Paramasivam (1979, Chapter 3) analyzes the semantic contrasts between morphological and syntactic causatives in detail, and should be consulted for further information.

GRAMMATICAL FORMATIVES

The denotational function of the AVC requires that a verb base be present in every auxiliate. As noted in Chapter 2, earlier stages of Tamil had AVCs in which the bare verb base with no suffix was a free form and could function as an auxiliate (p. 39); however, Modern Tamil no longer allows this possibility. Therefore, all verb forms of the modern language, including those that appear in an AVC, must be accompanied by a grammatical formative.

Finite and nonfinite forms

Grammatical formatives, suffixed to the verb base, comprise two classes. The first includes formatives that mark finite verb forms (*muṟṟu viṉai*); the second, those that mark nonfinite forms. As Chapter 2 notes, finiteness is a syntactic property of the Tamil sentence, which is morphologically interpreted according to which part

9 Fedson (1981) includes these periphrastic causatives among her set of compound verbs; however, they may better be analyzed as instances of complementation.

10 Several forms that descend from earlier causative stems, e.g., *kāṇ-pi* 'cause to see', no longer respect causative entailments, functioning as ordinary noncausatives (*kāmmi* < *kāṇpi* now means 'show' rather than 'cause to see'; because the phonological assimilation has obscured the identity of both the root and the suffix, the form no longer contrasts with a noncausative counterpart, and is simply taken as a synonym of *kāṭṭu* 'show').

of speech the predicate belongs. Though finite verbs are commonly defined as those verbs which mark tense and Subject-Verb Agreement, this definition founders on the analysis of certain forms such as the optative; as invariant forms, they cannot be said to explicitly contrast for the categories of tense, person or number.[11] The two main classes of finite verbs are those that mark nondeclarative illocutionary force, and those that do not.

Markers of illocutionary force

The formative suffixes that signal nondeclarative illocutionary force include the imperative,[12] singular and plural, affirmative and negative; the optative;[13] the *-aṭṭum* permissive (Asher 1985: 170); the *-lām* hortative (Asher 1985: 170); and the *-āṉēṉ* supine.[14] These forms have the same distribution as other finite predicates (Steever 1988). And since the distribution of finite predicates in Modern Tamil is restricted so that no serial verb constructions may occur, all of these markers are effectively ruled out as forms an auxiliate may assume. Their analysis is not pursued further; consult Lehmann (1989) for further discussion.

The remaining finite verb forms

The second class of finite verbs is divided into two subsets: affirmative and negative, each of which has a slightly different morphological characterization. Affirmative finite verbs are those that simultaneously mark tense and Subject-Verb Agreement, a definition which does not, however, adequately cover the negative paradigm.[15] Consider first the affirmative finite paradigms.

Tamil has three simple tense-forms, past (*iṟanta kālam*), present (*nikaẓcci kālam*) and future (*etir kālam*).[16] The primary use of the tense-forms is to convey time reference. Tense is a shifter that characterizes the time of E^n with respect to the time of E^s, hence Jakobson's symbolization of E^s/E^n. Reichenbach's (1947) logical model is also helpful in visualizing the content of tense and time reference: it

11 Although they might be said to covertly mark tense, so that the imperative encodes present (or it is future?) tense, they can at best encode time reference, but not formally defined tense. They must be listed as finite forms by virtue of their capacity to appear where the rules of Tamil permit finite predicates to occur (Steever 1988).

12 It could be claimed that the imperative consists solely of the verb base; however, a zero morph must be postulated to account for those cases in which the verb base (*varu-* 'come') and the singular imperative (*vā* 'come!') are distinct.

13 For example, *varu-ka* 'may X come', *vāẓ-ka* 'may X live, long live X'.

14 See (39b) for an illustration of this form.

15 In Old Tamil (Steever 2004) negative finite verbs did bear personal endings which, except for a few idioms, were lost in subsequent stages of the language.

16 Besides these simple forms, there are also several compound tense-forms, some of which are analyzed in subsequent chapters. There are at least three complex tenses, all of which are expressed by modal and nonmodal AVCs, but none of which is recognized in traditional grammar. An example of the former is the prospective tense form, consisting of the infinitive of the main verb and an inflected form of the auxiliary verb *irukka* 'be', e.g. *avaṉ pōka irukkiṟāṉ* 'he is to go'.

recognizes event time, speech time and reference time, located on a time line which begins in the past, intersects the present and proceeds into the future. The time line may be viewed as consisting of temporal points or intervals: in fact, a point may be considered a special case of an interval where the values of its start and its end are nondistinct. In keeping with the inherent imperfectivity of verb bases noted above, tense distinctions in Tamil appear to locate events at intervals on a time line, rather than at specific points.

Tense-forms in Tamil are traditionally recognized as having two uses, primary and secondary. The primary use, as noted above, is to signal time reference. The secondary uses, called *kālamayakkam* 'confusion of tenses' or *kālavaḻuvamaiti* 'sanctioned deviations in tense' in Tamil grammar, have additional, nontemporal meanings that tend to occur in specific grammatical frames. Tradition recognizes four kinds of *kālamayakkam* (Pope 1855): *viraivu* 'swiftness', *mikuti* 'emphasis', *teḷivu* 'perspicuity' and *iyalpu* 'influence'.

Certain uses of the tense-forms, however, will make sense only on the assumption that they encode the verbal category of mood. Mood characterizes the ontological status of the narrated event as potential or real through an opposition between modal forms and indicative[17] forms. If interpreted as a scalar opposition, mood defines a scale of ontological commitment from most real to least real. Because past tense forms represent events as part of an accepted history from the vantage point of the speech event, those forms make the strongest ontological commitment. Present tense-forms mark a weaker commitment; even though the events they represent are anchored in the reality of the speech event, their outcome is not fully assured. Future tense-forms, which represent events that are potential with respect to some reference time, make the weakest commitment.

Past tense

Table 3.1 enumerates the major allomorphs of the past tense, which are suffixed directly to the verb base. The primary use of past tense forms is to indicate that the event denoted by the verb base occurred at a time before the speech event.

(24) a *avaṉ nēṟṟu rāttiri va.n-t-āṉ.*
he-NOM yesterday night come-PST-3SM
'He came last night.'

b *nāṉ tiruviḻākku.p pō-ṉ-ēṉ.*
I-NOM festival-dat go-PST-1S
'I went to the festival.'

Consider some secondary uses, or *kālamayakkam*, of the past tense. Use of the past in (25a) indicates the speaker's strong conviction that he will carry out the act denoted by the verb; hence, it conveys an immediate future time reference (tradi-

17 Our use of of the term indicative differs from Asher's (1985), in which he contrasts indicative with imperative forms.

tionally classified under *viraivu* 'swiftness'). In this example the person answering the question literally says, 'I did come'; he is not misspeaking, but merely using a traditional, conventional device of Tamil to convey a strong commitment to perform that act (p. 46, Note 13). Use of the past in (25b) is meant to persuade the addressee of the speaker's determination. Figuratively speaking, the past tense-form is used to endow an event in the immediate future with the certainty and finality of one in the past. On our analysis, the past tense is marked for indicative mood and projects the strength of its ontological commitment onto the forthcoming action. Such secondary uses occur only in rhetorically marked settings; further examples appear in Andronov (1969: 168-70).

(25) a *eppo varu-kiṟ-āy? vantu viṭ-ṭ-ēṉ.*
when come-PRS-2s come-CP leave-PST-1s
'When are you coming? I'm coming right now (you can be sure).'

b *vara.v illai eṉṟāl cet.t-āy!*
come-INF IND-NEG say-CND die-PST-2s
'If you don't come right away, you're (as good as) dead.'

The secondary use of the past tense-form in (26) has not been remarked in the grammatical literature. When such a form is accompanied by a rising intonation and a future time adverb, it signals a paratactic relation with the following sentence. The result is a conditional proposition in which the clause with the past tense-form functions as a protasis and the following clause as an apodosis. It is figuratively an instruction for the addressee to imagine the situation in the first clause as given, then extrapolate what would ensue from it. So while past time reference is the dominant use of the past tense-form, it is not the only one.

(26) *avaṉ nāḷaikku iṅkē va.n-t-āṉ?* ↑ *eṉṉa paṇṇu-v-āy?*
he-NOM tomorrow here come-PST-3SM what do-FUT-2s
'Suppose he came here tomorrow, what would you do?'

Present tense

The primary use of the present tense-form is to indicate present time reference, where the time reference of E^n coincides with the time reference of E^s.

(27) a *nāṉ ippoẓutu paṭi-k.kiṟ-ēṉ.*
I-NOM now read-PRS-1s
'I am reading now.'

b *avaḷ cāppāṭṭai.c camai-k.kiṟ-āḷ.*
she-NOM meal-ACC prepare-PRS-3SF
'She is preparing the meal.'

Among its secondary uses, the present may convey future time reference when it occurs with a future time adverb (28a). This is in fact the predominant means of expressing future time reference in spoken Tamil. The present tense is also used in vivid historical narrative to relate past time reference. Once the past tense-form of the first verb in (28b) establishes the past time reference, the remaining two verbs appear in the present tense form.[18]

(28) a *avaṉ nāḷaikku varu-kiṟ-āṉ. eṉṉa pantāyam?*
he-NOM tomorrow come-pres-3sm what-NOM bet-NOM
'What will you bet he's coming tomorrow.'

b *rāmar ūril nuẓai-nt-ār. avar teruvil naṭa-k.kiṟ-ār.*
Rama-NOM town-LOC enter-PST-3H he-NOM road-LOC walk-PRES-3H
avar cītaiyai.p pār-k.kiṟ-ār.
he-NOM Sita-ACC see-PRES-3H
'Rama entered the town: (now) he's walking on the road, (now) he sees Sita.'

Future tense

Future tense-forms are used primarily to describe situations in which event time follows reference time: the event is not yet real or actual with respect to the reference time. As suggested above, the future tense-form is modal while its past and present counterparts are indicative; the future accordingly makes a weaker ontological commitment than the other two.

In the absence of any specific time expression, the reference time is set equal to the speech time so that event time follows speech time; in other words, it signals future time reference. However, a sentence such as (29) is general between two readings: 'The teacher will come to the house' and 'The teacher would come to the house.' While the first reading conveys simple future time reference, the second is a supposition: the speaker reasons from what he knows that the event will take place. Even insertion of the explicit time expression *nāḷaikku* 'tomorrow' cannot force one reading or the other.

(29) *vāttiyar vīṭṭukku varu-v-ār.*
teacher- NOM house-DAT come-FUT-3H
'The teacher will/would come to the house.'

A future tense-form need not invariably convey future time reference; it may occur with past time expressions, and when it does, it signals habitual action. The situation qualified by the future tense-form is then viewed as potential with respect to a set of past reference times. The act is seen as possible; therefore, the future tense-form is modal even with past time reference.

(30) *anta.k kālattil maṇi āṟu maṇikku.k kalūrikku.p pō-v-āṉ.*
that time-LOC Mani-NOM six o'clock college-DAT go-FUT-3SM
'In those days, Mani would go to college at six o'clock.'

18 See Herring (1991) for further examples of historical narration in Tamil.

Summary of simple tenses

The examples above suggest how different tense-forms make different ontological commitments. The past tense form makes the strongest; the present, a weaker one; and the future, the weakest.[19] Past and present events are presented as actual, while future events are not. Past events, since they are finished, project a stronger ontological commitment than present ones.

As will emerge from this analysis, the formal distinction between simple and periphrastic tense-forms in Tamil correlates with a semantic distinction between the kind of temporal indices that those tense forms denote. The three simple tense-forms, past, present and future, stand in formal contrast to several periphrastic tense-forms,[20] all of which are AVCs and include the perfect formed with *irukka* 'be' (Chapter 6) and the antiperfect formed with *kiẓiya* 'tear' and *kiẓikka* 'tear' (Chapter 8), as well as some modals AVCs not analyzed here. Simple tense-forms are marked for the feature [0 INTERVAL], i.e., unmarked for interval, while the compound tense-forms are marked [+INTERVAL], i.e., positively marked for interval.

Under this analysis, no basic form is inherently marked for [-INTERVAL], or a point of time, i.e., no basic form indicates an instantaneous event.[21] However, the value [-INTERVAL] may be derived by means of a conversational implicature (Levinson 2000). If a speaker uses a simple tense-form ([0 INTERVAL]) in a context where he could also have used a more informative periphrastic tense-form ([+INTERVAL]), he may conversationally implicate that he lacks the information to use such a form; hence, he implicates that an instantaneous reading ([-INTERVAL]) is intended. The speaker, however, should be able to cancel that reading, indicating it is a just a conversational implicature, not part of the form's conventional meaning.

Personal endings

Finite verbs agree with their subjects in person, number and gender. Agreement is signaled by personal endings suffixed to the tense marker. An uncommon instance of fusional morphology in Tamil, each ending simultaneously marks person, number and, where appropriate, gender and honorification.[22]

With only one personal ending for both, *-ōm*, the pronominal distinction between a first person inclusive plural *nām* 'we (and you)' and a first person exclusive plural *nāṅkaḷ* 'we (but not you)' pronoun is not reflected in the verb. The personal endings are presented in Table 3.2.

19 The variation in strength of ontological commitment reappears when the semantics of the perfect tense series is studied in Chapter 6.

20 The periphrastic tense-forms include both indicative and modal AVCs. The modal AVCs that convey tense include the prospective tense-forms with the auxiliaries *irukka* 'be' and *teriya* 'be clear'. As modal forms, these latter two fall outside the scope of our study, but relevant examples are found in Fedson (1981).

21 This accords with the characterization of Tamil verb bases as inherently durative in aspect, not punctual.

22 The rules governing the assignment of personal endings are somewhat more complex than this brief description would suggest, and are discussed in Steever (1981, Chapter 3).

Table 3.2 Personal endings of finite verbs

		Singular	Honorific	Plural
1st person		*-ēṉ*		*-ōm*
2nd person		*-āy*	*-īr* [a]	*-īrkaḷ*
3rd person	Masculine	*-āṉ*	*-ār* (Masculine and Feminine)	*-ārkaḷ* (Masculine and Feminine)
	Feminine	*-āḷ*		
	Neuter	*-atu*		*-aṉa* [b]

Notes
a Only in certain caste dialects, e.g. *caiva vellāḷa, aiyar*.
b Only in written Tamil; *-atu* is used in spoken Tamil.

Negative finite forms

Modern Tamil has two paradigms for negative finite verbs, future and nonfuture, illustrated in Table 2.2. Both are for the most part AVCs in which the auxiliate appears in its infinitival form. Note that future negative, formed with the auxiliary *māṭṭ-* 'will not',[23] has different forms for each cell of the paradigm, varying with the person, number and gender of the subject. The third person neuter, singular and plural, has a synthetic form, e.g. *varātu* 'it/they will not come', which preserves the simple negative paradigm of Old Tamil. The nonfuture negative, by contrast, is invariant for all persons, numbers and genders: it serves as the negative of both the past and the present affirmative paradigms, e.g., *vara.v illai* 'he, she, it, I, we, you, they do/did not come'. In the negative, the past and present finite paradigms function as a bloc over against their future counterpart. This formal distinction thus reflects the semantic distinction between nonmodal and modal, discussed below.[24] In the affirmative, therefore, the future tense form is modal while the past and present tense forms are nonmodal.

23 This auxiliary does not by itself show any variation in tense; it continues the nonpast negative paradigm of Old Tamil (Steever 2004). It gains its value of futurity by virtue of its contrast with the nonfuture negative paradigm.

24 What Kurylowicz (1973: 110) says about the Persian tense system applies equally well to the Tamil system: 'Mais ce qui importe, c'est l'inadmissibilité d'un traitement parallèle des opposition *moment de parler:moment passé* et *moment de parler:moment futur*. Il ne faut pas confondre la réalité linguistique avec la schéma logico-mathématique d'une ligne droite divisée par le point de présent en deux parties symmétriques, le passé et le futur. Si l'on veut s'en tenir à la réprésentation graphique, elle ne sera pas

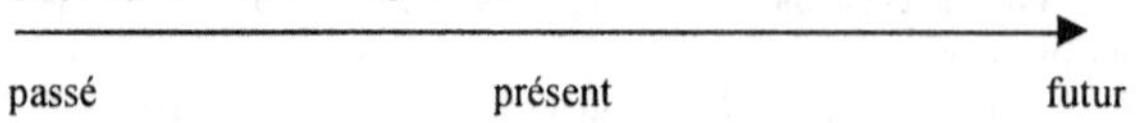

mais plutôt,

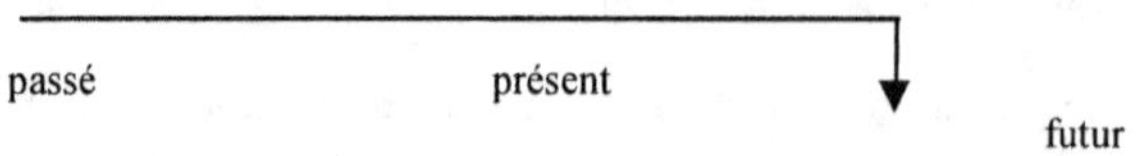

En face de la réalité, exprimée par le présent et le passé, le futur, designant l'éventualité, la possibilité, l'attent, etc. est un *mode*. A ce titre il s'oppose à *présent + passé* pris ensemble.'

NONFINITE VERB FORMS

While finite verb forms incorporate both a tense maker and a personal ending, nonfinite verbs do not: though some nonfinite forms inflect for tense, none inflects for personal endings. Since the constraint against serial verbs prevents finite forms from functioning as the auxiliate of an AVC, that task naturally falls to nonfinite verbs. Even so, not all nonfinite forms may function as auxiliates.

Nonfinite verb forms are traditionally divided into those that mark tense and those that do not. Those that mark tense include two subsets, adnominal forms (*peyareccam*) and verbal nouns (*viṉaippeyar*). The adnominal, often called a relative or adjectival participle,[25] is a verb that combines with a following noun to form such constructions as relative clauses. The traditional term *peyareccam* consists of *peyar* 'noun' and *eccam* 'deficiency': *eccam* describes those verb forms that necessarily combine with other forms, nouns or verbs. When the form is one that combines with a noun, or *peyar*, it belongs to the set of *peyareccam*; when it combines with a verb, or *viṉai*, it belongs to the set of *viṉaiyeccam*. All these forms are distinguished from such compounds as *kol-yāṉai* 'killer elephant' by the fact that other linguistic material—clitics or words—may come between any *eccam* and the word it combines with while nothing may intervene between the parts of compound words. Verbal nouns are called *viṉaippeyar*, a compound of *viṉai* 'verb' and *peyar* 'noun'. They represent the class of verbs that result from the combination of a verb marked for tense and an abstract noun such as 'the fact that V', 'the event that V' or, more generally, 'the N that V.'

viṉaiyeccam are nonfinite verb forms that combine with another verb, with or without additional intervening material. They bear a heavy syntactic load in the language; as noted in Chapter 1, they are crucial to the formation of coordinate and subordinate sentences, as well as compound verbs of all kinds.

The form that the auxiliary may assume in an AVC includes virtually any verb form in the language; however, the forms the auxiliate can assume are limited to *viṉaiyeccam*. *peyareccam* and *viṉaippeyar* are inappropriate forms for the auxiliate. Since by definition *peyareccam* must combine with a following noun, they cannot combine with a form that serves a verbal inflectional function within the AVC, viz., an auxiliary. *viṉaippeyar*, in combining with an abstract nominal head, are marked as representing a separate event, in contravention of the stipulation that an auxiliate should not mark taxis. This leaves the class of *viṉaiyeccam*.

peyareccam

Although *peyareccam* may not serve as an auxiliate in any AVC, they figure in many examples and arguments in this book. They are nonfinite verbs that anticipate or combine with a following noun; as such they are instrumental in the forma-

25 The term adjectival participle is avoided here. There is no major category of adjectives in the language so there can be no adjectives with verbal properties, that is, no participles.

tion of relative clauses (Annamalai 1969, 1997; Steever 1981: 152-75). They consist of a verb stem inflected for tense or negation, to which the adnominal marker *-a* is suffixed; e.g., *va-nt-a* 'which came', *varu-kiṟ-a* 'which is coming', *var-āt-a* 'which did/does not come'. In (31) *peyareccam* form relative clauses, combining with following head nouns that index an argument position in the subordinate clause. In (31a) the head noun *maṉitaṉ-ai* 'man' is coreferential with the (deleted) subject of the relative clause; in (31b) the head noun *ūr* 'town' is coreferential with the indirect object of the relative clause. In (32) *peyareccam* form adjuncts or adverbial clauses: the nouns that are modified by *peyareccam* have no θ-role in the subordinate clause. Annamalai (1997) discusses distinctions between the two kinds of clauses but their overall morphology is the same.

(31) a $_{S0}[_{NP}[_{S1}$[*nēṟṟu* *va.n-t-a*] *maṉitaṉ-ai.p*] *nāṉ* *pār.t-t-ēṉ*].
yesterday come-PST-ADN man-ACC I-NOM see-PST-1S
'I saw the man who came yesterday.'

b $_{S0}[_{NP}[_{S1}$[*nāṉ* *pō-kiṟ-a*] *ūr*] *maturai* *tāṉ*].
I-NOM go-PRES-ADN town-NOM Madurai-NOM PCL
'The town that I am going to is Madurai.'

(32) a $_{S0}[_{N}[_{S1}$[*avaṉ* *va.n-t-a*] *pōtu*] *nāṉ* *paṭi.t-t-ēṉ*].
he-NOM come-PST-ADN time I-NOM read-PST-1S
'I was reading at the time/when he came.'

b $_{S0}[_{N}[_{S1}$[*eṉakku.t* *teri-nt-a*] *varai*] *avaṉ* *pōka.v* *illai*].
I-DAT know-PST-ADN extent he-NOM go-INF IND-NEG
'As far as I know, he didn't go.'

viṉaippeyar and deverbal nouns

Paramasivam (1971) classifies three kinds of deverbal nouns, or *viṉaippeyar*. The first is a simple noun, cross-categorially derived from a verb root, e.g., *pēccu* 'speech' is derived from *pēca* 'speak'; it has the cooccurrence restrictions of a noun not a verb. It may be modified by a numeral, an adjectival expression or *peyareccam*, but not by a temporal adverb, so that **nēṟṟu pēccu* 'the yesterday speech' is unacceptable. The logical subject appears in the genitive not the nominative case, e.g., *uṉ pēccu* 'your speech', not **nī pēccu* 'id.' As a noun, it inflects for nominal morphology. This kind of *viṉaippeyar* is an unacceptable form for an auxiliate for three reasons. First, with the cooccurrence restrictions of a noun, and not a verb, it cannot adequately fulfill an auxiliate's denotational function. Second, its nominal morphology would introduce extraneous information into the AVC. Third, this kind of derivation is sporadic and subject to idiosyncratic variation in the lexicon, further compromising the auxiliate's denotational function.

The second kind of *viṉaippeyar* is simply called a verbal noun. It does not inflect for tense, but is clearly a reduction of a full clause. Its logical subject appears in the nominative not the genitive, e.g., *nī pēcu-tal* 'your speaking', not **uṉ pēcu-tal* 'id.' It appears to be modified by numerals, adjectival expressions and *peyareccam*, but it cannot cooccur with past time adverbs (Paramasivam 1971:

245), e.g., *avaḷ (*nēṟṟu) pāṭu-tal* 'her (*yesterday) singing'. This latter wrinkle in cooccurrence restrictions disqualifies it from use as the form of an auxiliate because it would vitiate the AVC's denotational function. Further, this form is lexically restricted in the modern spoken language so that many verbs lack a productive deverbal noun of this kind.[26]

While these verbal nouns may not ordinarily serve as auxiliates in the modern spoken language, they appear to have done so in the classical language, as well as in consciously archaizing modern prose. The modal AVCs *varutal kūṭum* 'the coming is possible' and *varutal vēṇṭum* 'the coming is necessary' occur in both these varieties of the language. These forms occur in modal AVCs which correlate with future time reference but not, it seems, in indicative AVCs which correlate with nonfuture time reference. This could be one reason why it does not cooccur with past time adverbials. Paramasivam (1971: 246) notes that over time many of these forms have become relexicalized as separate nouns no longer consciously or productively related to the nouns from which they originate, e.g., *viṭutalai* 'freedom' comes from the old verbal noun *viṭutal* 'release' (< *viṭa* 'leave') and the noun formative *-ai*. The more opaque their verbal source, the less able they are to fulfill the auxiliate's denotational function.

The most common deverbal noun in Modern Tamil is the nominalized verb. Like many *peyareccam*, it clearly has a sentential source and can be inflected for all three tenses, as well as the negative. Where the adnominal form has the suffix *-a*, the participial noun, as it is generally known, takes the suffix *-atu*, e.g., *va-nt-atu* 'that which came'. It preserves the cooccurrence properties of the verb from which it is productively derived; it takes the full array of satellites that the verb root has when it occurs in a finite form. At first blush, it would appear to be a good candidate for the auxiliate's form in an AVC. Yet, with a single exception discussed in Chapter 7, it virtually never occurs as the auxiliate in an AVC.

The reason for this exclusion may be attributed to the fact that such participial nouns are generally factive: the process of nominalization combines the verb base and tense marker with an abstract noun. As a result, the process denoted by the verb base is hypostasized as a separate event or action, so that the participial noun *varu-kiṟ-atu* may be translated as 'the event such that X is coming' or, more generally, as 'the N such that X is coming'. This form creates factive complements, as comparison of the two sentences below shows: (33a) is nonfactive, (33b) factive.

Nominalization thus has approximately the same effect on the verb base that would come from marking it for the verbal category of taxis: it would demarcate the process named by the verb base contained in the auxiliate as an event distinct and separate from other events. It therefore cannot appear within the interior of any AVC.

Moreover, the participial noun is inflected for nominal morphology, which might introduce extraneous information into an AVC. In general, no AVC will use a deverbal noun or adjective as the main verb unless there emerge very compelling

26 Nevertheless, this form is used as the citation form for verbs in the *Tamil lexicon*; we use the infinitive in that capacity.

circumstances to do so, e.g., if the formation rules prohibited two independent verb forms from entering into direct construction with each other.[27]

(33) a $_{S0}$[$_{S1}$[*karunaniti* *va-nt-ār*] *eṉṟu* *coṉṉāṉ*].
Karunaniti-NOM come-PST-3H say-CF tell-PST-3SM
'He said that Karunaniti came.'

b $_{S0}$[$_{S1}$[*karunaniti* *va-nt-at-ai.c*] *coṉṉāṉ*].
Karunaniti-NOM come-PST-VN-ACC tell-PST-3SM
'He told (us) the fact that Karunaniti came.'

viṉaiyeccam

Within the Tamil grammatical tradition, *viṉaiyeccam* are independent, nonfinite verb forms that combine with following verbs, with or without additional material intervening. This term and the concept that stands behind remain useful for the description of the present-day language. Modern Tamil has five, illustrated with the effective stem *piri-* 'separate', which has strong forms: the infinitive *piri-kka*, conjunctive *piri-ttu*, conditional *piri-ttāl*, negative combining form[28] *piri-kkāmal* (or *piri-kkātu*) and negative conditional[29] *piri-kkāviṭṭāl*.

viṉaiyeccam are likely to be the best candidates in Tamil to supply the form of the auxiliate in an AVC. Since they incorporate a verb base, they are able to satisfy the auxiliate's denotational function. As members of the category of verbs, they do not introduce extraneous categorial information, such as case, into the construction. Moreover, all are combining forms, and therefore not subject to the constraint against serial verb constructions in the modern language. However, as will be seen below, not all *viṉaiyeccam* can function as the form of the main verb: the infinitive, the conjunctive and, perhaps, the negative form are forms best suited to do so. The conditional and negative conditional, by virtue of the fact that they signal taxis, are disqualified.

27 The one apparent exception is the putative AVC in which auxiliary *āka* 'become' combines with the past participial noun of the auxiliate, e.g., *va-nt-atu āyiṟṟu* 'the coming has occurred'. Though an approximate paraphrase of the indicative AVC *vantu āyiṟṟu* '(X) has come', the two have not been shown to be semantically equivalent.

It should be noted that the present and future participial nouns never occur in this context, e.g., there are no well-formed phrases **varu-kiṟ-atu āyiṟṟu* or **varu-v-atu āyiṟṟu*. This suggests that in this context *va-nt-atu* does not have the same semantic value as it does elsewhere, viz., in contexts where it contrasts with the present and future counterparts.

It could thus be considered an idiosyncratic allomorph of the conjunctive in the environment of *āka* (see Chapter 7), which would be no surprise since the history of Tamil records several variants of the conjunctive, including *ceyyā* and *ceyyū* alongside *ceytu*.

28 This is often called the negative adverbial participle in the literature, but no demonstrations have ever been offered that its meaning is the sum of the adverbial participle (our conjunctive) and the negative operator.

29 This form is a contraction of an AVC in Middle Tamil, in which a now extinct negative form, *pirikkā* 'not separating', combined with the conditional of *viṭa* 'leave'. Such an analysis is not available in the modern language.

Conditional

In conditional sentences such as (34a), the verb of the protasis bears the conditional marker, connecting it to the apodosis. When the clitic particle *=um* 'all, and' combines with the conditional in the protasis and this is followed by a negative apodosis, as in (34b), a concessive conditional is formed. Examples (34c and d) illustrate a secondary use of the conditional form: when it is followed by the emphatic particle *tāṉē* 'indeed', it creates an indirect speech-act conveying a wish. The negative conditional form is illustrated in (34e).

(34) a $_{\text{S0}}$[$_{\text{S1}}$[*makaṉ poy co.ṉ-ṉ.āl*] *ammā aṭi.p-p-āḷ*].
son-NOM lie-NOM tell-CND mother-NOM beat-FUT-3F
'If a son lies, his mother will beat him.'

b $_{\text{S0}}$[$_{\text{S1}}$[*evvaḷavu kē.ṭ-ṭ.āl=um*] *avaṉ oṉṟum ceyya māṭṭāṉ*].
how.much ask-CND=AND he-NOM nothing do-INF FUT-NEG-3M
'No matter how much he's asked, he will do nothing.'

c $_{\text{S0}}$[$_{\text{S1}}$[*nāṉ co.ṉ-ṉ.āl*] *avaṉ kē.ṭ-ṭāl tāṉē*]!
I-NOM say-CND he-NOM listen-CND PCL
'If only he listened when I spoke.'

d $_{\text{S0}}$[*japu veḷiyē talai nīṭṭ-iṉ.āl tāṉē*]!
Jabu-NOM outside head-NOM stick-CND PCL
'If only Jabu would look outside!'

e $_{\text{S0}}$[$_{\text{S1}}$[*avaṉ var-āviṭṭāl*] *nāṉ avaṉai viṭa māṭṭēṉ*].
he-NOM come-NEG-CND I-NOM he-ACC leave-INF FUT-NEG-1S
'If he doesn't come, I won't leave him alone.'

The conditional appears—misleadingly—to combine the past tense marker with the instrumental case suffix *-āl*. On this hypothesis, the form *pirittāl* 'if separates' consists of the verb root *piri-*, the past allomorph *-tt-* and the instrumental case marker *-āl*. However, the naive segmentation this hypothesis implies is untenable. The segment following the root cannot be identified with the past tense marker because there are no present or future conditional forms to contrast with, i.e., there are no forms **pirikkiṟāl* 'if X is separating' or **pirippāl* 'if X will separate'. Nor can the segment *-āl* be identified with the instrumental case marker *-āl* because the two have distinct properties. The conditional never appears independently of the previous segment, which phonologically resembles the past tense; there is thus no motivation to introduce a morpheme boundary between the two. By contrast, the instrumental case marker *-āl* always combines with a noun, often the oblique stem. Lehmann's convention on morphophonemic adjustments may be extended to this form to clarify its internal structure, so that *vantālum* 'even if one comes' is segmented as *va-nt.āl=um* 'id.'.

Lehmann (1989: 378) adduces three examples where the concessive conditional appears to serve as the form of the auxiliate in an AVC. In all three, the putative auxiliary and auxiliate incorporate the same verb root. When the replicated verb inflects for past tense, as in (35a), it signals the speaker's disapproval of the action named by the verb base. When the replicated verb form is inflected for future tense, as in (35b), possibility and probability are expressed. And when in (35c), the replicated verb appears in the *-ālam* permissive form, possibility and probability are also expressed, though weaker than in (35b).

(35) a *kumar oru putu cāṭṭai.y-ai vāṅk-iṉ.āl=um vāṅk-iṉ-āṉ. atē cāṭṭai.y-ai*
Kumar-NOM one new shirt-ACC buy-CND=AND buy-PST-3SM same shirt-ACC
ippōtu tiṉam pōṭu-kiṟ-āṉ.
now daily put-PRS-3SM
'Kumar bought a new shirt; but now he wears the same shirt every day.'

b *kumar iṅkē va-nt.āl=um varu-v-āṉ.*
Kumar-NOM here come-CND=AND come-FUT-3SM
'Kumar may come here.'

c *kumar iṅkē va-nt.āl=um var-alām.*
Kumar-NOM here come-CND=AND come-PER
'Perhaps Kumar may come.'

As interesting as the sentences are, they are probably not examples of AVCs. The fact that the two verbs in these constructions must tautologously have the same root contravenes the separation of the denotational and inflectional functions between auxiliate and auxiliary envisaged by Auxiliary Formation.[30]

Negative nonfinite forms

Whether the negative forms in *-āmal* and *-ātu* can serve as the form of the auxiliate is debated in the literature. Although they seem to function as the negative of both the infinitive and the conjunctive, they cannot readily substitute for them in every context, particularly in AVCs. One of Annamalai's tests for auxiliaryhood (Chap-

30 Against our claim that the conditional form does not mark tense, it might be argued that in one context there appears to be a contrast between a past and present conditional form. Though these examples appear to constitute a minimal pair where the only contrast is in the tense marker before what appears to be the conditional marker, an alternative interpretation is indicated. With Vinson (1943), I believe these forms are hypercorrections in the written language that mistake what in the colloquial language is a collocation of the adnominal form and the noun *ap.pōla* 'that appearance, likeness' for the conditional. The literary forms in (i) and (ii) are pronounced in the colloquial variety as *peñjāppla* and *peyṟāppla*, respectively. Their correct analysis should be *peynta* + *ap.pōla* 'the appearance of having rained' and *peykiṟa* + *ap.pōla* 'the appearance of raining', respectively. The head noun in these clauses, *appōl* appearance, historically consists of the deictic marker *a-* 'that' and the noun *pōl* 'likeness'. Such a noun belongs to the set of forms that help to build adverbial adjuncts, e.g. *pōtu* 'time', *varai* 'limit' and *paṭi* 'manner'. The tense markers in (i) and (ii) are thus associated with the adnominal form of the verb, not its conditional form.

(i) *maẓai peytāl pōla irukkiṟatu.*
rain-NOM rain-PST-CND like be-PRES-3SN
'It looks like it rained.'

(ii) *maẓai peykiṟāl pōla irukkiṟatu.*
rain-NOM rain-PRES-CND like be-PRES-3SN
'It looks like it's raining.'

ter 2) holds that the auxiliate and auxiliary cannot be negated independently of each other; such a condition appears to preclude *-āmal* and *-ātu* as forms of the main verb. Fedson claims that two auxiliaries may combine with these negative forms: *irukka* 'be' (Fedson 1981: 24) and *pōka* 'go' (Fedson 1981: 164). She believes that (36b) alternates with (36a) below.

(36) a *avaṉ pō-y iru-kkiṟ-āṉ.*
he-NOM go-CF be-PRES-3SM
'He has gone.'
b *avaṉ pōk-āmal iru-kkiṟ-āṉ.*
he-NOM go-NEG-V be-PRES-3SM
'He is without going.' 'He stayed without going.'

That the two verbs in (36b) constitute a periphrastic form referring to a signal situation is far from clear; that it constitutes the negative of (36a) is an even more dubious claim. Even if (36b) were a compound verb, it would appear to alternate more closely with (37) below.

(37) *avaṉ pōka.v illai.*
he-NOM go-INF IND-NEG
'He didn't/doesn't go.'

The semantic difference between (36b) and (37) is one of relative scope; in (36b) tense has higher scope than negation, in (37) negation has higher scope than tense. The verb *irukka* in (36b) seems less an auxiliary chosen to convey a specific verbal category, and more a place holder syncategorematically inserted to bear the present tense marker *-(k)kiṟ-*. As such, *irukka* contributes no meaning to *pōkāmal irukka* 'be without going', and cannot therefore function as an auxiliary.

Annamalai (1982: 33-34) presents the alternative argument that the sequence (36b) is not an of AVC at all, but a coordinate structures meaning 'he remained without going' or 'he sat without going'. Each verb denotes a distinct event, thus disqualifying the sequence as an AVC. If this is so, then the negative verb form should be marked for taxis, a category that renders it unsuitable for use as an auxiliate in an AVC. If, however, it is merely the negative form of the infinitive and conjunctive form, it still cannot be semantically decomposed into the conjunctive form plus negative. Both counterarguments suggest that the status of such examples as (36b) is not as uncontroversial as Fedson's presentation would suggest. Finally, consider the following triad of examples.

(38) a *avaṉ vantu tolai-nt-āṉ.*
he-NOM come-CF lose-AF+PST-3SM
'He came, damn it.'
b * *avaṉ varāmal tolai-nt-āṉ.*
he-NOM come-NEGV lose-AF+PST-3SM
'He didn't come, damn it.'

c *avaṉ vantu tolai-y.a.v illai.*
he-NOM come-CF lose-AF+INF IND-NEG
'He didn't come, damn it.'

Twenty-three out of the twenty-five indicative auxiliaries that are treated in our corpus, which is to say all of the auxiliaries except *irukka* 'be' and *pōka* 'go', exhibit this pattern; they cannot grammatically combine with the negative verb form to create a coherent AVC.

Infinitive and conjunctive form

As we continue to close in on which forms are appropriate for the auxiliate, what remains are the infinitive and conjunctive, the two most common *viṉaiyeccam* in the language. Despite their frequency in texts and speech, their analysis has received little attention. Lindholm (1975) explores what motivates the use of the conjunctive; Steever (1981: 65-79) analyzes the semantic subsystem created by the opposition of these two forms. Deigner (1998) offers a study of the two forms, modeled on Latin, that sees the two in terms of perfectivity (see Steever 2000 for a review). For our purposes, the two basic kinds of AVC in Tamil differ according as one uses the infinitive for the auxiliate while the other uses the conjunctive.

Infinitive

The Tamil infinitive occurs in a wide range of constructions. In (39a) it joins two clauses of the same rank, in (39b) it marks a clause of circumstance. In (39c and d) it marks a subordinate clause under verbs of commanding and perception, respectively. In (39e) it is part of the future negative conjugation. In (39f) it has the illocutionary force of a rhetorical question and functions as a finite verb.[31] In (39g) it combines with a following noun, rather than another verb, serving as what McCawley (1988) calls an infinitival relative. In these last two the infinitive does not strictly exhibit the properties of a *viṉaiyeccam*: in (39f) it combines with nothing, behaving like a finite verb; in (39g) it combines with a noun.

(39) a [$_{S0}$ [$_{S1}$ *kamalā pāṭ-a*] [$_{S2}$ *carōjā āṭ-iṉ-āḷ*]].
Kamala-NOM sing-INF Saroja-NOM dance-PST-3SF
'As Kamala sang, Caroja danced.'

b [$_{S0}$ [$_{S1}$ *eytavaṉ iru.kk-a*] *ampai nō-vāṉēṉ*]?
archer-NOM be-INF arrow-ACC blame-SUP
'With the archer here, why blame the arrow?'

c [$_{S0}$ *nāṉ* [$_{S1}$ *avaṉai var-a.c*] *coṉ-ṉ-ēṉ*].
I-NOM he-ACC come-INF tell-PST-1S
'I told him to come.'

31 It is in this function more common in the spoken language than in the literary, where it is usually replaced by a future verbal noun, e.g. *eṅkē pōvatu* 'where is one to go?'

d $_{S0}$[$_{S1}$[*avaḷ* *pāṭ-a*] *nāṉ* *kēṭ-ṭ-ēṉ*].
she-NOM sing-INF I-NOM hear-PST-1S
'I heard her singing.'

e *kār* *ōṭ-a* *māṭṭ-ēṉ* *eṉkiṟatu.*
car-NOM run-INF FUT+NEG-1S say-PRES-3SN
'The car refuses to run.'

f *eṅkē* *pō.k-a?* *eṉṉa* *cey.y-a?*
where go-INF what do-INF
'Where is one to go? What is to be done?'

g $_{NP}$[$_{S0}$[*paṭi.kk-a*] $_{N}$[*nēram*]] *illai.*
study-INF time-NOM IND-NEG
'There is no time to study.'

Although the infinitive is commonly associated with notions of temporality, causality and purpose, none of these meanings invariably accompanies it. While it

(40) a $_{S0}$[$_{S1}$[*nel* *viḷai.y-a*] $_{S2}$[*maḻai* *pey-t-atu*]].
paddy-NOM result-INF rain-NOM fall-PST-3SN
'They paddy grew as/and the rain fell.'

b $_{S0}$[$_{S1}$[*maḻai* *pey.y-a*] $_{S2}$[*nel* *viḷai-nt-atu*]].
rain-NOM fall-INF paddy-NOM result-PST-3SN
'As the rain fell, the paddy grew.'

c $_{S0}$[$_{S1}$[*teyvattiṉ* *aruḷ* *kiṭai.kk-a.k*] $_{S2}$[*kaviñar* *uṇarcciyuṭaṉ* *pāṭ-iṉ-ār*]].
God-GEN grace obtain-INF poet-NOM emotion-SOC sing-PST-3H
'The poet sang with emotion to obtain God's grace.'
or
'The poet, having obtained God's grace, sang with emotion.'

d $_{S0}$[$_{S1}$[*makaṉ* *kallūrikku.c* *cel.l-a*] $_{S2}$[*appā* *vayalil* *pāṭupaṭ-ṭ-ār*]].
son-NOM college-DAT go-INF father-NOM field-LOC toil-PST-3H
'The father toiled in the fields so that his son could go to college.'
or
'As the son set off for college, his father was toiling in the fields.'

e $_{S0}$[$_{S1}$[*ceṅkai* *piṭittu* *maṇaceytōr=um* *pārttu* *iru.kk-a.k*]
fair.hand take-CF husband-NOM=AND see-CF be-INF
koṅkai *piṭittu* *iḻikkum* *kōmāṉē*]![32]
breast take-CF pull-FUT-ADN king-VOC
'O king who would fondle the breasts of a woman while her husband looked on.'

f $_{S0}$[$_{S1}$[*kākka* *uṭkār-a.p*] $_{S2}$[*paṉampaḻam* *viḻu-nt-atu*]].
crow-NOM sit-INF palmyra.fruit-NOM fall-PST-3SN
'The crow sat down and the palmyra fruit fell.'

joins two clauses to form coordinate or adjunct structures in (40a and b), the interchangeability of these two suggests that neither causality nor purpose can be part

32 This couplet comes from the *kūḷappa nāyakkaṉ viṟali viṭutūtu.*

of its invariant meaning. The time reference of the infinitival clause may be prior to (40c and d, second reading), simultaneous with (40e) or posterior to (40c and d, first reading) the time reference of the clause it combines with, suggesting the infinitive marks neither tense nor, most probably, taxis. The examples in (39a and b) and (40b, e, and f) do not support readings of causality or purpose. Example (40e) uses the infinitive to join a clause of circumstance to the main clause. Interestingly, example (40f) is a Tamil proverb which indicates that two events may happen coincidentally with no causal relation; significantly, the two clauses of the proverb are joined by an infinitive.

The infinitive occurs in a variety of matrix-complement constructions where one clause is subordinated to another according to the subcategorization features of the verb in the matrix clause. It typically occurs in the complements of verbs of ordering, telling (41a), aspectual verbs (41c—see Freed 1976), as well as verbs describing mental states or dispositions (41b and d).

(41) a *avar ilai pōṭ-a.c coṉ-ṉ-ār.*
he-NOM leaf put-INF tell-PST-3H
'He told (her) to set the leaves out (for a meal).'

b *eṉakku nīnt-a teriyum.*
I-DAT swim-INF know-FUT-3SN
'I know how to swim.'

c *mantiri cāṭcapaiyil pēc-a ārampi-tt-ār*
minister-NOM assembly-LOC speak-INF begin-PST-3H
'The minister began to speak in the assembly.'

d *avaṉukku.t tōcai cāppiṭ-a.p piṭikkum.*
he-DAT dosai eat-INF like-FUT-3N
'He likes to eat dosais.'

Infinitives may also combine with a following verb to form a lexical compound, a process somewhat more common in the written language than the spoken. Recall from Chapter 1 that in lexical compounds, the second verb has the basic denotational function which the first verb modifies, adding some specification of manner or direction. In example (42c), for example, *uẓala.k kaṭa* 'roam' refers to a single activity; the compound is a hyponym of the verb *kaṭa* 'cross'. Importantly, the fact that the infinitive appears in lexical compounds indicates that it is not marked for taxis, a conclusion buttressed by evidence from the remaining AVCs below.

(42) a *rāvaṇaṉ viyappil kaṇṇai [akal-a virittu.p] pār-tt-āṉ.*[33]
Ravana-NOM amazement-LOC eye-ACC widen-INF open-CF look-PST-3SM
'Ravanan looked (at them), his eyes wide open in amazement.'

b *avaṉ akal-a niṉ-ṟ-āṉ.*
he-NOM wide-INF stand-PST-3SM
'He stood apart/aloof.'

33 This example is from Andronov (1969: 188).

c *nī curāmīṉ vaṭivaṅ koṇṭu kaṭalil* [*uḻal-a.k kaṭavāy*]
you-NOM shark form take-CP sea-LOC whirl-INF cross-FUT-2S
eṉa.c cāpittu aruḷ-ṉ-ār.[34]
say-CF curse-CF grace-PST-3H
'(Siva) cursed him to roam the seas in the form of a shark.'

d *makaṉ aruk-a varu-v-āṉ.*
son-NOM near-INF come-FUT-3SM
'His son will approach.'

e *avaṉ niṟai.y-a.p pēc-iṉ-āṉ.*
he-NOM fill-A+INF speak-PST-3SM
'He gabbed,' 'He spoke a lot.'

In numerous auxiliary compounds, the auxiliate appears in its infinitival form. The modal auxiliaries *muṭiyum* 'be able, possible' in (43a) and *vēṇṭum* 'be necessary' in (43b) combine with just such an auxiliate. The auxiliary of a prospective tense series, *irukka* 'be' (43c), does so as well. The negative conjugation in Tamil is conspicuously expressed by a series of AVCs in which the auxiliate appears in the infinitive, as the future negative in (39a, 43d) shows (see also Table 2.2 on p. 35). Passive voice is signaled by an AVC whose auxiliate appears in infinitival form, e.g. (43e). In the emphatic construction illustrated in (43f), the auxiliary verb *ceyya* 'do, make', which serves as the marker of emphasis, combines with the infinitival form of the auxiliate of *vara* 'come'.

(43) a *ennāl pō.k-a muṭiyum.*
I-INSTR go-INF be.able-FUT-3N
'I can go.'

b *nīṅkaḷ eṅkaḷ vīṭṭukku var-a vēṇṭum.*
you-NOM our house-DAT come-INF need-FUT-3N
'You must come to our house.'

c *avaṉ pō.k-a iru-kkiṟ-āṉ.*
he-NOM go-INF be-PRES-3SM
'He is to go.'

d *avaṉ var-a.v=ē māṭṭ-āṉ*
he-NOM come-INF=PCL FUT+NEG-3SM
'He will not come.'

e *rāvaṇaṉ rāmarāl aṭi.kk-a.p paṭ-ṭ-āṉ*
Ravana-NOM Rama-INSTR beat-INF befall-PST-3sm
'Ravanan was beaten by Ramar.'

f *avaṉ vara.c cey-t-āṉ.*
he-NOM come-INF do-PST-3SM
'He did come.'

34 From the *tiruviḷaiyāṭal*, verse 286.

These examples further confirm our claim that the infinitive does not invariantly mark taxis or tense, causality or purpose. Furthermore, it does not mark aspect since the generality between imperfective and perfective readings, discussed above, is unaffected by the presence of an infinitive. Nor is voice at issue: the infinitive does not alter the valency of the verb base.

The great syntactic and semantic versatility of the infinitive leads us to the preliminary conclusion that it is the least marked verb form of Tamil. Although it functions primarily as a nonfinite verb (*viṉaiyeccam*), it also serves as a finite verb (*viṉai muṟṟu*) in certain circumstances (39f). It may combine syntactically with other clauses, with another verb, with a noun (39g) or with nothing at all (39f). No other *viṉaiyeccam* exhibits such a broad range of combinatoric properties. Saying the infinitive is the least marked verb form of Tamil is not the same thing as determining its invariant meaning, but it is suggestive nonetheless. Jakobson's model provides no verbal category that is more basic than mood, the qualifier of E^n.

Conjunctive form

The conjunctive form, also called the adverbial participle,[35] occurs in many syntactic structures, suggesting a meaning nearly as broad as the infinitive's. We attempt to define its meaning and how it contrasts with the infinitive. Lindholm's (1975) proposed meaning of "natural relevance" is vague and helps little to determine the conjunctive form's semantic contribution to the structures it occurs in.[36] The conjunctive may combine with a following clause to form coordinate (44a and b) or subordinate (44c) structures. It may combine clauses with different subjects as (44a-d). It combines most frequently with a following verb, justifying its membership in the set of *viṉaiyeccam*; but in (44f) it combines with a following predicate nominal. While it is used to subordinate a clause to verbs of perception, as in (44c and j), such uses appear more limited than the infinitive's. And in no case can the conjunctive function as a finite verb (*viṉai muṟṟu*), as the infinitive can (39f).

(44) a $_{S0}$[$_{S1}$[*rattiri* *pō-y*] $_{S2}$[*pakal* *va-nt-atu*]].
night-NOM go-CF daylight-NOM come-PST-3SN
'Night departed and daylight came.'

b $_{S0}$[$_{S1}$[*maḻai* *pey-tu*] $_{S2}$[*veyil* *aṭi.t-tu*] $_{S3}$[*vāṉavil* *tōṉṟ-i.y-atu*]].
rain-NOM rain-CF sunshine-NOM beat-CF rainbow-NOM appear-PST-3SN
'It rained, the sun shone and a rainbow appeared.'

c $_{S0}$[$_{S1}$[*nāṉ* *col.l-i*] *avaḷ* *kēṭ.k-a.v* *illai*].
I-NOM say-CF she-NOM listen-INF IND-NEG
'She didn't listen to what I was saying.'

35 The term adverbial participle is doubly noxious because Tamil does not include basic adverbs among its major parts of speech and it also has no basic class of adjectives, of which participles would be a subclass. We avoid it in preference to the term conjunctive form.

36 More to the point, Lindholm pointedly excluded from his definition the use of this form with indicative AVCs.

d $_{S0}$[$_{S1}$[*inta.p paṭattai srīdar ḍairekt paṇ.ṇ-i*] $_{S2}$[*cāvitri naṭi-tt-āḷ*]].[37]
this picture-ACC Sridhar-NOM direct do-CF Savitri-NOM act-PST-3SF
'This film was directed by Sridhar and stars Savitri.'

e $_{S0}$[$_{S1}$[*anta.c ceyti terivi.t-tu*] *oru kaṭitam va-nt-atu*].
that news announce-CF one letter-NOM come-PST-3SN
'A letter came, announcing that news.'

f $_{S0}$[$_{S1}$[*kavalaippaṭ-ṭu*] *eṉṉa payaṉ*]?
worry-CF what use-NOM
'What's the use of worrying?'

g *eṅkaḷ kuṭumpam cāstrattukku añc-i naṭa.k-kiṟ-atu.*[38]
our family-NOM sastras-DAT fear-CF conduct-PRES-3SN
'Our family is conducted in accordance with (lit. "fearing") the sastras.'

h *rikṣākkāraṅkaḷ avaḷai iṟaṅka viṭāmal taṭa.t-tu niṉ-ṟ-ārkaḷ.*[39]
rickshaw.drivers-NOM she-ACC descend-INF let-NEGV block-CF stand-PST-3H
'The rickshaw drivers stood about preventing her from getting out.'

i *pāmpu kaṭi.t-tu.p paiyaṉ cettuppō-ṉ-āṉ.*
snake-NOM bite-CF boy-NOM die-PST-3SM
'A snake bite the boy and he died.'

j *nāṉ avaḷai kār ōṭṭ-i.p pār-tt-ēṉ.*
I-NOM she-ACC car drive-CF see-PST-1S
'I saw her driving a car.'

Until Lindholm (1975) presented incontrovertible counterevidence, it was almost universally held that use of the conjunctive was constrained by a same-subject condition. Examples (44a, b, c, d, i, and j) are *prima facie* evidence against this claim; note especially that conjunctive forms link three clauses in (44b), each with a different subject.[40] Further, as evidence from compound verbs shows, it is meaningless to define the conjunctive by a same-subject constraint since such a constraint presupposes that each clause have its own subject, and a compound verb has only one subject, no matter how many independent verb forms it contains. In this sense, the conjunctive does not mark voice.

Anterior taxis has also been posited as the meaning of the conjunctive, and while such an interpretation is consistent with examples (44a and i), it is not for the remaining examples. An interpretation of simultaneity seems more appropriate for

37 Lindholm (1975: 33).
38 Lindholm (1975: 41).
39 Lindholm (1975: 1).
40 Lindholm (1975) detailed the conditions that motivate the conjunctive in certain constructions of Tamil syntax, but not in AVCs (Lindholm 1975: 2, 46, 48, 51). Despite the formal identity of the conjunctive in AVCs with the conjunctive elsewhere, he dismissed it as an automatic morphophonemic adjustment of the main verb in the presence of an auxiliary, forcing him to posit two homophonous conjunctive forms. Thus, the most this analysis could hope to determine was a circumstantial meaning (*Sonderbedeutung*) of the conjunctive in one of its principal contexts. Overlooking this discrepancy, Fedson (1981) uncritically applied Lindholm's meaning of the conjunctive to a group of constructions that he consciously excluded from his analysis.

examples (44b, c, d, g, h, and j). Example (44e) even suggests posterior taxis; the letter must first arrive and be opened before its contents can be known. The fact that the conjunctive is consistent with all three interpretations suggests it is general among all and, therefore, marked for none. Instrumentality and accompaniment may work for (44i) but not for (44a, b, or f). Behind these proposals lurks the assumption that the conjunctive should mark taxis: anteriority, simultaneity, instrumentality, etc. are inherently tactic notions, describing relations purported to hold between two events.[41] The lexical and auxiliary compound verbs below provide solid evidence against attributing taxis to the conjunctive form.

The conjunctive may link two verb forms to create a lexical compound. As above, the second verb denotes a basic activity that the first further specifies with such qualifications as manner or direction. In (45a) *nimirntu* 'straightening (the head)' specifies the direction of the basic activity *pār-tt-ār* 'he looked at'. The entire lexical is a hyponym of the second verb: *etirntu pēca* 'speak back, contradict' (45b) is thus a hyponym of *pēca* 'speak'. Certain compounds are idiomatic: the meaning of *piṭittu viṭa* 'massage' (45c) is not wholly predictable from the meaning of its two components, *piṭikka* 'take, grab' and *viṭa* 'leave, depart'; in isolation, both are semelfactive while the compound denotes an iterative activity. In keeping with its specifying function, the first verb may be reduplicated to add intensity (45d), a possibility denied to auxiliary compounds (pp. 130-32). Finally, two semantically similar verbs in a lexical compound may on occasion switch positions (45e and f), a permutation which the denotational and inflectional functions of the AVC prevent in auxiliary compounds.[42]

(45) a	*avar*	*maṉaviyai*	*nimir.n-tu*	*pār-tt-ār.*	
	he-NOM	wife-ACC	lift-CF	look-PST-3H	
	'He looked up at his wife.'				
b	*peṇ*	*puruṣaṉ*	[*etir.n-tu*	*pēca.k*]	*kūṭātu.*
	wife-NOM	husband	oppose-CF	speak-INF	should-NEG-3N
	'A wife must not challenge/speak back to her husband.'				

41 Lindholm takes the conjunctive to be a connector, specifically one marked for taxis. His labels include "causal," "sequential," "resultative," "descriptive" and "naturally relevant," all of which assume that the conjunctive marks taxis. In doing so, he failed to distinguish between the morphosyntactic category of *viṉaiyeccam* and the semantic category of taxis. He ultimately settled on the term "natural relevance" to describe the relation purported to hold between the two events linked by the conjunctive; any two clauses linked by the conjunctive are deemed to be "naturally relevant" to each other. He did not make any proposal as to how the criterion of natural relevance was to be restricted so it applied only to those clauses linked by the conjunctive. It could, at best, be a necessary condition for the appearance of the conjunctive since the language provides additional ways to express natural relevance. And it fails as a sufficient condition because not all uses of the conjunctive represent a tactic notion such as relevance. In short, natural relevance is merely an alternative label for the conjunctive, not an explanation of it.

42 It is in such instances, I suspect, that new auxiliary verbs may enter the auxiliary system. The first verb of a lexical compound, conveying some modifying meaning, is transposed rightward over the second verb so that the order of modifier-modified is reversed to match the order of main and auxiliary in an AVC.

c   *avaḷ   eṉ   kālai.p   [piṭi.t-tu viṭa]   māṭṭēṉ   eṉkirāḷ.*
    she-NOM my leg-ACC take-CF leave-INF FUT-NEG-3F say-PRES-3F
    'She refuses to massage my leg.'
d   *avaṉ   tuḷai.t-tu.t tuḷi.t-tu.k   kēṭ-ṭ-āṉ.*
    he-NOM dig-CF   dig-CF   ask-PST-3SM
    'He interrogated (someone) persistently.'
e   *avaṉ   uẓa.n-tu   puraṭṭ-iṉ-āṉ.*
    he-NOM whirl-CF   overturn-PST-3SM
    'He rolled about.'
f   *avaṉ   puraṭṭ-i   uẓa-nt-āṉ.*
    he-NOM overturn-CF   whirl-PST-3SM
    'He rolled about.'

Despite the two independent verb forms in the lexical compound, it behaves as a unit, describes a single situation and effectively militates against ascribing taxis to the conjunctive form's invariant meaning. While the compound has but one set of satellites, it is probable that both verbs may influence the selection restrictions of the whole compound. This process of "derivation" distinguishes lexical compounds from AVCs, where the nature of the modification is inflectional in nature.

Finally, the conjunctive functions as a component in many AVCs, where the second verb inflects the first with a specific verbal category. The combination of conjunctive and auxiliary *irukka* 'be' in yields the perfect tense series (46a). In the same context, auxiliary *viṭa* 'leave' produces disjunctive taxis (46b) while auxiliary *tolaikka* 'lose' gives rise to pejorative attitude (46c). Comparison of (43c) and (46a) clearly reveals that the conjunctive contributes to the AVC's meaning. Both contain AVCs with the lexeme *irukka* as auxiliary, but wheras (43c) conveys present prospective tense, (46a) conveys present perfect tense. Since the only apparent difference between them is the choice of form for the auxiliate, the infinitive or conjunctive, the difference in meaning must reside in that formal difference.

(46) a *avaṉ   ūrukku.p   pō-y   irukkirāṉ.*
        he-NOM   town-DAT   go-CF   be-PRES-3SM
        'He had gone to town.'
   b   *avaṉ   pō-y   vi.ṭ-ṭu   vantāṉ.*
        he-NOM   go-CF   leave-CF   come-PST-3SM
        'He left, then came back.'
   c   *contakkāraṅkaḷ   niṉaitta   nērattil   va.n-tu   tolaippārkaḷ.*
        relatives-NOM   think-PST-ADN   time-LOC   come-CF   lose-FUT-3P
        'Our relatives come here whenever they damn well please.'

Each AVC in (46) has just one set of satellites; despite the fact that each one consists of two or more independent verb forms, it denotes a single situation. Tamil *vantu irukkirāṉ* no more denotes two separate events than its English counterpart *he has come*; these examples constitute additional evidence that the conjunctive form does not invariantly mark taxis.

As the data from the compound verbs above has shown us, the conjunctive form in Tamil does not mark the verbal category of taxis or any concept that presupposes taxis, such as anteriority. Its use in constructions is clearly not governed by a same-subject condition, or any other phenomenon that would suggest that it marks the category of voice. As a suffix, it does not change the inherent aspectual class of the verb base, and so is cannot be marked for aspect. Like the infinitive, it is a highly unmarked form in Tamil.[43]

Despite the apparent homophony of the allomorphs of the conjunctive and those of the past tense, e.g. *cey-tu* 'doing' versus *cey-t-āṉ* 'he did, *pēc-i* 'speaking' versus *pēc-i.ṉ-āṉ* 'he spoke', the conjunctive does not encode tense. There are no present or future conjunctive forms to contrast with the "past" conjunctive, i.e., Tamil simply has no verb forms of the shape **cey-kiṟ-u* 'doing' or **cey-v-u* 'doing' to contrast with *cey-t-u* 'doing'.[44] Examples have shown that the conjunctive is consistent with anterior (44a), simultaneous (44j) or posterior time reference (44e), which is to say that it is not marked for tense.

Although the infinitive and conjunctive are among the least marked verb forms of Tamil, closer inspection is required to determine how they minimally contrast with each other syntactically and semantically. The major syntactic difference between the two is that the infinitive, but not the conjunctive, may occur alone functioning as a finite verb and may also modify a noun. The infinitive thus has a wider distribution than the conjunctive, suggesting it is the less marked of the two. Since neither form marks tense, taxis, voice or aspect, what we are left with is mood, the qualifier of E^n. This leads us to the proposal that the infinitive and conjunctive constitute an opposition of two terms within the category of mood.

OPPOSITION OF INFINITIVE VS. CONJUNCTIVE FORM

The following minimal pairs directly contrast the infinitive and conjunctive. Examples (47a and b) have similar meanings, and are interchangeable in many con-

43 Lindholm fails to contrast the infinitive with the conjunctive even though both belong to the set of *viṉaiyeccam*, a fact which invites comparison. Because both occur in similar contexts, they might be supposed to contrast minimally with each other. This gap undermines his argument, since the meaning of a form is often determined by its position in a system of grammatical oppositions. Instead, he contrasts the bald use of the conjunctive with two indicative AVCs: one with auxiliary *viṭa* 'leave', the other with auxiliary *koḷḷa* 'hold'. The former signals disjunctive taxis, the latter conjunctive taxis; both are taken as the lower and upper bounds, respectively, on the use of the conjunctive. While one might argue that a situation that motivates disjunctive taxis precludes natural relevance, it is difficult to see how situations that motivate conjunctive taxis do so. There is a glaring methodological error: both these AVCs already use the conjunctive form. Here forms containing the conjunctive are being used to define the conjunctive, a circular argument. The use of the conjunctive is not limited by these two AVCs; instead, it is consistent with both.

44 Despite the fact Tamil has no present or future conjunctive forms to contrast with, Lindholm (1975: 51) claims the conjunctive marks past tense, without explaining the relation between past tense and natural relevance. Subsequent analyses which rely on Lindholm's analysis, such as Fedson (1981), are heir to the same criticisms.

texts, but (47a) has a circumstantial reading (47b) lacks, viz., 'as it rained, the paddy grew.' The infinitive may suggest that the two events are coincidental, that the paddy could have grown without rain, say, by means of irrigation; the conjunctive, however, suggests a less circumstantial link between the two events.

(47) a *maẓai pey.y-a nel viḷaintatu.*
rain-NOM rain-INF paddy-NOM result-PST-3SN
'It rained and the paddy grew.'
b *maẓai pey-tu nel viḷaintatu.*
rain-NOM rain-CF paddy-NOM result-PST-3SN
'It rained and the paddy grew.'

Examples (48a and b) are both used to tell time. In (48a) the hour is yet to strike, and is treated as an event subsequent to the reference time; in (48b), the hour has already struck (ten minutes) before the reference time.

(48) a *pattu aṭi.kk-a.p pattu nimiṣam irukkiṟatu.*
ten-NOM strike-INF ten minute-NOM be-PRES-3SN
'It is ten minutes to (i.e. before) ten o'clock.'
b *pattu aṭi.t-tu.p pattu nimiṣam irukkiṟatu.*
ten-NOM strike-CF ten minute-NOM be-PRES-3SN
'It is ten minutes after ten o'clock.'

Use of sentence (49a) does not commit the speaker to the position that the subject ate any food, only that he intended to sample some food by tasting it. Example sentence (49b), however, does commit the speaker to the position that the subject did consume food.

(49) a *oru tōcai cāppiṭ-a.p pārttēṉ.*
one dosai eat-INF look-PST-1S
'I tried to eat a dosai (but couldn't).'
b *oru tōcai cāppiṭ-ṭu.p pārttēṉ.*
one dosai eat-CF look-PST-1S
'I tried eating a dosai (to see what it was like).'

Example (50a) can be uttered even if the Chola king did not succeed in ruling the country, it merely indicates that he intended or planned to rule. But in (50b) the speaker is committed to the truth of the proposition that he ruled the country.

(50) a *cōẓar inta nāṭṭai aḷ-a vantārkaḷ.*
Chola-NOM this land-ACC rule-INF come-PST-3P
'The Cholas came to rule this land.'
b *cōẓar inta nāṭṭai ā.ṇ-ṭu vantārkaḷ.*
Chola-NOM this land- ACC rule-CF come-PST-3P
'The Cholas were ruling this land.'

The form *irukkiṟāṉ* 'he is' establishes present reference time in both (51a and b); in the former, the act of coming is held to take place after that reference time, while in the latter, it is held to have taken place before it. As in (48a and b), the infinitive looks forward, the conjunctive backward.

(51) a *avaṉ iṅkē var-a irukkiṟāṉ.*
he-NOM here come-INF be-PRES-3SM
'He is (about) to come here.'
b *avaṉ iṅkē va.n-tu irukkiṟāṉ.*
he-NOM here come-CF be-PRES-3SM
'He has come here.'

The AVC in (52a) conveys permission, a notion commonly associated with modality, while (52b) shows no trace of modality. It serves in this context as an emphatic form that affirms the reality of the event of speaking (see the discussion in Chapter 6). Whether or not someone spoke in the situation in (52a) is besides the point; permission was granted to speak and that is all that is conveyed. But (52b) commits the speaker to vouching for the occurrence of an act of speaking.

(52) a *avaḷ pēc-a viṭṭāḷ.*
she-NOM speak-INF leave-PST-3SF
'She let (someone) speak.'
b *avaḷ pēc-i viṭṭāḷ.*
she-NOM speak-CF leave-PST-3SF
'She did speak.'

The construction in (53a) has not been analyzed in the literature; its approximate meaning, noted in the gloss, is 'they carried on no such activity of which speaking is a particular instance from a general range'. In this respect, it resembles echo compounds (see Steever 1993), but appears not to convey the contemptuous psychological tone of the *ki*-echo compound (pp. 136-39). This compound clearly contrasts with that in (53b).

(53) a *avarkaḷ pēc-a.k koḷḷa.v illai.*
they-NOM speak-INF hold-INF IND-NEG
'They didn't speak or do any such thing.'
b *avarkaḷ pēc-i.k koḷḷa.v illai.*
they-NOM speak-CF hold-INF IND-NEG
'They didn't speak among themselves.'

Example (54a) expresses an abilitative meaning: the subject was able or not, as the case may be, to write a novel. Whether the subject exercised that ability is not at issue here. The AVC in (54b) is marked for accelerative aspect (see Chapter 8), and the speaker is committed to the proposition that the subject wrote a novel, and quickly at that.

(54) a *avar nāvalai eẓut-a.t taḷḷ-a.v illai.*
he-NOM novel-ACC write-INF push-INF IND-NEG
'He was unable/not strong enough to write the novel.'

b *avar nāvalai eẓut-i.t taḷḷ-a.v illai.*
he-NOM novel-ACC write-CF push-INF IND-NEG
'He didn't write the novel extra quickly.'

This series of minimal pairs indicates that when a verb is inflected for the infinitive, the situation it denotes is viewed as possible or unrealized; when it is inflected for the conjuctive, the event is viewed as actual or realized. This contrast finds ready expression in the grammatical opposition between modal and nonmodal (or indicative). The infinitive in the a-sentences above is responsible for the semantic features of modality, contingency, possibility and unreality, while in the b-sentences, the conjunctive is responsible for the meanings of actuality, reality and noncontingency.

Verbal category of mood

The invariant meanings of the infinitive and conjunctive involve the category of mood, the qualifier of E^n which Aronson (1978) defines as "... a verbal category expressing the ontological evaluation of the process denoted by a given verb." As noted in Chapter 1, mood is minimally opposed to aspect, the quantifier of the narrated event.[45] Mood distinguishes primarily between modal and nonmodal (or indicative). Modal verb forms, in Aronson's words, characterize situations that "do not denote a real process," while indicative verb forms characterize those that do. This contrast aptly captures the observed contrasts between the Tamil infinitive and conjunctive, leading us to conclude that they contrast according to the category of mood with the infinitive as modal and the conjunctive as indicative.

The opposition between modal and indicative is privative; modal is the unmarked and indicative the marked term. Unmarked modal forms need not designate the real world, but neither are they inconsistent with it. The relative markedness is reflected in the facts that the infinitive appears in more syntactic frames than the conjunctive and that the infinitive is what is syncategorematically inserted in the formation of the passive and the *ceyya*-emphatic. More generally, the infinitive is the least marked modal verb form in Tamil while the conjunctive is the least marked nonmodal form.

The distinction between modal and nonmodal is applicable throughout the entire verbal system of Tamil. Only the infinitive and conjunctive are marked solely for mood alone; all remaining verb forms, whatever additional categories they

45 No study before (Steever 1981) had proposed invariant meanings for the infinitive and conjunctive or argued they constitute the terms of a grammatical opposition. Ignoring this study, Deigner 1998 attempted to characterize the contrast in aspectual terms. See Steever (2000) for a review of his methodology and results.

mark, are classified as modal or indicative. Forms such as the future, the conditional (negative and positive) and the negative conjugation are modal; the past and present affirmative forms are nonmodal.

To buttress this claim, note that Tamil has polarity items which are sensitive to the modal-indicative distinction: for example, the indefinite quantifier *=āvatu* 'some, any' cooccurs with modal forms while the indefinite quantifier *=ō* 'some, any, or' cooccurs with nonmodal forms (see Asher 1985: 193).

(55) a *yār=ō* *va-nt-ārkaḷ.*
who-NOM=SOME come-PST-3P
'Someone came.'

b *yār=āvatu* *varu-v-ārkaḷ.*
who-NOM=SOME come-FUT-3P
'Someone will/would come.'

The polarity items cannot be substituted for each other in in these examples without giving rise to unacceptable utterances.

Both may occur in the present tense; when they do, the modal polarity item *=āvatu* 'some, any' conveys a rhetorically charged nuance.

(56) a *yār=ō* *varu-kiṟ-ārkaḷ.*
who-NOM=SOME come-PRES-3P
'Someone is coming.'

b *yār=āvatu* *varu-kiṟ-ārkaḷ.* *uṉakku* *eṉṉa?*
who-NOM=SOME come-PRES-3P you-DAT what-NOM
'Yeah, someone or other is coming. What's it to you?'

Modal polarity items make less of an ontological commitment than their nonmodal counterparts do. Their distribution is not restricted to tense forms, but includes nonfinite forms as well: *=āvatu* 'some, any' occurs within domains defined by the conditional and the infinitive while *=ō* 'some, any' occurs within domains defined by the conjunctive.

The category of modality, whose existence has not heretofore been recognized in the grammar of Tamil, will be shown in the ensuing chapters to perform a goodly amount of work in the grammar of the language. To anticipate one result from Chapter 4, it will be demonstrated that the *ki*-echo construction and its distribution in Tamil utterances is sensitive to the distinction between modal and nonmodal, or indicative, contexts.

The semantic distinction between modal and indicative, as represented by the formal contrast between the infinitive and the conjunctive form, may also be used to classify AVCs. If we assume that the process of Auxiliary Formation respects semantic compositionality, then the meanings of modal and indicative auxiliates are projected to the AVCs in which they occur, permitting us to analyze them as modal and indicative AVCs, respectively. In short, those AVCs with an infinitival auxiliate are classified as modal AVCs while those with a conjunctive auxiliate are classified as indicative AVCs. It is for this reason that we describe the AVCs analyzed in this book as indicative.

Recall that the contrast between modal and indicative categories is a privative opposition, with modal as the unmarked and indicative as the marked member of the opposition. The meaning of the unmarked modal forms is thus consistent with that of indicative forms, and in contexts of neutralization it is the modal forms that are predicated to occur. So while modal auxiliaries involving such concepts as possibility, necessity and prospective tense typically require their auxiliates to assume an infinitival form, not all instances of an infinitive in a compound verb need to signal modality. Thanks to the fact that it is the unmarked member of the opposition, the infinitive also occurs in constructions where modality is not at issue and into which a verb form has to be transformationally inserted (and not base-generated), such as the *ceyya*-emphatic construction or the passive.[46]

By contrast, indicative AVCs are semantically unified in a way that modal AVCs are not. All indicative auxiliaries typically comment on the internal composition of the narrated event, whose component parts are viewed as real with respect to each other. This may provide us with a partial explanation as to why several scholars have characterized what we call indicative auxiliaries as aspectual. Strictly speaking, the category of aspect, the quantifier of the narrated event, characterizes the internal (temporal) composition of the narrated event. Taking some liberties, we might treat the term aspect as a metonym for all verbal categories that chartacterize the internal structure of the narrative event in one way or another, embracing such different categories as voice (P^nE^n), taxis (E^nE^n), tense, (E^s/E^n), attitude (P^s/E^n) and, of course, aspect proper (E^n). Since, however, this chapter has shown that mood, the qualifier of E^n is less marked than aspect, the quantifier of E^n, and since the infinitive and conjunctive contrast in terms of modality, projecting that contrast to the AVCs in which they occur, we will continue to classify AVCs as modal or indicative. As we consider various phenomena in the following chapters, the distinction between modal and indicative forms will be seen to pervade the grammar of Tamil AVCs.

46 Steever (1981: Chapter 6) argues that the passive sentence *rāvaṇaṉ rāmarāl aṭikka.p paṭṭāṉ* 'Ravana was beaten by Rama' is truth-functionally equivalent to its active counterpart *rāmar rāvaṇaṉai aṭittār* 'Rama beat Ravana'. The decision to apply Passive is motivated for reasons of syntax or pragmatics, not semantics. The passive auxiliary *paṭa* 'befall' does not therefore have any semantic function to convey a grammatical category. Both active and passive sentences issue from the same underlying structure.

When Passive applies, it inserts the auxiliary marker *paṭa*, and Chomsky-adjoins it to create a compound verb. The existing verb base in the structure, *aṭi-* 'beat', must appear in some form of the language that can be pronounced since the root by itself is not a free form; therefore, it assumes the least marked form, the infinitive, to introduce the least amount of extraneous meaning into the construction. While the result now conforms to an existing template for modal AVCs, the motivation to use the infinitive in this instance is syntactic, not semantic.

Similar arguments may be made for the *ceyya* 'do' emphatic construction. Though Fedson (1981) argues it marks taxis, it appears truth-functionally equivalent to the nonemphatic forms. The apparent difference in meaning may be ascribed to an M-implicature (see Levinson 2000).

4 The internal syntax of the Tamil indicative AVC

DISTINGUISHING THE AVC FROM OTHER STRUCTURES

According to our model, the AVC is a syntactic object in its own right and may be analyzed without reference to the lexical identity of the individual auxiliaries that appear in it. Its syntactic properties may be classified as internal and external (see McCawley 1988: 188): internal syntax treats its morphosyntactic composition; external syntax, its grammatical behavior in larger syntactic structures (see Chapter 5). In studying the indicative AVC's internal syntax, we identify it with a set of derivations to summarize its intrinsic properties, distinguish it from other, apparently similar constructions and describe its interaction with other phenomena.

The indicative AVC is syntactically distinct from complex clauses, lexical compound verbs and modal AVCs. In complex clauses, subordinate or coordinate, each verb has a separate denotational function and governs its own satellites. The sentences in (57a and b) are two variants of a sentence with a subordinate clause. (57a) includes a sequence of two verbs, *colli.k ... kēṭka*, the first of which is in the conjunctive. This sequence is not an AVC since each verb has its own subject: the subject of *colli* 'saying' is *nāṉ* 'I', the subject of *kēṭka.v illai* 'didn't listen to' is *avaḷ* 'she'. Further, the two verbs may be separated by other lexical material. Scrambling (see p. 111ff.) has moved *avaḷ* in (57b) so that it interrupts the sequence of the two verbs. Such a possibility is not open to indicative AVCs.

(57) a $_{S0}$[*avaḷ* $_{S1}$[*nāṉ* *colli.k*] *kēṭka.v* *illai*].
she-NOM I-NOM tell-CF hear-INF IND-NEG
'She didn't listen to what I was saying.'

b $_{S0}$[$_{S1}$[*nāṉ* *colli.k*] *avaḷ* *kēṭka.v* *illai*].
I-NOM tell-CF she-NOM hear-INF IND-NEG
'She didn't listen to what I was saying.'

An approximate constituent structure for (57a and b) is proposed in Figure 4.1 where each verb combines with its own satellites to form two separate clauses, S_0 and S_1. In this instance, the subordinate clause S_1 functions as the direct object of the verb *kēṭka.v illai* in S_0.

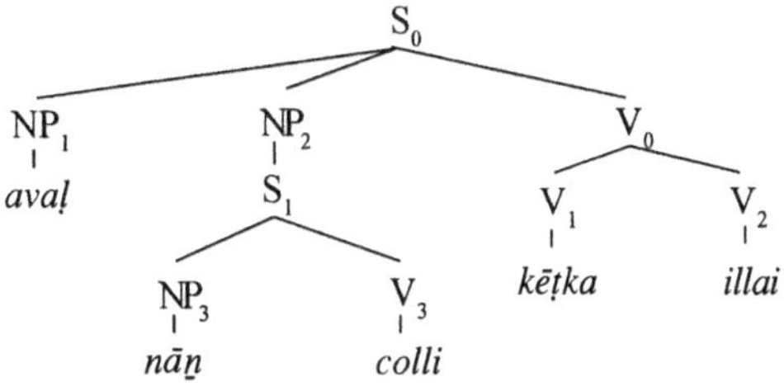

Figure 4.1 Constituent structure of a matrix-complement sentence.

Coordinate sentences also differ syntactically from compound verbs. In the sequence of verbs *peytu ... viḷaintatu* in (58a), the first verb has a conjunctive form; however, this sequence does not constitute an AVC since each verb has a separate denotational function and a separate set of satellites. The variant in (58b), which undoes the effects of Scrambling, shows this structure more transparently.

(58) a $_{S0}$[*nel* $_{S1}$[*maḻai* *pey-tu*] *viḷaintatu*].
paddy-NOM rain-NOM rain-CF result-PST-3SN
'It rained and the paddy grew.'

b $_{S0}$[$_{S1}$[*maḻai* *pey-tu*] $_{S2}$[*nel* *viḷaintatu*]].
rain-NOM rain-CF paddy-NOM result-PST-3SN
'It rained and the paddy grew.'

An approximate constituent structure is posited for such structures in Figure 4.2. As before, each verb and its satellites constitute separate clauses, S_1 and S_2. The two sentences combine to form a single sentence, S_0, which is the domain over which the rule that governs the distribution of finite predicates applies (Steever 1988). Since the verb V_2 occurs in the position designated for finite predicates, it assumes a finite form; even though V_1 has the same syntactic rank as V_2 in S_0, it does not occupy the position stipulated for finite predicates and must assume a nonfinite form, here the conjunctive. It is unclear at this point whether the conjunctive form instantiates an underlying operator with the semantics of a conjunction, such as AND, or whether the surface structure templates for Tamil simply permit two sentences to combine without the need for any such operator at all.[1]

Distinguishing lexical compound verbs from auxiliary compounds is trickier since both appear to be periphrastic forms with only a single set of satellites. Recall that the rules of thumb introduced in Chapter 1 indicated that the component verbs have different rankings in each kind of structure: in lexical compounds the first verb "modifies" the second while in auxiliary compounds the second verb modifies the first. Comparison of the two variants of a lexical compound verb in (59a and b) reveals another way we can distinguish between them. The sequence

1 In fact, the variant (58a) suggests the latter interpretation; if the two clauses were joined by a conjunction, this sentence could very well constitute a violation of the Coordinate Structure Constraint which, as examples below show, applies in other Tamil contexts.

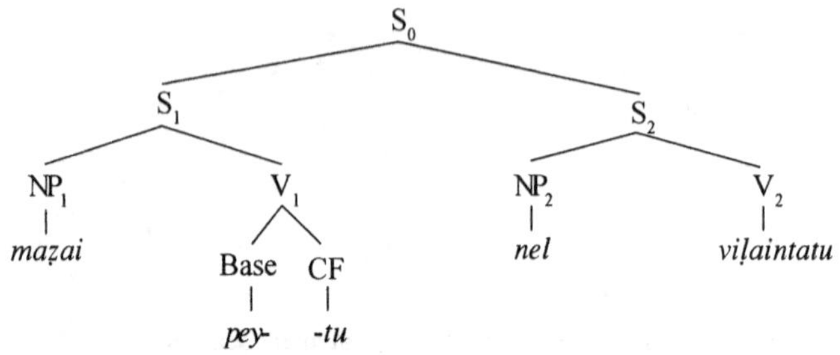

Figure 4.2 Constituent structure of a coordinate sentence.

of two verbs, *ōṭi vantāṉ* 'he came running', in (59a) is linked by the conjunctive *ōṭi* 'running'. The variant in (59b) presents a departure from this canonical form in which the first verb is postposed over the second. Such rightward movement is not possible for auxiliary compound verbs (see pp. 118-20).

(59) a *avaṉ nērattukku ōṭ-i vantāṉ.*
he-NOM time-DAT run-CF come-PST-3SM
'He came running/ran here on time.'
b *avaṉ nērattukku vantāṉ ōṭ-i.*
he-NOM time-DAT come-PST-3SM run-CF
'He came running on time.'

A number of arguments below indicate that the surface structure of what we have been calling lexical compounds is approximately as given in Figure 4.3, one quite distinct from the constituent structures associated with auxiliary compounds.[2] Tamil syntactic operations will thus be invoked to distinguish between complex clauses, subordinate and coordinate, and compound verbs. Further syntactic differences separate lexical and auxiliary compound verbs. Still further tests divide the set of AVCs into modal and indicative AVCs. Finally, indicative AVCs are subdivided into nonattitudinal and attitudinal subsets by a variety of syntactic and pragmatic criteria presented in this chapter and the next.

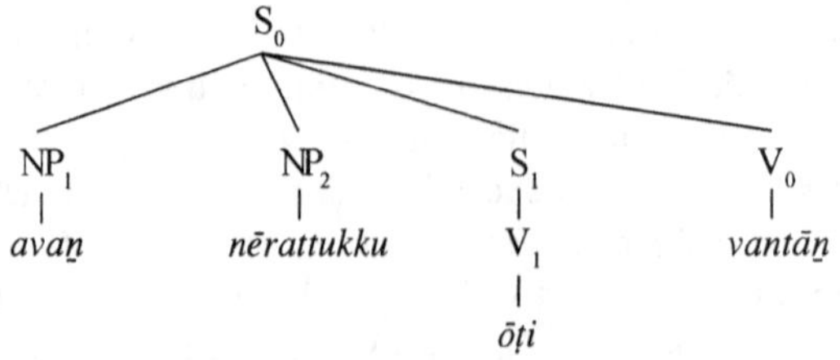

Figure 4.3 Surface structure of a lexical compound verb.

2 In fact, according to the structure in Figure 4.3, applying the term 'compound verb' to such structures is something of a misnomer in that the verb originating in the subordinate clause appears not to be directly dominated by the same V node that dominates the verb in the main clause. However, the term has been retained as a taxonomic convenience.

THE INDICATIVE AVC'S INTERNAL SYNTAX

Grammatical arguments are now presented for the derivation in Figure 4.4, confirming by induction what was proposed by deduction in Chapter 1. These arguments will show that neither the underlying nor the surface structure that we propose for the AVC corresponds with any of the constituent structures that we have postulated for compound clauses or lexical compound verbs. Accordingly, differences in their syntactic behavior are attributed to differences in their derivations.

Tamil has at least twenty-five indicative AVCs, each distinguished by its auxiliary; however, for any given argument, only a handful of auxiliaries will be illustrated. Where a particular grammatical argument does not apply to a specific auxiliary, that gap is noted in the text.

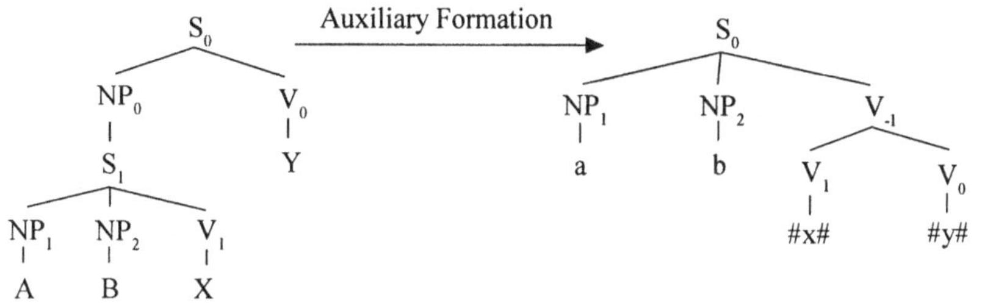

Figure 4.4 Proposed derivation of the AVC.

Subject of the AVC

Strict subcategorization

The derivation in Figure 4.4 claims that the verb base of the auxiliate is primarily responsible for subcategorizing the AVC's surface subject, a process in which the auxiliary plays no direct role. The underlying structure in Figure 4.5 contains a sentential complement (S_1) that includes the AVC's auxiliate (V_1) and subject (NP_1), but excludes the auxiliary (V_0): it is in this constituent that subcategorization of the subject takes place. Consider (60a) with the AVC *vantu āyiṟṟu* '(X) came, as expected' whose subject is *tapālkāraṉ* 'postman'. The base of the auxiliate *vara* 'come' determines the subject; it is the same one subcategorized when *vara* occurs nonauxiliated, as in (60b). Auxiliary *āka* 'become' does not participate in this process: combining *tapālkāraṉ* 'postman' and *āyiṟṟu* 'became', as in (60c), yields an unacceptable sentence. Where *āka* occurs in a nonauxiliated context, it typically subcategorizes subjects that denote time expressions, such as *maṇi* 'hour' in (60d).

(60) a *tapālkāraṉ va.n-tu āyiṟṟu.*
postman-NOM come-CF become-PST-3SN
'The postman came, as expected.'

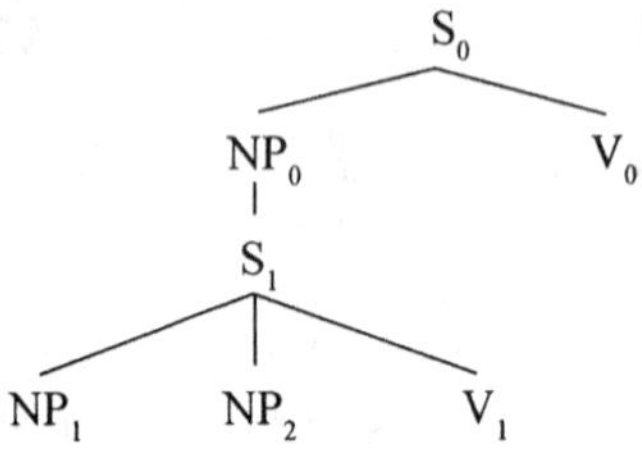

Figure 4.5 The underlying structure of an auxiliary verb construction.

b *tapālkāraṉ va.n-t-āṉ.*
postman-NOM come-PST-3SM
'The postman came.'

c * *tapālkāraṉ āyiṟṟu.*
postman-NOM become-PST-3SN
* 'The postman, as expected.'

d *maṇi āyiṟṟu.*
hour-NOM become-PST-3SN
'The time has come (to V).'

The subject of the AVC thus varies with the auxiliate's verb base, not the auxiliary's, indicating a structure in which the AVC's subject and the auxiliate, but not the auxiliary, form a constituent, as represented by S_1 in Figure 4.5. From a different view, if the auxiliary influenced the subcategorization of the AVC's subject, the ungrammaticality of (60c) should be projected to the AVC in (60a); but since (60a) is grammatical, we may conclude that *āka* 'became' does not bear the same relation to the subject of the AVC in (60a) as it does to the subject in (60d).

The underlying structure in Figure 4.5 makes another claim about subjects and AVCs: the auxiliary subcategorizes a sentential subject complement (S_1) in underlying structure, permitting selection restrictions to apply between the auxiliary and the *entire* sentential complement with which it combines. Example (61a) is grammatical but (61b) is not.

(61) a *tapālkāraṉ vēṇṭumeṉṟē va.n-tāṉ.*
postman-NOM deliberately come-PST-3SM
'The postman deliberately came.'

b * *tapālkāraṉ vēṇṭumeṉṟē va.n-tu āyiṟṟu.*
postman-NOM deliberately come-CF become-PST-3SN
'The postman deliberately came, as expected.'

As explained in Chapter 7, auxiliary *āyiṟṟu* combines with a sentential complement that refers to an event or happening, not a directed action. The presence of the agentive expression *vēṇṭumeṉṟē* 'deliberately' in (61a and b) forces a directed action reading on the sentences, rendering the latter ungrammatical. This same condition prevents *āyiṟṟu* from combining with effective verbs, which also represent directed actions. What endows a sentence with a directed action reading may depend on a variety of factors, such as an adverbial expression, an effective verb or some other expression of agentivity. This reading is thus taken to be a property of the entire clause.

So saying that an auxiliary does not determine the AVC's subject means that it does not subcategorize the subject NP that ultimately appears with the AVC in surface structure. The auxiliary does, of course, subcategorize a subject: an underlying sentential complement which refers to an entire situation or event. This further suggests that auxiliate and auxiliary reflect different logical categories; in the terminology of categorial grammar, auxiliates belong to the category of expressions that combine with arguments to form a sentence while auxiliaries belong to the set of expressions that combine with a sentence to form a sentence. This semantic difference is mirrored in their syntactic behavior with regard to the subcategorization of subjects and different underlying positions in Figure 4.5.

Figure 4.5 militates against deriving AVCs from an underlying coordinate structure; accordingly, no auxiliary may introduce into the sentence its own separate surface subject of the same rank or categorial status as the subject subcategorized by the auxiliate, although this is commonplace for compound clauses. Even though *āka* 'become' may combine with an NP referring to time to form a sentence (60d), it cannot introduce such a subject where it functions as an auxiliary (62).

(62) * *maṇi avaṉ va.n-tu āyiṟṟu.*
hour-NOM he-NOM come-CF become-PST-3N

Examples with attitudinal auxiliaries exhibit the same pattern of grammatical behavior. In (63a) *avaṉ* 'he' is the surface subject of the attitudinal AVC *uruki vaẓintāṉ* 'he melted away'. Auxiliary *vaẓiya* 'drip' conveys the speaker's attitude that the subject gives into his emotional states or bodily processes, like sleep (p. 246ff.). Example (63a) entails (63b) but not (63c). which is ungrammatical because in stand-alone contexts *vaẓiya* selects only NPs that denote viscous liquids, such as oil or saliva (63d), not ones that denote humans. However, *vaẓiya* and a human NP may cooccur in the same clause (63) just so long as that NP properly combines with another verb which serves as an auxiliate to auxiliary *vaẓiya*. Conversely, even though the verb *vaẓiya* may subcategorize certain subjects in stand-alone contexts, as in (63d), it cannot introduce them into a structure such as (63e) where it functions as an auxiliary.

(63) a *avaṉ uruk-i vaẓi.n-t-āṉ.*
he-NOM melt-CF drip-PST-3M
'He melted away/gave into his emotions.'

b *avaṉ uruk-i.n-āṉ.*
he-NOM melt-PST-3M
'He melted/gave into his emotions.'

c * *avaṉ vaẓi.n-t-āṉ.*
he-NOM drip-PST-3SM
'He dripped.'

d *eccil* *vaẓi.n-t-atu.*
saliva/water-NOM drip-PST-3SN
'Saliva/water dripped.'

e * *eccil* *avaṉ* *uruk-i* *vaẓintāṉ.*
saliva-NOM he-NOM melt-CF drip-PST-3SM

This pattern of grammaticality judgments makes sense only on two assumptions. First, a verb may occur in a variety of different frames, each with different syntactic properties, only one of which is the AVC. Second, subcategorization of the AVC's surface subject is entrusted solely to the auxiliate.

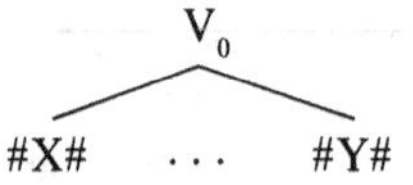

Figure 4.6 The surface structure of the AVC.

Subject-Verb Agreement

The rule of Subject-Verb Agreement (SVA) provides an argument for the AVC's surface structure in Figure 4.6. Each sentence usually has one finite verb which is located at the extreme right boundary of the sentence and c-commands all other verbs in the sentence. SVA makes the verb in that privileged position verb agree with its subject in person, number and, in the third person, gender, as marked by personal endings. All remaining verbs are nonfinite.

In (64a-c) only the rightmost verb is inflected by SVA; all other verb s are nonfinite. In the coordinate sentence (64a), only the rightmost verb *tōṉṟiyatu* 'it appeared' is finite. In (64b) *kēṭṭāḷ* 'she listened' bears inflections for the third person singular feminine, agreeing with its subject *avaḷ* 'she'; the subordinate clause verb *colli* 'saying' appears in the nonfinite conjunctive form which shows no agreement with its subject *nāṉ* 'I'. In (64c) the main clause verb *paṭittēṉ* 'I read' agrees with its subject *nāṉ* 'I' in person and number; the lower clause predicate *varukiṟatukku*, a verbal noun, shows no agreement whatsoever.

(64) a $[_{S0}$ $[_{S1}$ *mazai* *pey-tu*] $[_{S2}$ *veyil* *aṭi.t-tu*] $[_{S3}$ *vāṉavil* *tōṉṟ-i.y-atu*]].
rain-NOM rain-CF sun-NOM beat-CF rainbow-NOM appear-PST-3N
'It rained, the sun shined, and a rainbow appeared.'

b $[_{S0}$ *avaḷ* $[_{S1}$ *nāṉ* *coll-i*] *kē.ṭ-ṭ-āḷ*] .
she-NOM I-NOM say-CF listen-PST-3F
'She listened to what I was saying.'

c $[_{S0}$ $[_{S1}$ *avaṉ* *varukiṟatukku* *muṉṉāl*] *nāṉ* *paṭi.t-t-ēṉ*].
he-NOM come-PRS-VN-DAT before I-NOM read-PST-1S
'I was reading before he came.'

Application of SVA is constrained: the subject must c-command the finite verb with which it agrees; in no case may a subject in a lower clause control agreement in a higher clause. In (64b), for example, the subordinate clause subject *nāṉ* 'I', though closer to the finite predicate *kēṭṭāḷ* in the linear string, does not control its agreement features. On this assumption, only the surface structure of the AVC in Figure 4.6 makes the correct predications about SVA's application to AVCs; the underlying structure in Figure 4.5 would put the auxiliary out of the reach of SVA.

In (65a) the auxiliary *viṭa* 'leave' agrees with the subject *nīṅkaḷ* 'you' in person and number, as marked by the personal ending *-īrkaḷ*, the same agreement marker that the nonauxiliated verb in (65b) exhibits. The auxiliary bears the marker despite the fact that the previous section showed that the AVC's subject occurs in the same clause as the auxiliate while the auxiliary appears in a superordinate clause. The pair in (66a, b) shows the same pattern: the subject of the AVC, *paiyaṉ* 'boy', in (66a) triggers SVA on the attitudinal auxiliary, not the main verb.

(65) a *nīṅkaḷ* *vantu* *vi.ṭ-ṭ-īrkaḷ.*
you-NOM come-CF leave-PST-2P
'You did come.'

b *nīṅkaḷ* *va.n-t-īrkaḷ.*
you-NOM come-PST-2P
'You came.'

(66) a *paiyaṉ* *pēci.t* *tolaintāṉ.*
boy-NOM speak-CP lose-AF-PST-3SM
'The boy spoke, damn it!'

b *paiyaṉ* *pēc-iṉ-āṉ.*
boy-NOM speak-PST-3SM
'The boy spoke.'

The underlying tree structure in Figure 4.5 does not provide the correct topological relationship between subject and finite verb because the auxiliary appears in a higher clause than the one that contains the subject NP. The obvious solution, then, is that SVA applies at surface structure, as represented in Figure 4.6, where the AVC's structure conforms with the constraint requiring the subject to c-command the finite verb.

The differences between the AVC's deep and surface combinatorics help us to elucidate some otherwise mysterious facts. Recall from (63d) that when the verb *vaẓiya* 'drip' stands alone, it subcategorizes only subjects referring to viscous liquids; if that is the case, then it should never cooccur with a subject that requires animate agreement markers on it as a finite verb (63c). But it does so in (63a), bearing the ending for a third person singular masculine subject, precisely in the grammatical context where it functions as an auxiliary verb. In this example, the auxiliated verb *uruka* 'melt', which may subcategorize a human subject *avaṉ* 'he', is subsequently daughter-adjoined to the same clause that contains auxiliary *vaẓiya* 'drip', thereby allowing it to cooccur with an agreement marker it would not otherwise bear. Thus, *vaẓiya*, whose cooccurrence restrictions would normally require inanimate subject-verb agreement, can have animate agreement just in case it functions as an auxiliary verb in an AVC (whose auxiliate does subcategorize an animate subject).[3]

Other satellites of the AVC

Similar cooccurrence arguments may be made based on the AVC's other satellites, such as its adverbial adjuncts, complements and objects, which support the underlying structure in Figure 4.5. The presence or absence of such satellites in the AVC varies directly with the auxiliate, not the auxiliary. The auxiliate's verb base governs the strict subcategorization and selection restrictions for the entire AVC, which are the same as when the verb base appears in a simple, nonauxiliated verb form.

Adverbial adjuncts

The auxiliary, not the auxiliate introduces adverbial adjuncts into sentences with AVCs. Sentence (67a) with an AVC entails (67b), but not (67c). The denominal adverbial adjunct *cīkkiramāy* 'early' (from the noun *cīkkiram* 'earliness') is introduced into (67a) by the main verb *vara* 'come' just as in (67b) where *vara* 'come' is not auxiliated. Sentence (67c) shows that *irukka* 'be' does not subcategorize

(67) a *avaṉ cīkkiramāy* $_{\text{AVC}}$[*vantu irukkiṟāṉ*].
he-NOM early-ADV come-CF be-PRS-3SM
'He has come early.'

b *avaṉ cikkiramāy va.n-t-āṉ.*
he-NOM early-ADV come-PST-3SM
'He came early.'

c * *avaṉ cikkiramāy irukkiṟāṉ.*
he- NOM early-ADV be-PRS-3SM
'He is as earliness.'

cīkkiramāy 'early' on its own; *cīkkiramāy* normally cooccurs with verbs of motion, not verbs of state or location.[4] Thus, when *cīkkiramāy* cooccurs in a sentence with *irukka*, as in (67a), it has been introduced by the AVC's auxiliate, not its auxiliary.

This pattern also distinguishes AVCs from lexical compounds. Sentence (68a) contains the lexical compound *ōṭi vara* 'come running' and the time expression *nērattukku* 'on time'. The second verb in the sequence, not the first, introduces the time expression *nērattukku* into the sentence; the second verb (68b), but not the

3 Only auxiliary *āka* 'become' fails to illustrate this argument: a defective verb, it inflects only for third person neuter agreement, regardless of the person, number and gender of the subject NP. The subject NP *tapālkāraṉ* 'postman' normally triggers third person singular masculine agreement, as in (60b); but in (60a) the auxiliary verb bears the inflections for the third person singular neuter form (*āyiṟṟu* historically descends from *āy-iṉ-tu* in which *-tu* is the neuter ending.

4 The ungrammaticality of this sentence likely follows from the ungrammaticality of the embedded equational sentence **avaṉ cīkkiram* 'he (is) earliness'.

first (68c), subcategorizes it independently. AVCs exhibit the opposite pattern, where it is the first verb, not the second, that introduces such adjuncts.

(68) a *avaṉ* *nērattukku* *ōṭ-i* *va.n-t-āṉ.*
he- NOM time-DAT run-CF come-PST-3SM
'He came running/ran here on time.'

b *avaṉ* *nērattukku* *va.n-t-āṉ.*
he-NOM time-DAT come-PST-3SM
'He came on time.'

c * *avaṉ* *nērattukku* *ōṭ-iṉ-āṉ.*
he- NOM time-DAT ran-PST-3SM
'He ran on time.'

Direct object

Consistent with the underlying structure in Figure 4.5, the auxiliate (V_1), and not the auxiliary (V_0), determines the transitivity of the AVC, i.e., whether or not it takes a direct object. The AVC in (69c), *tolaittu.t tolaintēṉ* 'I lost (it), damn it', cooccurs with the accusative NP *pāspārṭṭai* 'passport'. Examples (69b and c) show that it is the auxiliate *tolaikka* 'lose', and not the auxiliary *tolaiya* 'be lost', that introduces the direct object into the sentence with the AVC, thereby determining its transitivity. In stand-alone contexts, the auxiliate's base is independently transitive; the auxiliary's, intransitive. If the auxiliary determined the AVC's transitivity, (69a) would be ungrammatical because the lexeme *tolaiya* 'get lost' does not independently subcategorize a direct object; however, its grammaticality suggests the auxiliary does not influence the AVC's transitivity.[5]

(69) a *nāṉ* *eṉ* *pāspārṭṭai.t* $_{AVC}$[*tolaittu.t* *tolai.n-t-ēṉ*].
I- NOM my passport-ACC lose-EF-CF lose-AF-PST-1S
'I lost my passport, damn it.'

b *nāṉ* *eṉ* *pāspārṭṭai.t* *tolai.t-t-ēṉ.*
I- NOM my passport-ACC lose-EF-PST-1S
'I lost my passport.'

c * *nāṉ* *eṉ* *pāspārṭṭai.t* *tolai.n-t-ēṉ.*
I- NOM my passport-ACC lose-AF-PST-1S
'I was lost my passport.'

The following triplet confirms that it is the auxiliate, not the auxiliary, that subcategorizes the AVC's object. In (70a) the direct object *paṭattai* 'picture' of the AVC, *varaintu irukkiṟīrkaḷ* 'you have sketched', is independently subcategorized by *varaiya* 'sketch' in (70b), and not by *irukka* 'be' which cannot subcategorize an

5 Since verbs in Tamil do not show agreement with their objects, a corresponding argument from object-verb agreement about surface constituency is not available. However, in the related languages Kui, Kuvi, Manda, and Pengo, which do have object-verb agreement, such an argument would be available.

accusative NP in (70c). On our model, these strict subcategorization rules are part of the AVC's denotational function and therefore invested in the auxiliate.

(70) a *nīṅkaḷ paṭa.tt-ai varaintu iru.k-kiṟ-īrkaḷ=ā?*
you-NOM picture-ACC sketch-CF be-PRS-2P=INT
'Have you sketched the picture?'
b *nīṅkaḷ paṭa.tt-ai varai.n-t-īrkaḷ=ā?*
you-NOM picture-ACC sketch-PST-2P=INT
'Did you sketch the picture?'
c * *nīṅkaḷ paṭa.tt-ai iru.n-t-īrkaḷ=ā?*
you-NOM picture-ACC be-PST-2P=INT
'Did you be the picture?'

This argument has a converse. When not auxiliated, *viṭa* 'leave' subcategorizes a direct object (71a). But as an auxiliary (71b), it cannot introduce a direct object into the AVC and override the auxiliate *pōka* 'go' never subcategorizes a direct object (71c).

(71) a *appā maturai.y-ai viṭṭār.*
father-NOM Madurai-ACC leave-PST-3H
'Father departed Madurai.'
b * *appā maturai.y-ai.p pōy viṭṭār.*
father-NOM Madurai-ACC go-CF leave-PST-3H
'Father did go Madurai.'
c * *appā maturai.y-ai.p pōṉār.*
father-NOM Madurai-ACC go-PST-3H
'Father went Madurai.'

Here again, lexical compounds differ in that the second verb tends to determine the entire collocation's direct object. In (72a) *nimirntu pārkka* 'look up at' cooccurs with the direct object *maṉaivi.y-ai* 'wife'. The transitivity of the compound varies with the second verb's transitivity: *pārkka* 'look at' (72b), not *nimira* 'rise' (70c), introduces the direct object into (72a). This is because the former, not the latter, subcategorizes a direct object regardless of whether it occurs in an AVC; *nimira* 'rise' cannot do so because it is intransitive.

(72) a *avaṉ maṉaiviyai nimirntu pār.t-t-āṉ.*
he-NOM wife-ACC rise-CF look-PST-3SM
'He looked up at his wife.'
b *avaṉ maṉaiviyai.p pār.t-t-āṉ.*
he-NOM wife-ACC look-PST-3SM
'He looked at his wife.'
c * *avaṉ maṉaiviyai nimir.n-t-āṉ.*
he-NOM wife-ACC rise-AF-PST-3SM
'He rose his wife.'

Complement clauses

Annamalai (1982: 29-30) observes that no auxiliary may introduce its own complement clauses into a sentence with an AVC. This is consistent with the derivation in Figure 4.4: the auxiliary has no independent complements because the sentential subject which it combines with *is* its (subject) complement. It is the auxiliate, and not the auxiliary, that introduces subordinate clauses into a sentence with an AVC. The AVC in (73a), *niṉaittu.t tolaikkiṟākaḷ* 'they believe (it), damn them', cooccurs with a sentential object complement introduced by the complementizing verb *eṉṟu* 'saying'. This same complement cooccurs with a nonauxiliated form of *niṉaikka* 'think' in (73b), but not with a stand-alone form of the *tolaikka* 'lose' in (73c). The former, but not the latter, is a verb of propositional attitude that subcategorizes such complements.

(73) a $_{\text{SO}}$[*araciyalvāti* $_{\text{SI}}$[*tāṅkaḷ* *teyvaṅkaḷ*] *eṉṟu* $_{\text{AVC}}$[*niṉaittu.t* *tolai.k-kiṟ-rkaḷ*]].
politician-NOM self-P-NOM god-P-NOM say-CF think-CF lose-EF-PRS-2P
'Politicians believe that they are gods, damn them.'

b $_{\text{SO}}$[*araciyalvāti* $_{\text{SI}}$[*tāṅkaḷ* *teyvaṅkaḷ*] *eṉṟu* *niṉai.k-kiṟ-ākaḷ*]
politician-NOM self-P-NOM god-P-NOM say-CF think-PRS-3P
'Politicians believe that they are gods.'

c * $_{\text{SO}}$[*araciyalvāti* $_{\text{SI}}$[*tāṅkaḷ* *teyvaṅkaḷ*] *eṉṟu* *tolai.k-kiṟ-ārkaḷ*].
politician-NOM self-P-NOM god-P-NOM say-CF lose-EF-PRS-3P
? 'Politicians lose that they are gods.'

Indirect object

If an AVC has an indirect object, it is the auxiliate, not the auxiliary, that subcategorizes it. In (74a) the AVC *pōy viṭṭār* 'he did go' cooccurs with the dative NP *maturaikku* 'to Madurai'. It is *pōka* 'go' (74b), the auxiliate in (74a), not the auxiliary *viṭa* 'leave' (74c), that independently subcategorizes an indirect object.

(74) a *appā* *maturaikku.p* *pōy* *viṭṭār*.
father-NOM Madurai-DAT go-CF leave-PST-3H
'Father did go to Madurai.'

b *appā* *maturaikku.p* *pōṉār*.
father-NOM Madurai-DAT go-PST-3H
'Father went to Madurai.'

c * *appā* *maturaikku* *viṭṭār*.
father-NOM Madurai-DAT leave-PST-3H
'Father left to Madurai.'

Annamalai (1982: 78-79) presents apparent counterexamples to this argument. The benefactive auxiliary *koṭukka* 'give' (Chapter 7) appears to introduce an indirect object into a clause with a AVC even though the auxiliate cannot do so independently. In (75a) the AVC *meṉṟu koṭuttāḷ* 'she chewed X for Y/on Y's behalf' cooccurs with the direct object *kaṟiyai* 'meat' and the indirect object *kuẓantaikku* 'for the child'. The auxiliate cannot independently subcategorize an indirect object (75b), while the auxiliary *koṭukka* 'give' can (75c). So it seems that in this case the auxiliary introduces an indirect object into the clause that contains the AVC.[6]

(75) a *ammā kuẓantaikku.k kaiyai meṉṟu koṭuttāḷ.*
mother-NOM child-DAT meat-ACC chew-CF give-PST-3SF
'The mother chewed the meat for the child.'

b *ammā (*kuẓantaikku.k) kaṟiyai meṉṟāḷ.*
mother-NOM child-DAT meat-ACC chew-PST-3SF
'The mother chewed the meat (*to her child).'

c *ammā kuẓantaikku.k atai.k koṭuttāḷ.*
mother-NOM child-DAT it-ACC give-PST-3SF
'The mother gave it to the child.'

This apparent inconsistency dissolves, however, when we distinguish between case marking and grammatical relations. All dative-marked NPs in sentences with benefactive auxiliaries may alternate with an expression of the form N-DAT+*āka* 'on N's behalf'; but not all dative NPs can have this alternant. NPs that exhibit this alternation mark beneficiaries, which are adjuncts to the clause; those that do not, mark another relation such as an allative indirect object or a dative subject. In this instance, then, the dative introduces a sentential adjunct, not an NP with a grammatical relation to the verb.

(76) a *nāṉ kumārukku.p puttakattai viṟṟu.k koṭuttēṉ.*
I-NOM Kumar-DAT book-ACC sell-CF give-PST-1S
'I sold the book to/for Kumar.'

b *nāṉ kumārukk-āka.p puttakattai viṟṟu.k koṭuttēṉ.*
I-NOM Kumar.behalf book-ACC sell-CF give-PST-1S
'I sold the book on Kumar's behalf.'

c ?? *ammā kuẓantaikk-āka atai.k koṭuttāḷ.*
mother-NOM child-behalf it-ACC give-PST-3SF
'The mother gave it on behalf of the child.'

Auxiliary *koṭukka* 'give' permits this alternation between (76a and b); as a nonauxiliated verb, it does not permit an alternation between (75c) and (76c). The dative NP in a sentence like (75c) denotes the recipient of the action, but the dative NP that cooccurs with the AVC in (75a)c denotes a beneficiary, not a recipient.[7] In

6 Although *koṭukka* 'give' can introduce a direct object when not auxiliated (75c), it cannot introduce an direct object into an AVC when it functions as an auxiliary.

7 The benefactive auxiliary *koṭukka* 'give' and the dative expression that names the beneficiary appear to be two parts of a discontinuous constituent: the first names a general range of beneficiaries of the action named by the AVC, the second specifies exactly who it is. In this it resembles the relation between a tense morpheme and a temporal adverb. See McCawley (1988: 250ff.).

short, the dative expression that *koṭukka* introduces into an AVC as an auxiliary is not the same kind of dative expression that it introduces when it is not auxiliated.

Selection restrictions

Arguments from selection restrictions confirm the AVC's underlying structure in Figure 4.5, which locates the AVC's denotational function in the auxiliate (V_1). The AVC in (77a), *eẓuti.t taḷḷiṉār* 'he wrote faster than expected', cooccurs with the direct object *oru katai* 'a story'. Both components, *eẓuta* 'write' and *taḷḷa* 'push', are transitive verbs that subcategorize direct objects in stand-alone contexts. While *eẓuta* selects objects referring to things that are written (77b), *taḷḷa* cannot do so (77c), selecting instead objects referring to something that can be physically pushed (77d). The paradigm below confirms that the verb which determines the AVC's subcategorization, the auxiliate, also determines its selection restrictions.

(77) a *avar oru katai eẓuti.t taḷḷiṉār.*
he-NOM one story write-CF push-PST-3H
'He wrote a story faster than expected.'

b *avar oru katai eẓutiṉār.*
he-NOM one story write-PST-3H
'He wrote a story.'

c ?* *avar oru katai taḷḷiṉār.*
he-NOM one story push-PST-3H
'He pushed a story.'

d *avar oru vaṇṭi taḷḷiṉār.*
he-NOM one cart push-PST-3H
'He pushed a cart.'

Attitudinal auxiliaries illustrate the same paradigm. In (78a) *poṭintu kiẓintatu* 'X won't be pulverized' cooccurs with the subject NP *pāṟai* 'rock'. Both components of the AVC are verbs of destruction, but in stand-alone contexts they differ as to the kinds of subjects they select: *poṭiya* 'be pulverized' selects subjects denoting friable materials such as rock or chalk, *kiẓiya* 'be torn' selects subjects denoting materials such as cloth or paper that can be rent. Thus, (78c) is ungrammatical while (78d) is grammatical. Since *poṭiya* selects a subject that refers to a friable material independently in (78b), it is responsible for the selection of the same kind of subject in the AVC in (78a).

(78) a *pāṟai poṭintu kiẓintatu.*
rock-NOM pulverize+AF-CF tear+AF-PST-3N
'The rock won't be pulverized.'

b *pāṟai poṭintatu.*
rock-NOM powder+AF-PST-3N
'The rock was pulverized.'

c ?**pāṟai* *kiḻintatu.*
rock-NOM tear+AF-PST-3SN
'The rock was torn.'

d *cāṭṭai* *kiḻintatu.*
shirt-NOM tear+AF-PST-3SN
'The shirt was torn.'

The auxiliate thus governs the subcategorization and selection of the AVC's satellites, indicating that at some stage of derivation, the auxiliate and the satellites form a constituent which excludes the auxiliary. It is thus the lower clause in Figure 4.4 over which the AVC's strict subcategorization and selection restrictions are held to range. More precisely, it is the verb base of the auxiliate that governs these combinatoric patterns, and not the entire form of the main verb. First, the subcategorization and selection restrictions are the same whether the verb appears in a simple or an auxiliated form. Second, only the verb base is shared in common between the simple and auxiliated counterparts of a single verb. Thus, in underlying structure, the predicate of the lower clause (V_1), which ultimately surfaces as the auxiliate, corresponds only to the verb base, not to the verb base and inflections that follow it.

The well-formedness of the lower clause S_1 in Figure 4.4 proves to be a necessary but not a sufficient condition of the well-formedness of the entire clause in which the AVC ultimately winds up. As the contrast between (61a and b) above shows, the auxiliary can impose selection restrictions on the entire lower clause. What the auxiliary verb selects, however, may be construed as global properties of the lower clause, whether, for example, it expresses a state or an accomplishment. The selection restrictions that may hold between an auxiliary and its underlying sentential complements are explored in further depth for individual auxiliaries in Chapters 6 through 8.

Causative Formation

Tamil has two kinds of causative formations, morphological and periphrastic (Chapter 3). The morphological causative is formed by suffixing the markers *-vi-/-ppi-* to the verb base, augmented by a morpheme for effectivity or not. The periphrastic causative is a matrix-complement construction in which one of three causative verbs, *ceyya* 'do, make', *paṇṇa* 'make', or *vaikka* 'place', combines with the infinitive of the verb that denotes the caused event.

We assume with McCawley (1976a) and Davidson (1980) that causative operators are two-place predicates whose argument positions are occupied by expressions that denote events. Dowty (1979) observes further that the expression which occupies the position of the causing event is generally subject to radical reduction, usually leaving behind nothing more than its subject NP. This kind of reduction commonly occurs in the examples of Tamil causatives presented below.

Periphrastic causation and the AVC

Sentence (79a) presents a noncausative sentence and (79b) a causative counterpart. When (79a) is embedded in a causative formation as the caused event in (79b), the finite verb *ninṟāṉ* 'he stood' assumes the infinitival form *niṟka* 'stand', and the subject of the caused event, *māṇavaṉ* 'student', appears in the accusative case, *māṇavaṉ-ai*.

(79) a *māṇavaṉ veḷiyil niṉṟāṉ.*
student-NOM outside stand-PST-3SM
'The student stood outside.'

b *āciriyar māṇavaṉ-ai veḷiyil niṟka vai.t-t-ār.*
teacher-NOM student-ACC outside stand-INF place-PST-3H
'The teacher made the student stand outside.'

Where a single cause has several effects, each clause denoting a separate effect is set off from the others by adding the clitic *=um* 'and' to each infinitive, as in (80).

(80) *kamalā [latāvai.p pāttiram kaḻava.v]=um*
Kamala-NOM Lata-ACC pots wash-INF=AND
[cārōjav.ai vīṭu kūṭṭa.v]=um vaittāḷ.
Saroja-ACC house sweep-INF=AND place-PST-3SF
'Kamala made Lata wash the dishes and (made) Saroja sweep the house.'

When a causative verb is applied to a sequence of two verbs that are joined by the conjunctive form, two distinct patterns emerge, depending as the sequence is interpreted as a compound clause or a compound verb. In Annamalai's (1982: 36-37) examples of causativized compound clauses, each verb denotes a separate situation. For example, the compound clause in (81a) has two verbs, each with its own set of satellites. In its causative counterpart (81b), each verb appears in the infinitive and has its own causative verb *vaikka* 'place'. When *vaikka* is added just to the second verb in the sequence, as in (81c), only that verb represents a caused event; the first verb, *koṭukka* 'give' is not in construction with *vaikka*. Thus, (81c) cannot mean 'I made (someone) give him the book and made him read it', with the causative operator applying to both verbs.

(81) a $[_{S0}$ $[_{S1}$ *avaṉ puttakattai eṭuttu.p*] $[_{S2}$ *paṭittāṉ*]].
he-NOM book-ACC take-CF read-PST-3SM
'He took the book and (he) read (it).'

b $[_{S0}$ *nāṉ* $[_{S1}$ *avaṉai.p puttakattai eṭukka vaittu.p*] $[_{S2}$ *paṭikka vaittēṉ*]]
I-NOM he-ACC book-ACC take-INF place-CF read-INF place-PST-1S
'I made him take the book and (I) made him read it.'

c *nāṉ avaṉukku.p puttakam koṭuttu.p paṭikka vaittēṉ.*
I-NOM he-DAT book give-CF read-INF place-PST-1S
'I gave him the book and made him read it.'

Where a sequence of two verbs constitutes an AVC, its syntactic behavior vis-à-vis causatives differs markedly from this pattern. Although the causative follows the second verb, it is the first verb, the one with the denotational function, and not the second, that refers to the caused event. As discussion of (81c) showed, such a pattern cannot be used to describe compound clauses with two verbs. As it turns out, the causative may skip over an intervening verb just in case that verb functions as an auxiliary in an AVC. A noncausative sentence, (82a), is embedded in a causative sentence, (82b), as the caused event; (82a) contains the complex AVC *ni<u>n</u><u>r</u>u koṇṭu iruntā<u>n</u>* 'he was standing'.[8] The causative verb *vaikka* 'place' applies to the entire complex AVC, not merely the immediately preceding verb form. It is the auxiliate in the most deeply nested AVC, *ni<u>n</u><u>r</u>u* 'standing', that supplies the denotational function for the entire complex AVC, as well as for the causative operator. Since causative operators subcategorize arguments that denote events, they must semantically combine with the AVC's auxiliate since that component carries the AVC's denotational function.

(82) a *māṇava<u>n</u> veḷiyil ni<u>n</u><u>r</u>u koṇṭu iruntā<u>n</u>.*
student-NOM outside stand-CF hold-CF be-PST-3SM
'The student was standing outside.'

b *āciriyar māṇava<u>n</u>-ai veḷiyil ni<u>n</u><u>r</u>u koṇṭu irukka vaittār.*
teacher-NOM student-ACC outside stand-CF hold-CF be-INF place-PST-3H
'The teacher had the student standing outside.'

Example (81b) showed us that each verb in a compound clause may be causativized independently of the others, a pattern which AVCs do not follow. The AVC *paṭittu vantāḷ* 'she kept reading' in (83a) is causativized in (83b) by adjoining a causative verb to the auxiliary's infinitive. But the causative *vaikka* 'place' cannot be distributed in (83c) opposite, where a separate token modifies the auxiliate and auxiliary each. Sentence (83c) is not the causative of (83a) because it makes reference to an event of coming, which the noncausative counterpart lacks.

A causative operator may thus be distributed over a sequence of two verbs only where that sequence is analyzed as a compound clause, not an AVC. Since only the auxiliate has a denotational function, (83a) refers only to an event of (continuous) reading. Because the causative verb takes as its direct object an expression that denotes an event, it combines semantically with an AVC's auxiliate. However, as the placement of the infinitive shows, it combines morphologically and syntactically with the auxiliary, in accordance with the latter's inflectional function. This pattern of interaction between causative constructions and AVCs would thus appear to coincide with Benveniste's precise attribution of the denotational and inflectional functions within the AVC: every verb with a denotational function may be causativized; an auxiliary, because it serves an inflectional function, may not be causativized independently.

8 In this form, the auxiliate *ni<u>n</u><u>r</u>u koṇṭu* 'standing' is internally complex, itself an AVC nested within a larger AVC. Within the nested AVC, *ni<u>n</u><u>r</u>u* is the auxiliate, *koṇṭu* the auxiliary.

(83)a *avaḷ puttakattai.p paṭittu vantāḷ.*
she-NOM book-ACC read-CF come-PST-3SF
'She kept reading the book.'

b *avaṉ avaḷai.p puttakattai.p paṭittu vara vaittāṉ.*
he-NOM she-ACC book-ACC read-CF come-INF place-PST-3SM
'He made her keep reading the book.'

c ?* *avaṉ avaḷai.p puttakattai.p paṭikka vaittu vara vaittāṉ.*
he-NOM she-ACC book-ACC read-INF place-CF come-INF place-PST-3SM
'He made her read the book and made her come.'

Causative Formation also serves to classify auxiliary verbs. Not all indicative auxiliaries may appear within the scope of a causative verb; as general rule, nonattitudinal auxiliaries may appear in the scope of a causative verb while attitudinal auxiliaries may not. In my corpus, the auxiliaries *irukka* 'be', *koḷḷa* 'hold', *koṭukka* 'give', *vara* 'come', *viṭa* 'leave', *pārkka* 'look at', *tolaiya* 'get lost' and, marginally, *tolaikka* 'lose' may all occur within a causativized construction. Even though the last two are attitudinal, the remaining ten attitudinal auxiliaries may not be causativized.[9] In (84) nonadditudinal auxiliaries are felicitously embedded un-

(84) a *avaṉ avarkaḷai.p* $_{AVC}$[*pēci.k koḷḷa*] *ceytāṉ.*
he-NOM they-ACC speak-CF hold-INF do-PST-3SM
'He made them speak among themselves/converse.'

b *avaḷ kuḻantaiyai.c cāppāṭṭai* $_{AVC}$[*rucittu.p pārkka*] *vaittāḷ.*
she-NOM child-ACC food-ACC taste-CF see-INF place-PST-3SF
'She had the child taste the food (to see what it was like).'

c *avar avaḷukku.k kaṭitattai* $_{AVC}$[*eḻuti.k koṭukka.c*] *ceytār.*
he-NOM she-DAT letter-ACC write-CF give-INF make-PST-3H
'He had a letter written on her behalf.'

(85) a *cantarpam eṉṉai.c* $_{AVC}$[*colli.t tolaikka*] *vaittatu.*
circumstance-NOM me-ACC tell-CF lose-INF place-PST-3SN
'Circumstance made me blurt (it) out, damn it.'

b ?* *avar avaṉai ellarraiyum colli.t tolaikka.c ceytār.*
he-NOM he-ACC all-ACC=AND tell-CF lose-INF do-PST-3H
'He $_i$ made him $_j$ blurt everything out, damn him $_j$.'

c * *cantarppam avaṉai vēlai ceytu kiḻikka vaittatu.*
circumstance-NOM he-ACC work do-CF tear-INF place-PST-3SN
'Circumstance made him unable/unwilling to work.'

der a causative verb; in (85) attitudinal auxiliaries are also embedded under a causative, but with varying degrees of acceptability.

Note that (85a) and (85b) form a near minimal pair; both use auxiliary *tolaikka* 'lose', which encodes the speaker's antipathy toward the action of the narrated

9 The overlap between attitudinal and nonattitudinal auxiliaries in this context is an indication that the two subgroups are not strictly segregated but both belong to the set of indicative auxiliaries. The two attitudinal auxiliaries in this case are among the most general in the subset.

event and, particularly in the effective version, toward the subject of that action. (85b) is deemed unacceptable because the speaker cannot fairly blame an undesirable act on the patient *avaṉai* 'him'; the agent that is purported to have caused the event, *avar* 'he', should shoulder that responsibility. The agent in (85a), on the other hand, is inanimate. Since the subject of the caused event, the referent of *eṉṉai* 'me', is animate and can be expected to prevail over inanimate forces, the speaker may more sportingly ascribe blame to the subject through the use of this attitudinal auxiliary. The animate causee subject is responsible for his actions in a way an inanimate object, say a rock, never can be. However, auxiliary *kiẓikka* 'tear' seems incapable of appearing inside a causative verb's scope in (85c). This appears to follow from its semantics: *kiẓikka* conveys the speaker's opinion that the subject of the action is too lazy or incompetent to carry it out, and seems to express the speaker's belief that that incapacity is an internal flaw, not subject to external influence. Thus, (85c) is odd because it holds both the causing subject (through the causative verb) and the caused subject (through the attitudinal auxiliary) responsible for the caused event. This makes use of *kiẓikka* 'tear' impossible within the scope of the causative verb.

What these examples show is that auxiliate and auxiliary behave as a unit—a single verb, in fact—under causative verbs. The auxiliate denotes the event which is purported to have been caused while the auxiliary bears the infinitival inflections that the causative verb imposes on the verbs it combines with. This division of labor agrees with our ascription of the AVC's denotational function to the auxiliate and inflectional function to the auxiliary.

Morphological causation and the AVC

Sentence (86a) presents a noncausative sentence, (86b) a morphological causative (see Paramasivam 1979: 55). This formation saw its heyday during Middle Tamil but is no longer productive in the modern language.

(86) a *toẓilaḷikaḷ* *tañcāvūr* *kōyilai.k* *kāṭṭ-iṉ-ārkaḷ.*
laborers-NOM Tanjore temple-ACC build-PST-3P
'Laborers built the Tanjore temple.'

b *cōẓaṉ* *tañcāvūr* *kōyilai.k* *kāṭṭu-vi-tt-āṉ.*
Chola-NOM Tanjore temple-ACC build-CAUS-PST-3SM
'The Chola caused the Tanjore temple to be built.'

Several of the lexemes that may function as indicative auxiliary verbs in Modern Tamil have retained their morphological causative stems from the medieval period, but as auxiliaries they cannot be inflected for it. Current auxiliaries with morphological causatives[10] are *vara* 'come' (*varuvikka* 'cause to come'), *viṭa* 'leave'

10 In Medieval Tamil, additional lexemes had morphological causatives: *irukka* 'be' (*iruppikka* 'cause to be'), *koḷḷa* 'hold' (*koḷvikka* 'cause to hold') and *pārkka* 'look at' (*pārppikka* 'cause to look at').

(*viṭuvikka* 'cause to leave'), *pōṭa* 'put' (*pōṭuvikka* 'cause to put'), *tolaikka* 'lose' (*tolaippikka* 'cause to lose'), and *koṭukka* 'give' (*koṭuppikka* 'cause to give').

In the following examples, only the periphrastic causative (87b), not the morphological causative (87c), may be construed as a causative version of (87a). Sentence (87c), with *viṭuvittāṉ* 'he caused X to leave', is a causative version of a compound clause in which the first verb denotes the subject's coming and the second verb the release of a captive. Further, (88b) is not the causative of (88a): whatever reading (88b) has, the causative operator is associated only with the lexeme *koṭukka* 'give', not with what serves as the auxiliate of the AVC in (88a).

(87) a *avaḷ vantu viṭṭāḷ.*
she-NOM come-CF leave-PST-3SF
'She did come.' or 'She came unexpectedly.'

b *avaṉ avaḷai vantu viṭa.c cey-t-āṉ.*
he-NOM she-ACC come-CF leave-INF do-PST-3SM
'He made her come unexpectedly.'

c *avaṉ avaḷai vantu viṭu-vi.t-t-āṉ.*
he-NOM she-ACC come-CF leave-CAUS-PST-3SM
'He came and (he) released her.'
not
'He made her come unexpectedly.'

(88) a *avaṉ avaḷukkāka kaṭitattai eẕuti.k koṭuttāṉ.*
he-NOM she-BEN letter-ACC write-CF give-PST-3SM
'He wrote a letter on her behalf.'

b * *avar avaṉai avaḷukkāka kaṭitattai eẕuti.k koṭu-ppi-tt-ār.*
he-NOM he-ACC she-BENE letter-ACC write-CF give-CAUS-PST-3H
'He caused him to give to X, he having written a letter on her behalf.'

Morphological causatives thus appear to be subject to the following stipulation: the verb base with which the causative markers *-vi-* and *-ppi-* morphologically combine must have a denotational function.[11] This effectively blocks them from attaching to indicative auxiliary verbs, which have only an inflectional function.

Negation

Under Negation AVCs behave as a unit: no single component can be negated separately from the others. As noted in Chapter 3, Negation is an exponent of Tamil verbs and is expressed in two ways. The first, morphological negation, involves

11 Another possible explanation for the inability of auxiliaries to inflect for the morphological causative is the formation's nonproductivity the modern language. Many verbs that appear to be morphologically causative are not so semantically, e.g., *kāṇpikka* 'show' (formerly, 'cause to see', which historically was the causative of *kāṇa* 'see') is no longer causative, but merely a synonym of *kāṭṭa* 'show' (Paramasivam 1979). This process of idiomaticization among morphological causatives may well undermine their applicability and successively restrict their domain.

suffixation of the morph *-ā-* to the verb base in a variety of forms, as *var-ā-tu* 'it will not come' (89a), *var-ā-ta* 'which will not come', *var-ā-mal* 'not coming' and *var-ā-tē* 'don't come'. The second, syntactic negation, involves the formation of modal AVCs with a negative auxiliary: *illai* 'not' in the present and past (89b), *māṭṭ-* 'will not' in the future (89c).

(89) a *kaṭitam iṅkē var-ā-tu.*
letter-NOM here come-NEG-3SN
'The letter will not come come here.'

b *avaṉ vara.v illai.*
he-NOM come-INF IND-NEG
'He did/does not come.'

c *avaṉ vara māṭṭāṉ.*
he-NOM come-INF FUT-NEG-3SM
'He will not come.'

Tamil indicative AVCs readily undergo Negation, as evidenced by the alternation between affirmative (90a, 91a) and negative (90b, 91b), morphological (90) and syntactic (91) counterparts. This property distinguishes Tamil AVCs from Hindi compound verbs (Hook 1974), which are rarely negated.

(90) a *kaṭitam vantu irukkum.*
letter-NOM come-CF be-FUT-3SN
'The letter will/would have come.'

b *kaṭitam vantu irukkātu.*
letter-NOM come-CF be-FUT-NEG-3SN
'The letter will/would not have come.'

(91) a *avaṉ vantu iruppāṉ.*
he-NOM come-CF be-FUT-3SM
'He will/would have come.'

b *avaṉ vantu irukka māṭṭāṉ.*
he-NOM come-CF be-INF FUT-NEG-3SM
'He will/would not have come.'

Annamalai (1982:34) argues that Negation distinguishes AVCs from compound clauses. In a compound clause, but not an AVC, the scope of negation can be restricted to the second verb by cliticizing *=um* 'and, all' to the first verb, thereby insulating the first clause. In (92b) the negative operator *illai* 'not' takes only the second verb *paṭikka* 'read' in its scope, not the first verb *eṭukka* 'take'; in (93b) *illai* 'not' applies only to *cāka* 'die', not to *kuṭikka* 'drink'.

(92) a *avaṉ pustakam eṭuttu.p paṭittāṉ.*
he-NOM book take-CF read-PST-3SM
'He took the book and (he) read it.'

b *avaṉ pustakam eṭutt=um paṭikka.v illai.*
he-NOM book take-CF=AND read-INF IND-NEG
'Even though he took the book, he did not read it.'

(93) a *paiyaṉ viṣam kuṭittu.c cettāṉ.*
boy-NOM poison drink-CF die-PST-3SM
'The boy drank some poison and died.'

b *paiyaṉ viṣam kuṭitt=um cāka.v illai.*
boy-NOM poison drink-CF=AND die-INF IND-NEG
'The boy drank some poison, and didn't die.'

This pattern does not apply to AVCs even though, as shown below (pp. 132-34), the main verb of an AVC may under other circumstances host the clitic *=um*. The second verb in an AVC cannot be negated independently of the first: attempts to do so result in unacceptable sentences or a semantic jumble. In neither case may such sentences be construed as the negative of an affirmative AVC. The AVCs in (94) and (95) cannot mimic the alternation witnessed above without gross unacceptability, as both (94b) and (95b) show. Thus, Negation may not disturb the unity of the auxiliate and the auxiliary.

(94) a *avarkaḷ pēci.k koṇṭārkaḷ.*
they-NOM speak-CF hold-PST-3P
'They spoke among themselves.'

b ?* *avarkaḷ pēci.y=um koḷḷa.v illai.*
they-NOM speak-CF=AND hold-INF IND-NEG
'Even though they spoke, they didn't hold.'

(95) a *maṇṇal tuṟaimukattai.t tūrttu vaittatu.*
sand-NOM harbor.mouth-ACC silt-CF place-PST-3SN
'Sand silted up the harbor.'

b * *maṇṇal tuṟaimukattai.t tūrtt=um vaikka.v illai.*
sand-NOM harbor.mouth-ACC silt-CF=AND place-INF IND-NEG
'Even though sand silted the harbor, it didn't place.'

Annamalai (1982: 33) also presents the converse of this argument. He observes that the first verb in a compound clause may be negated independently of the second, in which case the first verb assumes the negative verbal form. The negative expressions (96a and b) are based on the affirmative sentences (92a) and (93a), respectively. In (96b), then, the act of taking poison is negated while the event of dying is affirmed.

(96) a *avaṉ puttakattai.k kaiyil eṭukkāmal=ē paṭittāṉ.*
he-NOM book-ACC hand-LOC take-NEG-VF=EMP read-PST-3SM
'He read the book without holding it in his hand.'

b *avaṉ viṣattai.k kuṭikkāmal=ē cettuppōṉāṉ.*
he-NOM poison-ACC drink-NEG-VF=EMP die-PST-3SM
'He died without drinking the poison.'

As before, indicative AVCs do not follow the paradigm established for compound clauses: the auxiliate cannot be negated independently of the auxiliary. Example (97a), based on the AVC in (94a), and (97b), based on that in (95a), corroborate this claim. The auxiliate of an indicative AVC cannot normally host the negative verb form.

(97) a * *avarkaḷ* *pēcāmal=ē* *koṇṭārkaḷ.*
they-NOM speak-NEG-VF=EMP hold-PST-3P
'They held without speaking.'

b * *maṉṉal* *tuṟaimukattai.t* *tūrkkāmal=ē* *vaittatu.*
sand-NOM harbor.mouth-ACC silt-NEG-VF=EMP place-PST-3SN
'Sand placed without silting up the harbor.'

The discussion of examples (36-38) in Chapter 3 raised three apparent counterexamples to the claim that the auxiliate of an indicative AVC cannot take the form of the negative verb. Annamalai's (1982) analysis there indicated the putative counterexamples were not systematic negations of affirmative AVCs and, moreover, they were actually examples of compound clauses, with structures much like (96a and b) above. With these apparent counterexamples accounted for, we may conclude that the entire AVC acts as a unit under Negation. This is again consistent with Benveniste's assignment of the denotational and inflectional functions to the main and auxiliary verbs in the AVC: Negation applies only to verbs with a denotational, not an inflectional, function. These arguments further confirm that AVCs do not originate in a compound clause structure.

The next two sets of examples illustrate further interactions between indicative AVCs and Negation. The attitudinal auxiliary *tolaiya* 'get lost' in (98) conveys the speaker's antipathy toward the event the auxiliate denotes: in (98a) that antipathy is directed against the train's early arrival, in (98b) against its failure to arrive at all. What *tolaiya* comments on in both examples is the ensemble formed by the

(98) a *ṭirēṉ* *(cīkkiramāy)* *vantu* *tolaintatu.*
train-NOM early come-CF lose+AF-PST-3SN
'The train came early, damn it all.'

b *ṭirēṉ* *(iṉṉum)* *vantu* *tolaiya.v* *illai.*
train-NOM still come-CF lose+AF-INF IND-NEG
'The train (still) doesn't/didn't come, damn it all.'

main verb and the negative operator. The negative operator in (98b) does not negate the conventional content of the auxiliary *tolaiya*, and thus cannot mean either, 'The train came, but it is not the case that I dislike it,' or 'The train didn't come, and it is not the case that I dislike it'.[12] The negative operator negates just the auxiliate's content, not the auxiliary's.

12 Since *tolaiya*'s meaning is invariant under negation, it may well be treated as a presupposition or conventional implicature.

Auxiliary *viṭa* 'leave' signals a disjunction between two events: the event modified by *viṭa* departs from what has been accepted as given in the context. Its presence in (99a) indicates that on the basis of what was known from the context, the subject's running to the entrance was not expected to occur. When in (99b) the negative verb *illai* combines with the AVC *ōṭi viṭa* 'do run', only the content of the main verb is negated; the conventional content of the auxiliary remains unaffected by the negative operator. The auxiliary's presence in (99b) thus indicates that the subject's not running to the entrance was unexpected.

(99) a *avan̲ vācalukku ōṭi viṭṭān̲.*
he-NOM entrance-DAT run-CF leave-PST-3SM
'He ran to the entrance (after all).'

b *avan̲ vācalukku ōṭi viṭa.v illai.*
he-NOM entrance-DAT run-CF leave-CF IND-NEG
'He didn't run to the entrance, after all.'

These observations further reinforce the contention that the negative operator negates the meaning of the auxiliate, not the auxiliary. It combines semantically with the auxiliate, because that form fulfils the AVC's denotational function, but morphologically with the auxiliary because that serves its inflectional function. These various patterns show that the AVC functions an as indivisible unit under Negation, and differs from compound clauses in this ability.

Bounded movement rules

Four bounded movement rules, Scrambling, Clefting, Right Dislocation and CF-Postposing, provide evidence that the AVC functions as a unit, not two separate verbs. While the first three rules primarily target NPs and the fourth conjunctive clauses, their structural descriptions all make reference to a clause-final verb which acts as a boundary marker delimiting the rightward movement of the targeted constituent. Clefting and Right Dislocation, for example, do not ordinarily move an NP rightward over more than one verb; they may do so, however, if all the verbs in their path constitute a single AVC.

These rules thus serve to distinguish AVCs from compound clauses. Scrambling and CF-Postposing distinguish AVCs from lexical compounds: they may apply to separate a sequence of two verbs if it constitutes a lexical compound, but not an AVC. In these four cases, the indicative AVC behaves as a single verb with respect to the movement rule, not as a sequence of two stand-alone verbs.

Scrambling and the AVC

The rule of Scrambling in Tamil (Annamalai 1969) permutes the linear order of the individual constituents within a single clause to the left of the clause-final verb, yielding different surface word orders. The order of constituents in (100a) is taken as unmarked while the order in (100b and c) are permutations of it. In all cases, the verb remains at the extreme right boundary of the clause.[13] Scrambling may not break up a constituent, so that the NP *oru periya puttakam* 'a big book' is Scrambled as a unit and may not be interrupted by the insertion of another element, say *nēṟṟu* 'yesterday'. Similarly, a relative clause would necessarily accompany its head when the latter is Scrambled.

(100)a *avaṉ nēṟṟu eṉakku oru periya puttakam koṭuttāṉ.*
he-NOM yesterday I-DAT one big book give-PST-3SM
'He gave me a big book yesterday.'

b *oru periya puttakam nēṟṟu avaṉ eṉakku.k koṭuttāṉ.*
one big book yesterday he-NOM I-DAT give-PST-3SM
'He gave me a big book yesterday.'

c *nēṟṟu eṉakku oru periya puttakam avaṉ koṭuttāṉ.*
yesterday I-DAT one big book he-NOM give-PST-3SM
'He gave me a big book yesterday.'

Scrambling is bounded: it may not move a constituent into a higher or lower clause, nor may it move an element from one conjunct of a coordinate structure into another. Sentence (101a) illustrates a matrix-complement structure with unmarked word order: Scrambling may apply within each clause as long as each verb holds final position in its respective clause, as in (101b). In the higher clause of (101b) the subject *nāṉ* 'I' and the complement clause have been permuted; within

(101)a $_{S0}$[*nāṉ* $_{S1}$[*avaṉ iṅkē vantāṉ*] *eṉṟu niṉaittēṉ*].
I-NOM he-NOM here come-PST-3SM say-CF think-PST-1S
'I thought that he came here.'

b $_{S0}$[$_{S1}$[*iṅkē avaṉ vantāṉ*] *eṉṟu nāṉ niṉaittēṉ*].
here he-NOM come-PST-3SM say-CF I-NOM think-PST-1S
'I thought that he came here.'

c * $_{S0}$[*avaṉ nāṉ iṅkē vantāṉ eṉṟu niṉaittēṉ*].
he-NOM I-NOM here come-PST-3SM say-CF think-PST-1S

(102)a $_{S0}$[$_{S1}$[*maḻai peytu*] $_{S2}$[*veyil aṭittu*] $_{S3}$[*vāṉavil tōṉṟiyatu*]].
rain-NOM rain-CF sun-NOM beat-CF rainbow-NOM appear-PST-3SN
'It rained, the sun shined, and a rainbow appeared.'

b ?* *veyil maḻai peytu aṭittu vāṉavil tōṉṟiyatu.*
sun-NOM rain-NOM rain-CF beat-CF rainbow-NOM appear-PST-3SN

the lower clause the subject *avaṉ* 'he' and the adverbial *iṅkē* 'here' have also been permuted. But Scrambling cannot move an element from one clause into another, as the ungrammaticality of (101c) shows. Even though two possible bracketings could be applied to this structure, one that includes the upper clause subject *nāṉ* in the lower clause and one that includes the lower clause subject *avaṉ* in the upper

13 Scrambling may be informally stated as $_S$[X Y Z V] → $_S$[Y X Z V] or $_S$[Y Z X V], where V remains clause final and X, Y and Z are directly dominated by S.

clause, both are equally unacceptable for the same reason: an element has moved across a clause boundary. This restriction applies similarly to the coordinate structures: Scrambling cannot move the NP *veyil* 'sun, sunshine' in (102a) outside its original clause, as the unacceptability of (102b) shows.

Scrambling distinguishes AVCs from lexical compounds by separating the components of the latter, but not the former. The two parts of the lexical compound *nimirntu pārkka* 'look up at' (103a) may be separated when Scrambling moves the direct object *maṉaiviyai* 'wife' between them (103b). Similarly, the two parts of *etirttu.p pēca* 'contradict' (104a) may be separated when Scrambling moves the subject *maṉaivi* 'wife' between them (104b).

(103)a *avaṉ maṉaiviyai nimirntu pārttāṉ.*
he-NOM wife-ACC lift-CF look.at-PST-3SM
'He looked up at his wife.'

b *avaṉ nimirntu maṉaiviyai.p pārttāṉ.*
he-NOM lift-CF wife-ACC look-PST-3SM
'He looked up at his wife.'

(104)a *maṉaivi puruṣaṉai etirttu.p pēca.k kūṭātu.*
wife-NOM husband-ACC oppose-CF speak-INF ought-NEG-3SN
'A wife ought not speak against/contradict her husband.'

b *puruṣaṉai etirttu maṉaivi pēca.k kūṭātu.*
husband-ACC oppose-CF wife-NOM speak-INF ought-NEG-3SN
'A wife ought not speak against/contradict her husband.'

The alternations in the lexical compounds in (103) and (104) recalls the alternation observed in the matrix-complement structures in (101a and b). Comparison of Figure 4.7, which presents an approximate constituent structure for (101a), with Figure 4.3 above, which presents the constituent structure of a lexical compound, shows how closely their gross surface structures resemble each another.

In (101b), the constituent structure is the same as in Figure 4.7 except that nodes NP_0 and S_1 have been transposed by Scrambling. Similarly, (103b) resembles (103a) except that nodes NP_2 and S_1 in Figure 4.3 have been transposed, also by Scrambling. On this analysis, the two components of the lexical compound are not in

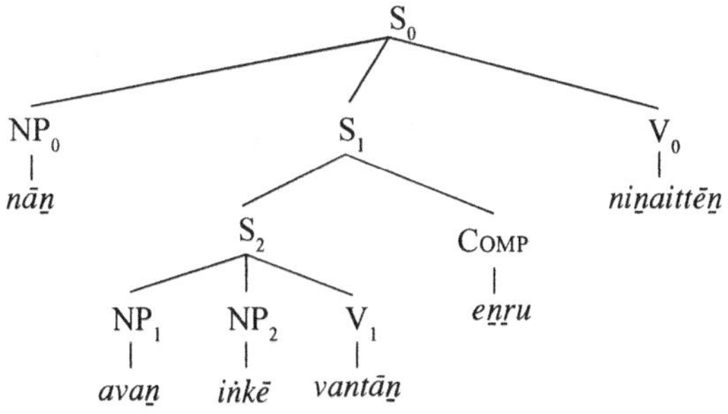

Figure 4.7 Constituent structure of a matrix-complement clause.

immediate constituency to the exclusion of all other parts of the sentence. Evidence from Scrambling, CF-Postposing and Reduplication suggest that Figure 4.3 is likely the correct approximate surface structure for what we have been calling lexical compound verbs.

Scrambling treats indicative AVCs differently: it cannot separate the sequence of auxiliate and auxiliary. The AVC *eẓuti.t taḷḷiṉāṉ* 'he wrote quickly' in (105a) cannot be split up by Scrambling through the interpolation of another constituent of the clause, as the unacceptability of (105b) shows. The same pattern holds true for the attitudinal verbs in (106a and b); indeed, for all remaining indicative AVCs.

(105)a *avaṉ oru nāvalai eẓuti.t taḷḷiṉāṉ.*
he-NOM one novel-ACC write-CF push-PST-3SM
'He wrote a novel quickly/dashed off a novel.'

b * *oru nāvalai eẓuti avaṉ taḷḷiṉāṉ.*
one novel-ACC write-CF he-NOM push-PST-3SM
?'Writing a novel, he pushed.'

(106)a *kāḷai tōṭṭattil vaḷarntu pōyiṟṟu.*
weeds-NOM garden-LOC grow-CF go-PST-3SN
'Some weeds went and grew in the garden.'

b * *tōṭṭattil vaḷarntu kāḷai pōyiṟṟu.*
garden-LOC grow-CF weed-NOM go-PST-3SN
?'Growing in the garden, some weeds went.'

Given the AVC's close-knit constituent structure, we would not expect Scrambling to break it up any more than it would separate a relative clause and its head or a noun and its modifiers. Scrambling thus transposes only elements that are directly dominated by the sentence within which they are Scrambled. On our analysis, in surface structure the auxiliate and auxiliary are not directly dominated by the sentence, but by the intermediate V_{-1} node which arises in the course of the derivation in Figure 4.4. Scrambling is sensitive to this (derived) verb, and effectively leaves the AVC in clause-final position.

Clefting and the AVC

Clefting in Tamil (Lindholm 1971) moves an NP rightward over the clause-final finite verb, Chomsky-adjoining it to the sentence from which it originates.[14] Two morphological adjustments ensue: the original clause-final verb becomes a verbal noun and the clefted NP appears (optionally) in the nominative case. Both adjustments help make the transformed sentence conform more nearly to the surface templates of Tamil: the resulting construction has the overall form of a so-called equational sentence consisting of two NPs, with the clefted NP playing the part of the predicate nominal. Example (107b) is a clefted version of (107a): the subject

14 Clefting may be informally stated as $_{S0}$[NP X V] → $_{S}$[$_{NP}$[X V] $_{NP}$[NP]], where NP is Chomsky-adjoined to S_0, V becomes a verbal noun and NP optionally assumes the nominative case.

NP moves rightward over the finite verb and is Chomsky-adjoined to the host clause. Simultaneously, the finite verb assumes the form of a verbal noun, which agrees in number and gender with the clefted NP.[15] The output of Clefting in sentence (107b) superficially resembles the structure of the equational sentence in (107c) which contains a predicate nominal.

(107)a $_{S}$[*contakkāraṉ nēṟṟu vīṭṭukku vantāṉ*].
relative-NOM yesterday house-DAT come-PST-3SM
'A relative came to the house yesterday.'

b $_{S}$[$_{NP1}$[*nēṟṟu vīṭṭukku vantavaṉ*] $_{NP2}$[*contakkāraṉ*]].
yesterday house-DAT come-PST-VN relative-NOM
'It was a relative who came to the house yesterday.'

c *avaṉ contakkāraṉ.*
he-NOM relative-NOM
'He is a relative.'

Clefting may not move an NP over a sequence of two verbs if they constitute a compound clause, either a coordinate or a matrix-complement structure. Example (108b) shows that the clefted NP cannot be moved from a subordinate into a matrix clause. This is a specific constraint on Clefting and not a general constraint on movement of NPs since in Relative Clause Formation (p. 120ff.) movement is unbounded. Although the unacceptability of (109b), which shows that no NP may be clefted out of one conjunct in a series into another, can be explained by appeal to the boundedness of Clefting, it alternatively could be explained as a violation of the Coordinate Structure Constraint.

(108)a $_{S0}$[*nāṉ* $_{S1}$[*contakkāraṉ nēṟṟu vantāṉ*] *eṉṟu niṉaittēṉ*].
I-NOM relative-NOM yesterday come-PST-3SM COMP think-PST-1S
'I thought that my relative came yesterday.'

b * [[*nāṉ* [*nēṟṟu vantāṉ*] *eṉṟu niṉaittatu*] *contakkāraṉ*].
I-NOM yesterday come-PST-3SM COMP think-PST-VN relative-NOM
'It is my relative that I thought came yesterday.'

(109)a $_{S0}$[$_{S1}$[*kāṭu muṭintu*] $_{S2}$[*pātai toṭaṅkiṉatu*]].
forest-NOM end-CF path-NOM begin-PST-3SN
'The forest ended and the path began.'

15 Clefting optionally transforms a nonnominative case NP into a nominative case NP, the unmarked case in Tamil. In (ii) the Clefted NP *oru puttakam* 'a book' appears without the accusative case marking its nonclefted counterpart in (i) has.

(i) *salīm oru puttakattai.k koṭuttāṉ.*
Salim-NOM one book-ACC give-PST-3SM
'Salim gave a book.'

(ii) *salīm koṭuttatu oru puttakam.*
Salim-NOM give-PST-3SN one book-NOM
'What Salim gave is a book.'

b * [[*muṭintu*] [*pātai* *toṭaṅkiṉatu*]] *kāṭu*].
end-CF path-NOM begin-PST-VN forest-NOM
* 'It is the forest that the path began and ended.'

However, Clefting may move an NP over a sequence of two verbs where it constitutes a compound verb, particularly an indicative AVC. In (110b) the subject NP *contakkāraṉ* 'relative' has been Clefted over the AVC *vantu tolaikka* '(someone) came, damn him'; in (111b) the direct object *oru nāval* 'a novel' has been Clefted over the complex AVC *paṭittu.k koṇṭu irukka* 'to be reading'.

(110)a $_{S0}$[*contakkāraṉ* *nēṟṟu* $_{AVC}$[*vantu* *tolaittāṉ*]].
relative-NOM yesterday come-CF lose+EF-PST-3SM
'My relative came yesterday, damn him.'

b $_{S0}$[$_{NP1}$[*nēṟṟu* $_{AVC}$[*vantu* *tolaittavaṉ*]] $_{NP2}$[*contakkāraṉ*]].
yesterday come-CF lose+EF-PST-VN relative-NOM
'It is my relative who came yesterday, damn him.'

(111)a $_{S0}$[*nāṉ* *oru* *nāvalai.p* $_{AVC}$[$_{AVC}$[*paṭittu.k* *koṇṭu*] *irukkiṟēṉ*]].
I-NOM one novel-ACC read-CF hold-CF be-PRS-1S
'I am reading a novel.'

b $_{S0}$[$_{NP1}$[*nāṉ* $_{AVC}$[$_{AVC}$[*paṭittu.k* *koṇṭu*] *irukkiṟatu*]]] $_{NP2}$[*oru* *nāval*]].
I-NOM read-CF hold-CF be-PRS-VN one novel-NOM
'It is a novel that I am reading.'

This behavior shows that the AVC functions as a single verb form under Clefting, supporting our proposed surface structure in Figure 4.6.

Right Dislocation and the AVC

As noted in Chapter 2, Tamil syntax generally requires a finite verb to appear at the extreme right boundary of a sentence. The rule of Scrambling was seen straightforwardly to obey this condition on the overall well-formedness of Tamil surface structures. Nor does the rule of Clefting violate the spirit of this condition since the finite verb is replaced by a verbal noun, and the output structure thus resembles an equational sentence. However, a few structures, along with the rules that generate them, do appear to violate this principle: one is Right Dislocation which moves the subject rightward over the finite verb, bringing the subject into sharp focus (Steever 1988: 16).[16] This rule is a focusing operation that typically applies to a salient subject NP whose referent is often a protagonist in a narrative.[17] It treats compound clauses and AVCs differently. Right Dislocation has applied in the derivation of (112b), based on (112a).

16 Examples of this appear in Old Tamil: *kāṅku ivaṉ* 'I will see' (*puṟanāṉūṟu*) derives from *ivaṉ kāṅku* 'id.' with normalized word order. In Steever (1988), this rule is called Heroic NP Postposing.

17 Informally stated as $_{S}$[NP X V] → $_{S}$[X V NP], where NP is a subject referring to a protagonist.

(112)a *aracar talainakarukku varukiṟār.*
king-NOM capital-DAT come-PRS-3H
'The king comes into the capital.'

b *talainakarukku varukiṟār aracar.*
capital-DAT come-PRS-3H king-NOM
'Into the capital comes the king.'

Right Dislocation may not transport a subject NP rightward over a sequence of two verbs if that sequence forms a compound clause, such as the matrix-complement structure in (113b) or the coordinate structure in (114b). The ungrammaticality

(113)a $_{S0}$[$_{S1}$[*avaḷ vantāḷ*] *eṉṟu niṉaittēṉ*].
she-NOM come-PST-3SF say-CF think-PST-1S
'I thought that she came.'

b * *vantāḷ eṉṟu niṉaittēṉ avaḷ.*
come-PST-3SF COMP think-PST-1S she-NOM
? 'She, I thought that came in.'

(114)a $_{S0}$[$_{S1}$[*paẓaiya ēyjeṇṭu pōy.p*] $_{S2}$[*putu ēyjeṇṭu vantāṉ*]].
old agent-NOM go-CF new agent-NOM come-PST-3SM
'The old agent went and the new agent came.'

b * *pōy.p putu ēyjeṇṭu vantāṉ paẓaiya ēyjeṇṭu.*
go-CF new agent-NOM come-PST-3SM old agent-NOM
* 'The new agent came and went the old.'

of these sentences may be ascribed to the boundedness of Right Dislocation or, alternatively, to violations of island constraints (see Annamalai 1969, 1997). For example, (114b) could also be a violation of the Coordinate Structure Constraint. What matters for present purposes, however, is that where a sequence of two verbs constitutes an indicative AVC, it lacks the structural description in which either kind of violation could arise.

Right Dislocation may move a subject across a sequence of two or more verbs where they form a single AVC. In (115b)[18] and (116b)[19] the subjects appear to the right of the finite verbs they agree with, having been moved there by Right Dislocation. In both instances, they have been transported across two separate verb forms; in each case, the two verbs constitute a single AVC.

(115)a $_{S}$[*uṟumiyavāṟē māriyāyi* $_{AVC}$[*niṉṟu iruntāḷ*]].
growl-ADN-way Mariyayi-NOM stand-CF be-PST-3SF
'Mariyayi was standing, growling.'

b *uṟumiyavāṟē niṉṟu iruntāḷ māriyāyi.*
growl-ADN-way stand-CF be-PST-3SF Mariyayi-NOM
'There stood Mariyayi, growling.'

18 From Jeyakantan's (1958) short story "*oru piṭi cōṟu.*"
19 From Jeyakantan's (1958) short story "*poṟukki.*"

(116)a $_S$[*inta ecciṟpoṟukki capāpati oru rūpāy kācakkāka*
this scavenger Sabhapati-NOM one rupee cash-ADV
atai $_{AVC}$[*nampi.t tolaikkiṟāṉ*]].
it-ACC trust-CF lose+EF-PRS-3SM
'For the price of one rupee, this scavenger Sabhapati trusts it, damn him.'

b *oru rūpāy kācakkāka atai nampi.t tolaikkiṟāṉ*
one rupee cash-ADV it-ACC trust-CF lose+EF-PRS-3SM
inta ecciṟpoṟukki capāpati.
this scavenger Sabhapati-NOM
'For the price of one rupee, this scavenger Sabhapati trusts it, damn him.'

The condition that prevents this rule from moving a subject outside its own clause treats the two components of the AVC as a single verb, indicating that this condition is sensitive not to the verb nodes that directly dominate the auxiliate and auxiliary, but to the single V node that joins them into a single constituent.

CF-Postposing and the AVC

The rule of Conjunctive Form Postposing (see Steever 1988: 15), or CF-Postposing, moves a conjunctive verb along with any accompanying material to the right of a finite verb.[20] Example (117) contains structures with two clauses joined by a conjunctive: (117a) gives the unmarked order while (117b)[21] exhibits the output of CF-Postposing, which has moved the conjunctive clause *tiṭcai eṭuttu.k koṇṭu* 'having taken a vow' rightward across the finite verb *ceykiṟār* 'he does'. The pair of sentences in (118a and b)[22] exhibits a similar alternation. Note *eṉṟu*, sometimes glossed as *that* or as a complementizer, is formally the conjunctive form of *eṉa* 'say, think', allowing us to treat *ippaṭi veṭṭi.p pozutu pōkkātē eṉṟu* 'saying, "Don't fritter your time away like this" ' as a conjunctive clause.

(117)a $_{S0}$[$_{S1}$[*tiṭcai eṭuttu.k koṇṭu*] *civa pūjai kūṭa ceykiṟār*].
vow take-CF hold-CF Siva puja even do-PRS-3H
'He even performs a Siva puja, having taken a vow (to do so).'

b $_{S0}$[*civa pūjai kūṭa ceykiṟār,* $_{S1}$[*tiṭcai eṭuttu.k koṇṭu*]].
Siva puja even do-PRS-3H vow take-CF hold-CF
'He even performs a Siva puja, having taken a vow.'

(118)a $_{S0}$[$_{S1}$[*ippaṭi veṭṭi.p pozutu pōkkātē eṉṟu*] *uṉakku*
this.way cut-CF time pass-NEG-IMP say-CF you-DAT
lakṣam taram colli irukkiṟēṉ].
100,000 time tell-CF be-PRS-1S
'I've told you 100,000 times not to fritter away your time wastefully like this.'

20 CF-Postposing may be informally stated as $_S$[NP [X]-CF Y V] → [NP Y V [X]-CF], where [X]-CF represents a conjunctive form and any material accompanying it.

21 Fedson (1981: 184).

22 Fedson (1981: 40).

b $_{S0}$[*uṉakku lakṣam taram colli irukkiṟēṉ,* $_{S1}$[*ippaṭi*
you-DAT 100,000 time tell-CF be-PRS-1S this.way
veṭṭi.p poẕutu pōkkātē eṉṟu]].
cut-CF time pass-NEG-IMP say-CF
'I've told you 100,000 times not to fritter away your time wastefully like this.'

The postposed material must be immediately dominated by the sentence node. On this hypothesis, CF-Postposing may apply to the first verb in a lexical compound because its overall shape resembles that of a matrix-complement clause, but not to an indicative AVC. The first verb in Figure 4.3, V_1, occupies a position in the tree structurally analogous to that occupied by *eṉṟu* in Figure 4.7. CF-Postposing does apply to the first verb in the lexical compound *ōṭi pōka* 'go running' in (119a), moving it rightward over the second verb, resulting in (119b). Similarly, CF-Postposing has applied in (120b),[23] altering the unmarked order in (120a). Comparing the structures in Figures 4.3 and 4.7, we may thus stipulate that the node moved by this rule is an S node directly dominated by the matrix sentence; further, the target S node directly dominates a conjunctive form. The similarity of behavior between lexical compounds[24] and compound clauses under CF-Postposing confirms this convergence of their syntactic structures.

(119)a *avaṉ vīṭṭukku ōṭi pōṉāṉ.*
he-NOM house-DAT run-CF go-PST-3SM
'He went running to the house.'

b *avaṉ vīṭṭukku.p pōṉāṉ ōṭi.*
he-NOM house-DAT go-PST-3SM run-CF
'He went running to the house.'

(120)a *pāpu avaḷai orumuṟai nimirntu pārttāṉ.*
Babu-NOM her-ACC strangely lift-CF look.at-PST-3SM
'Babu looked up at her strangely.'

b *pāpu avaḷai orumuṟai pārttāṉ nimirntu.*
Babu-NOM her-ACC strangely look.at-PST-3SM lift-CF
'Babu looked up at her strangely.'

However, the ungrammaticality of the b-variants in (121) and (122) indicates that CF-Postposing cannot extract a conjunctive form from an indicative AVC. It cannot extract either the auxiliate by itself or the auxiliate and the material that precedes and accompanies it. Only the former case is illustrated below.

(121)a *nī ceytatu ūr ellām* $_{AVC}$[*nāṟi.k kiṭakkiṟatu*].
you-NOM do-PST-VN town all stink-CF lie-PRS-3N
'What you did is (still) stinking all over town.'

23 Janakiraman (1976: 372).

24 Idiomatic lexical compounds such as *piṭittu viṭa* 'massage' and *eẕuntu irukka* 'get up' may not, however, be broken up by CF-Postposing.

b * *nī ceytatu ūr ellām kiṭakkiṟatu nāṟi.*
you-NOM do-PST-VN town all lie-PRS-3N stink-CF
'What you did is (still) stinking all over town.'

(122)a *avaṉ oru nāvalai $_{AVC}$[ezuti.t taḷḷiṉāṉ].*
he-NOM one novel-ACC write-CF push-PST-3SM
'He wrote a novel more quickly than expected.'

b * *avaṉ oru nāvalai.t taḷḷiṉāṉ eẓuti.*
he-NOM one novel-ACC push-PST-3SM write-CF
'He wrote a novel more quickly than expected.'

If the condition that the postposed node must be directly dominated by an S node is correct, then the ungrammaticality of these sentences follows because no indicative AVC can meet the structural description for CF-Postposing. The main verb of the AVC is directly dominated by a V node, not an S node.

These four bounded rules thus distinguish AVCs from other, apparently similar constructions. Clefting and Right Dislocation cannot move an NP across more than one verb, but they count the AVC as a single verb, no matter how internally complex it is. Scrambling requires verbs to remain clause-final and moves only constituents that are directly dominated by the S in which it applies. Its failure to interrupt the components of an AVC indicates that auxiliate and auxiliary are not directly dominated by the S node and, further, that since they remain clause final, they are dominated by an intermediate V node. CF-Postposing moves a conjunctive form only if it is directly dominated by an S node, and not the V node of an AVC. If we wish to formulate the conditions on these rules without resorting to disjunctions in their structural descriptions, e.g., the NP may cross only one "main" verb *or* one AVC, we must then posit the verb node that dominates both the auxiliate and auxiliary in the AVC. The rules and the conditions on them heed only that superordinate verb node, not its internal branching into auxiliate and auxiliary, nor its potential nesting. Thus, the verb node that arises in the course of derivation, labeled as V_{-1} in Figure 4.4, is the verb node to which these rules apply and according to which they are constrained.

Relative Clause Formation and the AVC

Relative Clause Formation (RCF) treats the AVC as a single unit. While RCF does not distinguish AVCs from lexical compounds or even matrix-complement structures, it does distinguish them from coordinate clauses, further buttressing the claim that AVCs do not originate in coordinate structures.

Tamil has four relative clause-forming strategies Annamalai (1969, 1997): two that use the adnominal form and two that use correlative strategies. The adnominal relative clause in (123b), the most frequent and the least marked in the language, is based on the simple sentence in (123a). The tense marking of the finite verb is retained in the adnominal form, but the personal ending is replaced by the adnominal suffix *-a*. For a variety of reasons (Steever 1981: 152-75), not all NPs are accessible on the plain adnominal strategy. Example (123c) is a variant of the adnominal strategy, the equi-strategy, in which the phrase *mēcaikku muṉṉālē* 'in front of the table' in the lower clause, which is ordinarily inaccessible on the plain adnominal strategy, is deleted under identity with the same phrase in the upper clause. (123d and e) present two kinds of correlative clauses in Tamil in which the clitics *=ō* 'or, some' and *=ē* 'even, all' embed finite verbs. Apart from Ramasamy (1978), little is known about them: their function seems to be to create relative clauses from sentences that cannot undergo the adnominal strategies for a variety of syntactic or pragmatic reasons. For example, a noun inflected for the bound postposition *-ōṭu* 'with' cannot be relativized on the adnominal strategy, and must be relativized on a correlative strategy (Steever 1981: 158-59). Correlative strategies are set aside here, and the adnominal strategy becomes the focus.[25]

(123)a *oru paiyaṉ nēṟṟu va.n-t-āṉ.*
one boy-NOM yesterday come-PST-3SM
'A boy came yesterday.'

b *nēṟṟu va.n-t-a oru paiyaṉ-ai.p pārttēṉ.*
yesterday come-PST-ADN one boy-ACC see-PST-1S
'I saw the boy who came yesterday.'

c $_{NP}$[$_{S}$[*nāṉ ni.ṉ-ṟ-a*] *mēcaikku*] *muṉṉālē oru nāṟkāli iruntatu.*
I-NOM stand-PST-ADN table-DAT before one chair-NOM be-PST-3SN
'There was a chair in front of the table that I stood (in front of).'

d *enta.p paiyaṉ* $_i$ *nēṟṟu va.n-t-āṉ=ō anta.p paiyaṉai.p* $_i$ *pārttēṉ.*
which boy-NOM yesterday come-PST-3SM=OR that boy-ACC see-PST-1S
'I saw the boy who came yesterday.'

e *nēṟṟu va.n-t-āṉ=ē oru paiyaṉ* $_i$ *avaṉai.p* $_i$ *pārttēṉ.*
yesterday come-PST-3SM=EVEN one boy-NOM he-ACC see-PST-1S
'I saw a boy who came yesterday.'

Tamil RCF obeys the Coordinate Structure Constraint (CSC): no NP may be relativized across verbs that belong to different conjuncts of a coordinate clause. The b-versions in (124) through (126) are ungrammatical, Annamalai (1969) argues, because they violate the CSC.

(124)a $_{S0}$[$_{S1}$[*iravu pōy.p*] $_{S2}$[*pakal vantatu*]].
night-NOM go-CF daylight-NOM come-PST-3SN
'Night went and daylight came.'

b * *pōy.p pakal va.n-t-a iravu*
go-CF daylight-NOM come-PST-ADN night
'The night that went and day came…'

(125)a $_{S0}$[$_{S1}$[*kār mōti.p*] $_{S2}$[*paiyaṉ cettuppōṉāṉ*]].
car-NOM dash-CF boy-NOM die-PST-3SM
'The car dashed against the boy and he died.'

25 The adnominal strategy is unbounded while the correlative strategies are most likely bounded.

b * *mōti.p paiyaṉ cettuppōṉ-a kār…*
dash-CF boy-NOM die-PST-ANP car
'The car that dashed against the boy and died.'

(126)a $_{S0}$[$_{S1}$[*nāṉ kāppi kuṭittu viṭṭu.p*] $_{S2}$[*pēciṉēṉ*]].
I-NOM coffee drink-CF leave-CF speak-PST-1s
'I drank some coffee, and then I spoke.'

b * *nāṉ kuṭittu viṭṭu.p pēc-iṉ-a kāppi…*
I-NOM drink-CF leave-CF speak-PST-ANP coffee
'The coffee that I drank and then spoke.'

An NP may be relativized out of a lower clause over indefinitely many higher clauses on the adnominal strategy as long as no island or other constraints are violated. In (127b) the NP *oru pēṉā* 'a pen' has been relativized out of two subordinate clauses, whose source is represented in (127a). RCF thus distinguishes between coordinate and matrix-complement clauses.

(127)a $_{S0}$[*nāṉ* $_{S1}$[*nī oru pēṉā vāṅkuvāy*] *eṉṟu niṉaittēṉ*].
I-NOM you-NOM one pen buy-FUT-2s say-CF think-PST-1s
'I thought that you would buy a pen.'

b $_{S0}$[*nāṉ* $_{S1}$[*nī vāṅkuvāy*] *eṉṟu ninai.t-t-a*] *oru pēṉā…*
I-NOM you-NOM buy-FUT-2s say-CF think-PST-ANP one pen
'A pen that I thought you would buy.'

RCF can move an NP across two verbs if they constitute a single compound verb, lexical or auxiliary. The sentences in (128) contain the lexical compound *ōṭi vara* 'come running', across which a NP may be relativized (128b). RCF also treats the elements of an indicative AVC as a unit, as in (129) and (130), differentiating them from coordinate structures.

(128)a *anta maṉitaṉ ōṭi va.n-t-āṉ.*
that man-NOM run-CF come-PST-3SM
'That man came running.'

b *ōṭi va.n-t-a anta maṉitaṉ…*
run-CF come-PST-ADN that man
'That man who came running…'

(129)a *vaḷavaṉ* $_{AVC}$[*vantu iru.k-kiṟ-āṉ*].
Valavan-NOM come-CF be-PRS-3SM
'Valavan has come.'

b *vantu iru.k-kiṟ-a vaḷavaṉ oru contakkāraṉ…*
come-CF be-PRS-ADN Valavan-NOM one relative-NOM
'Valavan who has come (here) is a relative.'

(130)a *nāṉ kōyilukku.p paṇam* $_{AVC}$[*koṭuttu aẓu-t-ēṉ*].
I-NOM temple-DAT money give-CF cry-PST-1s
'The money I went and gave to the temple.'

b *nāṉ kōyilukku.k koṭuttu aẓu-t-a paṇam…*
I-NOM temple-DAT give-CF cry-PST-ADN money
'The money I went and gave to the temple…'

All indicative auxiliaries except *āka* 'become' freely appear in adnominal relative clauses; *āka*, as an auxiliary, lacks the adnominal form this strategy requires.

Some further observations may be made concerning RCF which will set the stage for the analysis of the AVC's external syntax in Chapter 5 as well as the lexical semantics of individual auxiliaries. Annamalai (1969: 89) observes that "one does not find as many aspectual, modal and temporal distinctions in the surface forms of adjectival [= relative] clauses as he does in finite sentences." In fact, an AVC is often replaced by its simple, nonauxiliated counterpart in such a context. As shown in Chapter 6, finite reflexive clauses usually require the presence of auxiliary *koḷḷa* 'hold' so that (131a) would be odd if the auxiliary *koṇṭāṉ* 'he held' were absent. But in nonfinite context, while both (131b and c) are judged grammatical, the latter, with no auxiliary, is generally preferred over the former.

(131)a *avaṉ taṉukku oru mēcai* $_{\text{AVC}}$*[ceytu koṇṭāṉ].*
he-NOM self-DAT one table make-CF hold-PST-3SM
'He made a table for himself.'

b *avaṉ taṉukku.c ceytu ko.ṇ-ṭ-a mēcai*
he-NOM self-DAT make-CF hold-PST-ADN table
'The table that he made for himself…'

c *avaṉ taṉukku.c cey-t-a mēcai*
he-NOM self-DAT make-PST-ADN table
'The table that he made for himself…'

The adnominal form *ceyta* 'which made' in (131c) bears a strict relation to the AVC in (131b) on which it is modeled: it incorporates the auxiliate's lexical root and the auxiliary's inflections. This is precisely what Benveniste's theory predicts in the event of a neutralization between unmarked simple verbs and their marked periphrastic counterparts. The relative clause seems to favor such neutralization, although as the grammaticality of (131b) shows, the neutralization is a tendency here, and not a hard and fast rule. Annamalai conjectures that the information in a relative clause may generally be assumed or taken for granted so that additional specification of aspectual or modal distinctions through auxiliaries is otiose, drawing attention away from the head noun, which is the focus of the relative clause. In any event, the lower frequency of AVCs in relative clauses would appear to reflect a pragmatic rather than a syntactic or semantic constraint (Chapter 5).

S-deletion and the AVC

In the indicative AVC's underlying structure in Figure 4.5, the auxiliary stands outside the constituent formed by the auxiliate and the AVC's satellites. Further evidence for this structure comes from a phenomenon in which one sentence, an anaphor, is deleted under identity with another, its antecedent. The rule of S-deletion in Tamil deletes a sentence in a lower clause under identity with one in a higher clause; given the head-final nature of Tamil constituents, the antecedent may often follow the anaphor.[26]

When S-Deletion applies in sentences with indicative AVCs, the deleted constituent may be one that includes the AVC's main verb and satellites, but excludes the auxiliary verb.[27] Assuming this rule applies to constituents and is governed by a condition of identity between antecedent and anaphor up to alphabetic variance, we conclude that at one stage of the AVC's derivation the auxiliary occurs outside of the clause that contains the auxiliate and the AVC's satellites, as in Figure 4.4.

S-Deletion is illustrated below with examples that contain adjuncts which consist of an adnominal clause followed by the head noun *paṭi* 'way, manner, as'. These are generally rendered in English by 'as X V-ed'. In specific instances, material in the adnominal clause is deleted under identity with the material in the main clause; here, φ marks what is assumed to be the deletion site.

Example (132a) contains the negative compound *uruḷa.v illai* 'did/does not roll' in its main clause. The sentence may have two readings. On the preferred reading, the speaker of (132a) reports that the subject failed to complete the vow she promised to perform. As (132b) makes explicit, her vow was to roll around six shrines. Hence, the deleted material in the subordinate clause includes the lexical content of *uruḷa* 'roll', but not the negative operator *illai* 'not'. The other, less preferred, reading of (132a), in which a negative operator has been deleted from the subordinate clause, is nonsensical in this setting. To vow not to roll around six shrines to obtain a boon from the deity is thought to be absurd. What is important for present purposes, however, is not whether cultural knowledge licenses one reading or the other, but that the preferred reading, the one which excludes the negative operator from the deleted material, is available at all. The antecedent thus includes the auxiliate *uruḷa* but excludes the negative operator.

(132)a $[_{S0}$ $[_{S1}$ φ *coṉṉa* *paṭi*] *āṟu* *caṉṉatiyai.y=um* *cuṟṟi* *uruḷa.v* *illai*].
say-PST-ADN manner six shrines-ACC=AND around roll-INF IND-NEG
'(She) didn't roll around six shrines, as she said she would.'

b $[_{S0}$ $[_{S1}$ *āṟu* *caṉṉatiyai.y=um* *cuṟṟi* *uruḷa.c*] *coṉṉāḷ*].
six shrines-ACC=AND around roll-INF say-PST-3SF
'She said she would roll around six shrines.'

To provide an antecedent for S-deletion of the preferred reading, the underlying structure must segregate the negative auxiliary verb outside of and superordinate to the clause that contains the main verb and the satellites, as in Figure 4.5. A

26 S-Deletion may be informally stated as follows: In [[[S_0] [V-ADN]+*paṭi*] S_N], S_0 is deleted if it is identical with, and c-commanded by, S_N.

27 The deleted material may also contain the auxiliary (corresponding to a second reading), but the discussion will focus on instances where it does not.

surface structure such as Figure 4.6 cannot provide an appropriate antecedent for these deletions, since (the interpretation of) the deleted material does not contain an auxiliary.

Example (133a) presents an instance in which a subordinate S has been deleted under identity with a superordinate S which in surface structure contains the indicative AVC *uruṇṭu muṭittāḷ* 'she finished rolling'. Examples (133b and c), corresponding to two different readings, are attempts to recover the content of the deleted material which was embedded under the matrix verb *nēra* 'vow'. The reading in (133b) includes *uruḷa* 'roll' but excludes *muṭikka* 'finish' while (133c) includes both *uruṇṭu* as an auxiliate and auxiliary *muṭikka.* Although both interpretations are possible, (133b) is strongly preferred over (133c), again largely for cultural reasons.[28] What matters for our purposes is that (133b), which excludes the auxiliary, is a possible reading of the deleted material in (133a). While on this reading the antecedent in (133a) appears within an indicative AVC in surface stucture, the underlying structure points to an antecedent without the auxiliary, i.e., the structure in Figure 4.5.

(133)a [$_{S0}$ [$_{S1}$ φ *nērnta paṭi*] *kōyilai.c cuṟṟi uruṇṭu muṭittāḷ*].
VOW-PST-ADN manner temple-ACC around roll-CF finish-PST-3SF
'She finished rolling around the temple as she vowed.'

b *kōyilai.c cuṟṟi uruḷa nērntāḷ.*
temple-ACC around roll-INF VOW-PST-3SF
'She vowed to roll around the temple.'

c ?? *kōyilai.c cuṟṟi uruṇṭu muṭikka nērntāḷ.*
temple-ACC around roll-CF finish-INF VOW-PST-3SF
'She vowed to finish rolling around the temple.'

The following sentences also consist of a main clause with an indicative AVC and a subordinate clause that has been reduced under S-deletion. As above, in one of the possible readings, the deleted S includes the AVC's auxiliate but not its auxiliary. Where this reading occurs, a structure must be postulated in which the AVC's auxiliary occurs outside of and superordinate to the clause with the AVC's auxiliate and satellites, which serves as the antecedent for the deletion. In (134a) a *eṉṟu*-complement has been deleted from the subordinate clause under identity with a constituent in the main clause. The deleted material on one reading is made explicit in (134b); the verb form in the deleted material is the simple future tense of *vara* 'come', *varuvāṉ* 'he will/would come'. However, the verb in the main clause is inflected for the present perfect tense of *vara*, realized by an indicative AVC

28 In (133a) the speaker states that the subject *avaḷ* 'she' has finished a vow she promised to undertake. The original vow is, under normal expectations, understood as stipulating only the undertaking of this austerity, not the conclusion of the activity involved. For (133c) to be understood as the deleted material in (133a), the subject should have been rolling around a temple, ceased the activity, and then made (another) vow to take up this activity anew. But such vows are almost always to undertake an activity or penance, failure to complete which requires undertaking a new penance, not finishing an old one.

with the perfect tense auxiliary *irukka* 'be', *vantu irukkiṟāṉ* 'he has come'. The tense of the verb in the deleted subordinate S cannot have been present perfect because the verb of propositional attitude *etirpārkka* 'expect' selects future-oriented complements, and thus requires a complement verb to appear in the simple future, the prospective future or the future perfect tense, but not a present perfect. Example (134c) is judged strange because expectations are generally held about future events, not past ones that the most straightforward reading of (134c) seems to suggest. To provide an antecedent for the deletion, the tense must be segregated from the verb in (134a); in fact, the tense must be segregated from the deleted verb in the subordinate clause, as well. In both instances, tense is an operator that applies to a tenseless sentence which contains the lexical root of the verb *vara* 'come'. What is deleted under identity with the antecedent in the main clause is a tenseless sentence; and, of course, the antecedent must also be a tenseless sentence. This means that the lexical root of *vara* in *vantu irukkiṟāṉ* 'he has come' must appear in a clause without auxiliary *irukka* 'be'. The proposed underlying structure in Figure 4.5 provides us with just such a constituent.

(134)a $_{S0}$[$_{S1}$[φ *etirpārtta paṭi*] *maturaikku vantu irukkiṟāṉ*].
expect-PST-ADN manner Madurai-DAT come-CF be-PRS-3SM
'As (we) expected, he has come to Madurai.'

b $_{S0}$[$_{S1}$[*avaṉ maturaikku varuvāṉ*] *eṉṟu etirpārttōm*].
he-NOM Madurai-DAT come-FUT-3SM say-CF expect-PST-1P
'We expected that he will/would come to Madurai.'

c ?? $_{S0}$[$_{S1}$[*avaṉ maturaikku vantu irukkiṟāṉ*] *eṉṟu etirpārttōm*].
he-NOM Madurai-DAT come-CF be-PRS-3SM say-CF expect-PST-1P
?'We expected that he has (already) come to Madurai.'

The examples in (135) corroborate this argument and the derivation it implies, this time with the help of attitudinal auxiliaries. The main clause in (135a) contains the attitudinal AVC *eẓuti vaittu.k kiẓikka* which embeds the AVC *eẓuti vaittu* as its auxiliate (see Chapter 8 for *kiẓikka* 'tear'); as above, S-Deletion has removed some material from the adjunct. Auxiliary *kiẓikka* cannot be part either of the constituent that has been deleted or of the antecedent, for several reasons. First, at least one reading, namely that in (135d), excludes the meaning of this auxiliary. Second, the attempt to reconstruct the deleted material in (135b) with *kiẓikka* 'tear' is ill-formed: as shown in Chapter 5, attitudinal auxiliaries may not be embedded in indirect discourse constructions. Third, even if direct discourse were used to reconstruct the deleted material, as in (135c), it would be distinctly odd: it is highly marked for auxiliary *kiẓikka* to appear in the first person (see Chapters 5 and 8). Only (135d), without the attitudinal auxiliary, avoids these objections, and only it can represent the deleted material. This means that the main clause in (135a) must provide an identical constituent to serve as the antecedent for the deletion. It must furnish a constituent that contains the (internally complex) auxiliate *eẓuti vaikka* 'to will' but excludes the attitudinal auxiliary *kiẓikka*.

(135)a $_{S0}$[$_{S1}$[(φ *conna* *paṭi*] *uyilil* *eẓuti* *vaittu.k* *kiẓittār*].
say-PST-ADN manner will-LOC write-CF give-CF tear+EF-PST-3H
'Oh sure, he wrote me into his will like he said he would, sure.'

b * $_{S0}$[$_{S1}$[*uyilil* *eẓuti* *vaittu.k* *kiẓikka.c*] *connār*].
will-LOC write-CF place-CF tear+EF-INF say-PST-3H
'He said he would, oh sure, write me into his will.'

c ?? $_{S0}$[$_{S1}$[*uyilil* *eẓuti* *vaittu.k* *kiẓikkiṟēṉ*] *eṉṟu* *coṉṉār*].
will-LOC write-CF place-CF tear-PRS-1S say-CF say-PST-3h
'He said, "I will, oh sure, write you into my will."'

d $_{S0}$[$_{S1}$[*uyilil* *eẓuti* *vaikka.c*] *coṉṉār*].
will-LOC write-CF place-INF say-PST-3H
'He said he would write me into his will.'

The underlying structure proposed for AVCs in Figure 4.5 provides a constituent that can serve as the antecedent for those readings that exclude the auxiliary.

Conjunction and the AVC

Several arguments have already presented support for our contention that AVCs are not adequately represented by a coordinate construction in either underlying or surface structure. Dale (1975: 59) cites the following passage from Corre (1967: 73) concerning the impossibility of paraphrasing Tamil AVCs by means of coordinate structures.

> The auxiliary is a verb occurring after another verb ... in a sentence such that the sentence is not transformable into two sentences, each containing one of the verbs, that may stand together in discourse.

Corre's observation is correct but requires further precision because it applies equally well to lexical and to auxiliary compound verbs. Even so, the interaction of AVCs and coordinate structures sheds further light on the AVC itself. Conjunction combines several expressions of the same categorial status to create a coordinate structure; two expressions of different categorial status typically may not conjoin. Tamil examples below show that though they both may be morphological verbs, auxiliary and auxiliate belong to different logical or syntactic categories and cannot be reduced to, paraphrased by or derived from coordinate structures.[29]

Example (136a) contains two sentences, each with its own AVC, *pōṭṭu vaittu irukkiṟāḷ* 'she has put out X for subsequent use' and *ūṟṟi vaittu irukkiṟāḷ* 'she has poured (water) for subsequent use', respectively. Both AVCs are nested, with *irukka* 'be' (Chapter 6) as the auxiliary in the outer AVC and *vaikka* 'place' (Chapter 7) as

29 This incidentally argues against the proposal that an auxiliary verb system arises as certain verbs in coordinate structures lose their lexical context and coalesce with the verb in the other conjunct, forming an AVC.

the auxiliary of the inner AVC. The restriction against more than one finite verb form per sentence prohibits the bald conjoining of the two auxiliaries *irukkiṟāḷ* 'she is', both of which are finite, by the clitic =*um* 'and, all'. So in the conjoined sentence in (136b), the first instance of *irukkiṟāḷ* is deleted while =*um* is attached to both instances of the nested auxiliary *vaittu*. Although the perfect tense marker

(136)a $_{S1}$[*ilai pōṭṭu vaittu irukkiṟāḷ*.] $_{S2}$[*taṇṇīr ūṟṟi vaittu irukkiṟāḷ*].
leaf put-CF place-CF be-PRS-3SF water pour-CF place-CF be-PRS-3SF
'She has set leaves (for a meal). She has poured the water (for a meal).'

b $_{S0}$[$_{S1}$[*ilai pōṭṭu vaitt=um* φ] $_{S2}$[*taṇṇīr ūṟṟi vaitt=um irukkiṟāḷ*]].
leaf put-CF place-CF=AND water pour-CF place-CF=AND be-PRS-3SF
'She has set leaves and (has) poured the water (for a meal).'

irukka is pronounced only in the last clause, its meaning is attributed to both clauses. This example illustrates an important restriction on conjoining auxiliaries in Tamil: they must be the same auxiliary.[30]

This pattern is repeated in (137a and b): two instances of auxiliary *koḷḷa* 'hold' are conjoined by =*um* 'and', and are nested in a larger AVC as a part of the auxiliate. Example (138) illustrates a different case in which two subordinate clauses have AVCs and have the attitudinal auxiliary *tolaikka* 'lose' in nonfinite form; both may be conjoined by =*um*.

(137)a $_{S1}$[*āṭi.k koṇṭu irukkiṟāḷ*.] $_{S2}$[*pāṭi.k koṇṭu irukkiṟāḷ*.]
dance-CF hold-CF be-PRS-3SF dance-CF hold-CF be-PRS-3SF
'She is dancing. She is singing.'

b $_{S0}$[$_{S1}$[*āṭi.k koṇṭ=um* φ] $_{S2}$[*pāṭi.k koṇṭ=um irukkiṟāḷ*]].
dance-CF hold-CF=AND sing-CF hold-CF=AND be-PRS-3SF
'She is dancing and (is) singing.'

(138) $_{S0}$[$_{S1}$[*pala taṭavai eḻuti.t tolaitt=um*] $_{S2}$[*paṇam koṭuttu.t tolaitt=um*]
many times write-CF lose-CF=AND money give-CF lose-CF=AND
faiyal nakara.v illai].
file-NOM move-INF IND-NEG
'Even though I wrote so goddamn many times and gave so goddamn much money, the file didn't move off his desk.'

Attempts to conjoin an auxiliary (139a) to a homophonous, nonauxiliated verb in (139b) by means of =*um* ... =*um* 'and ... and', as in (139c), yield ungrammatical results because the two tokens of *vaittu* 'placing'in these sentences serve different categorial functions: the auxiliary has an inflectional, the auxiliate a denotational function.

30 There appear to be no Tamil counterparts to the English Right-Node Raising construction *Bill may, and Bernie must, go to the convention*, where two different modal auxiliaries have been conjoined.

(139)a *nāṉ oru kaṭitam eẕuti vaittu irukkiṟēṉ.*
I-NOM one letter-NOM write-CF place-CF be-PRS-1S
'I have written a letter (for subsequent use).'

b *nāṉ oru kaṭitam mēcaikku mēlē vaittu irukkiṟēṉ.*
I-NOM one letter-NOM table-DAT on place-CF be-PRS-1S
'I have placed a letter on the table.'

c * *nāṉ oru kaṭitam eẕuti vaitt=um mēcaikku mēlē vaitt=um irukkiṟēṉ.*
I-NOM one letter-NOM write-CF place-CF=AND table-DAT on place-CF=AND be-PRS-1S
'I have written a letter for subsequent use and place it on the table.'

All indicative auxiliaries except *viṭa* 'leave' and *taḷḷa* 'push' conform to this pattern. In (140a) *taḷḷi* 'pushing' functions as a simple, nonauxiliated verb; in (140b) as an auxiliary. When the two are conjoined in (140c), the resulting sentence is a (grammatical) pun, one that derives its humor from juxtaposing two homophonous but syntactically different forms of *taḷḷa*. The order must as in (140c), and cannot be reversed, as the unacceptability of (140d) shows. Example (141) is also considered a pun; like (140c), the order of the two verbs must be simple, nonauxiliated verb followed by auxiliary.

(140)a *katavai.t taḷḷi.k kōpattai.k kāṭṭiṉāṉ.*
door-ACC push-CF anger-ACC show-PST-3SM
'He showed his anger by slamming the door.'

b *cikkireṭṭu ūti.t taḷḷi.k kōpattai.k kāṭṭiṉāṉ.*
cigarette blow-CF push-CF anger-ACC show-pst-3SM
'He show his anger by chain-smoking.'

c *katavai.t taḷḷi.y=um cikkireṭṭu ūti.t taḷḷi.y=um kōpattai.k kāṭṭiṉāṉ.*
door-ACC push-CF-AND cigarette blow-CF push-CF=AND anger-ACC show-PST-3SM
'He showed his anger by slamming the door and by chain-smoking.'

d * *cikkireṭṭu ūti.t taḷḷi.y=um katavai.t taḷḷi.y=um kōpattai.k kāṭṭiṉāṉ.*

(141) *maṉacu viṭṭ=um colli viṭṭ=um pōṉāṉ.*
mind leave-CF=AND tell-CF leave-CF=AND go-PST-3SM
'He opened his mind and spoke freely.'

While the order in these two puns is invariable, in coordinate structures, the order of conjuncts may ordinarily be reversed; (142) is thus an acceptable alternant for (137b).

(142) *pāṭi.k koṇṭu=um āṭi.k koṇṭ=um irukkiṟāḷ.*
sing-CF hold-CF=AND dance-CF hold-CF=AND be-PRS-3SF
'She is singing and dancing.'

So aside from the two verbs noted above, no auxiliary may conjoin with its homophonous, nonauxiliated "main" verb. This restriction suggests that AVCs do not derive from coordinate structures, and that auxiliate and auxiliary have different status, as graphically illustrated in Figure 4.5.

Reduplication and the AVC

Annamalai (1982: 31-35) appeals to Reduplication to distinguish AVCs from compound clauses. Reduplication copies a nonfinite verb form,[31] creating an output with an iterative or distributive meaning. Finite verbs do not undergo this process; and while Reduplication applies to infinitives and conjunctive forms alike, only the latter are treated here. Examples (143b) and (144b), Annamalai's examples (8a and b), respectively, illustrate this process. Both contain compound clauses, so the reduplicated verb is a nonfinite verb without an auxiliary.

(143)a *māṇavarkaḷ pustakaṅkaḷai eṭuttu.p paṭittārkaḷ.*
students-NOM books-ACC take-CF read-PST-3P
'The students took the books and read them.'

b *māṇavarkaḷ pustakaṅkaḷai eṭuttu eṭuttu.p paṭittārkaḷ.*
students-NOM books-ACC take-CF take-CF read-PST-3P
'The students kept taking the books and reading them.'

(144)a *jaṉaṅkaḷ viṣattai.k kuṭittu.c cettuppōṉārkaḷ.*
people-NOM poison-ACC drink-CF die-PST-3P
'People took poison and died.'

b *jaṉaṅkaḷ viṣattai.k kuṭittu.k kuṭittu.c cettuppōṉārkaḷ.*
people-NOM poison-ACC drink-CF drink-CF die-PST-3P
'One after another, people kept taking poison and dying.'

Lexical compounds readily undergo Reduplication, as (145b) and (146b) show; the first verb is the one reduplicated since it is always nonfinite and because the second may occur in contexts that require it to be finite.

(145)a *avaṉ ōṭi vantāṉ.*
he-NOM run-CF come-PST-3SM
'He came running.'

b *avaṉ ōṭi ōṭi vantāṉ.*
he-NOM run-CF run-CF come-PST-3SM
'He came running and running.'

(146)a *avaḷ nimirntu uṭkārntāḷ.*
she-NOM lift-CF sit-PST-3SF
'She sat up straight.'

31 Reduplication may apply iteratively; however, for the sake of brevity, only examples with two verb forms are shown. Forms such as *ōṭi ōṭi ōṭi uṭkalanta cōti* 'running, running, running, (searching for) the light within…', with three forms, are common in literature and speech. Reduplication applies to whole words, not parts of a word as in some languages. It is not yet clear whether this process is the same one which applies to nouns to generate distributive compounds.

b *avaḷ nimirntu nimirntu uṭkārntāḷ.*
she-NOM lift-CF lift-CF sit-PST-3SF
'She sat up straight many times (fidgeting).'

All lexical compound verbs, except fixed idiomatic ones like *piṭittu viṭa* 'massage' and *eẓuntu irukka* 'get up', exhibit this pattern. However, indicative AVCs present a different picture. First, the auxiliary never reduplicates, even when it occurs in a content that permits nonfinite verb morphology. Second, with three possible exceptions, the auxiliate in an indicative AVC is never reduplicated.

(147)a *puttakattai.p paṭittu irukkiṟāṉ.*
book-ACC read-CF be-PRS-3SM
'He has read the book'.

b * *puttakattai.p paṭittu.p paṭittu irukkiṟāṉ.*
book-ACC read-CF read-CF be-PRS-3SM
'He has read and read that book.'

(148)a *avaṉ kōyilukku.p paṇam koṭuttu aẓutāṉ.*
he-NOM temple-DAT money give-CF cry-PST-3SM
'He grudgingly gave money to the temple.'

b * *avaṉ kōyilukku.p paṇam koṭuttu.k koṭuttu aẓutāṉ.*
he-NOM temple-DAT money give-CF give-CF cry-PST-3SM
'He kept grudgingly giving money to the temple.'

(149)a *kaṭitam vantu āyiṟṟu.*
letters-NOM come-CF become-PST-3SN
'Letters came, as expected.'

b * *kaṭitam vantu vantu āyiṟṟu.*
letters-NOM come-CF come-CF become-PST-3SN
'Letters kept coming, as expected.'

These examples permit formulation a more explicit condition on the application of Reduplication: it must apply to a nonfinite verb that is immediately dominated by an S node (Figure 4.3). As a result, any V node that is directly dominated by another V node, as in the AVC, is ineligible. This same pattern was seen above in Scrambling and CF-Postposing where the first verb in a structure may undergo some rule if and only if it is directly dominated by an S node. The proposed surface structure for indicative AVCs has a (derived) V node that dominates both the main and auxiliary verbs, blocking them from undergoing any of these rules.

In our corpus of 25 indicative auxiliaries, three permit Reduplication of the auxiliate: *tolaiya* 'get lost' (but not effective *tolaikka* 'lose'), *taḷḷa* 'push' and, seldom, *viṭa* 'leave'. The preponderance of the corpus indicates, however, that the auxiliate and auxiliary in an AVC are directly dominated by a V node, not an S node.

(150)a *contakkāraṉ vantu tolaintāṉ.*
relative-NOM come-CF lose+AF-PST-3SM
'My relative came, damn it.'

b *contakkāraṉ vantu vantu tolaintāṉ.*
relative-NOM come-CF come-CF lose+AF-PST-3SM
'My relative kept visiting and visiting, damn it.'

Reduplication of modal AVCs

Though Fedson (1981) holds that indicative and modal AVCs exhibit no major differences, the two sharply contrast in their ability to reduplicate the auxiliary verb. For example, many modals have emphatic reduplicated forms, e.g., *māṭṭa.v=ē māṭṭēṉ* 'I absolutely will not' from *māṭṭēṉ* 'I will not'; *muṭiuya.v=ē muṭiyātu* 'it really cannot' from *muṭiyātu* 'it cannot'; and *illa.v=ē illai* 'it really is/was not' from *illai* 'not be'.[32] No indicative auxiliary permits such Reduplication: there are thus no reduplicated indicative auxiliaries, such as **viṭa.v=ē viṭṭatu* 'it really did' from *viṭṭatu* 'it did' or **tolaiya.v=ē tolaintatu* 'it really got lost' from *tolaintatu* 'it got lost'. If our stipulation that a reduplicated verb must be directly dominated by a S node, and not a V node, holds up under further scrutiny, this would be proof that the surface structure of modal AVCs does not resemble that of indicative AVCs, where a single V node dominates both the main and auxiliary.[33] Reduplication shows us that despite their apparent surface similarities, indicative and modal AVCs do have notable syntactic differences.

Particle insertion and the AVC

Much of the evidence considered so far indicates a strong grammatical bond between the auxiliate and auxiliary in an indicative AVC, one so robust that we might ask whether they are not really two bound forms in a larger synthetic formation instead of two independent components in a periphrastic verb. The two elements of an AVC may, however, be separated by the insertion of clitic particles, in which the auxiliate hosts the clitic. The clitics that may be inserted include *=ē* 'even', *=tāṉ* 'indeed', *=um* 'and', interrogative *=ā* and, for some speakers, *=vēṟu* 'also' and *=illaiyā* 'isn't it' (spoken *=illā*). In (151a) the particle *=tāṉ* 'indeed' separates the main verb *vantu* 'coming' from the perfect tense auxiliary *irukkiṟār* 'he has V-ed'; in (151b) the particle *=ē* 'even' separates the main verb *eẓuti* 'writing' from the auxiliary verb of accelerative aspect *taḷḷiṉāṉ* 'he pushed'. Since clitics combine only with full words, not bound forms, i.e., they are not infixes, this shows that the main and auxiliary verbs are morphologically independent forms.

32 The emphatic differs from the homophonous infinitive: *māṭṭ-* has an emphatic form *māṭṭa(v.=ē)*, but no infinitive. The emphatic does not appear in other contexts that govern the infinitive. The same holds for *illai*.

33 If anything, the surface structure of these modal AVCs would resemble more the underlying structure of the indicative AVC in which the main and auxiliary verbs are in different clauses and both are directly dominated by different S nodes. If this holds true for modal AVCs at the point in their derivation where Reduplication applies, then their auxiliaries would satisfy the rule's structural description.

Table 4.1 Insertion of clitic particles between auxiliate and auxiliary

Auxiliary	=*ē* 'even'	=*tāṉ* 'indeed'	=*um* 'and'	=*ā* 'interrogative'
irukka 'be'	✓	✓	✓	✓
koḷḷa 'hold'	*	*	✓	*
koṇṭu irukka 'be V-ing'	✓	✓	✓	✓
viṭa 'leave' (WT)	✓	✓	✓	✓
viṭa 'leave' (ST)	*	*	*	*
āyiṟṟu 'become'	*	*	✓	*
vaikka 'place'	*	✓	✓	✓
vara 'come'	WT ✓			
	ST *	✓	✓	✓
koṭukka 'give'	WT ✓			
	ST *	✓	✓	✓
tīrkka 'exhaust'	*	✓	✓	✓
oẓiya 'purge'	✓	?	?	✓
pōṭa 'put'	✓	✓	✓	✓
aẓa 'cry'	✓	✓	✓	✓
vaẓiya 'drip'	✓	✓	✓	✓
kiẓiya 'get torn'	*	✓	*	✓
kiẓikka 'tear'	*	*	*	*
pōka 'go'	✓	✓	*	✓
taḷḷa 'push'	✓	*	*	✓

Key

WT Written Tamil, ST Spoken Tamil.
✓ grammatical, * ungrammatical, ? questionable.

(151)a *appā vantu=tāṉ irukkiṟār.*
father-NOM come-CF=INDEED be-PRS-3H
'Father has too come!'

b *oru mācattil oru nāvalai eẓuti.y=ē taḷḷiṉāṉ.*
one month-LOC one novel-ACC write-CF=EVEN write-PST-3SM
'He even wrote a novel in a single month.'

Clitic particles are never inserted into a sequence of two bound morphs; instead, they follow all inflectional suffixes on the host, here the auxiliate. The future form *varuvāṉ* 'he will come' consists of three bound morphs: the verb stem *varu-* 'come', the future tense marker *-v-* and the third person masculine singular personal ending *-āṉ*. The insertion of the clitic =*tāṉ* 'indeed' anywhere in this simple verb would result in an ill-formed word: **varu=tāṉ.u.v-āṉ* is not a possible word since tmesis is not found in Tamil.[34] Different auxiliaries permit or prohibit the insertion of different clitics. The cooccurrence possibilities for sixteen auxiliaries and one complex auxiliary are tabulated above with four clitics in Table 4.1.

34 Tamil clitics are thus not infixes; they do not behave, for example, as infixable particles in English, which permit *out-bloody-rageous* from *outrageous* or *fan-frickin'-tastic* from *fantastic*.

These clitics then are the only grammatical material that may interrupt the sequence of auxiliate and auxiliary in a Tamil indicative AVC.[35] As Chapter 1 notes, this is a language-specific property; English, for example, permits the interpolation of a considerably wider range of material within its AVCs.

Auxiliary Formation and the AVC

If the node directly dominating the auxiliate and auxiliary in an indicative AVC belongs to the category of verbs, it should naturally undergo any process that apply to verbs. Auxiliary Formation is itself one such process: it takes as its input two verb forms to create a periphrastic verb, the AVC. The resulting compound, which belongs to the category of (derived) verbs, should therefore be able to undergo another application of Auxiliary Formation. This predicts the existence of complex AVCs, which have one AVC nested inside another as one of the larger AVC's component parts. Since every AVC has a denotational function, when nested inside a larger AVC as a component part, it will function as the auxiliate because of that denotational function.[36] Examples of such nesting have already appeared; additional ones are given in (152).[37]

(152)a *avaḷ kuẓantaikku.k kaṟiyai* $_{\text{AVC0}}[$ $_{\text{AVC1}}[$*meṉṟu koṭuttu*] *irukkiṟāḷ*].
she-NOM child-DAT meat-ACC chew-CF give-CF be-PRS-3SF
'She has chewed the meat for the child.'

b *avar uyilil* $_{\text{AVC0}}[$ $_{\text{AVC1}}[$ $_{\text{AVC2}}[$ $_{\text{AVC3}}[$*eẓuti vaittu.k*] *kiẓittu.k*] *koṇṭu*] *iruntār*].
he-NOM will-ACC write-CF place-CF tear-CF hold-CF be-PST-3H
'Oh sure, he's written me into his will, sure.'

c *tapālkāraṉukku oru rūpāy* $_{\text{AVC0}}[$ $_{\text{AVC1}}[$*koṭuttu aẓutu.t*] *tolaittēṉ*].
postman-DAT one rupee give-CF cry-CF lost-PST-1S
'I gave that damn mailman a rupee, though I didn't want to (now others will come around for money).'

d *avaṉ tāṉiyāka niṟka muṭiyum eṉṟu*
he-NOM self stand-INF be.able-FUT-3SN say-CF
$_{\text{AVC0}}[$ $_{\text{AVC1}}[$ $_{\text{AVC2}}[$*kāṇpittu.k koṇṭ=ē*] *tāṉ vantu*] *irukkiṟāṉ*].
show-CF hold-CF-EMP indeed come-CF be-PRS-3SM
'He has been showing me all along that he can stand on his own.'

35 The inability of even clitics to appear between auxiliate and auxiliary in some AVCs, e.g., those with auxiliary *viṭa* 'leave' in spoken Tamil, may well be a prelude to an impending change in the verbal system, one which would in effect incorporate the auxiliary as a bound morpheme. Such changes are noted in Steever (1993). For the present, however, the WFRs for Tamil verbs, as well as the alternation with the diglossic high variety, continue to motivate a word boundary between auxiliary and auxiliate.

36 A further prediction of this model is that auxiliaries should not be able to nest inside one another.

37 This is one instance where the auxiliate differs significantly from the traditional term main verb, as noted in Chapter 1. An auxiliate may itself be internally complex, consisting of multiply nested AVCs while one cannot speak about main verbs in such a way.

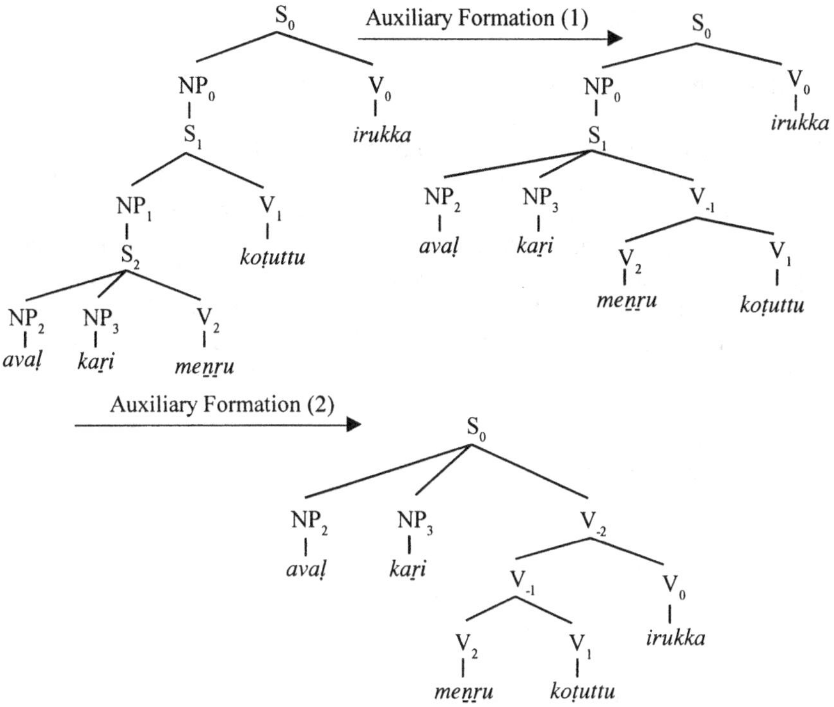

Figure 4.8 Derivation of a nested AVC.

Take (152a) where the AVC *meṉṟu koṭuttu* 'chewing for someone's behalf' is nested within the larger AVC, *meṉṟu koṭuttu irukkiṟāḷ* 'she has chewed for some someone's behalf', as its auxiliate. Figure 4.8 illustrates the derivation of (152), omitting the explicit benefactive phrase.

The process of Auxiliary Formation applies cyclically in Figure 4.8, first targeting S_2, then targeting S_1. As the derived structure shows, *koṭukka* 'give' is the auxiliary of the AVC *meṉṟu koṭukka*, which is labeled as V_{-1}. That constituent in turn serves as auxiliate of the AVC *meṉṟu koṭuttu irukka*, labeled V_{-2}. In the lower AVC, *koṭukka* conveys benefactive voice; in the upper AVC, *irukka* conveys perfect tense. Since V_{-1} is a member of the category of (syntactically derived) verbs, it can participate in any process which targets verbs as its operand. The examples in (152b-d) may also be analyzed as recurring nestings. No matter how complex these AVCs become, there is only one denotational function associated with the topmost AVC, projected from the most deeply embedded auxiliate. This forces us to analyze the so-called complex auxiliary *koṇṭu irukka* 'be V-ing' as two successively embedded auxiliary verbs since at no stage in their derivation do they form a constituent which excludes an auxiliate. Thus, such sequences of two auxiliaries does not constitute a separate auxiliary (as Herring 1991 suggests), and their meaning is to be construed as a function of their individual meanings. The order among multiple indicative auxiliaries in a complex AVC and the factors that govern this order are taken up in Chapter 5.

ki-echo Formation and the AVC

ki-echo Formation has been discussed in comparative Dravidian phonology, e.g., Emeneau (1938, 1939), and in the generative literature, e.g., Steever (1988: 48-50). Its most insightful treatment for Tamil is Keane (2001). Before demonstrating its relevance to the indicative AVC, we must discuss some of its properties. *ki*-echo Formation is in some ways a variation on the process of Reduplication; however, the *ki*-echo form, instead of being an exact copy of the word on which it is based, replaces the initial syllable of the echoed word with the syllable *ki*- or *kī*-, depending as the initial syllable of the echoed word is short or long. For example, the *ki*-echo word *kīṭu* in (153b) is Chomsky-adjoined to the word it echoes, viz. *māṭu* 'cattle': the resulting compound functions syntactically as a single noun.

(153)a *māṭu varum.*
cattle-NOM come-FUT-3N
'Some cows will come.'
b *māṭu kīṭu varum.*
cattle-NOM *ki*-ECHO come-FUT-3N
'Some cows or the like will come.'

(154)a *paṇam koṭuppāṉ.*
money-NOM give-FUT-3SM
'He will give some money.'
b *paṇam kiṇam koṭuppāṉ.*
money-NOM *ki*-ECHO give-FUT-3SM
'He will give some money or something.'

ki-echo Formation applies to verbs as well, targeting both finite and nonfinite forms. The finite verb *uṭaittāy* 'you broke' in (155a) serves as the basis for the echo compound *uṭaittāy kiṭaittāy* in (155b).[38]

(155)a *pāttirattai uṭṭaittāy eṉṟāl tōlai urippēṉ.*
pots-ACC break-PST-2s say-CND kin-ACC peel-FUT-1s
'If you broke the pots, I'll skin you alive.'
b *pāttirattai uṭṭaittāy kiṭaittāy eṉṟāl tōlai urippēṉ.*
pots-ACC break-PST-2s *ki*-PST-2s say-CND skin-ACC peel-FUT-1s
'If you broke the pots or did any such dumb thing, I'll skin you alive.'

Words beginning in either *ki*- or *kī*- do not undergo *ki*-echo Formation because the result would be indistinguishable from an ordinary reduplicated compound: *kiḷi kiḷi* 'parrots', a compound based on *kiḷi* 'parrots', can only mean 'parrots, parrot after parrot', not 'parrots and the like'. In such instances, some speakers may form echo words with the alternative syllables *hi*- and *hī*-, giving the echo com-

38 Such compounds are the only example I know in Modern Tamil of serial verbs (see Chapter 2). Unlike Reduplication, this process may apply to finite verb forms.

pound *kiḷi hiḷi* 'parrots and the like'; many speakers, however, prefer not to form any echo compound with these alternative syllables.

ki-echo Formation is best suited to modal contexts such as future tense, conditional, negative and interrogative clauses; it does not readily occur in such indicative contexts as (156). This restriction is semantic and global, not strictly morphological or local: example (155b) has an echo compound verb inflected for the past tense form, but it is embedded directly under the conditional verb *eṉṟāl* 'if (say)', a modal form.

(156) * *māṭu* *kīṭu* *vantatu.*
cattle-NOM *ki*-ECHO come-PST-3N
'Some cattle-shmattle came.'

In analyzing the cognate construction in Toda, Emeneau (1938: 41ff.) makes the following remarks about the meaning of the echo compound verb.

> The function of the formation is to refer to a specimen which the speaker does not care to identify from among a hypothesized collection of identical discrete entities of infinite number or from a hypothesized infinite extension of a non-discrete handleable entity .... This verb formation is found in negative statements, prohibitions, and questions .... The function of the forms is, parallel to the function of the noun formations, to denote a specimen, unidentified by the speaker, of the action denoted by the verb, separated from a hypothesized infinite extension of the verbal action, discrete extension if the verb stem refers to an action regarded as punctual, non-discrete if to an action regarded as durative.

The Tamil *ki*-echo Formation produces a similar meaning, with two distinct components. First is its distributive meaning: the compound means "entities or actions from a general range, of which the echoed word is a random example." Second is a pejorative meaning to the effect that the speaker cannot be bothered to characterize the entity or action any more precisely (see Steever 1993).

The following examples show how *ki*-echo Formation interacts with compound clauses. The first verb in a sequence may undergo *ki*-echo Formation if that sequence constitutes a compound clause (157b, 158b).

(157)a *maḻai* *peytu* *nel* *viḷaintat=ā?*
rain-NOM rain-CF paddy-NOM result-PST-3N=INT
'So it rained, did the paddy grow?'

b *maḻai* *peytu* *kiytu* *nel* *viḷaintat=ā?*
rain-NOM rain-CF *ki*-ECHO paddy-NOM result-PST-3N=INT
'So it rained and everything, did the paddy grow?'

(158)a *pāmpu* *kaṭittu.p* *paiyaṉ* *cettuppōṉāṉ* *eṉṟāl* *yārukku.p* *poṟuppu?*
snake-NOM bite-CF boy-NOM die-PST-3SM say-CND who-DAT responsibility-NOM
'If the boy died because a snake bit him, whose responsibility is it?'

b *pāmpu katittu.k kiṭittu.p paiyaṉ cettuppōṉāṉ eṉṟāl*
snake-NOM bite-CF *ki*-ECHO boy-NOM die-PST-3SM say-CND
yārukku.p poṟuppu?
who-DAT responsibility-NOM
'If the boy died because a snake bit him or something, whose responsibility is it?'

ki-echo Formation also applies to lexical compound verbs so that the first verb in a lexical compound may undergo this process. Examples (159b) illustrates the echoed version of (159a); similarly, (160b) illustrates the echoed version of (160a).

(159)a *ōṭi.p pōkātē!*
run-CF go-NEG-IMP
'Don't go running.'

b *ōṭi.k kīṭi.p pōkātē!*
run-CF *ki*-ECHO go-NEG-IMP
'Don't go running or anything.'

(160)a *eṭṭi.p pārkka.k kūṭātu!*
dart-CF look.at-INF must-NEG-3N
'You mustn't peek.'

b *eṭṭi.k kiṭṭi.p pārkka.k kūṭātu!*
dart-CF *ki*-ECHO look.at-INF must-NEG-3N
'You mustn't peek or anything.'

In an indicative AVC, the auxiliary verb never undergoes *ki*-echo Formation. This may be attributed to the fact that the echoed verb must have a denotational function, in keeping with Emeneau's observations that felicitous use of this construction requires reference to a particular action or entity within the general range denoted by the echo compound. Since the auxiliary has no denotational function, it may not participate in this process. Neither *irukka* 'be' in (161a) nor *tolaiya* 'get lost' in (161b) undergoes *ki*-echo Formation when it serves as an auxiliary in an AVC, although, of course, as nonauxiliated verbs they could.

(161)a **avaṉ puttakattai.p paṭittu irukkiṟāṉ kirukkiṟāṉ eṉṟāl …*
he-NOM book-ACC read-CF be-PRS-3SM *ki*-ECHO say-CND
'If he has or shmas read that book...'

b **contakkāraṉ vantu tolaintāṉ kilaintāṉ eṉṟāl …*
relative-NOM come-CF lose-PST-3SM *ki*-ECHO say-CND
'If my relative came, damn it, shmamn it.'

While no auxiliary may undergo *ki*-echo Formation, some auxiliates may, and which ones do appears to be determined by the identity of the auxiliary it combines with. Fifteen auxiliaries provide clear evidence for this interaction. In our corpus the following eight allow their auxiliate to undergo this process (162): *irukka* 'be', *vaikka* 'place', *tolaiya* 'get lost', *pōṭa* 'put', *oẓiya* 'purge', *tīrkka* 'exhaust', *pōka* 'go', and *koṭukka* 'give'; the remainder do not (163): *viṭa* 'leave',[39] *koḷḷa* 'hold', *āyiṟṟu* 'become', *vara* 'come', *taḷḷa* 'push', *kiẓikka* 'tear' and *aẓa* 'cry'. No discernible pattern has emerged from this set; data on the remainder is inconclusive.

(162)a *colli.k killi iruntāl kaṣṭam varum.*
tell-CF *ki*-ECHO be-CND difficulty-NOM come-FUT-3N
'If he said something or did anything else, there'll be a problem.'

b *vantu kintu tolaippāṉ.*
come-CF *ki*-ECHO lose-EF-FUT-3SM
'He'll come here or do some fool thing.'

c *kaṭitam eẓuti.k kiẓuti vaittāl faiyal nakarum.*
letter write-CF *ki*-ECHO place-COND file-NOM move-FUT-3N
'If I wrote them a letter or did something, the file would move.'

(163)a * *pāṭṭi katai colli.k killi vantāl bōr aṭikkum.*
grandmother-NOM story tell-cf *ki*-ECHO come-COND bore strike-FUT-3N
'If grandmother went on telling stories or anything, I'd be bored stiff.'

b * *paṇam koṭuttu.k kiṭuttu aẓa.v illai eṉṟāl eṉṉai.c cummāka viṭa māṭṭāṉ.*
money give-cf *ki*-ECHO cry-INF NEG say-CND I-ACC alone leave-INF FUT-NEG-3SM
'If I don't give him some money or something (for all the good it will do), he won't leave me alone.'

ki-echo Formation therefore reminds us how much variation the set of indicative auxiliaries embraces. The failure of any auxiliary verb to undergo *ki*-echo Formation is further evidence that it has no denotational function, and cannot therefore serve as the basis of an echo compound.

Further grammatical phenomena

Closer study of the grammatical properties of individual AVCs will put us in a better position to hone the meaning of the various auxiliaries. That meaning may in turn affect the grammatical behavior of the AVC so that it does not behave uniformly with other AVCs even though it otherwise patterns with them over against other constructions, such as compound clauses.

For example, only auxiliaries with an imperfective or durative meaning, such as *vara* 'come' (Chapter 7) or *kiẓiya* 'be torn' (Chapter 8) can take the durative suffixal complex *-(k)kai.y-il* 'while (X) was V-ing'; on the other hand, auxiliaries with a punctual meaning such as *viṭa* 'leave' cannot.

39 Keane (2001: 97) notes that her subjects permitted *ki*-echo Formation of *viṭa* if the entire AVC were echoed, e.g., *pāṭiṭṭu* 'after singing' (<*pāṭi viṭṭu*) could be acceptably echoed as *pāṭiṭṭu kīṭiṭṭu*, which would in our transcription correspond to *pāṭi viṭṭu kīṭi viṭṭu* 'after singing or the like'. This pattern did not appear in our original data.

(164)a *cōẓāṉ āṇṭu varu-kai.y-il...*
Chola-NOM rule-CF come-while
'While the Cholas were ruling, ...'
b * *avaṉ colli viṭu-kai.y-il...*
he-NOM tell-CF leave-while
? 'While he was doing saying,...'

Conversely, only punctual auxiliaries may occur in grammatical frames that have a punctual meaning, e.g., in the adnominal form plus *uṭaṉē* 'as soon as V-ed', or verbal noun plus *=um* 'id.'; nonpunctual auxiliaries cannot.

(165)a *avaṉ colli vi.ṭ-ṭ-a uṭaṉē...*
he-NOM tell-CF leave-PST-ADN immediacy
'As soon as he did tell...'
b *avaṉ colli viṭṭat=um...*
he-NOM tell-CF leave-PST-VN=AND
'As soon as he did say...'
c ?* *avaṉ colli.k koṇṭu iruntat=um...*
he-NOM tell-CF hold-CF be- PST-VN=AND
'As soon as he was speaking...'

Further individual variation is found in Chapters 5-8. For example, Chapters 5 and 8 show that attitudinal auxiliaries do not usually occur in the first or second persons without a marked rhetorical effect, the basis for which appears to be pragmatically motivated.

DIFFERENCES BETWEEN MODAL AND INDICATIVE AVCs

Auxiliaries in questions and answers

Reduplication (p. 132) has already illustrated one way in which modal and indicative AVCs may differ; a further difference is discussed here. Unlike English auxiliaries, Tamil indicative auxiliaries do not usually occur without their auxiliate, so that Tamil lacks direct counterparts to English forms such as *John was going home and Bill was, too* (i.e., there is no VP-deletion in Tamil). The strong bond between auxiliate and auxiliary in the Tamil indicative AVC discourages such patterns.

(166) *avaṉ vantu irukkiṟāṉ=ā? *(vantu) irukkiṟāṉ.*
he-NOM come-CF be-PRS-3SM=INT come-CF be-PRS-3SM
'Has he come? He has.'

The stigmata in example (166) shows that the reply to the question is grammatical only if the auxiliate *vantu* 'coming' is present. Only two indicative auxiliaries are exceptions to this pattern of grammatical behavior: *āyiṟṟu* 'become' and *kiẓikka* 'tear' (but not its affective counterpart *kiẓiya* 'get torn').

(167) *cāppiṭṭu āyiṟṟ=ā ammā? āyiṟṟu.*
eat-CF become-PST-3N=INT mother become-PST-3N
'Have you eaten yet, ma'am? I have.'

What is exceptional for indicative auxiliaries, however, is commonplace for modal auxiliaries: they need not occur with their main verbs in such contexts. Fedson (1981: 202) cites the following example (168a) in which the main verb *taṭavi koṭukka* 'stroke' has been deleted from a modal AVC *taṭavi koṭukka vēṇṭum* 'must strike', leaving behind only the modal auxiliary verb *vēṇṭum* 'must'. Examples such as (168b) are commonly encountered in everyday speech.

(168)a *kālai vēṇṭum āṉāl taṭavi koṭukkaṭṭum=ā pāṭṭi.*
leg-ACC must-FUT-3N become-CND stoke give-INF-may-INT grandmother
'If you want me to, grandmother, I'll massage your leg.'

b *pōka muṭiyum=ā? muṭiyum.*
go-INF be.able-FUT-3N=INT be.able-FUT-3N
'Can (you) go? (I) can.'

These differences show that we cannot equate the grammar of the modal AVC with that of the indicative AVC; their differences go much deeper than simply the presence of the conjunctive versus the infinitive.

SUMMARY

One of this chapter's primary results is that we can now analyze the indicative AVC's syntax without having constantly to specify the lexical identity of an auxiliary verb each time a question of the AVC's syntax arises. Its syntactic properties are not merely projections of individual auxiliaries' lexical properties, but characteristics of an independently motivated construction in which individual lexemes may appear as auxiliaries. The claim that the indicative AVC has a syntax of its own gains support from the grammatical observations and arguments in this chapter that distinguish it from constructions with which it might otherwise be confused: coordinate structures, matrix-complement structures, lexical compounds and modal auxiliary compound verbs. For example, strict subcategorization, Causation, Negation, Clefting, Right Dislocation and Reduplication distinguish the behavior of indicative AVC from that of coordinate and matrix-complement structures. Scrambling, CF-Postposing, Reduplication, *ki*-echo Formation, the order of modifier and modified, and selection restrictions distinguish the behavior of indicative AVC from lexical compound verbs. Finally, Reduplication and the ability of the auxiliary verb to stand alone distinguish the indicative from the modal AVC.

Taken together, these rules also reveal that the indicative AVC behaves as it if has two different constituent structures, one that groups the AVC's auxiliate and auxiliary together and one that groups the AVC's auxiliate and satellites together but excludes the auxiliary. To reconcile these two analyses, a derivation was proposed to link an underlying with a corresponding surface structure. Certain arguments pointed to the underlying structure proposed in Figure 4.5: selection restrictions, strict subcategorization, S-deletion, Conjunction and *ki*-echo Formation support the conclusion that auxiliate and auxiliary are in fact generated in different clauses. Accordingly, the two would appear to belong to different logical categories: the auxiliate combines with satellites such as NPs to form an S, while the auxiliary combines with an S to form another S. Buttressing this underlying categorial difference are arguments from Conjunction, Relative Clause Formation, Negation and Clefting, which show that auxiliate and auxiliary cannot originate from a coordinate structure. The majority of the arguments that confirm this underlying structure are, not surprisingly, semantic in nature.

Other grammatical arguments point to the surface structure in Figure 4.6. Arguments adduced in Chapter 3 establish that both auxiliate and auxiliary belong to the morphological category of verbs. Particle Insertion and *ki*-echo Formation, which both refer to word boundaries, show that the auxiliate and auxiliary are independent words, not lexical base and suffix. Subject-Verb Agreement, Scrambling and Clefting indicate that the auxiliary occurs in the same surface clause as the AVC's subject.[40] Scrambling, Right Dislocation, Negation and Auxiliation show that the auxiliate and auxiliary cooccur in the same surface clause, behaving as a single grammatical unit labeled verb. The verbhood of the AVC may further be inferred from the fact that AVCs can themselves undergo Auxiliary Formation and are generated everywhere that simple, nonauxiliated verbs are (but see Chapter 5 for pragmatic restrictions). These rules pertain to relatively superficial levels of linguistic structure, such as word order (Scrambling, CF-Postposing), morphology (Subject-Verb Agreement) and postsyntactic word formation (*ki*-echo Formation). The evidence from *ki*-echo Formation and morphological causation suggests that auxiliaries have no denotational function; they further suggest, by the same token, that the auxiliate has a denotational function.

The process of Auxiliary Formation, as it applies in these derivations, conflates three separate syntactic processes. The first and most important of these three involves the Chomsky-adjunction of the auxiliate to the auxiliary; in Figure 4.4 this results in the creation of the derived V node V_{-1}. Since this step gives rise to a verb node that directly dominates the auxiliary and the auxiliate, it is the process most closely identified with Auxiliary Formation. Chomksy-adjunction is the most economical way to relate the two tree structures, it preserves the constituency of the host and it introduces no new node labels into the resulting tree structure. This step is accompanied by Tree Pruning, which eliminates now extraneous nodes and branches in the tree structure, and Lexical Insertion, which replaces semantic primes with word and morphemes of Tamil.

40 Since the last two rules cannot extract a NP from a subordinate clause at the time of their application, the subject and auxiliary must be in the same clause.

Neither the underlying nor the surface structure in the derivation in Figure 4.4 corresponds closely to the constituent structures proposed for compound clauses or lexical compound verbs, indicating that AVCs are syntactically distinct from these other Tamil structures.

The derivation in Figure 4.4 does not intrinsically rely on the model of AVCs developed in Chapter 1: the arguments in this chapter show that it can be independently established without direct reference to Benveniste's theory. However, the derivation inferred by deduction in the earlier chapter and the one demonstrated by induction here felicitously converge, with each approach confirming the other. The convergence between Benveniste's theory and our particular analysis of the Tamil indicative AVC suggests that the two are nontrivially related. Since on Benveniste's theory the AVC is a periphrastic verb, it can be expected to behave like a single unit under the application of certain rules, e.g., Scrambling, Clefting, Relative Clause Formation. These rules are sensitive to the V node that directly dominates the auxiliary and auxiliate, treating them as one unit, despite their internal elaboration. Auxiliary Formation assigns a denotational function to the main verb, an inflectional one to the auxiliary. This functional difference is bound to be reflected in the differential application of certain rules, e.g., auxiliates, but not auxiliaries, undergo *ki*-echo Formation which requires a denotational function, and auxiliaries, but not auxiliates, undergo Subject-Verb Agreement. It is not necessary, therefore, to describe each and every facet of the Tamil indicative AVC *sui generis*: much of its syntax follows from Benveniste's theory of Auxiliation as adjusted for the parameters of Tamil morphosyntax. In turn, by separating what is specific about the Tamil AVC from what is incidental may help us begin to abstract a general theory of Auxiliary Formation.

Our arguments incidentally uncover a degree of variation among the individual auxiliaries, distinguishing primarily between attitudinal and nonattitudinal auxiliaries, as evidence from Causation shows; further, some AVCs permit their main verbs to undergo *ki*-echo Formation, while others do not. Future research may wish to return to the program initiated in Annamalai (1982) to establish more precisely the cline according to which a given verb is more or less auxiliary-like.

Finally, this chapter has presented many different syntactic phenomena of Tamil, some of which have gone unremarked even in the specialist literature. It exploits the richness of Tamil syntax and, frustratingly, exposes the limited extent to which it has been recognized and studied. Some of the rules and phenomena discussed have already been mentioned in the literature, with differing degrees of thoroughness, e.g., Scrambling, Clefting, Causation; others have been proposed here for the first time, e.g., CF-Postposing, S-Deletion, Right Dislocation. Further, the relevance of many phenomena for the indicative AVC has never been adequately explored before, such as strict subcategorization, Scrambling and *ki*-echo Formation. And, importantly, this is the first time that the interaction between these different grammatical phenomena and the indicative AVC has been made explicit by referring it to a derivation. In doing so, it gives the syntax of the indicative AVC its proper due rather than viewing it as an extension of the lexical semantics of individual auxiliaries.

5 The external syntax of the Tamil indicative AVC

INTRODUCTION

From the claim that the AVC is a (periphrastic) verb form, it should follow that an AVC may occur in any grammatical context where a simple, nonauxiliated verb form may occur, and *vice versa*. Any departure from this correspondence between the distribution of AVCs and that of simple verbs would give rise to a skewing which would tend to compromise the analysis of the AVC as a verb, unless that discrepancy could be attributed to some independent grammatical principle.

Instances where AVCs and simple verbs do exhibit a skewed distribution in Tamil have already been observed. Chapter 4 provided us with evidence that simple, nonauxiliated verb forms occur in relative clauses more frequently than AVCs do (p. 123). Appeal was made there to the relative markedness of unmarked simple verbs and marked AVCs to explain the difference; doing so helped us preserve the general formulation of both Auxiliary Formation and Relative Clause Formation. Further grammatical contexts are identified in this chapter which permit simple verbs, but not their auxiliated counterparts. Conversely, contexts that require AVCs, but disallow their simple, nonauxiliated counterparts are also noted and analyzed. To maintain the generality of Auxiliary Formation, pragmatic and semantic explanations are offered to account for these skewed distributions.

Our model of Auxiliary Formation also claims that since the AVC belongs to the set of (derived) verbs, it should participate in the same grammatical processes as ordinary verbs. In particular, once formed, an AVC may itself undergo repeated applications of Auxiliation Formation to create multiply nested structures. Chapter 4 illustrated such multiple nestings, up to four levels deep (pp. 134-35). Impressive as they are, none of them approaches in complexity the multiple nestings that 25 indicative auxiliaries theoretically imply. There appear, however, to be limits on the nesting of AVCs; such a limitation, however, could also call into question both the category membership of the AVC and the generality of Auxiliary Formation. To account for those nestings that occur, and those that do not, we will have recourse not to syntactic factors, but to semantic ones, in particular to the verbal categories conveyed by AVCs in nested structures. Such explanations, if successful, will relieve us of the need to inscribe the order of auxiliaries directly into the rules that generate AVCs.

Pragmatic constraints on syntactic structures

On the hypothesis that the AVC is itself a verb, it should occur wherever a simple, nonauxiliated verb form can occur. Yet, data below indicate some apparent departures from this proposed correlation. Instead of attributing their disparity in distribution to a categorial difference between simple verbs and AVCs, we trace it to independent pragmatic factors.

The claim that pragmatics may influence how Tamil syntactic structures are construed is certainly not a new one. The following examples taken from Lindholm (1975) illustrate how context may influence Tamil sentences without necessarily involving rules of syntax. The sentences in (169a and b) conjoin two clauses by means of the conjunctive form; but despite the virtual structural identity of the two, speakers find (169b) more acceptable than (169a).

(169)a ?* $_{S0}$[$_{S1}$[*maẓai* *peytu*] $_{S2}$[*āṟṟil* *pattu* *pēr* *muẓuki.c*
rain-NOM rain-CF river-LOC ten people-NOM drown-CF
cettuppōṉārkaḷ]].
die-PST-3P
'It rained and ten people died by drowning in the river.'

b $_{S0}$[$_{S1}$[*romba* *maẓai* *peytu*] $_{S2}$[*āṟṟil* *pattu* *pēr* *muẓuki.c*
much rain-NOM rain-CF river-loc ten people-NOM drown-CF
cettuppōṉārkaḷ]].
die-PST-3P
'It rained heavily and ten people drowned in the river.'

As analyzed in Chapter 3, the conjunctive form marks indicative mood and joins two expressions only when the relation between them is perceived as real, rather than potential. The relation between normal rainfall and people drowning in a river is generally perceived to be circumstantial, and therefore not strong enough to motivate use of the conjunctive in (169a). This likely contributes to speakers' judgments of this sentence as questionable. But when ordinary rain is replaced by a heavy downpour, as during the monsoon season, flash floods can suddenly erupt, drowning those who happen to be camped along the river bank or in an otherwise dry riverbed. In such a situation, it is easier to construct a mental picture of events in which excessive rainfall is connected with people's deaths closely enough to motivate use of the conjunctive form. What makes this a pragmatic rather than a syntactic account of the difference in acceptability between (169a and b) is the fact the acceptability varies not with the syntactic structure involved but with the richness of contextual information, no matter what structures are used to convey it. The information that the rainfall is torrential could just as easily be conveyed by reduplicating the verb form *peytu* 'raining', giving rise to an intensive compound, as by intensifying the noun *maẓai* 'rain' with the modifier *romba* 'much' as in (169b). Thus, rather than inscribe all the possible morphosyntactic loopholes in the protocols that govern the distribution of the conjunctive, we may attribute them to factors that govern the use of the language.

DISCURSIVE AND NONDISCURSIVE SPEECH

The distribution of simple and periphrastic verbs in Tamil is in fact skewed; there are certain contexts that readily host simple verbs but not AVCs and, conversely but less commonly, contexts that host AVCs but not simple verbs. To explain this discrepancy without compromising the syntactic generality of Auxiliary Formation, appeal is made to pragmatic factors to classify these contexts and explain their differential behavior.

Benveniste (1959, 1966) draws a fundamental distinction between two kinds of utterance which will permit us to classify those frames that allow AVCs and those that do not. He observes that there are two basic means available to present an utterance (*modes d'énonciation*): discursive speech (*discours*) and nondiscursive speech (*récit historique*, historical narrative). He further shows that each is able to govern the inventory and distribution of grammatical forms within the utterance. In the following passages, Benveniste (1966: 239-42) contrasts discursive speech with nondiscursive speech.

> Il faut entendre discours dans sa plus large extension: toute énonciation supposant un locuteur et un auditeur, et chez le premier l'intention d'influencer l'autre en quelque manière ... brefs tous les genres où quelqu'un s'adresse à quelqu'un, s'énonce comme locuteur et organise ce qu'il dit dans la catégorie de la personne.[1]

> Nous définirons le récit historique comme le mode d'énonciation qui exclut toute forme linguistique « autobiographique » ... On ne constatera donc le récit historique strictement poursuivi que des formes de « 3e personne. »[2]

The distinction between discursive and nondiscursive speech is thus made to turn on the presence or absence, respectively, of the category of person.[3] However, this condition may be broadened for present purposes: making use of Jakobson's terminology, discursive speech involves any category that makes crucial reference to the speech event. In this context, then, the category of person serves as a convenient metonym for all categories that refer to the speech event. Nondiscursive speech, by contrast, makes reference only to the narrated event. One immediate corollary of these definitions is that discursive speech has shifters while nondiscursive speech does not. In general and as seen below, discursive speech

1 'Discourse is to be understood in its broadest extent as all utterances that presuppose a speaker and a listener, and with the former the intention of influencing the latter in some way ... in short, all those genres where someone addresses himself to another, expresses himself as the speaker and organizes what he say according to the category of person [SBS].'

2 'We define nondiscursive speech as the way to present an utterance which excludes all autobiographical linguistic forms ... We recognize nondiscursive speech strictly speaking only in forms of the "third person" [SBS].'

3 Benveniste (1946) had already argued that only the first and second persons properly belong to the category of person; the third 'person' does not.

admits more grammatical categories than nondiscursive speech does.

This distinction naturally affects the distribution of linguistic forms and categories, a point which Benveniste (1966) illustrates with the tense forms of Modern French. Nondiscursive speech, he argues, permits only three tenses: an aorist (*passé simple*), imperfect (*imparfait*) and pluperfect (*plus-que-parfait*). Two other tense forms may appear on occasion: a prospective future and a present of definition; all others are excluded. Discursive speech, on the other hand, permits all tense-forms except the aorist. It allows, among others, the present, the future and the perfect tense series. This distinction goes deeper than this mere listing would suggest. What the tense forms really convey in nondiscursive speech is relative tense, or taxis, E^nE^n: they do not convey tense as it is properly understood, E^s/E^n. The aorist, for example, conveys anterior taxis: one event is presented as having taken place before another. The time reference of the narrated event is calculated relative to the other narrated events in the discourse, not relative to a speech event. Discursive speech, however, may use verb forms that convey tense as well as taxis.

From what has been said, it is obvious that the organization of tense-forms in an utterance may be subject to the distinction between discursive and nondiscursive speech. The temporal organization of successive narrated events within the utterance, which Benveniste calls *l'éffectif*, reflects the influence of these two different ways of framing and presenting an utterance. Benveniste (1966: 239-41) describes the influence of nondiscursive speech on the temporal organization of events in the following terms.[4]

> L'énonciation *historique* ... caracterise le récit des événements passés ... Il s'agit de la présentation des faits survenus à un certain moment de temps, sans aucune intervention du locuteur dans le récit ... dès lors qu'ils sont enrégistrés et énoncés dans une expression temporelle historique, ils se trouvent caracterisés comme passés.
>
> [D]ans ce mode d'énonciation, l'éffectif et la nature des temps demeurent les mêmes. Il n'y a aucune raison pour qu'ils changent aussi longtemps que le récit historique se poursuit, et il n'y a d'ailleurs aucune raison pour que celui-ci s'arrête, pusiqu'on peut imaginer tout le passé du monde comme un récit

4 'Nondiscursive speech characterizes the narrative of past events ... It is a matter of present facts happening at a certain moment in time without any intervention by the speaker in the narrative... once they are set down and expressed in a historical temporal expression, they are characterized as past.

'In this means of expression, the succession of events and the essence of time are the same. There is no reason for them to change as long as the historical narrative proceeds; moreover, there is no reason for the narrative to stop since one may imagine the entire past of the world as a continuous narrative and which can be based on a threefold distinction of aorist, imperfect and past perfect. It is necessary and sufficient that the author remain true to his historical purpose and eliminate everything which is alien to the narration of events (address, reflection, comparisons). Truly speaking, there is no narrator. Events are presented as they develop to the extent they appear on the horizon of history. No one speaks here; events appear to narrate themselves. The basic tense is the aorist which is the tense of an event outside of the person of a narrator [SBS].'

> continu et qui serait entièrement construit sur cette triple fonction temporelle: aoriste, imparfait, plus-que-parfait. Il faut et il suffit que l'auteur reste fidèle à sons propos d'historien et qu'il proscrive tout ce qui est étranger au récit des événements (discours, réflexions, comparaisons). A vrai dire, il n'y a même plus alors de narrateur. Les événements sont posés comme ils se sont produits à mesure qu'ils apparaissent à l'horizon de l'histoire. Personne ne parle ici; les événements semblent se raconter eux-mêmes. Le temps fondamental est l'aoriste, qui est le temps de l'événement hors de la personne d'un narrateur.

Nondiscursive speech thus presents the sequence of events "objectively," without reference to a speaker or his audience. Discursive speech, as Benveniste then proceeds to show, frames it "subjectively," relativizing its content to the speaker, the addressee and their goals in conversation.

Subjectivity in this context is to be understood as the ability to assume the role of speaker, defined over against the role of addressee, and the concomitant ability to exchange the two roles in the course of conversation. The two roles are mutually dependent, and both are dependent on the speech event. Perhaps the most obvious manifestation of subjectivity in natural language is the grammatical category of person, which opposes and an *ego* to a *tu*. Subjectivity should not in this context be taken to mean being under the sway of one's emotions, desires or interests any more than the grammatical category of person should be taken to imply a psychological entity; both here are grammatical concepts.

In practice, discursive and nondiscursive speech anchor opposite poles in a continuum. Benveniste cites examples from the work of historians to show how an individual narrator's opinions, properly restricted to discursive speech, can intrude into a historical narrative for rhetorical effect. Some of the Tamil examples noted below also exhibit an admixture of the two kinds of utterance.

Nondiscursive speech treats narrated events impersonally, relegating the participants to minor, background roles. Discursive speech, by contrast, clearly reflects the active roles that speaker and addressee—the participants in the speech event—play in the construction of the narrated event. Here the narrated event is relativized to them and their circumstances by means of verbal categories such as tense and attitude. (It is, of course, also relativized to them by means of nonverbal categories such as person.) Nondiscursive speech tends to suppress verbal categories that draw attention away from the pure stream of events. Anything that detracts from simple narrative is precluded, including the participants' motivations, interests and opinions. Tense (E^s/E^n), person (P^s/P^n), and attitude (P^s/E^n), all of them shifters, are absent from nondiscursive speech because they refer directly to the speech event. Voice (P^nE^n) is to a lesser extent discouraged because it draws attention away from the narrated event to the participants in it. Even certain kinds of taxis (E^nE^n) are to a certain extent avoided: they view one narrated event in terms of another, rather than *a se*. Since, as Benveniste notes in the passage cited above, each narrated event has a fixed position in the sequence of events, so that the natural order of events and the grammatical representation of that order coincide, the information that taxis conveys tends to be superfluous.

In Tamil, mood, the qualifier of the narrated event, appears in nondiscursive speech through its two basic exponents, the infinitive and conjunctive forms. Mood is retained because it comments on the narrated event without reference to its participants or to other narrated events. There is another, perhaps more basic, reason for the presence of mood in nondiscursive speech: there are no verb forms in Tamil that do not mark mood.[5]

Frames that prohibit AVCs

This discussion prepares the following hypothesis: indicative AVCs tend not occur in certain frames because those frames are instances of nondiscursive speech and discourage the presence of the relatively complex verbal categories that AVCs encode. The following examples contain sequences of conjunctive forms; where the stigmata (*AUX) appears, however, the simple verb cannot be replaced by an AVC. In (170a) the simple, nonauxiliated verb *pōy* 'going' cannot be replaced by an AVC such as *pōy iruntu* 'having gone'; in (171a) *perukki* 'sweeping' cannot be replaced by an AVC such as *perukki.k koṇṭu* 'while sweeping'; in (172a) *uṭaittu* 'breaking' cannot be replaced by an AVC such as *uṭaittu viṭṭu* 'breaking off'.[6] This prohibition applies to all indicative auxiliaries, even though their semantics might otherwise seem to suit them to these sentences, e.g., the transition between night and day (170a) might ordinarily be thought to motivate the use of disjunctive taxis as conveyed by auxiliary *viṭa* 'leave' (see Chapter 6). The reason for this prohibition is shown to be pragmatic rather than syntactic or semantic.

(170)a $_{S0}$[$_{S1}$[*iravu* *pōy* (*AUX)] $_{S2}$[*pakal* *vantatu*]].
night-NOM go-CF daylight-NOM come-PST-3N
'Night went and daylight came.'

b $_{S0}$[$_{S1}$[*tamiẓ vakuppu muṭintu* (*AUX)] $_{S2}$[*iṅklīṣ vakuppu ārampittatu*]].
Tamil class-NOM end-CF English class-NOM begin-PST-3N
'Tamil class ended and English class began.'

c $_{S0}$[$_{S1}$[*iḷaimai pōy* (*AUX)] $_{S2}$[*muṭumai vantatu*]].
youth-NOM go-CF old.age-NOM come-PST-3N
'Youth departed and old age arrived.'

(171)a $_{S0}$[$_{S1}$[*viṭiyaṟkālaiyil vācalai.p perukki.c* (*AUX)] $_{S2}$[*cāṇi*
daybreak-LOC entrance-ACC sweep-CF dung
teḷittu.k (*AUX)] $_{S3}$[*kōlam pōṭa vēṇṭum*]].
sprinkle-CF figure put-INF need-FUT-3N
'At daybreak, one must sweep the entrance, sprinkle it with cow dung and draw auspicious figures on it.'

5 For certain forms, there are no satisfactory alternatives that do not mark, say, taxis (the conditional).

6 Note that in (172b) the verb *pōṭa* 'put' functions not as an auxiliary but as a nonauxiliated verb that subcategorizes an accusative NP *muḷḷai* 'thorn-acc' and a locative NP *mūñciyil* 'face-loc'.

b $_{S0}$[$_{S1}$[*inta mättirattai.t taṇṇīril karaittu* (*AUX)] $_{S1}$[*oru nāḷai mūṉṟu*
this tablet-ACC water-LOC dissolve-CF one day three
taṭavai cāppiṭavum]].
times eat-OPT
'This tablet is to be dissolved in water and taken three times a day.'

c $_{S0}$[*vētam kēṭkiṟa cūttiraṉiṉ kātil* $_{S1}$[*īyattai.k kāycci* (*AUX)]
Vedas hear-PRES-ANP Sudra-GEN ear-LOC iron-ACC melt-CF
ūṟṟa vēṇṭum].
pour-INF need-FUT-3N
'Lead must be melted and poured into the ear of any Sudra who hears the Vedas.'

(172)a $_{S0}$[$_{S1}$[*pallukku ellām uṭaittu* (*AUX) *kaiyilē koṭuttu viṭuvēṉ*],
teeth-DAT all break-CF hand-LOC give-CF leave-FUT-1s
jākkiratai eṉṟēṉ].
care say-PST-1s
'I warned, "Watch out, or I'll break your teeth and hand them to you."'

b $_{S0}$[*mūñciyil* $_{S1}$[*muḷḷai veṭṭi.p* (*AUX)] *pōṭuvēṉ*].
face-LOC thorn-ACC cut-CF put-FUT-1s
'I'll cut some thorns and shove 'em in your puss.'

Consider these examples in light of the distinction made between discursive and nondiscursive speech above. Example (170a) describes the natural procession of night and day; (170b), the prescribed class schedule in a school; and (170c), the natural process of aging. Example (171a) describes the established sequence of events in a daily domestic ritual, whose purpose is to invoke the blessings of Laksmi, goddess of prosperity. The sequence is determined by tradition, and not subject to improvisation. Example (171b) is a doctor's prescription; the sequence of steps in the course of medication is presented as invariable—the tablet will have no curative power unless first dissolved in water. Example (171c), from a Tamil version of the traditional Hindu law code *Manu Dharmasastra*, sanctions a transgression of a religious law; here the punishment is seen to follow from—to be determined by—the nature of the infraction.

Examples (172a and b) are conventional ways of expressing threats in Tamil. All threats consisting of two clauses behave this way, prohibiting AVCs at the juncture of the two clauses. How do threats, which initially appear to be instances of discursive speech (note the first person pronouns), behave more like nondiscursive speech? First, a threat is an ultimatum unilaterally imposed on one person by another; it does not develop from the cooperation of the participants in conversation, a hallmark of discursive speech. Someone who threatens another effectively gives his opponent no quarter, and is unwilling to change places with the object of the threat.[7] Second, to competently inspire fear and acquiescence, the order of events in a threat must seem inflexible, irresistible. To interpolate an AVC

7 In fact, part of the essence of a threat is to treat another person as an object, not as a subject potentially on the same footing as the speaker.

with its verbal category would give the threat an articulated joint presenting the person menaced with an opening to parry the verbal blow. In these respects, then, threats fall somewhat short of the norms of discursive speech. Whether or not threats can be decisively brought under the umbrella of nondiscursive speech is a question for further research in Tamil speech acts. For present purposes, however, what matters is that threats are a pragmatic, not a syntactic, classification of the frames in which simple verbs, but not AVCs may appear.

Instructions, laws, prescriptions, threats and natural processes are well suited to being represented by nondiscursive speech. The order of events (*l'éffectif*) is assumed to be given naturally, not artificially. Since nondiscursive speech tends to exclude more complex verbal categories, it naturally excludes the morphosyntactic forms that encode those categories: AVCs. Whatever the final solution for explaining the skewed distribution of AVCs in (170-172), their initial classification refers to pragmatic features of the utterance, not syntactic ones.

Frames that require AVCs

In contrast to frames that prohibit AVCs, certain frames appear to require AVCs and cannot host a corresponding simple verb form. Consider (173a) which illustrates a compound clause in which each verb has its own denotational function. Nowadays it is acceptable only in written Tamil; in that register, it is ambiguous between two readings: one in which the singing and bathing overlap, and another in which they do not. These two readings are paraphrased by (173b and c), respectively. In spoken Tamil, however, one must choose between (173b and c): (173a) sounds strange in the spoken language because there is generally not enough information to construe the two events as coherently related. As noted in Chapter 6, the auxiliaries *koḷḷa* 'hold' and *viṭa* 'leave' encode conjunctive and disjunctive taxis, respectively, providing the participants in conversation with enough information to construe the two events coherently.

(173)a *pāṭi.k kuḷittāṉ.*
sing-CF bathe-PST-3SM
'He sang and bathed.'

b $_{AVC}$[*pāṭi.k koṇṭu*] *kuḷittāṉ.*
sing-CF hold-CF bathe-PST-3SM
'He bathed while singing.'

c $_{AVC}$[*pāṭi viṭṭu.k*] *kuḷittāṉ.*
sing-CF leave-CF bathe-PST-3SM
'He bathed after singing.'

In the examples below, which replicate this pattern, the stigmata *(AUX) indicates that the sentence is unacceptable without an auxiliary in that position. The subject *atu* 'it' in (174) may refer to a piece of sculpture, a theodolite or a loudspeaker that was attached to a temple tower, broke away from it and fell to the ground. On the way down, it struck a projection, dislodging that as well. The three component sentences purport to describe the three events of breaking away, falling and dislodging another object. Sentence (174a) is generally regarded as unacceptable by speakers because it lacks sufficient information with which to construe these three events coherently. Therefore, the speaker must ordinarily choose between the two alternatives in (174b and c), both of which contain AVCs that further specify the relationships among the three events. Breaking away from a high perch and falling to the ground are two events that may be naturally related by the effects of gravity, information readily available to the participants in conversation. But the relation between these two events and the dislodging of another statue protruding from the tower is not as readily given; the first statue's fall to the ground need not entail its striking and dislodging some other object. Specific information must be introduced—here, via AVCs—to help the participants in conversation build a coherent overall mental picture of this event relative to the other two.

(174)a [$_{S0}$ [$_{S1}$ *atu* *kōpurattiliruntu* *pirintu*] [$_{S2}$ *pommaiyai uṭaittu* *(AUX)]
it-NOM temple.tower-ABL separate-CF statue-ACC break-CF
[$_{S3}$ *kīḻē* *viḻuntatu*]].
down fall-PST-3N
'It separated from the temple tower, broke off (another) statue and fell to the ground.'

b [$_{S0}$ [$_{S1}$ *atu* *kōpurattiliruntu* *pirintu*] [$_{S2}$ *pommaiyai* *uṭaittu.k* *koṇṭu*]
it-NOM temple.tower-ABL separate-CF statue-ACC break-CF hold-CF
[$_{S3}$ *kīḻē* *viḻuntatu*]].
down fall-PST-3N
'It separated from the temple tower and, in doing so, broke off another statue, and fell to the ground.'

c [$_{S0}$ [$_{S1}$ *atu* *kōpurattiliruntu* *pirintu*] [$_{S2}$ *pommaiyai* *uṭaittu* *viṭṭu*]
it-NOM temple.tower-ABL separate-CF statue-ACC break-CF leave-CF
[$_{S3}$ *kīḻē* *viḻuntatu*]].
down fall-PST-3N
'It separated from the temple tower and, after breaking off another statue, fell to the ground.'

Is the presence of auxiliaries in (174b and c) motivated by grammatical rules governing the construction of sentences or, alternatively, by pragmatic principles determining the richness of the informational relation between context and utterance? If pragmatic factors do in fact influence the acceptability of these sentences, it then should be possible to vary the context and discover some situations in which the unacceptable (174a) is actually found to be more acceptable. In fact, it is regarded as acceptable in the following scenario: a movie crew is finishing a scene in which an object is rigged to fall off a temple tower and knock off a statue as it plummets earthward. The special effects man could then utter a sentence such as (174a) to report the successful completion of his staged effect. The presence of AVCs in these sentences is thus motivated by pragmatic concerns dealing with the provision of adequate information,[8] not by syntactic ones dealing with the distribution of grammatical forms. On that hypothesis, we can still generate AVCs wherever we would generate simple verbs, and *vice versa.*

Conversely, but following the same logic, example (170a), which generally prohibits an AVC, may allow one in certain settings. Presented with an auxiliary in (175), it can be used to describe the procession of darkness and light in an artificial environment such as a sleep-chamber used in sleep experiments or on a space station where darkness and light—night and day—are regulated by human intervention at the flick of a switch.

(175) $_{S0}$[$_{S1}$[*iravu* $_{AVC}$[*pōy viṭṭu.p*]] $_{S2}$[*pakal* *vantatu*]].
night-NOM go-CF leave-CF daylight-NOM come-PST-3N
'Night went away, and then daylight came.'

If the acceptability of such sentences is subject to such contextual variation, that acceptability need not be regarded as a direct function of syntactic structure. Further, if the skewed distribution of AVCs and simple verbs in these examples is piggybacked on to such pragmatic factors, not syntactic ones, we need not write any special syntactic rules or place any riders on those rules to account for this distribution. The AVC can be generated wherever simple verbs are generated, without loss of syntactic generality, and the claim that AVCs function as single verbs is thus not vitiated by apparent counterexamples.

DIRECT AND INDIRECT DISCOURSE

Pragmatic factors may also apply more finely within the set of indicative auxiliaries, partitioning them into two distinct subsets. Causation in Chapter 4 has already established that there are two subsets of indicative auxiliary verbs: attitudinal and nonattitudinal. In general, nonattitudinal auxiliaries can appear in causative constructions while attitudinals cannot. While this distinction is reflected in the syntax, it is also motivated in other contexts by pragmatics. Other grammatical frames are also sensitive to this distinction, most notably reported speech. There are two basic varieties of reported speech in Tamil, direct and indirect discourse (see Steever 2002b). Study of the examples below demonstrates that while both attitudinal and nonattitudinal auxiliaries freely occur in direct discourse, only nonattitudinals appear in indirect discourse.

Jakobson (1971: 130) characterizes reported speech as "a speech within speech, a message within a message…" Reported speech may therefore be thought of as a

8 Such a scene for (174) would appear in a movie script that attempted to recreate a historical incident that occurred during Lampton's celebrated mapping of India in the nineteenth century. Surveyors placed a theodolite on the *vimāna* of Brihadeesvara Temple in Tanjore, one of the highest vantage points in the area, to triangulate their readings. The instrument broke away and fell to the ground dislodging a statue as it plunged to the ground (see Keay 2000: 60-62).

speech event whose narrated event is itself another speech event, one that has been displaced from its original context. Reported speech is commonly divided into direct and indirect discourse. Jespersen (1965: 292) adroitly characterizes indirect discourse by a shifting of person, tense and mood away from the forms it would have had in direct discourse. In this shifting, the deictic center of the reporting speech captures and assimilates the deictic center of the original, reported speech event. For example, an NP in indirect discourse is assigned first person if it refers to the speaker of the reporting speech event, second person if it refers to the addressee and third person in other cases. Any grammatical form that makes reference to the speech events or its participants, such as person P^s/P^n, tense E^s/E^n, attitude P^s/E^n, is affected by the deictic shift from direct to indirect discourse. Such a shift is illustrated in the English example of indirect discourse *he said that he would come home*: on the interpretation where the subject of the main clause is coreferential with the subject of the subordinate clause, the pronoun in the original speech would have been *I* and the verb phrase would have been *will come home*, as are preserved in the direct discourse counterpart *he said, "I will come home."*

Such changes do not occur in direct discourse. The original speech in (176a) is reported in (176b, c and d).

(176)a $_{S1}$[*nī* *vā!*]
you-NOM come-IMP
'You come!'

b $_{S0}$[$_{S1}$[*nī* *vā*] *eṉṟu* *coṉṉāṉ*].
you-NOM come-IMP saying-CF say-PST-3SM
'He said, "You come!"'

c $_{S0}$[*eṉṉai* *vara.c* *coṉṉāṉ*].
I-ACC come-INF say-PST-3SM
'He told me/said to me to come.'

d $_{S0}$[*eṉṉai* *varum* *paṭi* *coṉṉāṉ*].
I-ACC come-FUT-ADN manner say-PST-3SM
'He told me to come'

Example (176b) illustrates direct discourse in which the original speech is embedded by the so-called complementizer *eṉṟu* 'that': it is actually the conjunctive *eṉa* 'say', which does not alter the morphological features of the forms it embeds (see Steever 1988). The verb in the subordinate clause continues to bear the inflections of the imperative singular and the subject appears in the nominative case, the forms they would respectively have had in the original speech now being reported. But a marked shift takes place in the indirect discourse counterpart in example (176c): the finite imperative form is replaced by the nonfinite infinitive and the nominative case second person singular pronoun *nī* 'thou' of the original speech is replaced by the accusative case first person singular pronoun *eṉṉai* 'me'. Further, the accusative pronoun is now grammatically construed as the object of the verb of reporting *colla* 'tell, say' in the matrix clause. In (176d), the underlying second person subject pronoun has been shifted to a first person accusative pronoun, as in

Table 5.1 Direct and indirect discourse in Tamil

DIRECT DISCOURSE	INDIRECT DISCOURSE
[[REPORTED SPEECH] REPORTING SPEECH]	[[REPORTED SPEECH] REPORTING SPEECH]
└── NO ASSIMILATION ──↑	└── ASSIMILATION ──↑
1. TWO DEICTIC CENTERS	1'. ONE DEICTIC CENTER
2. FINITE EMBEDDED VERBS	2'. NONFINITE EMBEDDED VERBS
3. QUOTATIVE COMPLEMENTIZER *e<u>nr</u>u*	3'. INFINITIVAL COMPLEMENTIZER ADNOMINAL FORM + *paṭi* 'as'
4. IMPERATIVE AND OPTATIVE FORMS	4'. INFINITIVAL FORMS
5. AFFECTIVE LENGTHENING AND LEXIS	5'. NO AFFECTIVE LENGTHENING OR LEXIS
6. NON-SHIFTED DEIXIS	6'. SHIFTED DEIXIS
7. VOCATIVES AND EXCLAMATIONS	7'. NO VOCATIVES OR EXCLAMATIONS
8. INTERROGATIVE FORMS	8'. NO INTERROGATIVE FORMS
9. ATTITUDINAL AUXILIARY VERBS	9'. NO ATTITUDINAL AUXILIARY VERBS

(176c). Furthermore, the finite verb *vantā<u>n</u>* 'he came' has been replaced by the composite form *varum paṭi* 'manner of coming', which consists of the future adnominal form *varum* 'which will come', a nonfinite verb form, and the head noun *paṭi* 'manner'. The shift from finite to nonfinite form in both examples, as well as the change in the case and person of the pronoun, indicates that clause union has taken place to some extent, partially obscuring the fact that the reported speech originally consisted of two separate sentences which, on certain analyses, may derive from an underlying biclausal structure. It also obscures which noun phrases and which verbs originally appeared in the original speech being reported and which should be attributed to the speech reporting the original.

Subsequent research has come to treat the dichotomy between direct and indirect speech as a polar opposition, not a privative one. The phenomenon of semi-direct discourse, well known from Romance linguistics, exemplifies a kind of speech that falls between the two poles of direct and indirect speech. Semi-direct discourse does occur in Tamil (Steever 2002b: 103); for the time being, however, we will concentrate on bringing into sharper focus the grammatical contrasts between direct and indirect discourse as it occurs in Tamil. Table 5.1 summarizes some of the major differences between direct and indirect discourse in Tamil.

Any linguistic form that conventionally encodes the speaker's sentiments, opinions or the like are excluded from indirect discourse. Consider the curse *nācamāy pō* 'go to hell' in (177) and the exclamation *tīyai vai* 'holy smokes, no kidding' (lit. 'put the fire') in (178). Both occur in direct but not indirect discourse.[9] Both are highly affective utterances with relatively little propositional content. In the shift

9 An alternative explanation might argue that these are idioms whose frozen forms cannot be changed by the grammatical shifts that occur in indirect discourse.

from direct to indirect discourse, the original deictic center is eliminated and these forms lose their original frame of reference and are also eliminated. They cannot be properly attributed to the speaker of the reporting speech in which the original speech is embedded.

(177)a *nācamāy pō*!
hell-ADV go-IMP
'Go to hell.'

b $[_{S0}$ $[_{S1}$ *nācamāy pō*] *e<u>nr</u>u co<u>nn</u>ā<u>n</u>*].
hell-ADV go-IMP say-CF tell-PST-3SM
'He said, "Go to hell."'

c * *nācamāy pōka.c co<u>nn</u>ā<u>n</u>*.
hell-ADV go-INF tell-PST-3SM
?'He said that go to hell.'

(178)a *tīyai vai*!
fire-ACC place-IMP
'Holy smokes.'

b $[_{S0}$ $[_{S1}$ *tīyai vai*] *e<u>nr</u>u co<u>nn</u>ā<u>n</u>*].
fire-ACC place-IMP say-CF tell-PST-3SM
'He said, "Holy smokes!"'

c * *tīyai vaikka.c co<u>nn</u>ā<u>n</u>*.
fire-ACC place-INF tell-PST-3SM
? 'He said to holy smokes.'

Other expressions of the speaker's emotional state are removed in the shift from direct to indirect discourse. In (179c) and (180c), both instances of indirect discourse, the finite verb form of the original speech is replaced by a combination of the future verbal noun and the complementizer *āka* (the infinitive of *āka* 'become'). It contrasts with the complementizer *e<u>nr</u>u*, which occurs in direct discourse in (179b) and (180b). In (179a) the modifier *periya* 'big' is intensified and exaggerated by lengthening its second vowel to four times its original length as *perīiiya* 'reeeally big'.[10] Such lengthening is a conventional stylistic figure that expresses the speaker's feeling—surprise, astonishment, shock—that the subject of the conversation is extraordinarily important, abnormal, noteworthy, strange, etc. It is permissible in direct (179b) but not in indirect discourse (179c). Affective lengthening may also occur in the adverbial expression in (180a), *ittaṇūṇṭu* 'itsy-bitsy, teensy-weensy' (*tammātūṇṭu* 'id.' in and around Chennai). As before, it is permitted in direct (180b) but not indirect discourse (180c). Here it is not merely the affective lengthening that disqualifies this word from appearing in indirect discourse: the word itself, with or without affective lengthening, belongs to the vocabulary of affective speech, resembling baby-talk. These and similar elements of affective

10 The overlong vowel is approximately twice as long as ordinary long vowels in Tamil. The graphic convention used here to represent it mimics the traditional Tamil orthographic convention of one long vowel graph followed by two short vowel graphs.

lexis cannot occur in indirect discourse because they conventionally encode the speaker's attitudes or emotions, all reference to which is eradicated when the original speech is embedded in indirect discourse.

(179)a *perīiiya maṉuṣaṉ varuvāṉ.*
big-EXG man-NOM come-FUT-3SM
'A reeeally big man is coming/will come.'

b $[_{S0}$ $[_{S1}$ *perīiiya maṉuṣaṉ varuvāṉ*] *eṉṟu coṉṉāṉ*].
big-EXG man-NOM come-FUT-3SM say-CF tell-PST-3SM
'He said, "A reeeally big man is coming/will come."'

c * *perīiiya maṉuṣaṉ varuvatu āka.c coṉṉāṉ.*
big-EXG man-NOM come-FUT-VN become-INF tell-PST-3SM
'He said that a reeeally big man would come.'

(180)a *miṭṭāy ittaṇūṇṭu koṭu!*
sweets itsy.bitsy-EXG give-IMP
'Give me just an itsy-bitsy piece of candy.'

b $[_{S0}$ $[_{S1}$ *miṭṭāy ittaṇūṇṭu koṭu*] *eṉṟu coṉṉāḷ*].
sweets itsy.bitsy-EXG give-IMP say-CF tell-PST-3SF
'She said, "Give me just an itsy-bitsy piece of candy."'

c * *miṭṭāy ittaṇūṇṭu koṭuppatu āka.c coṉṉāḷ.*
sweets itsy.bitsy-EXG give-FUT-VN become-INF tell-PST-3SF
'She told me to give her just an itsy-bitsy piece of candy.'

Vocative phrases and exclamations are also removed from indirect discourse. The exclamation *aṭa* 'alas' and the vocative phrase *kaṭavuḷē* 'O God' occur in direct (181b) but not indirect discourse (181c). Other exclamations, such as *bēṣ* 'wow' or *cī* 'gee', and vocative phrases follow the same pattern. As indices of the speaker's emotional state, they are removed when indirect discourse erases the original speech's frame of reference.

(181)a *aṭa kaṭavuḷē! avaḷ ōṭippōy viṭṭāḷ.*
alas god-VOC she-NOM run.away-CF leave-PST-3SF
'O God, she's run away (from home).'

b $[_{S0}$ $[_{S1}$ *aṭa kaṭavuḷē! avaḷ ōṭippōy viṭṭāḷ*] *eṉṟu coṉṉāṉ*].
alas god-VOC she-NOM run.away-CF leave-PST-3SF say-CF tell-PST-3SM
'He said, "O God, she's run away (from home)."'

c (**aṭa kaṭavuḷē*) *avaḷ ōṭippōy viṭṭatu āka.c coṉṉāṉ.*
alas god-VOC she-NOM run.away-CF leave-PST-VN become-INF tell-PST-3SM
'He said that O God, she ran away from home.'

This discussion bears directly on the analysis of the Tamil indicative auxiliary system. Examination of the examples below reveals that some of the auxiliaries may freely occur in both direct and indirect discourse. For example, auxiliary *viṭa* 'leave' in (182) and auxiliary *vaikka* 'place' in (183) are equally at home in both direct and indirect discourse.

(182)a *pōy viṭu*!
go-CF leave-IMP
'Go away.'

b $_{S0}[_{S1}$[*pōy viṭu*] *eṉṟu coṉṉāṉ*].
go-CF leave-IMP say-CF tell-PST-3SM
'He said, "Go away."'

c *pōy viṭa.c coṉṉāṉ*.
go-CF leave-INF tell-PST-3SM
'He said to go away.'

(183)a *oru kaṭitam eẓuti vaippāṉ*.
one letter write-CF place-FUT-3SM
'He will write a letter for subsequent use.'

b $_{S0}[_{S1}$[*oru kaṭitam eẓuti vaippāṉ*] *eṉṟu coṉṉāḷ*].
one letter write-CF place-FUT-3SM say-CF tell-PST-3SF
'She said, "He will write a letter for subsequent use."'

c *oru kaṭitam eẓuti vaippatu āka.c coṉṉāḷ*.
one letter write-CF place-FUT-VN become-INF tell-PST-3SF
'She said that he would write a letter for subsequent use.'

This pattern does not apply to all indicative auxiliaries; speakers of conservative dialects do not generally permit attitudinal auxiliary verbs in indirect discourse. Instead, they replace them with either with a simple, nonauxiliated form of the auxiliate or an indicative AVC with the auxiliary *viṭa* 'leave', which marks disjunctive taxis (see Chapter 6). The attitudinal AVC *pōy tolaiya* 'go, damn it' appears in (184a) and *colli oẓintāṉ* 'he went and said (it)' in (185a). Most attitudinals may not occur in indirect discourse although *tolaiya* is marginally acceptable.

(184)a *pōy tolai*!
go-CF lose-IMP
'Go away, damn it!'

b $_{S0}[_{S1}$[*pōy tolai*] *eṉṟu coṉṉāṉ*].
go-CF lose-IMP say-CF tell-PST-3SM
'He said, "Go away, damn it."'

c ? *pōy tolaiya.c coṉṉāṉ*.
go-CF lose-INF tell-PST-3SM
'He said to go damn it.'

(185)a *colli oẓintāṉ*.
say-CF purge-PST-3SM
'He went and said it.'

b $_{S0}[_{S1}$[*colli oẓintāṉ*] *eṉṟu coṉṉāḷ*].
tell-CF purge-PST-3SM say-CF tell-PST-3SM
'She said, "He went and said it."'

c * *colli oẓintatu āka.c coṉṉāḷ*.
tell-CF purge-PST-3SM become-INF tell-PST-3SM
'She said that he went and said it.'

As defined here, the verbal category of attitude, symbolized as P^s/E^n, characterizes the speaker's subjective evaluation of the narrated event. However, the shift from direct to indirect discourse removes the original deictic center to which P^s refers, neutralizing the category of attitude in favor of mood, the least marked verbal category.[11] So in general, the attitudinal AVC is replaced by a simple, nonauxiliated form of the main verb (or by an AVC with *viṭa* 'leave'). The speaker who makes a report with indirect discourse does not vouch for the opinions and feelings of the person whose speech is being reported. Direct discourse, on the other hand, preserves the deictic center of the original speech within quotation marks, so to speak; consequently, attitudinal auxiliaries are retained. It is thus the loss of the original deictic center in indirect discourse that catalyzes the loss of attitudinal auxiliaries, along with other grammatical devices that convey the speaker's emotional state, e.g., affective vowel lengthening, exclamations, vocative phrases, etc. The difference in grammatical behavior between attitudinal and nonattitudinal auxiliaries can in these instances be referred to the pragmatic distinction between direct and indirect discourse, rather than inscribing it in the syntax of AVCs.

Hearsay clitic

Another kind of reported speech in Tamil is formed by cliticizing the hearsay particle *=ām* 'it is said that' to a sentence itself or to any major category within the sentence. It does not, however, combine with imperative verbs.[12] In (186b) the hearsay particle attaches to *vantāṉ* 'he came', in (186c) to the subject *avaṉ* 'he'. It is used when the speaker wishes to report a rumor or hearsay without claiming responsibility for the content of what was said.[13]

(186)a *avaṉ vantāṉ.*
he-NOM come-PST-3SM
'He came.'

b *avaṉ vantāṉ=ām.*
he-NOM come-PST-3SM=HRSY
'It is said that he came.'

c *avaṉ=ām vantāṉ.*
he-NOM=HRSY come-PST-3SM
'It is said that it was he who came.'

11 This discussion underscores the limitations of Herring's (1991) methodology, which emphasizes the nondiscursive genres, such as narrative, at the expense of discursive genres, such as conversation. Lack of attention to the categories characteristic of discursive speech may well be responsible for the almost total absence of attitudinal auxiliaries in her corpus, as well as the tendency in her analysis to assimilate tense to taxis.

12 It could be a matter of evidentiality since the phrase to which the clitic attaches may in fact not be thought of as reporting another utterance, but merely an approximation of its propositional content. See Steever 2002.

13 As Jespersen (1965: 294) notes, shifting of responsibility away from the speaker of the reported speech is a hallmark of indirect discourse.

Like indirect speech, the hearsay particle embeds nonattitudinal auxiliaries, but not—in conservative dialects—attitudinal auxiliaries. Accordingly, it readily embeds a nonattitudinal AVC such as *viṭa* 'leave' in (187b), but not attitudinal AVCs, as (188b) and (189b). Since by use of the hearsay particle the speaker disavows responsibility for the content of his report, he cannot fairly ascribe to the subject information or attitudes for which he, the speaker, would have had to be present.

(187)a *nī pōy viṭuvāy.*
you-NOM go-CF leave-FUT-2S
'You're going away.'

b *nī pōy viṭuvāy=ām.*
you-NOM go-CF leave-FUT-2S=HRSY
'Word has it you're going away.'

(188)a *nī pōy tolaivāy.*
you-NOM go-CF lose-AF-FUT-2S
'You're going away, damn it.'

b *? *nī pōy tolaivāy=ām.*
you-NOM go-CF lose-AF-FUT-2S=HRSY
'Word has it you're going away, damn it.

(189)a *avaṉ oru nāvalai eẓuti.t taḷḷiṉāṉ.*
he-NOM one novel-ACC write-CF push-PST-3SM
'He dashed off a novel in no time at all.'

b * *avaṉ oru nāvalai eẓuti.t taḷḷiṉāṉ=ām.*
he-NOM one novel-ACC write-CF push-PST-3SM=HRSY
'It is said he dashed off a novel in no time at all.'

These examples suggest that the principles which govern the external syntax of auxiliary verbs in Tamil, offered to explain skewed distributions, are pragmatic rather than syntactic in nature. This permits us to preserve our claim that the syntactic distribution of AVCs and simple verbs is essentially the same, and that both belong to the category of verb.

RELATIVE ORDER AMONG MULTIPLE AUXILIARIES

If AVCs and their simple, nonauxiliated counterparts both belong to the category of verbs, they should undergo the same grammatical processes. The possibility that indicative AVCs can, like their nonauxiliated counterparts, undergo Auxiliary Formation was raised in Chapter 4. Auxiliary Formation thus appears to be recursive, generating complex AVCs with one AVC nested inside another, theoretically without limit. Not all theoretically possible combinations occur, however, prompting us to ask what principles govern this nesting process. If the order of nested AVCs proved to be highly idiosyncratic, it might compromise our claim that the AVC is a (derived) verb that freely participates in the same sorts of activities that ordinary verbs participate in.

No one can read the generative linguistic literature since 1957 without getting the impression that the major goal of studying auxiliaries is to generate multiple auxiliary verbs in their correct, observed order. However, none of the analyses of the Tamil auxiliary system reviewed in Chapter 2 treats the problem of order among multiple auxiliary verbs. While certain frequently occurring collocations, such as *koṇṭu irukka* or *vaittu irukka*, are noted, they are often treated as idiomatic sequences. Bright and Lindenfeld (1968) is the only study dedicated to this issue. The authors researched the relative order among four auxiliaries: "reflexive" *koḷḷa* 'hold', "completive" *viṭa* 'leave', "perfective" *irukka* 'be' and "progressive" *koṇṭu irukka* 'be V-ing'. *koḷḷa* is a voice marker, *viṭa* 'leave' an aspect marker, *irukka* a tense marker and *koṇṭu irukka* a taxis or aspect marker. They present their results in two rules, which recall Chomsky's (1957) rules for the English AUX: rules (190a and b) come from Bright and Lindenfeld (1968: 32, 35).[14]

(190)a *VNuc → Verb (+Reflexive) (+Completive) (+Progressive) (+Perfective)*
b *Reflexive + Completive + Progressive + Tense*
→ Reflexive + Progressive + Completive + Tense

Rule (190b) applies obligatorily, switching the linear order of the completive and progressive auxiliaries in that specific environment. These two rules wear remarkably well, but account for only four auxiliaries (or three, on the analysis that *koṇṭu irukka* 'be V-ing' consists of the reflexive and perfective auxiliaries). Our study must contend with 25 indicative auxiliaries. If we assume that an auxiliary can occur but once in a complex AVC, the total number of combinations to be tested would be 25!. If, counterfactually, the auxiliaries were restricted to just one position within the AVC, the number of possible combinations would be 2^{25}. Such daunting numbers are motivation enough to discover some ways to reduce these figures and the combinations they represent to more manageable proportions.

Complex AVCs with several auxiliary verbs are commonplace in Tamil. In the following examples, the multiply nested AVCs are bracketed for ease of reference.[15] Complex AVCs with two (191a, b) or three (191c, d) auxiliaries are unremarkable in the spoken language; nor are those with four auxiliaries (191e) uncommon.

(191)a *anta.p paiyattiṉāl tāṉ nāṉ uṅkaḷiṭam* $_2$[$_1$[$_0$[*vantu*] *oẓintu*] *koṇṭēṉ*].
that child-INST EMP I-NOM you-SOC come-CF purge-CF hold-PST-1S
'It's because of that child that I came here to see you, damn it.'

14 The abbreviation VNuc in this formula stands for verbal nucleus.

15 In each example the verb bracketed by $_0$[. . .] is the most deeply embedded auxiliate: it combines with the following auxiliary to create the most deeply nested AVC, which is in turn bracketed by $_1$[. . .]. This AVC then functions as the auxiliate of the next higher AVC, bracketed by $_2$[. . .]. This process continues until the highest bracketing is reached. Consequently, the highest positive integer in these diagrams equals both the number of AVCs nested in the complex AVC and the number of individual auxiliary verbs.

b *āṉāl eṉ mukam eṉṉai.k* $[_2[_1[_0$ *[kāṭṭi.k] koṭuttu] viṭṭatu]*.
but my face-NOM I-ACC show-CF give-CF leave-PST-3SN
'But my face gave me away (to him), unexpectedly.'

c *inta.k kālam iṅkē* $[_3[_2[_1[_0$ *[vāẓntu] kiẓittu] āki] viṭṭatu]*.
this time here live-CF tear-CF become-CF leave-PST-3N
'We've been living here for all this time, for all the good it's done us, just as expected.'

d *avaṉ tāṉiyāka niṟka muṭiyum eṉṟu* $[_3[_2[_1[_0$ *[kāṇpittu.k] koṇṭ=ē] tāṉ vantu] irukkiṟāṉ]*.
he-NOM self-ADV stand-INF be.able-FUT-3N say-CF show-CF hold-CF=PCL EMP come-CF be-PRS-3SM
'He has been continuing to show me all along that he can stand on his own.'

e *avaṉ uyilil āyiram rūpāy* $[_4[_3[_2[_1[_0$ *[eẓuti] vaittu.k] kiẓittu.k] koṇṭu] iruntāṉ]*.
he-NOM will-LOC thousand rupee write-CF place-CF tear-CF hold-CF be-PST-3SM
'Oh sure, he was writing Rs.1,000 into his will for me.'

Working through (191e), which contains four nested AVCs, will be instructive. At level 0, the most deeply embedded auxiliate *eẓuti* is the conjunctive of *eẓuta* 'write' and specifies the denotational function for the entire complex AVC. At level 1 it combines with auxiliary *vaikka* 'place', creating the most deeply nested AVC. *vaikka* marks subsequent taxis (Chapter 7): it indicates that the action of the auxiliate prepares for some subsequent event. At level 2 this AVC combines with auxiliary *kiẓikka* 'tear' (Chapter 8), which marks the antiperfect tense, indicating the speaker's belief that the subject is so unwilling or incompetent that the action named by the auxiliate will never be accomplished. Skipping level 3, we note that at level 4 the perfect tense auxiliary *irukka* 'be' combines with the complex AVC at level 3: it signals that the action named by the auxiliate began at some time prior to the reference time, which here is the present, and moves toward completion at the reference time. However, a conflict arises between the meanings of the perfect auxiliary *irukka* 'be' at level 4 and the antiperfect auxiliary *kiẓikka* 'tear' at level 2: the former indicates that the action of the auxiliate moves towards completion, the latter that it will not. Auxiliary *koḷḷa* 'hold' combines with the AVC at level 2 to form, in effect, an "imperfective converb" (p. 201ff.); the combination of *koṇṭu* + *irukka* has the value of a progressive tense form. Since this progressive meaning does not conflict with the meaning of *kiẓikka* 'tear', the resulting complex AVC at level 4 is acceptable. The sentence can thus be roughly paraphrased: there is a prior interval of time (*irukka*) during some subinterval of which (*koḷḷa*) the subject is thought by the speaker to engage ineffectually (*kiẓikka*) in performing an action for a subsequent purpose (*vaikka*), namely writing (*eẓuta*) a will.

One obstacle complicates the attempt to fix the order of multiple auxiliaries in Tamil as was done for English auxiliaries in early generative studies: the order of auxiliaries appears to be variable in Tamil. Two auxiliary verbs appear in (192a and b): the modal auxiliary *vēṇṭum* 'be necessary' and the perfect tense auxiliary *irukka* 'be': in (192a) the modal operator has higher scope than tense while in (192b) the scope is reversed.[16] In fact, (193c) shows that modal auxiliaries may be interspersed among indicatives in a single complex AVC.

(192)a *avaṉ* $[_2 [_1 [_0$ *pōy*] *irukka*] *vēṇṭum*].
he-NOM go-CF be-INF need-FUT-3N
'He must have gone.'

b *avaṉ* $[_2 [_1 [_0$ *pōka* *vēṇṭi.y*] *irukkiṟatu*].
he-NOM go-INF need-CF be-PRES-3N
'He has had to go.'

c *nāṉ* *avarukku* *āyiram* *rūpāy* *uyilil* $[_3 [_2 [_1 [_0$ *eḻuti*] *vaittu*] *aḻa*]
I-NOM he-DAT thousand rupee will-LOC write-CF place-CF cry-INF
vēṇṭi.y] *irukkiṟatu*].
need-CF be-PRS-3N
'I've had to write Rs. 1,000 into my will for him, for all the good it will do.'

In (193a and b)[17] the two indicative auxiliaries *viṭa* 'leave' and *koḷḷa* 'hold' appear in different orders. As analyzed in the next chapter, both are connectors with circumstantial meanings of taxis and voice. In both examples, the lower auxiliary has a voice reading; the higher, a taxis reading. This suggests that the nesting of multiple auxiliaries in indicative AVCs is sensitive to the verbal categories conveyed, not the identity of the words that function as auxiliaries.

(193)a *rīcīvarai* *vaittu* *viṭṭu* *neṟṟiyil* *poṅki* *irunta* *viyarvaiyai.t*
receiver-ACC place-CF leave-CF brow-LOC boil-CF be-PST-ADN sweat-ACC
$[_2 [_1 [_0$ *tuṭaittu*] *viṭṭu.k*] *koṇṭāṉ*] *veṇu*.
wipe-CF leave-CF hold-PST-3SM Venu-NOM
'Venu put the receiver down and wiped away from his brow the sweat that had broken out.'

b *tōṟṟam=ē* *uḷ* *eṉṟ=um* $[_2 [_1 [_0$ *niṉaittu.k*] *koṇṭu*]
appearance-NOM=EMP being-NOM comp=AND think-CF hold-CF
viṭum] *atu*.
leave-FUT-3N it-NOM
'And it [= her childishness] would consider that outward appearance is inner being.'

Instead of burdening the syntax with specifications of individual auxiliaries, we propose appealing to semantics, following a proposal by McCawley (1988). Auxiliaries may be freely generated in any order. Rules of semantic construal, includ-

16 It should be noted that examples such as (192b) and (191d), where the perfect tense operator has higher scope than the necessity modal operator, are clear counterexamples to Dale's (1975: 234) claim that modal auxiliaries in Tamil always take higher scope than nonmodal auxiliaries.

17 Example (193a) comes from Akilan's 1951 novel *ciṉēkiti*, (193b) from Janakiraman's (1966: 73) novel *ammā vantāḷ*.

ing the selection restrictions of individual auxiliaries, would then rule out certain combinations as semantically deviant. First, the affective and effective versions of an auxiliary never cooccur in the same complex AVC; for example, neither *tolaiya* 'get lost' and *tolaikka* 'lose' nor *kiẓiya* 'get torn' and *kiẓikka* 'tear' ever appear in the same complex AVC as auxiliaries. The appearance of two identical stems would be redundant, the occurrence of two diametrically opposed voice markers, contradictory. Consider auxiliary *āyiṟṟu* 'become' and the attitudinal auxiliaries *tolaiya* 'get lost' and *tolaikka* 'lose'. *āyiṟṟu* may embed an AVC with auxiliary *tolaiya* but not *tolaikka.* This follows from *āyiṟṟu*'s selection restrictions: it combines only with verbs that denote events or happenings (194a), not directed actions (194b) (see p. 221). The affective verb *tolaiya* is consistent with an event interpretation; the effective verb *tolaikka* 'lose', with a directed action interpretation. Thus example (195b) is ruled out for the same reason as (194b): *āyiṟṟu* 'become' may not combine with effective verbs, whether auxiliates or auxiliaries.

(194)a *kaṇṇāṭi* [$_1$ [$_0$ *uṭaintu*] *āyiṟṟu*].
glass-NOM break-AF-CF become-PST-3N
'The glass broke, as expected.'

b * *kaṇṇāṭi* [$_1$ [$_0$ *uṭaittu*] *āyiṟṟu*].
glass-NOM break-EF-CF become-PST-3N
'Someone broke the glass, as expected.'

(195)a *avaṉ* [$_2$ [$_1$ [$_0$ *vantu*] *tolaintu*] *āyiṟṟu*].
he-NOM come-CF lose-AF-CF become-PST-3N
'He came here, as expected, damn it.'

b * *avaṉ* [$_2$ [$_1$ [$_0$ *vantu*] *tolaittu*] *āyiṟṟu*].
he-NOM come-CF lose-EF-CF become-PST-3N
'He came here as expected, damn him.'

The two auxiliaries *aẓa* 'cry' and *koṭukka* 'give' never cooccur in the same complex AVC due to the fact that they have diametrically opposed meanings.[18] Their cooccurrence would confuse the listener with an apparent contradiction and tend to cancel out each other's meaning. Auxiliary *koṭukka* 'give' signals benefactive voice (196a) while *aẓa* 'cry' conveys antibenefactive voice (196b). For this reason, speakers find (196c) highly unacceptable.[19]

(196)a *vāttiyar* *maṉuvāy* [$_1$ [$_0$ *eẓuti.k*] *koṭuttār*].
teacher-NOM petition write-CF give-PST-3H
'The teacher wrote the petition (on a student's behalf).'

b *nāṉ* *uyilil* [$_2$ [$_1$ [$_0$ *eẓuti*] *vaittu*] *aẓutēṉ*].
I-NOM will-LOC write-CF place-CF cry-PST-1S
'I wrote (X) into my will (for no benefit at all).'

18 On a more abstract analysis, the combination might be ruled out because the meaning of *aẓa* already incorporates the meaning of *koṭukka*.

19 Changing the relative order of auxiliaries in (196c) will not materially change the acceptability.

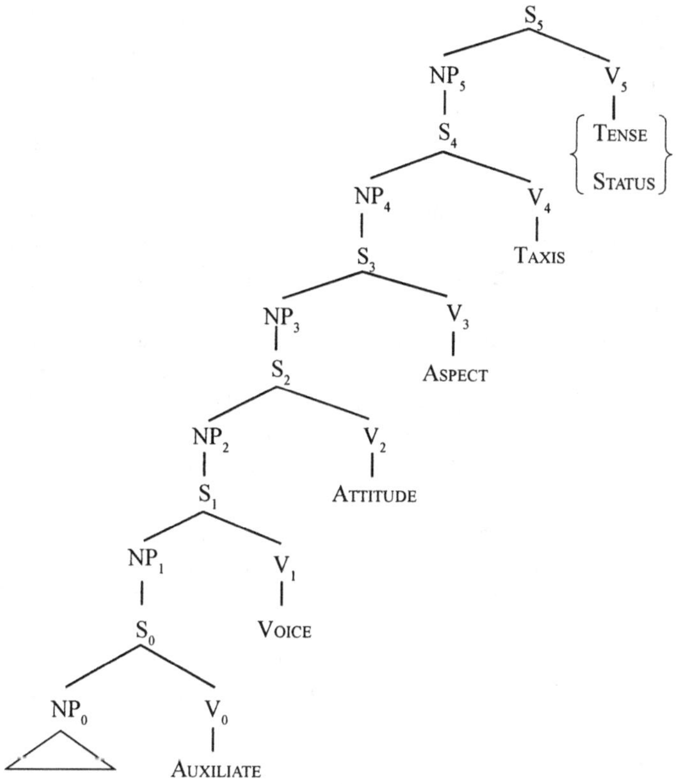

Figure 5.1 Unmarked order among multiple indicative auxiliaries.

c ?* *vāttiyar* *maṉuvay* [$_2$ [$_1$ [$_0$ *eẓuti.k*] *koṭuttu*] *aẓutār*].
teacher-NOM petition write-CF give-CF cry-PST-3H
'The teacher wrote the petition (on a student's behalf, for no benefit at all).'

The order of multiple auxiliaries in a complex AVC appears to fall out, in large part, from the semantics of individual verbs that appear in these constructions, particularly their selection restrictions. Further examples of such restrictions are discussed throughout the next three chapters.

The further possibility exists that additional semantic criteria, specifically the verbal categories that auxiliaries encode, govern their relative order in complex AVCs. As suggested earlier, no single complex AVC may contain two auxiliaries marked for the same verbal category. That hypothesis effectively reduces the number of potential combinations to 5!, where five is the number of major verbal categories, viz. voice, attitude, aspect, taxis and tense (with status as a sub-variety of tense). Figure 5.1 presents what is taken to be the general, unmarked order among multiple indicative auxiliaries.

The order in Figure 5.1 is provisional, pertaining only to indicative auxiliaries; the addition of the modal auxiliaries will doubtless occasion a revision. Two general tendencies may be noted. First, verbal categories that involve the participants in either the speech event or the narrated event generally stand closer to the most deeply embedded auxiliate than those that do not; hence, voice and attitude are more deeply nested than aspect or tense. Second, verbal categories that refer to the narrated event or its participants stand closer to the auxiliate than those that appeal to the speech event and its participants. Hence, voice P^nE^n and taxis E^nE^n stand closer to the auxiliate than do their counterparts which are shifters, attitude P^s/E^n and tense E^s/E^n, respectively.

Certain auxiliaries may be analyzed as encoding two categories, e.g., *aẓa* 'cry' marks voice and attitude. Thus *aẓa* 'cry' and *tolaiya* 'get lost' may cooccur in the same complex AVC because, although both encode attitude, *aẓa* 'cry' is additionally encodes for voice and can be assigned to that position while *tolaiya* 'get lost' appears in the slot for attitude. Example (191d) appears to contradict this formula: *vaikka* 'place', which marks taxis, precedes *aẓa* 'cry', which marks attitude. This may be due to the fact that voice, though not the invariant meaning of auxiliary *vaikka*, is a strong circumstantial meaning, perhaps one strong enough to motivate this order.[20] The order in Figure 5.1 accounts for the variation between (193a and b): auxiliary *viṭa* 'leave' can signal disjunctive taxis or, circumstantially, other-oriented voice; auxiliary *koḷḷa* 'hold' can signal conjunctive taxis or self-oriented. In (193a), where *viṭa* precedes *koḷḷa*, it marks voice while in (193b), where it follows, it signals taxis. While this preliminary analysis of the ordering of multiple auxiliaries will doubtlessly be revised under the impact of new research, especially through the addition of modal auxiliaries, it appears that circumstantial meanings of auxiliaries are chosen in accordance with the template in Figure 5.1.

20 Indeed, the presence of the dative-marked beneficiary *avarukku* 'for him' is likely to reinforce the voice interpretation in this sentence.

6 The major indicative auxiliary verbs of Tamil

INTRODUCTION

Here and in the next two chapters we analyze the semantics of the individual indicative auxiliary verbs. Those analyzed here are the most common; significantly, each exhibits multiple circumstantial meanings.[1] Those in Chapter 7 have a narrower compass and lack multiple circumstantial meanings. Finally, those in Chapter 8 encode the verbal category of attitude.

No study of Tamil verbs can ignore *irukka* 'be located', *viṭa* 'leave' or *koḷḷa* 'hold', the three most frequent indicative auxiliaries in the language. Not only are they the most common auxiliaries in conversation and texts, but their range of functions is broader than all the other indicative auxiliaries. So broad in fact that they appear to express several distinct categories, leading some to propose multiple, homophonous auxiliaries, e.g., *irukka*$_1$ for perfective, *irukka*$_2$ for progressive and *irukka*$_3$ for supposition. We will instead propose an invariant meaning for each auxiliary underlying its various circumstantial meanings and attempt to calculate how those multiple meanings may be derived from it.

Chapter 1 has already introduced one analytic tack we might take to reconcile the various, apparently different readings these three auxiliary verbs display. Take auxiliary *viṭa* 'leave' for example. It appears variously to mark disjunctive taxis, disjunctive status and other-oriented voice. To avoid the analytic embarrasment of having to posit three distinct, yet homophonous auxiliaries, *viṭa*$_1$ for taxis, *viṭa*$_2$ for status and *viṭa*$_3$ for voice, we suggest treating *viṭa* as general among these three categories. We propose to represent it symbolically as the generalized disjunctive connector XE^n, where X ranges over $\{E^n, E^s, P^n\}$. When E^n is substituted for X in this formula, the resulting category is taxis, E^nE^n; when E^s is substituted, the result is status, E^s/E^n; and when P^n is substituted, the result is voice, P^nE^n. In a similar vein, auxiliary *irukka* 'be located' variously marks tense and status; its meaning is analyzed here as general between the quantifier of E^s/E^n, tense, and its corresponding qualifier, status. Despite many apparent different readings, each auxiliary is argued to have an invariant meaning.

1 The use of the terms major and minor here is intended merely as classificatory; no value judgment should be attached to them.

Function of indicative auxiliaries

The meanings of indicative auxiliaries reflect the uses to which they are put in conversation. They encode verbal categories that elaborate the narrated event, anchoring it to the context of utterance. These categories indicate who is involved (voice), what relation it bears to other events (tense and taxis), how it is known (status) and what opinion the participants have of it (attitude). They enable the participants in conversation to construct a coherent mental picture of what is being said, acting as a kind of grammatical cement between the narrated event and other facets of the utterance. They are thus responsible for much of the cohesion (Halliday and Hasan 1976) in Tamil syntactic structures.

As proposed in Chapter 1, the paucity of parts of speech likely promotes the elaboration of auxiliaries marking taxis and attitude in Tamil. Since Tamil lacks primitive conjunctions or complementizers, AVCs signal the interclausal relations that these parts of speech supply in languages like English. Except for the conditional, which marks taxis, all other combining forms (*vinaiyeccam*) mark only mood; taxis is thus only minimally represented in the basic verb morphology. The absence of a primitive category of adverbs also encourages the proliferation of auxiliaries marking status and attitude. Where English uses sentential adverbs, e.g., *probably*, *doubtfully*, *likely*, *unlikely*, to represent the speaker's knowledge concerning the utterance, Tamil uses its auxiliaries.

Sources for auxiliaries

Chapter 1 also observed that many auxiliaries are typically motion verbs. As nonauxiliated verbs, these lexemes range over a concrete domain such as space; as auxiliaries, they range over abstract domains such as time or knowledge. Many of the verbs in Chapters 6, 7 and 8 have a strong motion or location component: *irukka* means 'be located'; *koḷḷa*, 'hold, contain'; *viṭa*, 'leave, depart from'; *kiṭakka*, 'lie'; *vara*, 'come'; *pārkka*, 'look at'; *koṭukka*, 'give'; *pōka* 'go'; *taḷḷa*, 'push'; *tolaiya*, 'get lost'; *pōṭa*, 'put'; etc.

AUXILIARY OF ANTERIOR INTERVAL: *irukka*

In our corpus, the Tamil verb *irukka* 'be (located)' serves three primary functions: as a nonauxiliated "main" verb, a modal auxiliary and an indicative auxiliary. It also appears in certain lexical compounds, e.g., *eẓuntu irukka* 'get up'. In (197a) *irukka* predicates a location of its subject, in (197b) it serves as an auxiliary of (present) prospective tense in a modal AVC and in (197c) it functions as an auxiliary of (present) perfect tense in an indicative AVC.

(197)a	*kaṇṇaṉ*	*vīṭ.ṭ-il*	*iru-kkiṟ-āṉ.*
	Kannan-NOM	house-LOC	be-PRES-3SM
	'Kannan is in the house.'		

b *avaṉ* *ceṉṉaikku.p* $_{AVC}$[*pōka* *iru-kkiṟ-āṉ*].
he-NOM Madras-DAT go-INF be-PRES-3SM
'He is (about) to go to Madras.'

c *avaṉ* *ceṉṉaikku.p* $_{AVC}$[*pōy* *iru-kkiṟ-āṉ*].
he-NOM Madras-DAT go-CF be-PRES-3SM
'He has gone to Madras.'

Several scholars have studied this verb's semantics, including Lindholm (1969), Schiffman (1969: 140ff.), Annamalai (1982: 147ff.) and Fedson (1981: 21, 40, 47, 130). In general, they attribute a core meaning of stativity to *irukka*. Our analysis posits a basic locational meaning that is common to all three of its uses: 'be located (in a place) (at a time)'.

Main verb use

As a main verb, that is as a simple, nonauxiliated verb or an auxiliate in an AVC, *irukka* 'be located' predicates a temporary location or state of its subject. In example (198a) it combines with two NPs, one in the nominative and one in the locative case,[2] so that the sentence predicates a location of the subject. In example (198b) it combines with a nominative NP and a denominal adverbial, predicating of the subject the state that is expressed by the adverbial. Both of these situations are viewed as temporary.

(198)a *avaṉ* *kaṭai.y-il* *iru-pp-āṉ*.
he-NOM store-LOC be-FUT-3SM
'He will/would be in the store.'

b *avaṉ* *cantōṣam-āy* *iru-nt-āṉ*.
he-NOM happy-ADV be-PST-3SM
'He was happy.'

While the sentences in (199a and b) are often treated as synonymous, they differ in an important way. Example (199a) is an equational sentence with a subject,

(199)a *avaṉ* *maṉitaṉ*.
he-NOM man-NOM
'He is a man.'

b *avaṉ* *maṉitaṉ-āka* *irukkiṟāṉ*.
he-NOM man-NOM-become-INF be-PRES-3SM
'He is a man (now).'

c *avaṉ* *maṉitaṉ* *ā-v-āṉ*.
He-NOM man-NOM become-FUT-3SM
'He will become a man.'

2 This is to be broadly understood. It is not necessary to explicitly mark locative case; use of an inherently locative word such as *aṅkē* 'there' is sufficient for a well-formed phrase.

avaṉ 'he', in the nominative case and a predicate nominal *maṉitaṉ* 'man', also in the nominative. It predicates manhood of the subject as an essential property. (199b), on the other hand, predicates manhood of the subject as an accidental property; it can describe a myth in which a god or an animal temporarily takes on human form. Despite its apparent brevity, its structure is involved: the so-called adverbial suffix *-āka* is actually the infinitive of *āka* 'become', just as the adverbial suffix *-āy* in (198b) is (historically) a contracted conjunctive form of the same verb. *āka* means 'become, assume a role' and is the most basic change-of-state verb in Tamil. It refers to two different states, one before and one after the change has occurred. To say the subject became a man is to imply that at some earlier time he was not a man, but a child, god or animal. *āka* thus conveys the notion that the property predicated of the subject is temporary because it is liable to change over time. Why then does *irukka* 'be located' appear in (198b) and (199b)? The morphology of modern spoken Tamil does not furnish *āka* with the finite forms necessary to bear tense and agreement markers; *irukka* is inserted as a morphological prop for them. It is probably chosen because as a common verb with a general meaning, it introduces the least amount of extraneous information into the structure. Example (199c), with *āka* inflected for the future tense, is possible only in written Tamil.

While the invariable predicate *uṇṭu* 'exists' in (200a) is used to assert God's existence,[3] (200b) illustrates how *irukka* 'be located' requires a locative expression. Without the material in brackets, (200b) strikes Tamil speakers as incomplete; indeed, the presence of *irukka* prompts them to ask where God is and, in effect, to complete the sentence with a locative expression. *irukka* thus appears to coordinate spatial and temporal dimensions: one is in a place at a time.

(200)a *kaṭavuḷ uṇṭu.*
god-NOM exist
'God exists,' 'There is a God.'

3 Lindholm (1969: 6) argues that *irukka* is an existential predicate used to assert the existence of the subject; however, the defective verb *uṇṭu* in (200a) more properly serves this function. He holds that *irukka* instantiates the existential quantifier, whose meaning would preclude its syncategorematic introduction. However, even if the logical structure of (200b) contained an existential quantifier, it would not necessarily be introduced by *irukka*. Tamil has no overt definite article and so must convey definiteness by other means. Consider the following sequence.

(i) *oru maṉitaṉ vantāṉ. appuṟam maṉitaṉ uṭkārntāṉ.*
one man-NOM come-PST-3SM then man-NOM sit-PST-3SM
'A man came in. Then the man sat down.'

The Tamil sequence *oru N . . . ø N* appears to behave just like the English sequence *a N . . . the N*: the indefinite article *oru* 'one' introduces a discourse referent (McCawley 1979b) which is subsequently treated as an existentially quantified expression for the purposes of the subsequent discourse. In Tamil, a subject NP without an indefinite quantifier, such as *oru* 'one' or *cila* 'some', is treated as definite and existentially quantified. Thus, if there is an existential quantifier in the logical structure of (200b), it is most likely expressed by the "phantom" definite article/existential quantifier combined with the noun *kaṭavuḷ* 'God', not by the verb *irukka*.

b *kaṭavuḷ* ??(*aṅkē*) *irukkiṟāṉ*.
god-NOM there be-PRES-3SM
'God is ??(there).'

Unless explicitly noted, the location that *irukka* 'be located' predicates of its subject is not a point but an extended area, a semantic component that accompanies all the verb's uses. Note in this regard that *irukka* forms part of the complex ablative case marker. In (201a and b), *iruntu*, the verb's conjunctive form, combines with the locative case markers, *-il* (inanimate) and *-iṭam* (animate), to form the inanimate and animate ablative case suffixes, respectively. The locative case marker provides the initial endpoint of the interval described by the ablative case, i.e., from X (to Y), while *iruntu* provides its final endpoint. Thus, *irukka* more precisely means 'be located (in an extended place) (at a time)'.

(201)a *avaṉ* *vīṭ.ṭ-il+iruntu* *vantāṉ*.
he-NOM house-LOC+be-CF come-PST-3SM
'He came from the house.'

b *avaḷ* *avaṉ-iṭam+iruntu* *pārsal* *vāṅkiṉāḷ*.
she-NOM he-LOC+be-CF parcel-NOM get-PST-3SF
'She got a parcel from him.'

Indicative auxiliary uses

The verb *irukka* 'be located' may serve as an indicative auxiliary. Depending on context, it appears to have four circumstantial meanings.

(202)a *kalamā* [$_{S1}$ [$_{S0}$*taṭittu*] *irukkiṟāḷ*]].
Kamala-NOM be.fat-CF be-PRES-3SF
'Kamala is fat.'

b *kumār* *tiṇaiyil* [$_{S1}$ [$_{S0}$*uṭkārntu*] *irukkiṟāṉ*]].
Kumar-NOM porch-LOC sit-CF be-PRES-3SM
'Kumar is sitting on the porch.'

c *avaṉ* *ceṉṉaikku.p* [$_{S1}$ [$_{S0}$*pōy*] *irukkiṟāṉ*]].
he-NOM Madras-DAT go-CF be-PRES-3SM
'He has gone to Madras.'

d *appā* *nēṟṟu* *vīṭṭukku* [$_{S1}$ [$_{S0}$*vantu*] *irukkiṟār*]].
father-NOM yesterday home-DAT come-CF be-PRES-3H
'Father came home yesterday (I have indirect proof).'

In (202a) *irukka* combines with the stative verb *taṭikka* 'be fat': the AVC expresses the (present) durative tense of *taṭikka*. In nonauxiliated form, *taṭikka* would be general between durative and punctual readings; *irukka* thus indicates that when the truth of the proposition it modifies is evaluated, it must be evaluated over an interval, not at a single point. In (202b) *irukka* combines with *uṭkāra* 'sit', which may express an activity or change of state. On the activity reading, the AVC is interpreted as the (present) progressive tense of *uṭkāra* 'sit': the truth of the embedded proposition is evaluated over an interval of time (anchored in the present). In (202c) *irukka* combines with (*ceṉṉaikku.p*) *pōy* 'going (to Madras)': the resulting AVC is construed as the present perfect of this expression. In Vendler's (1967) schema *ceṉṉaikku.p pōy* is an accomplishment, an aspectual class in which an activity, going, leads to a change of state, being in Madras. The perfect tense therefore describes a temporal interval during which an activity that precedes the reference time runs its course and culminates in a change of state.

All three examples thus crucially involve temporal intervals over which the truth of an embedded proposition is to be evaluated. The apparent semantic differences among them, we argue, vary directly with the aspectual class of the auxiliate, not the identity of the auxiliary. Neither stative nor activity verbs culminate in a change of state so when they combine with auxiliary *irukka,* the result is a durative or progressive tense reading, respectively. However, when achievement and accomplishment verbs, which do incorporate a change of state, combine with *irukka*, the result is a perfect tense reading. These observations provide evidence for the claim made in Chapter 3 that while the three simple tense forms are general between points and intervals of time, compound tenses, represented in general by AVCs and here by perfect, are positively marked for temporal intervals.

Reverting to the fourth usage, Tamil speakers understand (202d) in a different light: they regard its time reference as neither present progressive nor present perfect, but simply as past. What then does the auxiliary *irukka* contribute to the understanding of this AVC? Our analysis shows it indicates that the speaker has indirect evidence for what he is stating. In such instances, *irukka* indicates that there is an interval over which the truth of the embedded proposition is to be evaluated. But the difference between this example and the previous three lies in the fact that the interval connects epistemic values, not temporal ones. Here the auxiliary tells the participants in conversation that the evaluation of the proposition's truth is to be referred to a value that is epistemically or logically prior to the reference point, such as a premise in a logical argument. Examples below reveal that the directness of the evidence varies directly with tense marking.

In its temporal and the epistemic readings, then, auxiliary *irukka* crucially refers to an interval that precedes the reference point. Time and knowledge may be viewed as abstract, structured domains; the information that they provide helps the participants in conversation get a hold on what is being said by referring it to specific temporal and epistemic states. Accordingly, the definition of tense must be refined to accommodate this situation. Jakobson's representation of tense is E^n/E^s, a connector that characterizes the relation between the narrated event and the speech event. While tradition may have led linguists to interpret the relation between them as exclusively temporal, Tamil evidence shows that it can also be epistemic.[4] Where that relation is in fact epistemic, the auxiliary will be said to instantiate the verbal category of status.

4 The use of a perfect tense series for to convey inference has been attested in other languages. See Haugen (1987: 175) for a discussion of the inferential perfect in Scandinavian languages.

Negation and auxiliary irukka

Consider how auxiliary *irukka* 'be located' interacts with negation. AVCs with *irukka* have virtually no idiosyncratic restrictions in affirmative contexts, appearing wherever simple verbs do. Negative contexts, however, present a twist. The negative of auxiliary *irukka* is rare in the past and present tenses, and when it does occur, it is highly marked. Instead, the simple negative form appears. Thus, in the past and present negative paradigms, there is a neutralization between the AVC with *irukka* and its nonauxiliated counterpart in favor of the nonauxiliated form. In essence, one form, the indicative negative, does duty for the negative of the past and present, simple and perfect, tense forms. In (204a) it serves as the negative of both the simple form in (203a) and the AVC in (203b). When parents tell their children of events prior to their birth, for example, they use (204a), not (204b). (204b), which results from the mechanical application of negation to (203b), is rare.

(203)a *nī pir̠antāy.*
you-S-NOM be.born-PST-2S
'You were born.'

b *nī pir̠antu iruntāy.*
you-S-NOM be.born-CF be-PST-2S
'You had been born (when X occurred).'

(204)a *nī pir̠akka.v illai.*
you-S-NOM be.born-INF IND-NEG
'You weren't/hadn't/aren't/haven't been born.'

b *? *nī pir̠antu irukka.v illai.*
you-S-NOM be.born-CF be-INF IND-NEG
'You hadn't been born (yet).'

Observe what happens when a negative response answers a question with auxiliary *irukka*. The indicative AVC with *irukka* in the question (205a) is replaced by a simple negative form (205b). The form in (205c), generated by the blind application of the negative operator *illai* 'not be' to the AVC, is perceived by speakers as distinctly odd.

(205)a *avan̠ vantu irukkir̠ān̠=ā?*
he-NOM come-CF be-PRES-3SM=INT
'Has he come?'

b *avan̠ vara.v illai.*
he-NOM come-INF IND-NEG
'He didn't/hasn't come.'

c ?? *avan̠ vantu irukka.v illai.*
he-NOM come-CF be-INF IND-NEG
'He hasn't come.'

When a negative indicative perfect form does crop up on occasion, as in dime-store novels called *malivuppatippu*, its use is considered to be the mark of a poor writer. In examples such as (206), the negative indicative perfect form does not generally convey tense, but taxis, and is used to link the two clauses.

(206) *nāṉ pōṉa nērattil avaṉ vantu irukka.v illai.*
I-NOM go-PST-ADN time-LOC he-NOM come-CF be-INF IND-NEG
'He had not come by the time I left.'

A logical rationale may explain the lack of a formal negative counterpart to the past and present perfect AVCs. *irukka* 'be located' indicates the proposition expressed by the sentence is to be evaluated over an anterior interval. The negative indicative tells us that there is no time at which the proposition is true, which leads to the following conclusion: there can be no interval during which it was true because there was no single moment at which it was true.[5] Though the simple negative indicative usually serves as the negative for the past and present, simple and perfect tenses, examples such as (206) provide evidence of less conservative dialects where the prohibition against the negative indicative perfect is relaxed.

By contrast, in modal forms and modal contexts, such as the future tense (207a) or the conditional (207b), a negative perfect form is unexceptional.

(207)a *nī ittaṉai naẓi kaẓittu vantu irukka.v=ē māṭṭiyē.*
you-NOM this.much time pass-CF come-CF be-INF=EMP FUT-NEG-2S
'It is surprising that after all this time you would not have come.'

b *avaṉ vantu irukkāviṭṭāl...*
he-NOM come-CF be-NEG-COND
'If he had not come...'

It should be noted that the prohibition against a negative indicative perfect is not formally but semantically motivated. Speakers accept (208) where, with a rising intonation, it functions as the protasis of a conditional statement (see p. 63). This context endows the formally indicative *irukka.v illai* with a modal interpretation, making it acceptable.

(208) *avaṉ vantu irukka.v illai* ↑ *eṉṉa paṇṇuvāy?*
he-NOM come-CF be-INF IND-NEG what do-FUT-2S
'Suppose he hasn't come (by then), what will you do?'

Consider how Negative Raising interacts with the negative perfect. The preferred reading of (209a) is the first gloss, where the negative marker *illai* 'not be' is associated with the lower, not the upper, clause. However, the lower clause also contains the perfect tense operator *irukka*. While the preferred reading thus stipulates that both operators must be semantically associated with the lower clause,

5 This follows the quantificational analog to a De Morgan Law (McCawley 1993: 96-7): $\sim(\exists{:}fx)gx \rightarrow (\forall{:}\ fx)\sim gx$. From the proposition that there is no past or present time at which proposition Y is true, it follows that for all past and present times, proposition Y was not true.

(209c) shows that they both cannot be formally manifested on the same AVC. The only way the combination can be pronounced is as in (209b), where the perfect tense marking has been neutralized, or, less felicitously, in (209a) after Negative-Raising has lifted the negative operator into the matrix clause allowing perfect tense marking of the lower clause verb.

(209)a $[_{S0}$ $[_{S1}$*avaṉ vantu irukkiṟāṉ*] *eṉṟu avaḷ nampa.v illai*].
he-NOM come-CF be-PRES-3SM say-CF she-NOM believe-INF IND-NEG
'She believes that he hasn't come.' (preferred reading)
or
'She doesn't believe that he has come.' (alternate reading)

b $[_{S0}$ $[_{S1}$*avaṉ vara.v illai*] *eṉṟu avaḷ nampukiṟāḷ*].
he-NOM come-INF IND-NEG say-CF she-NOM believe-PRES-3SF
'She believes that he didn't/hasn't come.'

c ?? *avaṉ vantu irukka.v illai eṉṟu avaḷ nampukiṟāḷ.*
he-NOM come-CF be-INF IND-NEG say-CF she-NOM trust-PRES-3SF
'She believes that he hasn't come."

Durative and progressive readings of irukka

Examples below illustrate how *irukka* marks the durative/progressive tense series.[6] All auxiliates in (210) are stative verbs or verbs of habitual activity in the Vendler-Dowty scheme of aspectual classes (Dowty 1979: Chapter 2). These two classes are generally homogenous throughout their duration: to distinguish them from punctual events, they must be evaluated over an interval of time. Elsewhere Dowty notes that many activity verbs can be aspectually "strengthened" and interpreted as accomplishments. A similar strengthening occurs in Tamil, as evidenced below; for example, (210b) may be interpreted either as 'the clothes are bleached' (stative) or as 'the clothes have been bleached' (accomplishment). Likewise, (210c) can be interpreted as 'the brahmin is fat' (stative) or 'the brahmin has become fat' (accomplishment).

(210)a *kaṇṇāṭi* $[_{S1}$ $[_{S0}$*uṭaintu*] *irukkiṟatu*].
glass-NOM break+AF-CF be-PRES-3N
'The glass is broken.'

b *tuṇi* $[_{S1}$ $[_{S0}$*veḷuttu*] *irukkiṟatu*].
clothes-NOM be.white-CF be-PRES-3N
'The clothes are/have been bleached.'

c *aiyar* $[_{S1}$ $[_{S0}$*tatittu*] *irukkiṟār*].
Brahmin-NOM be.fat-CF be-PRES-3H
'The Brahmin is fat.'

6 No formal properties in Tamil appear to motivate a principled semantic distinction between durativity and progressivity. The first is used when the auxiliary combines with a stative predicate, the latter when it combines with an activity predicate.

Stative verbs in Tamil commonly occur in AVCs with *irukka* 'be located' since it is unmarked for them to be durative; by contrast, the simple past tense may be used when a punctual interpretation is sought. And when interpreted punctually, these stative verbs involve a change of state. As simple verbs are general between durative and punctual readings, with the latter a subcase of the former, the punctual interpretation of (211b) is not part of the invariant meaning of the form. However, when an inherently durative auxiliate occurs in and AVC with *irukka*, the following conversational implicature may arise. To use the simple tense form in a context where you could have but chose not to use the periphrastic form (AVC with *irukka*) is to invite the implicature that the meaning associated with the periphrastic form, durativity, is inappropriate, effectively ruling out the durative reading in favor of the punctual.

(211)a *avaṉ paṭuttu irukkiṟāṉ.*
he-NOM lie-CF be-PRES-3SM
'He is lying down/has lain down.'

b *avaṉ paṭuttāṉ.*
he-NOM lie-PST-3SM
'He lay down.'

The reading of durativity in these examples thus correlates with the aspectual class of the main verb. States and activities are inherently durative; it is in fact unmarked for them to be so. Achievements and accomplishments correlate with punctuality because both incorporate a change of state. In labeling *irukka* as the stative auxiliary, previous authors have often left unsaid what they mean by this term. Stativity is treated here as an aspectual class of the main verb, one which implies duration in time, and is thus attributed to the auxiliate not the auxiliary.

Perfect tense reading of irukka

Perhaps the most frequent use of *irukka* 'be located' in an indicative AVC is as a marker of the perfect tense series. A perfect tense reading arises when a nonstative auxiliate, one whose aspectual class is an achievement or accomplishment, combines with auxiliary *irukka*. This signals that the proposition is to be evaluated over an anterior interval of time. Accomplishments are activities that culminate in a change of state, while achievements involve a change of state, instantaneous or not. The notion change of state is crucial to both, implying two distinct moments, one at which some proposition X is not true and a subsequent one at which it is true. When such an auxiliate combines with auxiliary *irukka*, the implication is that both moments, before and after the change of state, are included in the interval. This gives rise to the present result of a past activity, which is one popular definition of the perfect tense series.

(212)a *āciriyar anta.p putu kataiyai eẓuti irukkiṟār.*
author-NOM that new story-ACC write-CF be-PRES-3H
'The author has written that new story.'

b *māriyammāḷ mattiyāṇa.c cāppaṭṭai.c camaittu iruppāḷ.*
Mariyammal-NOM afternoon meal-ACC cook-CF be-FUT-3SF
'Mariyammal would/will have cooked the afternoon meal.'

Benveniste (1959: 246-47) argues the perfect tense is a complex notion consisting of two parts, anteriority and accomplishment. It represents an interval of time that is anterior, and leads up, to the reference time. At the reference time, the accomplishment is held to be consummated. Reichenbach's (1947) analysis of the perfect tense claims that it refers to an interval of time, with event time preceding reference time. More recent analyses stress the notions of "current relevance," "result" or "accomplishment" (in Benveniste's term, *accomplissement temporalisé*) at the expense of the notion of anteriority. McCoard (1978) argues that "current relevance" is not the invariant meaning of the (English) perfect tense; in its place he proposes that the perfect tense represents an *extended now*, a proposal Dowty (1979) elaborates within model-theoretic semantics. McCoard's proposal agrees with ours in emphasizing the notion of termporal interval or extension. Nonetheless, it fails to specify the component of anteriority, concentrating only on the final endpoint of the interval. As it stands, this position would not suffice to distinguish the English progressive tense from the perfect tense series. Bennett (1981) does so by associating the notion of accomplishment to the perfect tense, but not to the progressive. As noted above, our analysis ascribes this distinction, not to the auxiliary, but to the aspectual class of the auxiliate. Thus, for the Tamil AVC with *irukka*, the readings of accomplishment, current relevance and the like are circumstantial meanings which vary with the aspectual class of the auxiliate.

The temporal interval that *irukka* signals is anterior to the reference time and extends forward into it. Two auxiliaries, *irukka* 'be located' and *viṭa* 'leave', often translate the English perfect. But *viṭa* signals disjunction (see below) while *irukka* does not. Both can on occasion have anterior taxis as a circumstantial reading, but while *viṭa* signals temporal disjunction or discontinuity, *irukka* does not. As a result, *viṭa* 'leave' often conveys punctual aspect, while *irukka* signals durative or iterative aspect. Example (213a) describes the visit of a celebrity: *irukka* implies some temporal continuity with the past event and present pride of the speaker about that event; (213b), on the other hand, describes the appearance of some unwelcome vistor: *viṭa* conveys disjunction in that the speaker wants to distance himself from the unpleasant event.

(213)a *avar oru taṭavai vantu irukkiṟār.*
he-NOM one time come-CF be-PRES-3H
'He has come here once.'

b *avar oru taṭavai vantu viṭṭār.*
he-NOM one time come-CF leave-PST-3H
'He has come here once.'

In (214a), use of *irukka* suggests that the undesirability which prompts the negative judgment embodied in *naṭakka.k kūṭātō* 'should not (happen)' extends from the past into the present, continuing to have consequences for the speaker. The use of *viṭa* in (214b) puts distance—temporal or epistemic—between the speaker and the undesirable event.

(214)a *eṉṉa naṭakka.k kūṭāt=ō atu naṭantu irukkiṟatu.*
what-NOM occur-INF should.not=OR that-NOM occur-CF be-PRES-3N
'What should not have happened, has happened.'

b *eṉṉa naṭakka.k kūṭāt=ō atu naṭantu viṭṭatu.*
what-NOM occur-INF should.not=OR that-NOM occur-CF leave-PST-3N
'What should not have happened, did happen.'

From what has been said so far, an auxiliate whose aspectual class happens to be an accomplishment or achievement cannot directly combine with auxiliary *irukka* 'be located' to yield a progressive tense reading, and this in fact is the case. To form the progressive tense of an auxiliate of either aspectual class, speakers use a complex AVC with the auxiliaries *koḷḷa* 'hold' and *irukka*. Kandaiah (1968) first proposed that "affixation" of auxiliary *koḷḷa* to an auxiliate creates, in effect, a progressive or stative "participle," called an imperfective converb here. As elaborated below in our discussion of *koḷḷa* (p. 201), when auxiliary *irukka* combines with this converb, what results is the progressive tense of the embedded auxiliate. This complex AVC indicates that there is an interval (*irukka*) which contains (*koḷḷa*) a sample of the auxiliate's activity, but not the final change of state. This reading coincides in large part with Dowty's (1979: 145) stipulations on the truth-conditions for English progressive tense forms.

Taxis thus need not be considered part of the invariant meaning of auxiliary *irukka* 'be located'; however, the fact that it describes a temporal interval suits it to a reading of taxis as a circumstantial meaning because an event that extends over an interval of time is likely to overlap the temporal coordinates of other events.

Epistemic use of irukka

Example (202d) illustrated *irukka* 'be located' in an epistemic, not a temporal function: it indicates the degree of evidence the speaker has for his assertion. Schiffman (1969), Ramanujan and Annamalai (1969: 159), Annamalai (1982: 154-56) and Fedson (1981: 47-52) note the epistemic potential of *irukka*, but fail to describe its full extent or systematic nature. All authors record it in the future tense; Fedson (1981) records it in the present. Its actual scope is broader, encompassing past, present and future: our examples reveal that the degree of evidence a speaker claims to have varies directly with the simple tense marking on the auxiliary. In (215a) *irukka* bears the past tense marker, indicating the speaker has strong, direct evidence, such as witnessing the event. In (215b) it takes the present tense, indicating indirect evidence, e.g., the speaker's knowledge derives from a report or such circumstantial evidence as seeing the subject's luggage. In (215c) it takes the future tense, indicating a conjecture. Finally, in (215) *irukka*'s approximate epistemic contribution is indicated within brackets in the gloss.

(215)a *avaṉ nēṟṟu vantu iruntāṉ.*
he-NOM yesterday come-CF be-PST-3SM
'He came yesterday (I have direct evidence).'

b *avaṉ nēṟṟu vantu irukkiṟāṉ.*
he-NOM yesterday come-CF be-PRES-3SM
'He came yesterday (I have indirect evidence).'

c *avaṉ nēṟṟu vantu iruppāṉ.*
he-NOM yesterday come-CF be-FUT-3SM
'He came yesterday (I conjecture).'
or
'He would have come yesterday.'

Although epistemic perfects are known in other languages (see Haugen 1987:175 for the Scandinavian languages), no one has remarked on the correlation between tense and status in Tamil.[7] Note that each sentence in (215) contains the temporal adverb *nēṟṟu* 'yesterday', which appears to block *irukka* from accessing a perfect tense reading. Bilingual informants confirmed that (215b) could not be construed as 'he has come yesterday', which struck them just as odd in Tamil as its English counterpart.

How is the epistemic use of *irukka* 'be located' reconciled with the temporal in our analysis? We retain the notion of an anterior interval relating two values in a structured domain; however, the epistemic use does not relate temporal values, but epistemic ones, such as propositions or information states. As a marker of status,[8] it indicates that a logically or epistemically prior state exists which is relevant to evaluating the truth of the proposition at the reference time, as signaled by the auxiliary's tense marking. What does it mean for one proposition to be epistemically prior to another? It can mean that the prior proposition functions as a premise in a logical argument whose conclusion is the later proposition, or, more weakly, that it is evidence which supports the later proposition. The degree of certainty with which the speaker advances his assertion varies directly with the tense marking.

As noted in the discussion of *kālavaḻuvamaiti* 'sanctioned deviations in tense use' in Chapter 3, each simple tense marks mood and makes an ontological commitment of varying strength. The past tense makes the strongest, the present tense a weaker one and the future tense the weakest. The past is viewed as the domain of events which are held to be real and which the participants in conversation accept as given and noncontroversial. The present marks a domain of events which are viewed as real but still unfolding before the participants; since the present is not yet history, its ontological commitment is less firm than the past. As a modal form,

7 This tripartite distinction was discovered by K. Paramasivam and the author in fieldwork, and later confirmed by E. Annamalai (personal communication).

8 We propose the term *status*, first introduced by Benjamin Lee Whorf, to describe the grammatical category to represent this distinction. Aronson (1978) uses status to describe the relation named by the formular P^s/E^n, which in Chapter 8 we reserve for *attitude*. I believe that the symbolic representation of what I call status should be the qualifier of E^s/E^n, opposed to tense the quantifier of E^s/E^n.

the future makes an even weaker ontological commitment than either the past or the present tense forms.

This discussion assumes that the propositions which serve as evidence do not float freely in some epistemic space, but are organized into structured groups. Perhaps the most important group is the *context set* of propositions, those noncontroversial propositions that the participants in the speech event accept as given and true (Karttunen 1976, McCawley 1979b). As used here, a proposition that is marked for the past fully belongs to this context set, one marked for the present stands on its threshold and one marked for the future stands outside this set. The gradient from past to future tense is thus paralleled by the gradient from least to most controversial status.

Consider further examples of the epistemic perfect. Example (216) presents a brief discourse from a novel,[9] divided here into its three component sentences. (216a) is a question that asks how the addressee came to know of a certain detail. (216b) answers using an AVC with *irukka* 'be located'. The temporal expression *nēṟṟu* 'yesterday', not the tense marker, establishes the time reference of the narrated event: it signals that *irukka* should be interpreted epistemically, not temporally. Note the remainder of the discourse (216c) continues in the simple past tense.

(216)a *uṅkaḷukku eppaṭi inta vivaram teriyum? eṉṟēṉ.*
you-DAT how this detail know-FUT-3SN ask-PST-1S
b *nēṟṟu.k kūṭa kāntam iṅkē vantu iruntāḷ.*
yesterday even Kantam-NOM here come-CF be-PST-3SF
c *ellavaṟṟai.y=um kūṟiṉāḷ.*
all-ACC=AND tell-PST-3SF
'I asked, "How do you know these details?" Kantam came here yesterday. She told (me) everything.'

Another conversational exchange from the same novel[10] is split into three sections to illustrate epistemic *irukka* 'be located'. (217a) sets the stage. In (217b), one speaker uses the present perfect tense form to tell his friend that his knowledge of the girl's deception is second-hand. In (217c) his friend cuts him short and,

(217)a *ivaḷ katai eḻutukiṟavaḷ alla: pattrikkai mutalāḷiyiṉ makaḷ;*
she-NOM story writer-3SN not newspaper owner-GEN daughter-NOM
b *uṉṉai nēṟṟu ēmāṟṟi irukkiṟāḷ.*
you-ACC yesterday deceive-CF be-PST-3SF
c *avaḷ kiṭattaṭṭum kātāl kēṭṭatai ippōtu col!*
she-NOM lie-OPT ear-INSTR hear-ACC now tell-IMP
'She's no storywriter, she's the daughter of the owner of this newspaper. She tricked you yesterday (I have indirect evidence). Never mind her. Now tell me what you have heard with your own ears.'

9 Akilan (1951: 37).
10 Akilan (1951: 40).

as if to offset the indirect evidence, asks what the first speaker has heard himself. Note that (217b), which uses the present perfect tense form evidentially, contains an explicit time expression, *nēṟṟu* 'yesterday', which specifies when the deception took place. (217c) reverts to the simple past tense.

Example (218) offers another connected discourse.[11] The second sentence gives the speaker's impression, which is then backed up by more direct evidence in the third. The speaker claims direct evidence that another member of the household, Rankam, was asking him about the subject's whereabouts. Note the presence of the temporal expression *pōṉa vāram* 'last week', which gives the time reference of the evidenced event. Explicit time expressions do not accompany all such examples in our corpus, but seem more common in the past and present epistemic perfect than the future.

(218) *nīṅkaḷ āttu.p pakkamē vara.v illai.y-ē vantu mācakkaṇakkāka*
you-NOM house side=EMP come-INF NEG-IND come-CF month.count-ADV
āyirukkum pōl irukkē. raṅkam kūṭa pōṉa vāram colli
become-FUT like be-PRES-3N Rangam-NOM even last week say-CF
uṇṭē iruntāḷ maṇiyai.k kāṇavē illaiyē eṉṉu ...
hold-CF be-pst-3SF Mani-ACC see-INF IND-NEG-EMP say-CF
'You haven't come around to the house... Why it seems like months since you last came. Even Rankam said so last week (I have direct evidence): Mani hasn't been seen at all.'

The contrast between a sentence with, and one without, the epistemic perfect highlights the semantic contribution of this auxiliary. Since the speaker in (219) was assumed to be asleep when the subject arrived, he cannot have directly witnessed the arrival. Hence, (219a) is inappropriate; (219b) with the inferential present perfect is used instead.

(219)a ?? *nāṉ tūṅkum pōtu avaṉ vantāṉ.*
I-NOM sleep-PST-ADN time he-NOM come-PST-3SM
'He came when I slept.'

b *nāṉ tūṅkum pōtu avan vantu irukkiṟāṉ.*
I-NOM sleep-PST-ADN time he-NOM come-CF be-PRES-3SM
'He came home when I was sleeping.'

Under the scope of predicates such as *teriyum* 'be known, clear', *kēḷvi* 'hearsay' and *vatanti* 'gossip', the distinction between direct and indirect evidence is neutralized. Use of the verb of propositional attitude *teriyum* 'be known, clear' in (220) asserts that there is direct knowledge of the event, so there can be no contrast between direct and indirect evidence in the subordinate clause. Similarly, in (221) the predicate *vatanti* 'gossip' indicates the speaker lacks direct evidence, again

11 Janakiraman (1966: 106). The auxiliary *uṇṭē* 'holding' is a Brahmin dialect variant of the auxiliary *koḷḷa* 'hold'. See below pp. 197-98.

neutralizing the contrast between direct and indirect evidence in the lower clause. Both contexts of neutralization lead to a formal neutralization: the distinction between simple and periphrastic verb forms is neutralized in favor of the simple forms, as predicted in our model.

(220)a *nēṟṟu vantatu ellārukkum teriyum.*
yesterday come-PST-VN all-DAT=AND know-FUT-3SN
'Everyone knows that he came yesterday.'

b *? *nēṟṟu vantu* { *irukkiṟatu* / be-PRES-3SN / *iruntatu* / be-PST-3SN } *ellārukkum teriyum.*
yesterday come-CF { be-PRES-3SN / be-PST-3SN } all-DAT-AND know-FUT-3SN
'Everyone knows that he came yesterday.'

(221)a *kuṭittu viṭṭu pāṉai ellām uṭaintatu eṉṟu vatanti.*
drink-CF leave-CF pots all break+EF-PST-VN that gossip-NOM
'The gossip (is) that he got drunk and smashed all the pots.'

b ?* *kuṭittu viṭṭu pāṉai ellām utaittu* { *irukkiṟatu* / be-PRES-VN / *iruntatu* / be-PST-VN } *eṉṟu vatanti*
drink-CF leave-CF pots all break-CF { be-PRES-VN / be-PST-VN } that gossip-NOM
'The gossip (is) that he got drunk and smashed all the pots.'

As the meaning conveyed by the epistemic perfect appears to be parasitic on the mood of tense-forms, where tense distinctions are neutralized, the epistemic distinctions dependent on them are also neutralized. In (222) the AVC *vantu irukka* 'be coming' cannot be interpreted epistemically; auxiliary *irukka* has a nonfinite form, the infinitive, which is unspecified for tense. The phrase is thus interpreted as the progressive tense of *vara* 'come'.

(222) *avaṉ vantu irukka ivaṉ pōṉāṉ.*
that.man-NOM come-CF be-INF this.man-NOM go-PST-3SM
'As that man was coming, this man went.'

Where other auxiliaries come between the most deeply embedded auxiliate and auxiliary *irukka* in a complex AVC, as in (223), an epistemic reading is available as long as a tense marker can be associated with the AVC.

(223) *avaṉ nēṟṟu* [$_{V2}$[$_{V1}$[$_{V0}$*vantu*] *tolaintu*] *irukkiṟāṉ*].
he-NOM yesterday come-CF lose+AF-CF be-PRES-3SM
'He came here yesterday, damn it (I have indirect evidence).'

The following examples demonstrate that *irukka* need not bear the tense inflections when it is nested inside a larger AVC inflected for tense. In (224a) the AVC *vantu irukka* 'to have come' nests within a larger construction, the *ceyya*-emphatic. The auxiliary *ceyya* 'do, make' bears the past tense marker, which may be associated to the auxiliary *irukka* to signal direct evidence. If the tense of *ceyya* changed to the present, it would combine with *irukka* to signal indirect evidence. In (224b)[12] the AVC *naṭantu irukka* 'to have occurred' nests within a modal AVC, signaled by the negative indicative auxiliary *illai* 'not be'. Since this modal AVC serves as the negative for both the past and present affirmative simple tenses, the three-way distinction in epistemic states appears to be reduced to a two-way distinction between conjecture (future tense) and evidenced (past and present tenses).[13]

(224)a *nēṟṟu vantu irukka.t tāṉ ceytāṉ.*
yesterday come-CF be-INF EMP do-PST-3SM
'He did come here yesterday (I have direct evidence).'

b *1947-il kūṭṭam naṭantu irukka.v illai.*
1947-LOC meeting-NOM occur-CF be-INF IND-NEG
'The meeting did not occur in 1947 (I have evidence).'

In the examples considered thus far, the speaker is credited with having evidence for the assertion. Our analysis of direct discourse (Chapter 5) necessitates some refinement. In direct discourse, it is the speaker of the original discourse, not the speaker of the report, who is credited with having evidence for what is being reported. Thus, the distinction between direct and indirect evidence in (225a and b) is attributed not to the speaker of these sentences, but to the speaker of the original speech, the referent of *avaḷ* 'she'.

(225)a $_{S0}$[*avaḷ* $_{S1}$[*avaṉ nēṟṟu vantu irukkiṟāṉ*] *eṉṟu coṉṉāḷ*].
she-NOM he-NOM yesterday come-CF be-PRES-3SM say-CF say-PST-3SF
'She said that he came yesterday (and she has indirect evidence).'

b $_{S0}$[*avaḷ* $_{S1}$[*avaṉ nēṟṟu vantu iruntāṉ*] *eṉṟu coṉṉāḷ*].
she-NOM he-NOM yesterday come-CF be-PST-3SM say-CF say-PST-3SF
'She said that he came yesterday (and she has direct evidence).'

This helps accounts for the oddity of (226). If responsibility for directly witnessing the event described in (226) were assumed by the speaker of that reporting speech, rather than the speaker of the original speech, *rāmaṉ*, the subject of *coṉṉār* 'he said', the sentence should contain no contradiction. The speaker could have known of *kiruṣṇaṉ*'s arrival without *rāmaṉ* knowing of it. It is only on the assump-

(226) ?* *kiruṣṇaṉ*$_{j}$ *nēṟṟu vantu iruntāṉ. āṉāl tāṉ*$_{i}$ *pārkka.v illai*
Krishna-NOM yesterday come-CF be-PST-3SM but self-NOM see-INF IND-NEG
eṉṟu coṉṉār rāmaṉ$_{i}$.
that say-PST-3H Raman
?? 'Raman said that (he had direct evidence that) Krishna came yesterday, but that he didn't see him.'

12 From Fedson (1981: 51).

13 Note the formal negative of the perfect is acceptable as long as it is interpreted epistemically.

tion that responsibility for the evidence is ascribed to the speaker of the original speech, namely *rāmaṉ*, that the oddity of this sentence can be explained.

This discussion has highlighted the past and present uses of the epistemic perfect because previous authors have treated its future use. Above (215c) presents one example; others are interspersed in the sections treating *irukka* in Schiffman (1969), Fedson (1981) and Annamalai (1982). In using the future epistemic perfect in (227), from Annamalai (1982: 155), the speaker indicates he is basing his statement on a hunch or general background knowledge, such as the frequency of rain during the monsoon. But he lacks direct or indirect evidence of this event, such as getting caught in a cloud burst. Use of the future epistemic perfect indicates here that the speaker's evaluation is not a random guess, but a conjecture based on background knowledge and general expectations.

(227) *nēṟṟu rāttiri maḻai peytu irukkum.*
yesterday night rain-NOM rain-CF be-FUT-3SN
'It would have/probably has rained last night.'

The epistemic perfect thus indicates that there is information epistemically prior to the narrated event, E^n, which is relevant for evaluating the truth of E^n. This epistemically prior proposition serves as evidence for E^n in much the way a proposition may serve as a premise in a logical proof. The strength of the evidence for E^n varies directly with the strength of the ontological commitment signaled by the tense marking on auxiliary *irukka* 'be located'. This suggests a symbolic representation for the epistemic perfect in Jakobson's system of grammatical categories: the connector E^s/E^n. While this formula is generally understood as the common representation for tense, nothing in Jakobson's system requires it to describe a temporal relation. Indeed, the Tamil epistemic perfect forces us to recognize the possibility that it can describe an epistemic as well as a temporal relation. For this purpose, the term status is used to describe the verbal category instantiated by the Tamil epistemic perfect, and treated as is the qualifier of E^s/E^n. As such, it is minimally opposed to tense, the quantifier of E^s/E^n. Status characterizes the evidential relation between the narrated event and the speech event.[14]

How do we determine when any given instance of auxiliary *irukka* 'be located' functions temporally or epistemically? Example (216b) contains three clues that the perfect tense form should be understood epistemically. First, the auxiliary is marked for tense. Second, a past time expression such as *nēṟṟu* 'yesterday' occurs, blocking a tense reading. Third, it answers the question how the addressee came by certain information, although this condition need not be explicitly stated.

In all its circumstantial uses, stative, progressive, perfect tense or status, auxiliary *irukka* crucially refers to an anterior interval connecting two points, one of which

14 And perhaps between the narrated event and the context set of propositions. Example (224b) above uses the epistemic perfect to signal a relation between two propositions, not necessarily organized on a time line.

precedes the reference point. When the auxiliary ranges over a temporal domain, the connected points are two times. The differences between the stative and progressive readings, on the one hand, and perfect tense, on the other, inhere in the aspectual class of the AVC's auxiliate, not the auxiliary. When the domain is epistemic, the connected points are two propositions connected by a relation of evidence. If our distinction between tense and status holds up to scrutiny, we can say that auxiliary *irukka* is general between the two: it characterizes the relation between the speech event and the narrated event without specifying either the qualitative or the quantitative aspects of that relation. It represents the connector E^s/E^n, general between a qualifier (status) and a quantifier (tense), which is positively marked for an interval rather than a single point.

DISJUNCTIVE CONNECTOR: *viṭa*

In the corpus of examples we collected, the verb *viṭa* 'leave, depart from, abandon' appears to have four primary functions. First, it serves as a transitive main verb in (228a and b), subcategorizing nominative and accusative arguments. Second, it serves as a component part in certain lexical compounds, e.g., *piṭittu viṭa* 'massage' (lit. 'grab and leave') in (228c).[15] Third, it serves as a quasi-modal verb in (228d), indicating permission. Finally, it serves as an indicative auxiliary. It is this last function whose analysis we will take up us in this section.

(228)a *avaḷ maturai.y-ai viṭṭāḷ.*
she-NOM Madurai-ACC leave-PST-3SF
'She left Madurai.'

b *nāṉ cikkareṭṭ-ai viṭa vēṇṭum.*
I-NOM cigarette-ACC leave-INF be.necessary-FUT-3N
'I have to give up cigarettes.'

c *avaḷ eṉ mutukai.p piṭittu viṭṭāḷ.*
she-NOM my back-ACC grab-CF leave-PST-3SF
'She massaged my back.'

d *avaṉ pantai uruḷa viṭṭāṉ.*
he-NOM ball-ACC roll-INF leave-PST-3SM
'He let the ball roll.'

Indicative auxiliary verb uses

As an indicative auxiliary, *viṭa* 'leave' marks disjunction and is symbolized by XE^n, where X ranges over $\{P^n, E^n, E^s\}$. Where E^n is substituted for X^n, the resulting verbal category is taxis, E^nE^n, which conveys temporal disjunction. Where E^s is

15 This compound is idiomatic because the action it describes is iterative, not semelfactive as both of its component parts are.

susbtituted, the result is status, E^s/E^n, with a disjunctive epistemic meaning. And where P^n is substituted, the resulting category is disjunctive voice, P^sE^n: the subject's action departs from a stereotypical activity. Auxiliary *viṭa* thus signals that the narrated event contrasts with another component of the utterance in terms of time, knowledge or stereotypical activity.

Auxiliary *viṭa* 'leave' appears in all major studies of the Tamil verb system, e.g., Schiffman (1969: 45, 114), Dale (1975: 210), Fedson (1981: 53, 80) and Annamalai (1982: 92-126). There and elsewhere, a variety of labels have been proposed to describe its meaning: completive, perfective, definitive, sequential and change of situation. These analyses do not generally seek to find an invariant meaning for these different uses; Fedson and Annamalai, for example, propose recognizing at least two different indicative auxiliary verbs *viṭa*.

When it is used temporally, *viṭa* 'leave' signals disjunctive anterior taxis, as in (229) where it signals temporal disjunction between the acts of returning home and eating, and the act of going to sleep. This disjunction distinguishes it from *irukka* 'be located'.

(229) *avaṉ vīṭṭukku vantu cāppiṭṭu viṭṭu.t tūṅkiṉāṉ.*
he-NOM home-DAT come-CF eat-CF leave-CF sleep-PST-3SM
'After he came home and ate, he slept.'

When used epistemically, *viṭa* signals disjunctive status, indicating that the narrated event contrasts with another proposition, either one in the context set (see above) or one that can be inferred from it. From epistemic disjunction arise the subsidiary nuances of unexpectedness or suddenness commonly attributed to this auxiliary. In (230), for example, *viṭa* informs us that the arrival of the speaker's relatives contrasts with what the speaker believed they would do.

(230) *contakkāraṅkaḷ nēṟṟ=ē vantu viṭṭārkaḷ.*
relatives-NOM yesterday-EMP come-CF leave-PST-3P
'My relatives unexpectedly came yesterday.'

In yet other contexts, *viṭa* functions as a voice marker: in (231b) it indicates that the auxiliate's action deviates from a stereotypical instance of the activity ordinarily denoted by the auxiliate. Unless otherwise noted, phrases such as *put on a shirt*, *comb one's hair*, *bathe*, *undress*, etc., are understood as pertaining to the subject: they are inherently self-directed. This is in fact the normal understanding of (231a): even without the reflexive pronoun *tāṉ* 'self', it describes an action the subject performed on herself. The presence of auxiliary *viṭa* in (231b), on the other hand, signals a departure from this norm so that the action is directed toward someone other than the subject.

(231)a *ammā oru cāṭṭai.p pōṭṭāḷ.*
mother-NOM one shirt-ACC put-PST-3SF
'Mother put a shirt on (herself).'

b *ammā oru cāṭṭai.p pōṭṭu viṭṭāḷ.*
mother-NOM one shirt-ACC put-CF leave-PST-3SF
'Mother put a shirt on someone else.'

Some properties of auxiliary viṭa

When it marks disjunctive taxis, *viṭa* 'leave' often signals punctual aspect so that one event is understood as ending before another begins. Recall from Chapter 3 that Tamil verb stems are inherently imperfective. Thus (232a) and (233a), without *viṭa*, are acceptable even though their closest English counterparts are unacceptable because English verbs are by comparison perfective. However, when these verbs combine with auxiliary *viṭa*, they are interpreted as perfective so that (232b) and (233b) are as anomolous as their English glosses. In such contexts, *viṭa* could be seen as an auxiliary of perfective aspect.

(232)a *nēṟṟu pustakam paṭittēṉ. āṉāl muṭikka.v illai.*
yesterday book read-PST-1S but finish-INF IND-NEG
'Yesterday I read *(from) the book; but I didn't finish it.'
b *? *nēṟṟu pustakam paṭittu viṭṭēṉ. āṉāl muṭikka.v illai.*
yesterday book read-CF leave-PST-1S but finish-INF IND-NEG
'Yesterday I read the book (through); but I didn't finish it.'
(233)a *ṭākṭar eṉ pallai.p piṭuṅkiṉār. āṉāl vara.v illai.*
doctor-NOM my tooth-ACC pull-PST-3H but come-INF IND-NEG
'The doctor pulled (at) my tooth, but it didn't come out.'
b *? *ṭākṭar eṉ pallai.p piṭuṅki viṭṭār. āṉāl vara.v illai.*
doctor-NOM my tooth-ACC pull-CF leave-PST-3H but come-INF IND-NEG
'The doctor pulled my tooth out, but it didn't come out.'

Annamalai (1982: 117) notes that trial verbs with generic readings, such as *tēṭa* 'seek', may cooccur with *viṭa* 'leave' without a perfective reading. In (234) *urukka* 'melt' denotes a gradual process of heating, not an absolute transformation. It cannot be understood as perfective; hence, *viṭa* is intepreted as epistemic disjunction. This contrasts with the pulling of a tooth in (233a), which is not a gradual process.

(234) *nāṉ veṇṇaiyai.p pattu taṭavai urukki viṭṭēṉ. āṉāl uruka.v illai.*
I-NOM butter-ACC ten times melt-EF-CF leave-PST-1S but melt-INF IND-NEG
'I melted the butter ten times, but it didn't melt.'

When it signals perfective aspect, *viṭa* 'leave' cannot appear in durative contexts, e.g., with the durative marker *-(k)kai.y-il* 'while V-ing' (235a) or the progressive tense complex AVC (235b).

(235)a * *colli viṭu-kaiyil . . .*
speak-CF leave-VN-LOC
'While (X) stopped saying . . .'

b * *colli viṭṭu.k koṇṭu iruntārkaḷ.*
say-CF leave-CF hold-CF be-PST-3P
'They were stopping saying.'

On the other hand, *viṭa* may itself combine with a complex durative AVC in *koṇṭu + irukka* 'be V-ing', but only in main clauses. When *viṭa* embeds *koṇṭu + irukka* in (236), it signals not punctual aspect, but rather an unexpected change of situation (status), glossed here by *instead.*

(236) *nāṉ eḻuti koṇṭu iruntu viṭṭēṉ. nīṅkaḷ varuvatai.k*
I-NOM write-CF hold-CF be-CF leave-PST-1S you-NOM come-FUT-VN-ACC
kavaṉikka.v illai.
notice-INF IND-NEG
'I didn't notice you come in; I was writing instead.'

The meaning that *viṭa* contributes to an AVC remains constant under negation, suggesting that its meaning is a conventional implicature. The negative auxiliary *illai* 'not be' does not negate the meaning of auxiliary *viṭa* 'leave', which lacks a denotational function, but *vara* 'come'; hence, (237) cannot mean 'he came, but it was not expected'.

(237) *avaṉ vantu viṭa.v illai.*
he-NOM come-CF leave-INF IND-NEG
'He didn't come (no one expected that he wouldn't come).'

In (238)[16] the doctor's failure to run immediately to the door on hearing a ruckus outside contrasts with general expectations, a contrast that evokes the status use of *viṭa*; the final sentence elaborates what motivates its use.

(238) *koṭṭu mēḷam cattam kēṭṭatu. ṭāktar uṭaṉē vācalukku ōṭi*
drum sound hear-PST-3N doctor-NOM suddenly entrance-DAT run-CF
viṭa.v illai. avaṉ inta.c cattattiṟku ellām acaikiṟavaṉ alla.
leave-INF IND-NEG he-NOM this sound-DAT all move-VN-3SM become-NEG-3N
'The sound of the drum was heard. The doctor did not run suddenly to the entrance (as you might have expected him to). He is not a man to be stirred by these sounds.'

Auxiliary *viṭa* 'leave' occurs in all three simple tense forms. In the present, it has a habitual interpretation rather than a present time one. Since the present describes an actual event whose time reference is the same as the speech event's, use of *viṭa* to mark temporal disjunction might be considered contradictory, signaling that a present event somehow contrasts with itself. This sitatution favors chosing a non-contradictory circumstantial meaning of present tense, viz. habitual action.

16 Janakiraman (1980: 3).

(239) *avaṉ vantu viṭukiṟāṉ.*
he-NOM come-CF leave-PST-3SM
'He does come (often).'

Although *viṭa* 'leave' may be modified by the necessity modal *vēṇṭum* 'be necessary' (240a), it cannot modify that modal in a complex AVC (240b). This restriction may be semantically based. In (240b) the proposition expressed by the sentence 'I go' is directly modified by *vēṇṭum*: the AVC means the proposition is true in all possible worlds. However, felicitous use of *viṭa* requires that the statement it modifies contrast with those in the context set. But because the statement is qualified by the necessity modal, there is no alternative that contrasts with the original statement. In this order, these two auxiliaries make contradictory demands on the interpretation of the modified proposition: it must be necessary (*vēṇṭum*), but it must also contrast with or depart from (*viṭa*) what is known to be the case.

(240)a *nāṉ pōy viṭa vēṇṭum.*
I-NOM go-CF leave-INF be.necessary-FUT-3N
'I really must go.'
b * *nāṉ pōka vēṇṭi viṭṭatu.*
I-NOM go-INF be.necessary-CF leave-PST-3N
'It turned out to have to go.'

Temporal uses of viṭa

In certain contexts, *viṭa* 'leave' signals disjunctive anterior taxis; this reading is more likely when the AVC is embedded under a main clause, less likely when it is finite and in the main clause. Because this correlation is a tendency, not a hard and fast rule, this interpretation cannot be absolutely restricted to a specific context. The event denoted by the AVC is interpreted as happening before the event named by the verb in the main clause; further, the time spans of the two events are represented as nonoverlapping, viz., temporally disjoint. In (241a) *viṭa* indicates that the singing stopped before the bathing began; in (241b), that the speaker will take a drag on a cigarette before passing it to a friend. In (242) the suffix *-(k)kuḷ* 'before

(241)a *avaṉ pāṭi viṭṭu.k kuḷittāṉ.*
he-NOM sing-CF leave-CF bath-PST-3SM
'After he sang, he bathed.'
b *oru dam aṭittu viṭṭu.t tarukiṟēṉ.*
one drag strike-CF leave-CF give-PRES-1S
'Once I've taken a drag from this cigarette, I'll give it to you.'

(242) *maḻai peykiṟatukkuḷ payir vaḷarntu* { *viṭṭatu.* / **? irukkiṟatu.* }
rain-NOM rain-VN-DAT crops-NOM grow-CF { leave-PST-3N / be-PRES-3N }
'By the time the rain was falling, the crops had (already) grown up.'

that, within the time that' signals temporal disjunction between the falling rain and the growing crops, which motivates the use of *viṭa* for disjunctive taxis, rather than *irukka* 'be located', which would signal a continuity between the two events.

This temporal disjunction may occasionally lead to the reading of perfective aspect noted earlier. It appears to derive from a conversational implicature based on general assumptions about how people deal with multiple tasks: one task is addressed and completed before moving on to another. All things being equal, temporal disjunction of two events suggests the completion of the earlier one (unless explicit information to the contrary is provided). Use of *viṭa* 'leave' over against *irukka* 'be located' also tends to imply that the action of the auxiliate is semelfactive, not iterative. Use of the adverbial *aṭikkaṭi* 'often' in (243) implies iteration and, perhaps, habitual practice; there is thus no single time or single event of coming that can be taken to contrast with some other event: the coming is repeated several times over an interval, requiring use of *irukka*.

(243) *aṭikkaṭi vantu* { *irukkiṟēṉ.* / * *viṭṭēṉ.* }
often come-CF { be-PRES-1S / leave-PST-1S }
'I have come (here) often.'

Consider further examples of the contrast between these two auxiliaries. Normal expectations are that the addressee should have finished reading the book before the speaker can borrow it; use of *viṭa* in (244a) signals temporal disjunction between the two events. It is not necessary to have finished reading a book to form an opinion of it; thus, in (244b) *irukka* suggests a continuous interval of time during which the reading occurred and the opinion emerged. Thus, *viṭa* is consistent with a disjunctive interpretation.

(244)a *pustakam paṭittu viṭṭīrkaḷ=ā? kaṭaṉāka.k koṭukkiṟīrkaḷ=ā?*
book read-CF leave-PST-2P=INT loan-ADV give-PRES-2P-INT
'Have you read the book? Would you loan it to me?'

b *pustakam paṭittu irukkiṟīrkaḷ=ā? atai.p paṟṟi uṅkaḷ karuttu eṉṉa?*
book read-CF be-PRES-2P=INT it-ACC about you-GEN opinion-NOM what
'Have you read the book? What's your opinion of it?'

Epistemic uses of viṭa

Others have noted the epistemic use of *viṭa* 'leave', most notably Annamalai (1982: 92-102), who calls it the verb of change of situation. The event denoted by the AVC is represented as departing from the natural, expected course of events. With what sort of object does the event expressed by the AVC contrast? It departs from the context set or those propositions that can be directly inferred from it. Together these two sets of assumptions describe a neutral situation and its natural course of development.

The border between the temporal and epistemic interpretations of *viṭa* is sometimes a porous one. For example, (242) can have an epistemic reading as well as a temporal one, namely that it is expected for the annual rains to provide the water for growing crops. Use of *viṭa* here might signal that this was not the case; that irrigation was used instead. As noted above, *viṭa* gives rise to an epistemic reading more frequently in main clauses than in subordinate ones. Its presence in (230) above thus indicates that the proposition expressed by the sentence, 'our relatives came yesterday', could not be deduced from the context set of propositions. In the same vein, *viṭa*'s use in the subordinate AVC in (245) also signals the speaker's surprise that a thief would leave without taking all the jewelry, an instance of unthief-like behavior. In (246) the speaker tells her friend to go to the movies without asking her husband's permission; in the imperative, *viṭa* serves as a suggestion to depart from the customary preparations for movie-going.

(245)	*tiruṭan̲*	*nakaiyai*	*ellām*	$[_{VI}$ $[_{VO}$*viṭṭu*$]$	*viṭṭu.p*$]$	*pōn̲ān̲.*
	thief-NOM	jewels-ACC	all	leave-CF	leave-CF	go-PST-3SM

'The thief went, leaving behind all the jewels.'

(246)	*collāmal*	*koḷḷāmal*	*pōy*	*viṭu!*
	tell-NEG-CF	ECHO	go-CF	leave-IMP

'Why not just go without telling or making any such fuss!'

The contexts of the two following sentences require the presence of *viṭa* 'leave'. The *yāḻi* in (247) is a mythological beast, a lion with an elephant's trunk, which is generally assumed not to exist in the real world. *viṭa* signals the speaker's belief that the image he saw was unreal or hallucinatory, a departure from normal expectations. Similarly, use of *viṭa* in (248) marks the speaker's belief that the subject's talking about everything as if he had personally witnessed it departs from what can be expected of any person; *viṭa* thus marks the contrast between the subject's behavior and what the speaker assumes to be the case.

(247)	*yāḻaiyai.k*	*kaṇṭu*	**(viṭṭār̲)*	*pōla*	*pārttēn̲.*
	Yari-ACC	see-CF	leave-PST-ADN	like	see-PST-1S

'It's as if I saw a Yari (and that can't be so).'

(248)	*ellārrai.y=um*	*kaṇṭu*	**?(viṭṭār̲)*	*pōla*	*pēcuvān̲.*
	all-ACC=and	see-CF	leave-PST-ADN	like	speak-FUT-3SM

'Oh sure, he'll talk like he's seen everything (knowing him, that can't be so).'

In (249) the first speaker makes a statement which the second speaker immediately corrects. The content of the first statement is temporarily added to the context set so the presence of *viṭa* in the second sentence serves both as an indication that his correction contrasts with the temporarily amplified context set and as an instruction to revise the context set according to that correction. In (250)[17] the immediate context also prepares the use of *viṭa* in the last sentence. If anyone other than

17 Akilan (1951: 85).

Narayanasami had asked this particular question of him, he would have answered without hesitation. But contrary to expectation, Narayanasami did ask him; hence, *viṭa* is required.

(249) *rāmaṉ pattu maṇikku.p paḷḷikkūṭattukku varuvāṉ.*
Raman-NOM ten o'clock school-DAT come-FUT-3SM
illai: eṉpatu maṇikku vantu viṭuvāṉ.
not ninc o'clock come-CF leave-PRES-3SM
'Raman would go to school at ten o'clock. No, he would go at nine.'

(250) *inta.k kēlvi eṉṉai.t tikaikka vaittatu. vēṟu yārāvatu*
this question me-ACC falter-INF place-PST-3N other any.who-NOM
kēṭṭu iruntāl yōciyāmal patalaḷittu iruppēṉ. nārāyaṇacāmiy=ē
ask-CF be-COND think-NEG-VF answer-CF be-FUT-1S Narayanasami-NOM=EMP
itai eṉṉiṭam kēṭṭu viṭṭār.
it-ACC me-SOC ask-CF leave-PST-3H
'This question made me hesitate. If anyone else had asked me, I probably would have answered without a second thought. But it was Narayanasami who asked me.'

In the following examples, *viṭa* marks an epistemic disjunction between the event denoted by the AVC and the context set. In (251) the onomatopoetic form *tiṭaitippeṉṟu* 'suddenly, with a bang' reinforces the use of *viṭa*: the relatives' sudden arrival departs from what was expected on the basis of the context set. In (252) *viṭa* contrasts the speaker's arrival with some third party's expectation that the addressee, not the speaker, would come. In (253) *viṭa* contrasts the subject's physical presence with the speaker's mental image of him: conjuring up an image of the subject was not expected to bring him physically into the speaker's presence.

(251) *tiṭatippeṉṟu contakkāraṅkaḷ vantu viṭṭārkaḷ.*
sudden-ONOM relatives-NOM come-CF leave-PST-3P
'All of a sudden, our relatives came.'

(252) *uṅkaḷai etirpārkkum camayattil nāṉ vantu viṭṭēṉ.*
you-ACC expect-FUT-ADN time-LOC I-NOM come-CF leave-PST-1S
'I came at the time you were expected (to come).'

(253) *inta.c camayam māttiram avaṉai.p paṟṟi niṉaittu.k*
this time only he-ACC about think-CF
koṇṭu irukkum pōt=ē avaṉ vantu viṭṭāṉ!
hold-CF be-FUT-ADN time=EMP he-NOM come-CF leave-PST-3SM
'Just as I was thinking about him, in he comes!'

Epistemic contrast is also evident in pairs of questions and answers. The question in (254a) asks for information, presupposing nothing about the arrival time. Thus, in (254b) an AVC with *viṭa* 'leave' is inappropriate since the context set contains no information about the arrival time with which information in the response might contrast; the nonauxiliated verb *vantēṉ* 'I came' is used instead. The question in (255a), on the other hand, introduces into the context set (if only temporarily) the assumption that the addressee arrived in the morning. But as the actual time of arrival differed from the assumed time, *viṭa* appears in the response in (255b) to mark this contrast.

(254)a *eppōtu vantāy?*
when come-PST-2S
'When did you come?'

b *nāṉ nēṟṟu* { *vantēṉ.* / *? *vantu viṭṭēṉ.* }
I-NOM yesterday { come-PST-1S / come-CF leave-PST-1S }
'I came/?did come yesterday.'

(255)a *iṉraikku.k kālaiyil vantāy=ā?*
today morning-LOC come-PST-2S=INT
'Did you come this morning?'

b *illai: nēṟṟu rāttiriyil* { *vantu viṭṭēṉ.* / *? *vantēṉ.* }
no yesterday night-LOC { come-CF leave-PST-1S / come-PST-1S }
'No, it was last night that I came.'

Use of *viṭa* in (256b) is inappropriate because there are no assumptions about anyone coming, and therefore nothing to motivate *viṭa*. This requires the simple, nonauxiliated verb in (256a). But both (256c and d) presuppose that someone came and asked for further specification of who came; in both cases, *viṭa* is used because there is some assumed information with which the contrast can be made.

(256)a *yār vantārkaḷ?*
who-NOM come- PST-3P
'Who came?'

b * *yār vantu viṭṭārkaḷ?*
who-NOM come-CF leave-PST-3P
?? Who did come?'

c *yāryār vantu viṭṭārkaḷ?*
who-who-NOM come-CF leave-PST-3P
'Which different people came?'

d *yār ellām vantu viṭṭārkaḷ?*
who-NOM all come-CF leave-PST-3P
'Who all came?'

Epistemic *viṭa* 'leave' also occurs in indirect commands. The imperative of auxiliary *viṭa* signals a displaced command, viz. a suggestion or warning. Example (257a), without *viṭa*, may be issued by a teacher to a student dozing off in class; it is a direct command issued in virtue of the authoritarian teacher-student relationship. Example (257b), with *viṭa*, amounts to an instruction, and is less direct in two ways. First, it anticipates a situation that may arise when the parents are absent and for which they have no present grounds for issuing a direct command. Second, since parents hire sitters, the relationship is somewhat flexible. Similarly, (258a), without *viṭa*, is a direct order to a child who has just fallen and begun to cry; (258b) is a parental warning to child before a long, dusty bus trip. The displacement between a possible situation and the reponse it might evoke motivates *viṭa*.

(257)a	*tūṅkātē!*	b	*tūṅki viṭātē!*
	sleep-NEG-IMP		sleep-CF leave-NEG-IMP
	'Don't sleep!'		'Don't fall asleep!'
(258)a	*aẓātē!*	b	*aẓutu viṭātē!*
	cry-NEG-IMP		cry-CF leave-NEG-IMP
	'Don't cry!'		'Don't go and cry.'

Because of their inherent lexical meaning, some verbs tend regularly to occur with auxiliary *viṭa* 'leave'. Use of *maṟaṅka* 'deny, forget' presupposes the existence of something that has been denied or forgotten. Similarly, *tolaikka* 'lose' can be used only when someone possessed something that was subsequently lost. *viṭa* may be thought of as an instruction to revise the set of assumptions with the information encoded by the AVC's auxiliate. For example, in (259a) it instructs the addresse to deny or forget what he knows (and what the speaker knows he knows), if anyone should ask him about it. Without *viṭa* in (259b), the bare imperative is judged as odd.

(259)a	*maṟantu viṭu!*	b *?	*maṟaṅku!*
	deny-CF leave-IMP		deny-IMP
	'Deny it (if someone asks you)!'		'Deny it.'

Object-orientation of viṭa

Annamalai (1982: 92) and Fedson (1981: 167) observe that when combined with certain kinds of auxiliates, auxiliary *viṭa* 'leave' indicates that the subject of the AVC directs the action away from himself to someone else. For Fedson, it is a marker of other-oriented voice; for Annamalai, it is not a separate auxiliary, but a circumstantial use of his category of "change of situation," corresponding roughly with our reading of disjunctive taxis. In this use *viṭa* 'leave' still signals disjunction or displacement; but instead of characterizing a relation between two narrated events, it characterizes a relation between the narrated event and one of participants, the subject, symbolically P^nE^e. Use of *viṭa* signals that the subject's participation departs from the activity stereotypically associated with the auxiliate. Note that in (260a) *oru cāṭṭai.p pōṭa* 'put on a shirt' is ordinarily construed as an action the subject performs on himself; the English phrase *she dressed* carries a similar implication. In Dixon's (1976) terminology, this verb is subject-oriented: in the absence of any indication to the contrary, it is understood as pertaining to the subject. But when auxiliary *viṭa* 'leave' combines with *pōṭa* 'dress' in (260b), the interpretation is that the subject dresses someone else; the act of dressing departs (*viṭa* 'leave') from the stereotypical activity of dressing oneself. Further, verbs such as *tēykka* 'rub (X's body or limb)', *eẓuppa* 'awaken (X's self)', *kaẓuva* 'wash (X's body)', *pēṉ pārkka* 'pick lice' and *kuḷippāṭa* 'bathe (X's body)' denote inherently subject-oriented activities, which when combined with *viṭa* in an AVC, denote an object-oriented activity.

(260)a *ammā oru cāṭṭai.p pōṭṭāḷ.*
mother-NOM one shirt-ACC put-PST-3SF
'Mother put a shirt on (herself).'

b *ammā oru cāṭṭai.p pōṭṭu viṭṭāḷ.*
mother-NOM one shirt-ACC put-CF leave-PST-3SF
'Mother put a shirt on someone else.'

A caveat, perhaps an important one, is in order. In most of its uses, auxiliary *viṭa* undergoes some phonological reduction: the initial *v-*, and often *vi-*, is lost in spoken Tamil, though it is retained in written Tamil and formal speech. But when *viṭa* signals object-orientation, the initial *v-* (or *vi-*) is not lost, which led Annamalai to propose two distinct auxiliaries. Different morphophonemic behavior of otherwise homophonous forms tends to suggest different lexemes; yet, despite this one difference, the many other parallels in grammatical behavior suggest that object-orientation is merely a circumstantial meaning of the disjunctive connector *viṭa*. We may thus symbolize *viṭa* 'leave', the disjunctive connector, as XE^n, where X ranges over $\{E^n, E^s, P^n\}$. Substitution of E^n for X in this formula gives rise to the subcategory of disjunctive temporal taxis; substitution of E^s yields disjunctive status. This resembles the generality between the temporal and epistemic uses noted in *irukka* 'be located'. Readings of perfectivity, punctuality and semelfactivity are parasitic on the auxiliary's tactic use; readings of suddenness, unexpectedness and novelty, on its status use. When P^n is substituted for X, the result is disjunctive voice; since *viṭa* usually combines with a subject-oriented activity in this capacity, what meaning it contributes in this context is tantamount to object-oriented voice.

CONJUNCTIVE CONNECTOR: *koḷḷa*

In our corpus, the verb *koḷḷa* 'hold, contain, keep, acquire' serves as a main verb, a modal auxiliary and an indicative auxiliary. As a main verb, *koḷḷa* is transitive: it combines with a nominative NP, the container, and an accusative NP, the thing contained (261). When it serves in this capacity, *koḷḷa* appears to exhibit defective, morphology, occurring primarily in the third person singular neuter form.

(261)a *inta.p peṭṭi attaṉai tuṇiyai.y=um koṇṭatu!*
this box-NOM so.many clothes-ACC=AND hold-PST-3N
'This box held so many clothes!'

b *oru tajaṉ iṭliyai.y=um uṉ vayiṟu koṇṭu kiṭum=ā?*[18]
one dozen idlies-ACC your stomach-NOM hold-CF hold-FUT-3N
'Can your stomach hold a dozen idlies?'

c *irunūṟṟuppattu vīṭukaḷ koṇṭa anta.t teru ...*[19]
210 houses-NOM hold-PST-ADN that street
'That street, which contained 210 households . . .'

koḷḷa 'hold' appears to function as a modal auxiliary, a usage not hitherto noted in the specialist literature. In (262a) it combines with an infinitive to form a modal AVC that functions like the *ki*-echo formation (p. 136ff.): the resulting compound denotes a range of events, of which the one named by the auxiliate is a typical example. In (262b) it combines with the negative verbal form in *-āmal* to form a similar construction. Both uses might be preliminarily classified as a kind of distributive aspect. In (263a) it combines with an infinitive to signal instrumental taxis. Instrumentality occurs in a circumstantial reading of the indicative auxiliary *koḷḷa*, noted below, as well as in the postposition *koṇṭu* 'with' (263).

(262)a *avaṉ colla.k koḷḷa.v illai.*
he-NOM say-INF hold-INF IND-NEG
'He didn't say (it) or do any such thing.'

b *collāmal koḷḷāmal pōy viṭu.*
say-NEG-VF hold-NEG-VF go-CF leave-IMP
'Why not go without telling or anything?'

c *avaṉ vara.k koṇṭu eṉakku.t teriyum.*
he-NOM come-INF hold-CF me-DAT know-FUT-3N
'I know about it through his coming (here).'

(263) *avaṉ kattiyai.k koṇṭu pūcaṉikkāyai veṭṭiṉāṉ.*
he-NOM knife-ACC with pumpkin-ACC cut-PST-3SM
'He cut the pumpkin with a knife.'

Indicative auxiliary use of *koḷḷa*

The commonest use of *koḷḷa* 'hold' in Modern Tamil, particularly the spoken variety, is as an indicative auxiliary. It has been variously labeled an auxiliary of reflexive voice, self-benefactive voice, self-affectivity, ego-benefaction and progressive tense,[20] suggesting a wide range of uses. Even a brief comparison shows that the two auxiliaries *viṭa* 'leave' and *koḷḷa* resemble each other in many ways. Like *viṭa, koḷḷa* has both temporal and epistemic uses, and appears to be general between them. Again like *viṭa, koḷḷa* may in certain contexts serve as a marker of voice. Factoring out what is common to all its uses, we arrive at another connector

18 This form belongs to the paradigm of *koḷḷa* 'hold'; but in this context, it is pronounced as a form of *kiṭa* 'hold'. See below for a discussion of this suppletion.

19 Janakiraman (1966: 12).

20 See Arden (1891), Schiffman (1969), Dale (1975), Fedson (1981) and Annamalai (1982).

XE^n, where X ranges over $\{E^n, E^s, P^n\}$. But while *viṭa* conveys a disjunctive meaning, *koḷḷa* conveys a conjunctive meaning.

The examples in (264) illustrate the tactic use of *koḷḷa* 'hold'; in (265), its use as a voice marker. Both sets of readings appear to have extended uses. In (264a) the auxiliary indicates that the activites of bathing and singing overlap in time. In (264b) it helps form the "stative participle," or imperfective converb, crucial to the formation of several complex AVCs. In (264c) the tactic relation between the two overlapping events is not temporal but epistemic, specifically, instrumental: *koḷḷa* indicates that opening the door was the means by which the subject entered the car. In its voice readings, *koḷḷa* is predominantly subject-oriented. It occurs in reciprocal (265a) and reflexive (265b) constructions. In (265c), an epistemic use, it indicates that the subject's involvement was unexpected.

(264)a *avaṉ kuḷittu.k koṇṭu pāṭiṉāṉ.*
he-NOM bathe-CF hold-CF sing-PST-3SM
'While bathing, he sang.'

b *avaḷ pāṭi.k koṇṭu irukkiṟāḷ.*
she-NOM sing-CF hold-CF be-PRES-3SF
'She is singing.'

c *avaṉ piṉsīṭṭiṉ katavai.t tiṟantu koṇṭu uḷḷē varukiṟāṉ.*
he-NOM back.seat-GEN door-ACC open-CF hold-CF inside come-PRES-3SM
'He opens the backseat door and, in doing so, comes inside.'

(265)a *avarkaḷ pēci.k koṇṭārkaḷ.*
they-NOM speak-CF hold-PST-3P
'They spoke among themselves/conversed.'

b *avaḷ taṉṉai.t tāṉē aṭittu.k koṇṭāḷ.*
she-NOM self-ACC self-EMP hit-CF hold-PST-3SF
'She hit herself.'

c *avaṉ cāppiṭṭu.k koṇṭāṉ.*
he-NOM eat-CF hold-PST-3SM
'He ate (of his own accord, though he wasn't expected to).'

Some properties of indicative koḷḷa

In careful speech and conscious imitation of the written language, such as *mēṭai pēccu* 'platform oratory', the auxiliary *koḷḷa* is instantiated by the class I verb *koḷḷa* 'hold' with the conjugational pattern *ko.ṇ-ṭ-ēṉ* 'I held', *koḷ-kiṟ-ēṉ* 'I hold', *koḷ-v-ēṉ* 'I will hold'. While this paradigm occurs in all writing, unguarded speech presents a different picture. In non-Brahmin Tamil, this auxiliary is the class IV verb *(k)iṭa* 'hold' with the conjugational pattern *(k)i.ṭ-ṭ-ēṉ* 'I held', *(k)iṭu-kiṟ-ēṉ* 'I hold', *(k)iṭu-v-ēṉ* 'I will hold', where the initial stop is often elided in rapid speech. Paramasivam (1979: 29) argues this form descends from Old Tamil *koṭa* 'hold', whose root appears in such compounds as *koṭu.p-pō* 'take' (< 'hold' + 'go', *akanāṉūṟu* 66.16). Rather than being a version of *koḷḷa* which lost the root-internal nasal in such forms as the conjunctive *koṇṭu* 'holding', Paramasivam proposes that *koṭa/kiṭa* is an affective stem in its own right, opposed to effective *koṭukka* 'give' (whose auxiliary use is analyzed in the next chapter). The meaning of affective *koṭa* 'hold, have, keep' was apparently similar enough to *koḷḷa* 'hold, keep, contain' to permit a suppletive relation to develop between the two over time, as well as in the diglossic variants of the language.[21] Spoken Brahmin Tamil, on the other hand, does possess reflexes of the class I verb *koḷḷa* 'hold', though with certain phonological changes. In rapid speech, the initial stop is usually lost and the root vowel is raised from *o* to *u*; literary *koṇṭu* 'holding' thus becomes spoken Brahmin *(k)uṇṭu* 'holding'. Modern writers portraying the speech of Brahmins, such as Jeyakantan and Asoka Mitran, use *uṇṭu* as the conjunctive form of this auxiliary: *uṇṭu*, thus reduced, appears homophonous with the conjunctive of *uḷḷa* 'be, exist, be contained', a source of some confusion in the specialist literature. One informant, a Brahmin married to a non-Brahmin, appears to have developed a mixed system: in indicative forms such as the conjunctive, she uses reflexes of class I *koḷḷa*; in modals forms such as the infinitive, reflexes of class IV *kiṭa*.

My transcription from spoken Tamil utilizes forms of *koḷḷa* 'hold' to maximize comparability between the spoken and written forms of the language. In any event, we should remember that the language is dynamic: the process of suppletion between the class I verb *koḷḷa* and the class IV verb *(k)iṭa* 'hold' may have progressed further phonologically and morphologically than semantically so that two homophonous auxiliary verbs might yet have to be distinguished in the modern language. The class I verb appears to be historically responsible for the readings of taxis; the class IV verb for readings of voice. It could turn out that the tactic and voice readings of *koḷḷa* and *(k)iṭa* are converging over time on a generalized connector whereas the tactic and voice readings of *viṭa* 'leave' may ultimately diverge into two auxiliaries.

Like other indicative auxiliary verbs, *koḷḷa* 'hold' freely occurs under the scope of a negative operator; in such contexts, the operator negates the event denoted by the auxiliate, not the meaning of the auxiliary.

(266)a *avarkaḷ pēci.k koḷḷa.v illai.*
they-NOM speak-CF hold-INF IND-NEG
'They didn't converse/speak among themselves.'

b *evvaḷavum coṉṉāl=um taṉṉai.c cariyāka alaṅkārittu.k koḷḷa.v illai.*
how.much say-COND=AND self-ACC well groom-CF hold-INF IND-NEG
'No matter how much I say to her, she will not look after her appearance.'

Tactic uses of koḷḷa

koḷḷa has two main tactic uses. In the first, it combines with an auxiliate to form an AVC which is not subsequently embedded by another auxiliary; in the second, it

21 The descent from two separate verb bases at an earlier stage of the language also helps to explain, from a historical perspective, why the auxiliary has so many varied uses in the modern language.

combines with an auxiliate to form an imperfective converb which then combines with another auxiliary. In the first, *koḷḷa* signals a temporal conjunction between two events, one named by the AVC of which *koḷḷa* is a part, the other named by the predicate in the following clause. The time-spans of two events are held to overlap, but need not be wholly coextensive.[22] In (267a-c), *koḷḷa* indicates that the relevant events overlap in time. In (267a) the singing coincides with the bathing; in (267b) sitting in the chair and refusing to get up are simultaneous; and in (267c) eating the food and planning a trip to the movies are also simultaneous. (267d) illustrates multiple simultaneous events linked by *koḷḷa*.

(267)a *rāju pāṭi.k koṇṭu kuḷittāṉ.*
Raju-NOM sing-CF hold-CF bathe-PST-3SM
'Raju was singing while he bathes.'

b *avaṉ eṉ iṭattil uṭkārntu koṇṭu eẕuntirukka māṭṭēṉ eṉkiṟāṉ.*
he-NOM my seat-LOC sit-CF hold-CF get.up-INF fut-NEG-1S say-PRES-3SM
'He is sitting in my seat and refuses to get up.'

c *āppattai.t tiṉṟu koṇṭ=ē mattiyāṉam enta.p paṭattukku.p pōkalām eṉṟa yōcaṉaiyil āẕntāṉ capāpati.*
appam-ACC gobble-CF hold-CF-EMP afternoon what picture-ACC go-HORT say-PST-ANP thought-LOC immerse-PST-3SM Sabhapati-NOM
'While gobbling down the appam, Sabhapati was engrossed in thoughts about which movie he should go see this afternoon.'

d *ōyāmal iruvarum taṅkaḷukkuḷ pēci.k koṇṭ=um cirittu.k koṇṭ=um caṇṭaiyiṭṭu.k koṇṭ-um poẕutai ōṭṭiṉārkaḷ.*
cease-NEG-VF two-NOM=AND self-PL-AMONG speak-CF hold-CF=AND laugh-CF hold-CF=AND banter-CF hold-CF=AND time-ACC drive-PST-3P
'The two of them passed the time of day ceaselessly conversing, laughing and bantering.'

In this use *koḷḷa* also admits circumstantial readings of simultaneity and sequentiality, among others. When the overlap is complete, the reading is simultaneous; when it is partial, the reading is sequential. In (267c and d), for example, the time-spans of the events linked by the auxiliary need not exactly coincide.

Further circumstantial readings are found, such as consequence and instrumentality, suggesting that *koḷḷa* 'hold' may apply in epistemic as well as temporal domains. In (268a) opening the door is presented as the means of entering the car. In (268b) asking directions at the bus station is the means of getting to the temple. Thus, in an epistemic domain, two events, X and Y, related by *koḷḷa*, may be understood as either 'Y is a consequence of X' or 'X is an instrument/means to Y'.[23]

22 Dale (1975: 189) analyzes it as a marker of simultaneity; Fedson (1981: 96), as a marker of non-disjunction, which may or may not be sequential (Fedson (1981: 105).

23 This resembles the way in which conversational implicatures may be used to strengthen logical operators (see Levinson 2000). Used temporally, *X and Y* is strengthened to *X and then Y*; used epistemically, it is strengthed to *X and thus Y*.

(268)a *avaṉ piṉsīṭṭiṉ katavai.t tiṟantu koṇṭu uḷḷē varukiṟāṉ.*
he-NOM back.seat-GEN door-ACC open-CF hold-CF inside come-pres-3SM
'He enters by opening the car door (and getting in).'

b *baṣ ṣṭāṇṭil vicarittu.k koṇṭu kōyilai aṭaintōm.*
bus stand-LOC inquire-CF hold-CF temple-ACC reach-PST-1P
'In asking (its whereabouts) at the bus terminal, we reached the temple.'

The AVCs with *koḷḷa* 'hold' in (269) appear in finite clauses: in such contexts, the tactic reading of instrumentality noted above is replaced by a reading of conjunctive status. *koḷḷa* indicates that the context set must contain the proposition denoted by its auxiliate to accommodate another proposition under consideration. Consider the first example. Several friends buy a lottery ticket, then start discussing how to spend the prize money. The cynic in the group utters sentence (269a), cautioning them against idle speculation until they have the money in hand. Here *koḷḷa* is used to say that winning the prize money is a prerequisite to spending it. In the second example a boy pesters his father to make a paper sailboat, but the father urges patience, uttering (269b). *koḷḷa* suggests that rain must first fall to replenish the empty pond. It links the means, viz. creating a body of water, with a goal, viz. sailing a toy boat.

(269)a *paricu mutalil viḻuntu koḷḷaṭṭum; appuṟam atai.p paṟṟi pēcalām.*
prize-NOM first fall-CF hold-OPT then it-ACC about speak-HORT
'Let's win the prize money first; then we can talk about (what to do with) it.'

b *maḻai peytu koḷḷaṭṭum; appuṟam pārppōm.*
rain NOM rain-CF hold-OPT then see-FUT-1P
'Let it rain first; then we'll see about it.'

Since finite predicates encode categories that refer to the speech event, E^s, while nonfinite predicates tend to refer to the narrated event, E^n, it is natural that a tactic relation, E^nE^n, should be replaced by one of status, E^s/E^n, in the finite contexts noted in (269).

Outside of its epistemic uses auxiliary, *koḷḷa* 'hold' tends not to combine auxiliates that denote a change of state and have inanimate subjects. Consider the sentences in (270).

(270)a *avaḷuṭaiya mukam* { *māṟiyatu.* / * *māṟi.k koṇṭatu.* }
her-GEN face-NOM { change-PST-3N / change-CF hold-PST-3N }
'Her face changed.'

b *pāṟai nilattil payir* { *vaḷarntatu.* / * *vaḷarntu koṇṭatu.* }
rock land-LOC crop-NOM { grow-PST-3N / grow-CF hold-PST-3N }
'The crops grew on rocky land.'

c *ūril veḷḷam pukuntu koṇṭatu. veḷḷam kāṟai uṭaittu.k*
town-LOC flood-NOM enter-CF hold-PST-3N flood-NOM bank break-CF
koṇṭatu. veḷḷam vaṇṭi ellām kaviḻttu.k koṇṭatu.
hold-PST-3N flood-NOM carts all overturn-CF hold-PST-3N
'The flood has just entered the town; it has just broken the embankments; it has just overturned all the carts.

However, an on-the-spot reporter can use auxiliary *koḷḷa* to narrate the sequence of events in (270c) as they unfold, each with an inanimate subject and change-of-state verb. Each instance of the auxiliary may be viewed as an instruction to add the proposition it modifies to the context set to build up a background and narrative for the news story. The connection is then considered epistemic so that *koḷḷa* may combine with a change-of-state verb with an inanimate subject.

koḷḷa and the imperfective converb

koḷḷa 'hold' figures as the first member of six auxiliary complexes : *koṇṭu + irukka* 'be V-ing', *koṇṭu + vara* 'keep V-ing', *koṇṭu + kiṭakka* 'be V-ing', *koṇṭu + pōka* 'go on V-ing', *koṇṭu + kiḻikka* 'being unable to V' and *koṇṭu + vaḻiya* 'do slowly'.[24] Kandiah (1967) was the first to claim that the auxiliary *koṇṭu* 'hold' combines with the conjunctive form of an auxiliate to form, in effect, a "stative participle," which then combines with another indicative auxiliary to form a complex AVC. Here the construction is called the imperfective converb.

As noted earlier, when it conveys a progressive tense reading, *irukka* 'be located' may not directly combine with an auxiliate whose aspectual class is an achievement or accomplishment because such a combination invariably yields a perfect tense reading (271). Instead, *koḷḷa* is interpolated to form an imperfective converb, after which *irukka* is added, as in (272).

(271)a *avaṉ oru nāvalai.p paṭittu irukkiṟāṉ.*
he-NOM one novel-ACC read-CF be-PRES-3SM
'He has read a novel.'

b *avaḷ mattiyāṉa.c cāppāṭṭai.c camaittu irukkiṟāḷ.*
she-NOM afternoon meal-ACC cook-CF be-PRES-3SF
'She has prepared the afternoon meal.'

(272)a *avaṉ oru nāvalai.p paṭittu.k koṇṭu irukkiṟāṉ.*
he-NOM one novel-ACC read-CF hold-CF be-PRES-3SM
'He is reading a novel.'

b *avaḷ mattiyāṉa.c cāppāṭṭai.c camaittu.k koṇṭu irukkiṟāḷ.*
she-NOM afternoon meal-ACC cook-CF hold-CF be-PRES-3SF
'She is cooking the afternoon meal.'

24 These expressions are shorthand for multiply nested AVCs. For example, auxiliary *irukka* does not combine directly with *koḷḷa* but with an AVC in which *koḷḷa* is the auxiliary. Further, our use of the term converb here and below is for descriptive convenience because it has fewer pernicious associations than the term participle does. Nothing theoretical turns on our use of converb.

How does "suffixation" of the auxiliary *koḷḷa* to an achievement or accomplishment predicate yield an imperfective converb? States and activities are homogenous throughout their duration, so that any slice from them resembles any other slice. Achievements and accomplishments, however, additionally incorporate a change of state, conventionally reckoned as the operator BECOME, which implies two distinct moments, one before and one after the change occurs. Consequently, achievement and accomplishment verbs are not homogenous throughout their duration: their onset and body differ from their coda.[25]

The complex *koṇṭu* + *irukka* 'be V-ing' is sensitive to the aspectual composition of the predicate with which it combines. It indicates that there is an anterior interval (*irukka* 'be') that contains (*koḷḷa* 'hold') a portion of the event denoted by the auxiliate. When it is combined with an auxiliate whose aspectual class is an achievement or accomplishment, *koṇṭu* + *irukka* focuses on the state or activity of that event prior to the change of state in the coda. This permits *irukka* to combine with a (complex) auxiliate to give rise to a progressive tense reading.

The following examples of *koṇṭu* + *irukka* 'be V-ing' suggest the underlying tactic meaning of *koḷḷa* 'hold' survives its use as an imperfective converb. In each sentence an event in the foreground occurs against another in the background, which is qualified by *koṇṭu* + *irukka*. In (273a)[26] the speaker wonders about his return home in relation to what his family expects; in (273b)[27] the newspaper advises readers to follow certain procedures for viewing an eclipse; in (274c)[28] a scientist predicts that ants will behave normally while the eclipse is occurring; in (274d)[29] flies are observed to be swarming while the narrator is taking a meal; and in (274e)[30] the speaker excuses himself during the middle of a conversation, telling his friends to continue while he leaves or until he returns. These examples suggest that the imperfective converb marks taxis whether the second event required for the tactic interpretation is made explicit or merely suggested (273a, d, e). These examples show that the second event may be suggested by another verb (273b) or even by a noun, such as *kirakaṇam* 'eclipse' in (274c).

(273)a	*ūril*	*yār*	*nammai*	*etirpārttu.k*	*koṇṭu*	*irukkiṟārkaḷ?*
	town-LOC	who-NOM	us-ACC	expect-CF	hold-CF	be-PRES-3P

'(I wonder) who in town is awaiting me/my arrival?'

25 State and activity predicates are respectively related to achievement and accomplishment predicates as follows: an achievement consists of a state that leads into to a change of state while an accomplishment consists of an activity that leads into a change of state. Achievements and accomplishments may thus be said to wholly contain a corresponding state and activity predicate, respectively, as their onset and body, but additionally incorporate the change of state operator as their coda.

26 Janakiraman (1966: 9).

27 From *āṉanta vikaṭaṉ*, 17 February 1980.

28 From *diṉamaṉi*, 16 February 1980.

29 Patmanapan (1977: 40).

30 Akilan (1951).

b *cūriyaṉ maṟaintu koṇṭu irukkum nērattil atai.p pārkka*
sun-NOM hide-CF hold-CF be-FUT-ADN time-LOC it-ACC see-INF
virumpukiṟavarkaḷ kīḻkkaṇṭapaṭi ceyya-lām.
wish-PRES-VN-3P as.seen.below do-HORT
'Those who wish to watch the eclipse while it is occurring (lit. when the sun is hiding) may do so in one of the ways noted below.'

c *kirakaṇam erumpukaḷai.c caṟṟum pātippatu illai. vaḻakkam pōla*
eclipse-NOM ants-ACC little disturb-VN IND-NEG usual like
avai vēlai ceytu koṇṭu irukkum.
they-NOM work do-CF hold-CF be-FUT-3N
'The eclipse will not bother ants in the slightest. They will be working as usual.'

d *mējai mītu īkkaḷ moyntu.k koṇṭu iruntaṉa.*
table on flies-NOM swarm-CF hold-CF be-PST-3NP
'Flies were swarming on the table (while we ate).'

e *itō, oru nimiṭattil vantu viṭukiṟēṉ. pēci.k koṇṭu iruṅkaḷ . . .*
here one minute-LOC come-CF leave-PRES-1S speak-CF hold-CF be-IMP
'I'm coming back in just a minute: keep on talking (while I step out).'

The two events do not have equal importance in the conversational goals: the one qualified by *koṇṭu + irukka* 'be V-ing' is the backdrop against which the more important of the two is played out. The durativity of *irukka* 'be' appears to contribute the relative subordination of the one event, indicating that there is an on-going event unfolding over an interval of time. The other event, not qualified by *koṇṭu + irukka*, is viewed as a simple action which advances the narrative whereas the action of the complex AVC is positively marked for durativity.

Fedson (1981) suggests that *koṇṭu + irukka* 'be V-ing' is "progressive" while *koṇṭu + vara* is "continuous." While she claims that continuous events have longer duration than progressive ones, our examples indicate that her generalization is spurious. *koṇṭu + irukka* is marked for taxis, while *koṇṭu + vara* is not.[31] Note the examples in (274)[32] do not set the backdrop for another event, but concentrate instead on the durativity of the event named by the auxiliate. Because it is not tactically related to another event, it can have circumstantial readings of intensity or relentlessness because no other event interrupts it. This intensity aptly describes the unabating pain in (274a), and may have led Fedson to ascribe longer duration to this complex form.[33]

(274)a *kuṭalai.p puraṭṭi.k koṇṭu vantatu ataṉ kacappu.*
bowels-ACC stir-CF hold-CF come-PST-3N it-GEN bitterness-NOM
'Its bitterness kept churning my insides.'

31 This difference is elaborated more fully in Chapter 7 when the semantics of auxiliary *vara* 'come' are analyzed in detail.

32 Example (274a) is from Akilan (1951: 130), (274b) from Akilan (1951: 82).

33 See Steever (1993: 182-88) for a historical linguistic criticism of micro- versus macro-durative aspect in Tamil.

b *vēṇṭumeṉṟē caṉyāciṉi.k kōlattiṟku.t tayār ceytu koṇṭu vantāḷ.*
deliberately recluse form-DAT prepare do-CF hold-CF come-PST-3SF
'She kept deliberately dressing in the guise of a recluse.'

Two other complex AVCs, *koṇṭu + pōka* 'go on V-ing' and *koṇṭu + kiṭakka* 'be V-ing', behave like *koṇṭu + irukka* and *koṇṭu + vara*. As noted in the next two chapters, these auxiliaries ordinarily combine with auxiliates denoting states and activities, but may combine with predicates denoting achievements and accomplishments only through the intermediary of the imperfective converb.

Like *koṇṭu + vara* 'keep on V-ing', *koṇṭu + pōka* 'go on V-ing' is not tactic; *koṇṭu + pōka*, however, marks pejorative attitude (see Chapter 8). *pōka* 'go' combines with main verbs denoting states or activities; *koṇṭu + pōka*, with main verbs denoting achievements or accomplishments. The main verb in (275a),[34] *taṭikka* 'be fat', is stative and may combine directly with *pōka*, which contributes a meaning that the auxiliate's action is undesirable. But the auxiliate in (275b),[35] *uyara* 'rise' is interpreted as an accomplishment with the meaning 'become higher', and so requires the interpolation of *koṇṭu* to form the imperfective converb before *pōka* may combine with it.

(275)a *ippō uṭampu taṭittu.p pōṉataṉālē kuḷḷam mātiri terikiṟatu.*
now body-NOM be.fat-CF go-VN-INST tank likeness appear-PRES-3N
'Because his body has gotten fatter, it now looks like a tank.'

b *kōpuviṉ kural uyarntu koṇṭ=ē pōyiṟṟu.*
Gopu's voice-NOM rise-CF hold-CF=EMP go-PST-3N
'Gopu's voice kept getting higher and higher.'

The ability of *koḷḷa* to form an imperfective converb thus appears to be related to its ability to mark conjunctive taxis where the time-spans of two events partially overlap. What appears to overlap in this case, however, are not the time-spans of two different events, but the time-spans of two discrete portions of a single event, such as an achievement or accomplishment.

Subject-orientation of koḷḷa

The complementarity of *viṭa* 'leave' and *koḷḷa* 'hold' appears to carry through into their use as markers of the category of voice: while *viṭa* signals object-oriented voice, *koḷḷa* signals subject-oriented voice.[36] However, the characterization of *koḷḷa*

34 Jeyakantan (1970: 132). The tank (*kuḷḷam*) referred to is a water tank, not an armored vehicle, although the latter image would not be an infelicitous rendering of the author's intent.

35 Fedson (1981: 125).

36 Several observers have noted that *koḷḷa* can as an auxiliary mark voice: Arden (1891) treats it as a marker of reflexive voice; Schiffman (1969) as a self-benefactive auxiliary; Dale (1975) as a self-affective auxiliary; Fedson (1981), as an actor focus auxiliary; and Annamalai (1982), as an auxiliary of ego-benefaction.

as a voice marker has not been without some contention in the literature. In refuting Schiffman's (1969) claim that *koḷḷa* marks self-benefaction, Dale (1975: 117) created examples to test Schiffman's claim as to whether or not this auxiliary does mark self-benefaction. On Schiffman's hypothesis, (276) should be grammatical when, in fact, none of Dale's informants found it acceptable.

(276) * *ammā kuẓantaiyai.k kuḷippāṭṭi.k koṇṭāl avaḷukku cantōṣamāy irukkum.*
mother-NOM child-DAT bathe-CF hold-CND she-DAT happy be-FUT-3SN
'If the mother bathes the child (for her own benefit), she will be happy.'

Dale (1975: 165) treats *koḷḷa* as a reflexive auxiliary generally, and a self-affective auxiliary more specifically. He argues the presence of a reflexive pronoun supports the presence of the auxiliary verb. If self-affectivity is a subspecies of reflexivity, it should, like a reflexive verb, denote a transitive relation. He claims that the following sentence bears his hypothesis out.

(277) *kuẓantai tāṉāka(.v=ē) kuḷittu.k koṇṭāl ammāvukku cantōṣamāy irukkum.*
child ? bathe-CF hold-CND mother-DAT happy be-FUT-3N
'If the child bathes *tāṉākavē*, its mother will be happy.'

Dale glosses *tāṉākavē* as 'self+adverb', but it is an idiom that means 'of one's own accord'. It is not a reflexive pronoun that is restricted to a third person antecedent, as the reflexive pronoun *tāṉ* 'self' is in Tamil. Also, the main verb *vara* 'come' in (278) is intransitive, but still cooccurs with *tāṉākavē*. Thus, the voice meaning of *koḷḷa* cannot be self-affectivity, if that notion involves transitivity.

(278) *nāṉ tāṉākavē vantu koṇṭēṉ.*
I-nom of.one's.own.accord come-CF hold-PST-1s
'I came of my own accord/my own free will.'

Dale fails to elaborate the concept of self-affectivity, and his proposal is superceded by Paramasivam's (1979) subseqent analysis of affective and effective verbs. Recall that historically *koḷḷa* 'hold' is the affective counterpart of the effective verb *koṭukka* 'give'. So whatever nuance of self-affectivity *koḷḷa* may exhibit likely derives from the fact that it is an affective verb; this, however, is insufficient to distinguish it from the numerous other affective verbs in Tamil. If *koḷḷa*'s function were to invest a verb with (self-)affectivity, it should be redundant to combine it with an affective verb, but examples such as (282b) show us that it is not.

Reflexivity is not an invariant component of *koḷḷa*'s meaning: both sentences in (279) are reflexive but only one (279b) has auxiliary *koḷḷa*; hence, *koḷḷa* is not a necessary component of a reflexive construction. Moreover, (279a) indicates that the presence of a reflexive pronoun is not sufficient to trigger the insertion of *koḷḷa*. How do the two differ? Fedson's (1981) proposal of "actor focus" is suggestive. The implication in (279b) is that the subject went out of his way to praise himself, drawing attention to the praise, whereas in (279a) the subject in the natural flow of events praised himself, perhaps unconsciously or inadvertantly. The auxiliary in (279b) focuses our attention on the subject's involvement in the action.

(279)a *karuṇaniti tannai.p pukaẓntār.*
Karunaniti-NOM self-ACC praise-PST-3H
'Karunaniti praised himself.'

b *karuṇaniti tannai.p pukaẓntu koṇṭār.*
Karnunaniti-NOM self-ACC praise-CF hold-PST-3H
'Karunaniti praised/congratulated himself.'

If *koḷḷa* indicates that the subject goes out of his way to perform the action of the auxiliate, further implications may arise that he does so on his own and without regard for others. In such circumstances, when the subject is plural, the presence of *koḷḷa* often accompanies a circumstantial meaning of reciprocity in which the action affects only the referents of the subject.

(280) *avarkaḷ pēci.k koṇṭārkaḷ.*
they-NOM speak-CF hold-PST-3P
'They spoke among themselves/conversed.'

Example (281) is set against the backdrop of traditional rules governing intercaste commensality, which generally prohibit members of a higher caste from accepting cooked food from members of a lower caste. A host belonging to a lower caste has invited to his house a guest who belongs to a higher caste, and offers his guest cooked food.

(281) *cāppiṭa māṭṭār eṉṟu niṉaittēṉ. āṉāl cāppiṭṭu.k koṇṭār.*
eat-INF FUT-NEG-1s that think-PST-1s but eat-CF hold-PST-3H
'I thought he wouldn't eat; but he took it upon himself to do so.'

When contrary to general expectations, the guest accepts the cooked food, the host may utter (281). Use of *koḷḷa* here signals that the subject—the guest—made a particular exception to a general set of expectations. The speaker, by using *koḷḷa*, may additionally express the feeling that he had been complemented or patronized by the subject.

Because *koḷḷa* draws attention to the subject's action, it may also indicate that the action stems from the subject's self-interest, without regard to other participants or their expectations. The presence of *koḷḷa* in (282a) signals that the subjects took it upon themselves to arrive at times they thought best, without considering the possible inconvenience to their hosts. Sentence (282b) may be said of a diplomat who goes overseas, leaving his wife behind: *koḷḷa* 'hold' signals that he went out of his way to bear this separation. Overtones of unpredictability, apparent in several examples, are a circumstantial use of this auxiliary, and arise from the fact that the auxiliary indicates that the subject is the primary agent of the action:

he does it for himself, by himself, with his own counsel, etc.

(282)a *niṉaitta nērattil avarkaḷ vantu koṇṭārkaḷ.*
think-PST-ADN time-LOC they-NOM come-CF hold-PST-3P
'They came when they felt like it (they didn't consult us).'

b *avaṉ nāṭṭukkāka maṉaiviyai.p pirintu koṇṭāṉ.*
he-NOM country-DAT wife-ACC separate-CF hold-PST-3SM
'He was separated from his wife for the sake of his country (it was a noble thing to do).'

In (283a) the car passes down a lane that seemed too narrow; use of *koḷḷa* suggests that something the driver—or metonymously, the car—did was responsible for the unexpected event. In (283b) use of *koḷḷa* once again suggests that something about subject—here, a nonagentive, dative-subject—is responsible for the unexpected situation.

(283)a *kār aṅkē pōy koṇṭatu.*
car-NOM there go-CF hold-PST-3N
'The car went there (the lane was so narrow I wouldn't have expected it).'

b *avaṉukku avaḷai.p piṭittu.k koṇṭatu.*
him-DAT her-ACC like-CF hold-PST-3N
'He liked her (I wouldn't have expected it/I thought I knew him/there's no accounting for taste).'

Thus, as a voice marker, *koḷḷa* signals the subject's keeping or holding our attention on the action of the auxiliate. The action is subject-oriented in that the subject is unusually involved in the action in some way, which leads to a variety of nuances such as one-sidedness, unexpectedness, etc.

AVCs with *koḷḷa* 'hold' often translate into English either as a verb with a latinate stem and prefix, such as *con-*, *re-*, or *ad-* (see Aronoff 1976: 11), or as a verb and particle combination, so that *kalantu koḷḷa*, composed of *kalantu* 'mixing' and auxiliary *koḷḷa*, may be translated as 'mix up' or 'combine' (284a).

(284)a *kalantu koḷḷa*
mix-CF hold-INF
'combine, circulate, mix up, mix with'

b *niṉaittu.k koḷḷa*
think-CF hold-INF
'consider, conceive, reflect'

c *kēṭṭu.k koḷḷa*
ask-CF hold-INF
'request, ask of'

d *pēci.k koḷḷa*
speak-CF hold-INF
'converse, speak together'

Due to the broad range of circumstantial meanings it conveys, *koḷḷa* 'hold, contain' is perhaps the most difficult of indicative auxiliaries to analyze. As suggested earlier, this may stem from the fact that the modern paradigm represents a suppletion from two historically distinct bases, *koḷḷa* and **koṭa*, the first giving rise to the auxiliary's temporal, and the second to its voice readings. Complicating matters further is the fact that both these uses appear to have extended epistemic uses.

Future research may be able to confirm whether all these different uses may be brought under a single auxiliary, or whether they have to be parceled out among two or more distinct, yet homophonous auxiliaries.

Like *viṭa* 'leave', *koḷḷa* 'hold' is a connector, specifically the conjunctive connector XE^n. When E^n is substituted for X, the result is a tactic category that characterizes the relation between two narrated events and is general between temporal and epistemic domains. When E^nE^n ranges over a temporal domain, we have temporal taxis, the quantifier of E^nE^n ; when it ranges over an epistemic domain, we have epistemic taxis, the qualifier of E^nE^n. As a marker of temporal taxis, it signals temporal conjunction: the time-spans of two events overlap, from which may arise subsidiary meanings of sequentiality or simultaneity. In an important subcase, *koḷḷa* forms the imperfective converb of an achievement or accomplishment verb. When we have epistemic taxis, *koḷḷa* signals that one event is a premise, precondition or instrument for a later event; it qualifies one event as the means to another. When E^s is substituted for X, the result is status. The auxiliary then indicates that the context set must contain the proposition modified by *koḷḷa* for some other proposition to be considered. When P^n is substituted for X, the result is conjunctive, or subject-oriented, voice, P^nE^n. The subject keeps or "holds" the action within his control or sphere of influence, going out of his way to undertake the action named by the main verb. His participation is in one way or other extraordinary. This suits *koḷḷa* to being used in reflexive voice to signal deliberateness and to being used as a marker of reciprocal voice. This use appears to have epistemic parallels, as well: the action of the main verb is unexpected, sudden, unpredictable, one-sided, etc.

SUMMARY

The three auxiliaries analyzed here, *irukka* 'be located', *viṭa* 'leave', and *koḷḷa* 'hold', each have meanings that range over what are conventionally thought to be two or three distinct grammatical categories. An analysis has been proposed in which these various uses may be related through the use of generalized connectors. One persistent distinction made is between the temporal and epistemic uses of these auxiliaries, which are treated here as circumstantial meanings that arise depending as the auxiliary ranges over the category of tense, the quantifier of E^s/E^n, or the category status, the corresponding qualifier. While future research will certainly refine specific details of the analysis here and may well present evidence for dividing *viṭa* 'leave' and *koḷḷa* 'hold' each into several distinct, yet homophonous verbs, we have shown that appeal may be made in principle to generalized connectors to express broad invariant meanings that appear to bridge what have traditionally been considered distinct verbal categories. Finally, whatever their ultimate analysis, these three auxiliaries are of interest not just in themselves but also for the roles they play in the system of indicative auxiliaries.

7 The minor indicative auxiliary verbs of Tamil

INTRODUCTION

This chapter analyzes the minor indicative auxiliaries of Tamil, which may be characterized as simple in that they neither exhibit the range of circumstantial readings of the auxiliaries in Chapter 6 nor encode the verbal category of attitude of the auxiliaries in Chapter 8. They include *āka* 'become', *kiṭakka* 'lie', *vara* 'come', *koṭukka* 'give', *tara* 'give to you or me', *vaikka* 'place', and *pārkka* 'look at', among others. These lexemes denote motions, transitions or changes of state; all are used in indicative AVCs to signal a variety of verbal categories.

AUXILIARY OF FULFILLMENT: *āka*

The verb *āka* 'become' has numerous uses in Modern Tamil; we discuss its main verb and auxiliary uses. As a main verb, i.e., a nonauxiliated form, the lexeme *āka* is predicated of a subject NP whose referent has assumed a new role or position signaled by the object NP.

(285)a *avaṉ mantiri āvāṉ.*
he-NOM minister-NOM become-FUT-3M
'He will become the minister.'

b *avaṉ periyavaṉ āki viṭṭāṉ.*
he-NOM big.man-NOM become-CF leave-PST-3SM
'He did become a big man'.

c *avaḷ tōṭṭakkāri āka irukkiṟāḷ.*
she-NOM gardener-NOM become-INF be-PRS-3SF
'She is now (in the role of) the gardener.

d *avaṉ rāmaṉ-āka naṭikkiṟāṉ.*
he-NOM Rama-NOM-become-INF act-PRS-3SM
'He plays (the role of) Rama.'

Sentences such as (285a) occur primarily in the written language; however, those such as (285b, c and d) commonly occur in spoken Tamil. The basic meaning 'fulfill a role, come to serve in a role' is evident in these examples. Note that while *āka* is a transitive verb, both its arguments must appear in the nominative case; under no circumstances may the object argument appear in the accusative case. Elsewhere (Steever 1988: 19-25) I have noted that this idiosyncracy, which it inherits from its Proto-Dravidian etymon, gives the verb specialized uses in the formation of complex sentences.

Examples demonstrate that as a main verb, *āka* also appears in temporal expressions denoting a lapse of time.

(286)a *uṅkaḷai.p pārttu rompa nāḷ āyiṟṟu.*
you-ACC see-CF many day-NOM become-PST-3SN
'It has been many days since (I) last saw you.'

b *maṇi āyiṟṟu.*
hour-NOM become-PST-3SN
'The time has come (to do it).'

c *paṭukaiyil viṭṭu eẓuntavuṭaṉ mutal kāppi āyiṟṟu.*
bed-LOC leave-CF rise-PST-ADN-as.soon.as first coffee-NOM become-PST-3SN
ippōtu maṇi ēẓarai.[1]
now hour-NOM eight.thirty-NOM
'As soon as I got up and out of bed, it was time for my first cup of coffee; it was now 8:30.'

The English present perfect is often used here and by other authors to translate the past tense form of *āka* 'become', *āyiṟṟu* 'it became/has become'. In these examples, *āka* seems to refer to an interval of time, a notion which was argued in Chapter 6 to have relevance for the analysis of the present perfect. Here, however, the formal tense marking of the verb is assigned according to the time reference of the initial endpoint of the interval, not the final one, as was the case with *irukka* 'be located'. The present state of affairs is thus viewed as the result of a prior configuration of events, with the earlier events prefiguring the later ones. Even the examples in (285) implicitly refer to a temporal interval: the operator BECOME, which *āka* instantiates, implies two moments in time, one before and one after which the change of state takes place. If in some of its uses the perfect tense with *irukka* may be considered retrospective, looking back at the seeds of an event from the standpoint of its present results, then the "perfect" with *āka* is prospective, anticipating a following event.

Chapter 6 observed that the temporal and epistemic uses of certain lexemes, as auxiliaries, may displace the spatial uses of those same lexemes when used as nonauxiliated verbs. Thus, auxiliary *irukka* does not refer to spatial location even though main verb *irukka* does. But what displaces what in the case of *āka*? As a main verb, it already has a temporal use, illustrated in (286); in its capacity as an auxiliary, its epistemic use displaces its temporal one.

1 Akilan (1951: 7). Here the author reflects, though only half-facetiously, on the habit of many modern Tamilians who measure out the times of day in cups of coffee.

Some grammatical properties of auxiliary *āka*

As an auxiliary (and as a main verb), *āka* has a defective paradigm. Prose texts show that it occurs more often in main clauses than in subordinate clauses, and that it has only third person forms. Even so, its morphology is not quite as defective as others (Dale 1975, Fedson 1981) have claimed. Fedson, for example, says it occurs only in the past tense. While its most common form is *āyiṟṟu* 'it became' (< *āy* + *-iṉ-* + *-tu*), the following examples confirm the existence of others.[2]

(287)a *veḷiyē kiḷampi ākiṟat=ā?*
outside start-CF become-PRS-3N=INT
'Are you getting ready to start outside?'

b *cāṭṭai māṭṭukiṟāṉ. iṉṉum koñcam nērattil kiḷampi ākum.*
shirt-ACC button-PRS-3SM still little time-LOC start-CF become-FUT-3SN
'He is buttoning his shirt. He'll start out in just a moment.'

c *eṅkaḷ vīṭṭil ettu maṇikku cāppiṭṭu ākum.*
our house-LOC eight o'clock eat-CF become-FUT-3SN
'In our house, we (can expect to) eat at eight o'clock'.

In (287a) *ākiṟatu* 'it becomes' is a futurate present tense form; the start outside is viewed as an immanent event from the present time; (287b) is a future tense form with a similar meaning; (287c) is a habitual future.

In terms of selection restrictions, auxiliary *āka* modifies events, not actions. Thus, in a constraint that has gone unnoticed in the literature, when a verb has both an affective and an effective stem, *āka* combines only with the affective stem.

(288)a *kaṇṇāṭi uṭaintu āyiṟṟu.*
glass-NOM break+AF-CF become-PST-3SN
'The glass broke, as expected.'

b * *kaṇṇāṭi uṭaittu āyiṟṟu.*
glass-ACC break+EF-CF become-PST-3SN
'He broke the glass, as expected.'

Some speakers who are unable to find an appropriate context might deem (288a) unacceptable; Annamalai (1982), for example, argues that *āka* modifies only change of state verbs with a positive outcome, a constraint which would effectively stigmatize (288a) as ungrammatical. However, this sentence is unexceptional when a technician studying the properties of a new kind of glass, say for car windshields, predicts that it will break at a certain level of stress. When the sample does break at the level he predicted, he is entitled to utter (288a). What matters then is not whether

2 These examples, elicited from native speakers of Tamil, show how Fedson's almost exclusive reliance on written sources can fail to uncover crucial examples. Indeed, her claim that *āyiṟṟu* is a marker of perfect tense would appear to be suspect if the form were not marked for any oppositions of tense: if it contrasted with no other tense-forms, it could not be truly said to mark tense.

the outcome is positive or not, but whether the outcome is what the speaker had anticipated.[3]

Annamalai (1982) recognizes the role that the speaker's expectations play in determining the conditions governing the use of auxiliary *āka*. Schiffman (1969: 106) also notes that it may convey an expected result. Fedson (1981: 36, 60) resorts to a listing: "… perfects of result, persistent situation and recent past …." In view of her earlier claim (Fedson 1981: 58) that *āka* occurs in just one tense, the past, her claim now that *āka* marks perfect tense is suspect since on that hypothesis it would not contrast with any other tense. She rejects as incomplete Schiffman's claim that expectation is an invariant condition on the use of *āka*, substituting instead a disjunction of terms: the event must be expected or be hoped for. She distinguishes between reporting an event and referring to it as a fact, claiming that a reported event must not be undesirable to motivate the auxiliary's use. Such distinctions seem more a feature of certain contexts in which *āka* occurs than a facet of its invariant meaning. Recourse to this distinction can be avoided if Annamalai's meaning of anticipation is taken as the basic meaning for the auxiliary's proper use. Expected events, hoped-for events, desired events and anticipated events are then treated as members of the same family without such dubious distinctions (in this context) as reported versus referred-to situations.

Although *āka* 'become' inflects for the third person singular neuter, it can be associated in surface structure with subject NPs of other persons and numbers, as in example (289) below.

(289) *nāṉ pōy āka vēṇṭum.*
I-NOM go-CF become-INF be.necessary-FUT-3SN
'I have got to go (it is expected of me).'

This auxiliary, unlike other indicative auxiliaries, combines not only with the conjunctive form of the auxiliate, but on occasion, also with verbal nouns.

(290)a *maṇ veṭṭi.k kūli tiṉal āyiṟṟu.*[4]
earth cut-CF wages eat-VN become-PST-3SN
'(They) dig the earth and eat up all their wages.'

b *vantatu āyiṟṟu.*
come-PST-VN become-PST-3SN
'One has come.'

c *colla vēṇṭiyatu āyiṟṟu.*
say-INF be.necessary-VN become-PST-3SN
'What needs to be said has been said.'

Such variants lack currency in the modern spoken language, and are restricted to

3 Annamalai (personal communication) now concurs on this point. Fedson (1981: 64) presents a similar observation.

4 From Bharattiyar's (1962: 184) poem, *maṟavaṉ pāṭṭu*.

the written register. It is not clear how they impact our analysis of auxiliary *āka*; if they are indicative AVCs, it would appear that in the derivations of (290b and c), Predicate Raising has not applied, and that *āka* combines with a sentential complement in surface structure as well as in underlying structure, in which case this verbal noun does not convey a meaning similar to taxis.

āka is one of two indicative auxiliaries (the other is *kiẓikka* 'tear') in our corpus that may occur without its auxiliate in a response to a question that contains the auxiliary.

(291) *cāppiṭṭu āyiṟṟu ammā? āyiṟṟu.*
eat-CF become-PST-3SN mother-VOC become-PST-3SN
'Have you eaten yet, ma'am? I have.'

Other than the collocation *āka vēṇṭum* 'have got to become' and the negative conjugation, e.g., *āka.v illai* 'does not become', auxiliary *āka* seems to lack an infinitive. Instead of the simple conditional form *āṉāl* 'if becomes', which is otherwise expected, the periphrastic construction *āyiṟṟu eṉṟāl* 'if become' is used. The conjunctive form *āy* 'becoming' seems not to occur outside of the perfect tense series *āy irukkum* 'it would be'. The auxiliary does have a verbal noun as part of the complex form *āṉatum* 'as soon as X becomes'. Although not an absolute prohibition, it tends not to appear in nonfinite contexts, perhaps because it necessarily refers the speech event and the speaker.

Since felicitous use of *āka* 'become' requires the speaker's anticipation of the event named by the auxiliate, it is ungrammatical to use *āka* in questions that ask for new information (292a).[5] In asking (292b), however, the speaker assumes that

(292)a *? *yār vantu āyiṟṟu?*
who-NOM come-CF become-PST-3SN
'Who came, as expected?'
b *yār-yār vantu āyiṟṟu?*
who-who-NOM come-CF become-PST-3SN
'Which different people came?'

someone came, permitting *āka*; the distributive interrogative pronoun *yār-yār* 'who all' seeks merely to discover the identity of the various individuals who did come.

Auxiliary *āka* 'become' is unacceptable with expressions of agentivity. The agentive adverbial in (293a) and the overt subject in (293b) are inconsistent with the event reading that *āka* combines with. What is anticipated to occur is an event, not a directed action.

(293)a *avaṉ (*?vēṇṭumeṉṟē) vantu āyiṟṟu.*
he-NOM deliberately come-CF become-PST-3SN
??'He deliberately came.'

5 Compare with example (256) in Chapter 6.

b *(*?avar) avaṉiṭam colli.t tolaintu āyiṟṟu.*
he-H-NOM he-SOC tell-CF lose-AF-CF become-PST-3SN
'Just as expected, he got told the story (??by him).'

Though Annamalai (1982: 132) states that *āka* 'become' occurs only in affirmative contexts, in the proper setting it may occur in negative contexts. Felicitous use of (294) occurs in the following setting: a medicant visits the speaker's house to beg for leftover food, which it is customary to give away. The speaker informs the mendicant that the family has not finished eating, even though the mendicant expected that they would have by that time.

(294) *oruttarum iṉṉum cāppiṭṭu āka.v illai. appuṟam vā.*
no.one-NOM yet eat-CF become-INF IND-NEG later come-IMP
'No one has eaten yet, as expected. Come back later.'

The failure to tabulate all occurring forms of auxiliary *āka* seems to have impeded attempts to determine its invariant meaning. What were thought to be formal constraints on the shapes this auxiliary could take, e.g., that it lacked a present or future tense form, are actually pragmatic constraints that limit the number and kind of appropriate contexts in which such a form might be used, and so limit the relative number of tokens of such forms in discourse. While such limitations could eventually lead to a diachronic reanalysis of its paradigm, Tamil speakers currently use the range of forms presented here.

Indicative auxiliary use of āka

Auxiliary *āka* 'become' marks status, indicating the event denoted by the auxiliate occurs in fulfillment of a prior expectation that it would take place. *āka* thus forges an epistemic link between the narrated event (E^n) and the speech event (E^s), and in this regard, resembles the epistemic use of *irukka* 'be' (Chapter 6). Since the use is primarily epistemic, not temporal, *āka* marks status, not tense.

In (295) *āka* indicates that the speaker had anticipated an event before it occurred. In (295a), therefore, the speaker cannot both say that he anticipated the

(295)a ?? *pālkārikku.p paṇam koṭuttu āyiṟṟu. atai ippō terintu koṇṭēṉ.*
milkmaid-DAT money give-CF become-PST-3SN that-ACC now know-CF hold-PST-1S
'The milkmaid has been paid, as expected, a fact that I learned just now.'

b *ettu maṇikku.t tāṉ kūṭṭam. eṉṉa āṟu maṇikku*
eight o'clock indeed meeting-NOM what six o'clock
vantu { *viṭṭīkaḷ!* / * *āyiṟṟu!* }
come-CF { leave-PST-2P / become-PST-3SN }
'The meeting is at eight o'clock. Why have you come at six!'

milkmaid would be paid and that he learned about this after the fact; the presence of *āka* puts the two statements at loggerheads. In (295b) the speaker expected no one to come to the meeting before eight o'clock: in such circumstances, he can felicitously use auxiliary *viṭa* 'leave', but not auxiliary *āka*.

As indicated above, the use of *āka* in an AVC is neutral with respect to whether the event denoted by the auxiliate is desirable. It is generally known that the sun sets every day; use of *āka* in (296a) signals that the speaker anticipated that the sun would go down. Its use further suggests, as a subsidiary implication, that the sun's descent itself anticipated another event, here, for astrological, esthetic or scientific reasons, the rising of the moon. Use of *āka* in such a frame can advance a narrative: an event, anticipated earlier, takes place and no longer has to be accounted for. In (296b), several children are playing hide-and-go-seek. One group, having hidden themselves, may yell out (296b) to say that they have done what was expected by the rules of the game. In (296c) the speaker uses *āka* not only to report that the fake gold bangle has tarnished but also to remind the addressee that he had predicted it would tarnish.

(296)a *cūriyaṉ maṟaintu āyiṟṟu. iṉṉum cantiraṉai.k kāṇōm.*
sun-NOM hide-CF become-PST-3SN yet moon-ACC see-NEG-1P
'The sun has set, but the moon has not yet risen.'

b *nāṅkaḷ oḷintu āyiṟṟu. kaṇṭupiṭi!*
we^{ex}-NOM hide-CF become-PST-3SN find-IMP
'Okay, we're hidden now. Come and get us!'

c *rōlṭu kōlṭu atukkuḷ karuttu āyiṟṟu.*
rolled gold-NOM that-LOC tarnish-CF become-PST-3SN
'The imitation gold has already tarnished (just as I predicted it would).'

Further examples bolster the claim that use of *āka* refers to expectations current at the time of the speech event. Dale (1975: 263) argues that sentences such as (297a) are ungrammatical; but framed in the appropriate context, speakers find

(297)a *avaḷ cirittu āyiṟṟu. appuṟam eṉṉa?*
she-NOM laugh-CF become-PST-3SN then what-NOM
'Okay, she laughed (at your joke, as expected). What happened next?'

b *māṭu karantu āyiṟṟ=ā?*[6]
cow-NOM milk-CF become-PST-3N=INT
'Have the cows been milked yet (it's your job).'

them acceptable. In relating an office story, the addressee told a friend how he plotted to tell a female coworker a joke so he could engage her in a lengthier conversation. The friend becomes impatient with the addressee and interrupts him by uttering (297a), indicating that the joke elicited laughter, as expected, and to get on with it. Here, the anticipation of the event in question is available to both the

6 Janakiraman (1966: 13).

addressee and the speaker, and as such, likely belongs to the context set of propositions (see Chapter 6). By using *āka* in (297b) the speaker, the employer in this story, communicates to the addressee, his employee, that he had expected him to milk the cows by a certain time. In using the interrogative clitic =*ā*, this sentence obliquely reminds the addressee of this prior expectation. A speaker using *āka* has access to, but not an exclusive claim on, the expectations in the context set, suggesting this auxiliary marks status, not attitude.

Auxiliary *āka* indicates that the event named by the auxiliate occurs at the reference time in fulfillment of a previous anticipation of its occurrence. It therefore characterizes an epistemic relation between the narrated event and the speech event, represented by E^s/E^n, which we may call prospective status. Depending on context, this anticipation could be further interpreted emotionally as a desire or intellectually as an expectation.

PERFECT OF NONDISCURSIVE SPEECH: *kiṭakka*

The verb *kiṭakka* 'lie, rest, remain' functions as an indicative auxiliary; in this capacity it closely resembles the perfect tense auxiliary *irukka* 'be' (Chapter 6). But while *irukka* appears in both discursive and nondiscursive discourse (Chapter 5), *kiṭakka* is restricted to nondiscursive discourse. It shares with *irukka* the circumstantial readings of progressive and perfect tense, and may therefore be considered a form that expresses (relative) tense and is positively marked for temporal intervals. But it differs from *irukka* in lacking an epistemic reading. This failure to mark status follows because reference to the speech event and its participants, who are the locus of knowledge, is absent in nondiscursive discourse.

Few have recognized *kiṭakka* as an auxiliary; Annamalai (1982) and Fedson (1981) alone acknowledge this use. The *Tamil lexicon* offers two examples of *kiṭakka* in what appear to be auxiliary usages, one a progressive auxiliary (298a), the other a modal auxiliary. (298c), from the medieval text *tirumantiram*, 258, prefigures the indicative auxiliary use in Modern Tamil.

(298)a *uṇṇā kiṭantēṉ.*
eat-CF lie-PST-1S
'I was eating.'

b *avaṉ ceyya.k kiṭappa.t tōṉr=um illai.*
he-NOM do-INF lie-FUT-INF appear-CF=AND IND-NEG
'He seems unable to do it.'

c *piṉṉi.k kiṭantatu eṉ pēr aṉpu tāṉē.*
entwine-CF lie-PST-3SN my great love-NOM indeed
'My supreme love is (inseparably) bound (with God).'

Both (298a and b) use archaic forms characteristic of Middle Tamil. The auxiliate in (298a) has the form *uṇṇā* 'eating', an obsolete form of the conjunctive that survives only as a relic frozen in the negative conditional, e.g., *ceyyāviṭṭāl* 'if X does not do, make'. (298b) contains an auxiliate in the obsolete future infinitive form, *kiṭappa,* as well as other archaisms; for example, the negative operator *illai* 'not be' governs the conjunctive, not the infinitive, something it has not been able to do for several hundred years. Neither AVC—if they are AVCs—appears in the modern language. Only (298c) survives to the present.

Main verb uses of kiṭakka

As a nonauxiliated verb, *kiṭakka* 'lie' denotes an entity's being and persisting in a static position. The entity, which appears in the subject position, may be concrete or abstract, animate or inanimate.

(299)a *eṉ putakam aṅkē kiṭantatu.*
my book-NOM there lie-PST-3SN
'My book was lying there.'

b [*nāṉ*] *caṟṟu nēram mēcaiyil talaiyai.k kaviḻttu.k koṇṭu kiṭantēṉ.*[7]
I-NOM little time table-LOC head-ACC overturn-CF hold-CF lie-PST-1S
'I was lying there for a little while with my head turned down on the table.'

c *nāṉ nampuvatu kiṭakkaṭṭum. ulakam nampa vēṇṭum.*[8]
I-NOM believe-VN lie-HORT world-NOM believe-INF be.necessary-FUT-3SN
'Let lie (to one side) what I believe. The world must believe.'

Morphological preliminaries

The verb root *kiṭa-* 'lie' has two different conjugations. One is a class VI verb with a geminate past tense marker, e.g., *kiṭa-tt-ēṉ* 'I was lying' (300a); the other, a class VII verb with a nasal in the past tense marker, e.g., *kiṭa-nt-ēṉ* 'id' (300b). Both are affective verbs paired with an effective counterpart, the class III verb *kiṭatta* 'make lie'. No semantic contrast has been found to accompany the formal distinction

(300)a *nāṉ kiṭattēṉ.*
I-NOM l ie-PST-1S
'I was lying'.

b *nāṉ kiṭantēṉ.*
I-NOM lie-PST-1S
'I was lying'.

between the two affective forms. Class VI forms generally occur in written Tamil, class VII forms in the spoken register. It seems likely that the semantic similarity between *kiṭakka* 'lie' and *irukka* 'be', itself a class VII verb, has over time attracted

7 Akilan (1951: 49).
8 Akilan (1951: 116).

kiṭakka from class VI into class VII in the spoken language through analogy. Examples below include forms from both classes, but since most of the crucial data comes from the spoken register, most reflect a class VII verb.

Indicative auxiliary uses

Auxiliary *kiṭakka* 'lie' conveys the progressive and perfect series in nondiscursive discourse. As Chapter 5 notes, nondiscursive speech obviates reference to the speech event and its participants, and so is used primarily in narrative genres. In lengthy, complex narrations, nondiscursive speech may mix with discursive speech to establish the backdrop against which the major actions of the narrative, those that advance the plot, are played out. Because nondiscursive speech does not refer to E^s or to P^s, several overtones may accompany *kiṭakka*. Fedson (1981) observes that in some instances, the action is viewed as "unchecked"; Annamalai (1982: 160) claims its use signals a casual manner or lack of care. These do not constitute part of the AVC's invariant meaning but arise because in nondiscursive speech the action is viewed as outside the influence of the participants in conversation. Conversational implicatures such as these are likely generated when one uses an AVC with *kiṭakka* in a context where he could have but chose not to use an AVC with *irukka* 'be'.[9] Because grammatical forms that are restricted to discursive speech cannot appeal to E^s or to P^s, *kiṭakka* cannot generate an epistemic circumstantial meaning. In this contracted universe of discourse, there is no recourse to alternative epistemic states representing the contrasting positions of the speaker and hearer.

Like *irukka* 'be', however, *kiṭakka* has both progressive and perfect circumstantial meanings depending as it combines with a verb that denotes a state or activity or with one that denotes an accomplishment or achievement. And like *irukka*, *kiṭakka* must combine with the imperfective converb of an accomplishment or achievement predicate to secure a progressive tense reading.

When a given verb root has both affective (301a, 302a) and effective (301b, 302b) stems, auxiliary *kiṭakka* combines grammatically only with the affective stem, a restriction not observed in previous studies.

(301)a *atu valaintu kiṭakkiṟatu.*
it-NOM bed-AF-CF lie-PRS-3SN
'It is/has bent.'

b * *avaṉ atai vaḷaittu.k kiṭakkiṟāṉ.*
he-NOM it-ACC bend-EF-CF lie-PRES-3SM
'He is bending/has bent it.'

(302)a *atu pirintu kiṭakkiṟatu.*
it-NOM split-AF-CF lie-PRS-3SN
'It is/has split.'

9 It may be such overtones that persuaded Lehmann (1989) to include this auxiliary among attitudinals; however, various grammatical tests point to its membership among nonattitudinal auxiliaries.

b * *avaḷ atai.p pirittu.k kiṭakkiṟāḷ.*
she-NOM it-ACC split-EF-CF lie-PRS-3SF
'She is splitting/has split it.'

In contrast to the use of *irukka* 'become', felicitous use of *kiṭakka* requires that the event denoted by the auxiliate be true at the reference time. A speaker may utter (303b) only when the fallen object, the referent *atu* 'it', still lies on the floor at the reference time. On the other hand, (303a) with *irukka* can be used even when the fallen object has been moved elsewhere by the reference time.

(303)a *atu mēcaiyiliruntu ippō viḻuntu irukkiṟatu.*
it-NOM table-ABL now fall-CF be-PRS-3SN
'It has fallen from the table.'

b *atu mēcaiyiliruntu ippō viḻuntu kiṭakkiṟatu.*
it-NOM table-ABL now fall-CF lie-PRS-3SN
'It has fallen from the table.'

The following examples support our claim that *kiṭakka* marks relative tense, specifying that the proposition it modifies is to be evaluated over an anterior interval of time.

(304)a *nī ceytatu ūr ellām nāṟi.k kiṭakkiṟatu.*
you-NOM do-PST-VN town all stink-CF lie-PRS-3SN
'What you did is (still) stinking all over town.'

b *vīṭṭu pūṭṭa.p paṭṭu.k kiṭantatu.*
house lock-INF befall-CF lie-PST-3SN
'The house was/remained/lay locked up.'

c *veyil naṉaitu kiṭakkum anta.k kuṉṟai.y=um kuḻai.y=um naṉṟāka.p pārvaiyiṭṭāṉ avaṉ.*[10]
sunshine-NOM wet-CF lie-FUT-ADN that hill=AND dale=AND well survey-PST-3SM he-NOM
'He surveyed those hills and dales that were glistening in the sunshine.'

d *pātai iruḷ maṇṭi.k kiṭantatu.*[11]
path-NOM darkness press-CF lie-PST-3SN
'The path lay/was surrounded in darkness.'

Examples (305a, b and c) convey negative connotations that the event denoted by the auxiliate persists heedless of the participants in conversation. In (305a) the subject is portrayed as prattling on, unaware of the boring effect his digressions are producing. In (305b) the plant withers despite all attempts to keep it well watered. In (305c) *kiṭakka* suggests that the children for whose benefit this advice is made constantly stay inside the house without any regard for external influence.

10 Patmanapan (1977: 51).
11 Janakiraman (1966: 12).

However, *kiṭakka* does not invariably convey such nuances in (305d) and, hence, is not marked for pejorative attitude (see Chapter 8).

(305)a *eṉṉeṉṉa.m=ō colli koṇṭu kiṭantāṉ.*
what.what=OR say-CF hold-CF lie-PST-3SM
'He was saying every sort of thing.'

b *ceṭi kāyntu kiṭantatu.*
plant-NOM dry-CF lie-PST-3SN
'The plant had become dry.'

c *vīṭṭil aṭaintu kiṭakkāmal veḷiyē pōṉāl nallatu.*
house-LOC contain-CF lie-NEG-CF outside go-CND good.thing-NOM
'It's a good thing to go outside without being (constantly) shut up in the house.'

d *maranizalil mētuvāka naṭantōm. vaẓiyellām veḷḷai veḷēreṉṟu*
tree.shade-LOC slowly walk-PST-1P way-all white white-EXG
vēppam pū koṭṭi.k kiṭantatu.
neem flower-NOM pour-CF lie-3SN
'We walked slowly in the shade of the trees. All along the way were strewn brilliantly white flowers of the neem tree.'

kiṭakka thus conveys progressive and perfect meanings in nondiscursive discourse. It focuses the participants' attention on the duration of the event without connecting it to the speech event and its participants or to any other narrated event. This lack of connection with external factors promotes occasional overtones of extreme, uninterrupted duration, which may or may not be viewed pejoratively.

DURATIVE AUXILIARY: *vara*

The verb *vara* 'come' functions as a main verb and an indicative auxiliary. As a main verb, it indicates that the subject moves towards the speaker or a deictic center designated by the speaker.

(306) *tarakar iṅkē vantār.*
broker-NOM here come-PST-3H
'The broker came here.'

In an indicative AVC, auxiliary *vara* indicates the process denoted by the main verb endures over a long interval of time. How then is this auxiliary to be distinguished from the complex auxiliary *koṇṭu* + *irukka* 'be V-ing' discussed in Chapter 6? Whereas the complex auxiliary marks taxis, *vara* does not. Auxiliary *vara* also contrasts with *kiṭakka* 'lie' in that it occurs in discursive speech while *kiṭakka* does not. Finally, in contrast to *pōka* 'go', it is not marked for the category of (pejorative) attitude (Chapter 8). As noted earlier, Fedson (1981) distinguishes *vara* from *koṇṭu* + *irukka* by claiming that the former has a longer duration than the latter. Our data show that Fedson's distinction does not systematically accompany the use of *vara*; instead, the absence of marking for taxis proves to be crucial. Further, Dale's (1975: 305) claim that *vara* occurs exclusively in written Tamil, but not in the spoken register, is contradicted by everyday speech.[12] As a nontactic form, it generally applies to descriptions in a narrative's background rather than to events that advance the story line. Example (307a) describes the speaker's pastime, representing a long-term activity repeated over time without connection to other events. In example (307b), the variant with *vara* is unacceptable to speakers because a tactic reading is required to coordinate two events: the Chola's reign and the invaders' arrival, a task for which *koṇṭu* + *irukka* is needed.

(307)a *uṅkaḷuṭaiya kataikaḷai nāṉ toṭarntu paṭittu varukiṟēṉ.*
your-H-GEN story-PL-ACC I-NOM continuously read-CF come-PRS-1S
'I have been reading your stories all along.'

b *vaṭanāṭṭiliruntu cēṉai vantapōtu cōẓā*
north.land-ABL army-NOM come-ADN-time Chola-NOM
āṇṭu { *koṇṭu iruntārkaḷ.* / hold-CF be-PST-3P / * *vantārkaḷ.* / come-PST-3P }
rule-CF
'When the invading army came from the north, the Cholas were ruling.'

In our corpus, auxiliary *vara* may inflect for the present perfect (308a) but not—somewhat surprisingly—for the past perfect (308b) tense.

(308)a *colli vantu irukkiṟēṉ.*
say-CF come-CF be-PRS-1S
'I go on saying.'

b * *colli vantu iruntēṉ.*
say-CF come-CF be-PST-1S
'I went on saying.'

While this gap seems puzzling at first, its explanation lies in the fact that the Tamil past perfect with *irukka* 'be' primarily serves a tactic function, one which would naturally disqualify it from cooccuring with the nontactic auxiliary *vara*.

Auxiliary *vara* generally combines with state or activity predicates; to combine with an accomplishment or achievement predicate, the imperfective converb with *koḷḷa* 'hold' is used. Consider the contrast between (309a and b); note the correlation between the auxiliary and the case-marking of the object NP. In (309a) the phrase *katai colla* 'tell stories' represents an activity; the phrase in (309b) (*oru*) *katai.y-ai colla* 'tell the story', an accomplishment: the former is imperfective, the latter perfective. To secure a durative reading for the latter, an imperfective converb

12 It was an auxiliary in Old Tamil (see p. 39), and appears in Middle Tamil in Cenavaraiyar's commentary to *tolkāppiyam, collatikāaram*, 98: *puli pōṟṟi vā* 'always beware the tiger'.

must first be constructed, to which the auxiliary *vara* is then appended, as in (313a and b) below.

(309)a *pāṭṭi tiṇṇaiyil uṭkārntu koṇṭu katai colli vantāḷ.*
grandmonther-NOM porch-loc sit-CF hold-CF story tell-CF come-PST-3SF
'Grandmother sat on the porch telling stories.'

b *pāṭṭi oru katai.y-ai.c colli.k koṇṭu vantāḷ.*
grandmother-NOM one story-ACC tell-CF hold-CF come-PST-3SF
'Grandmother kept telling a story.'

Use of auxiliary *vara* is appropriate when the activity it qualifies recurs over several periods, with each period containing a typical instance of that activity. This yields the iterative reading in (309a), one which describes many separate instances of story-telling. Use of *vara* in (310) is inappropriate to describe a single stretch of sleep; its presence indicates that the subject slept, awoke and fell asleep several times, which would describe someone with a sleep disorder, but not a normal sleeper. By contrast, the *koṇṭu+irukka* may describe a single phase of an action.

(310) *nēṟṟu pakal avaṉ tūṅki koṇṭu* { *iruntāṉ.* be-PST-3SM / ?* *vantāṉ.* come-PST-3SM }
yesterday morning he-NOM sleep-CF hold-CF
'He was sleeping yesterday morning.'

Auxiliary *vara* 'come' appears in (311a and b) in preference to the complex construction *koṇṭu + irukka* for two reasons. First, the activities are not continuous, but iterated over long periods of time, which is consistent with use of *vara*. Second, these activities are presented as occurring without interference from or connection to any other outside event, which tends to favor nontactic *vara* over tactic *koṇṭu + irukka*.

(311)a *anta maitāṉattil pattu varuṣamāy viḷaiyāṭṭi*
that field-LOC ten year-ADV play-CF
{ *varukiṟārkaḷ.* come-PRS-3P / ?* *koṇṭu irukkiṟārkaḷ.* hold-CF be-PRS-3P } *ippō eṉṉa kavalai?*
now what bother-NOM
'They've been playing in that field for ten years. What's all the fuss about now?'

b *ittaṉai varuṣamāy koṭuttu* { *vantu* come-CF / ?* *koṇṭu iruntu* hold-CF be-CF }
this.many year-ADV give-CF
tiṭēreṉṟu niṟutta muṭiyum=ā?
suddenly stop-INF be.able-FUT-3SN=INT
'When you've been giving for so many years, can you just stop all of a sudden?'

The apparent great length of events denoted by AVCs with *vara* may thus be a circumstantial reading that is implicated because there are no outside events against which its periodicity may be measured. Use of *vara* in the doctor's prescription in (312a) is doubly appropriate because the patient should both take the prescribed dosage at regular intervals and not let anything interrupt this regimen. In (312b) God instructs his devotee to continue observing a vow he took to the exclusion of other, possibly compromising activities. And in (312c) a king, about to depart on an expedition, leaves instructions for his regent to rule the kingdom in his absence, letting nothing interfere. The nontactic, durative and iterative facets of *vara* are all manifest in these examples, giving rise to such semantic overtones as singlemindedness and constancy.

(312)a *marantu cāppiṭṭu varuṅkaḷ!*
medicine eat-CF come-H-IMP
'Take the medicine (on a regular basis, without interruption).'

b *nī inta virutattai kaṭaippiṭittu vā!*
you-NOM this vow-ACC observe-CF come-IMP
'Keep observing this vow (don't let anything distract you)'.'

c *āṇṭu vā!*
rule-CF come-IMP
'Keep ruling (without lapse).'

Use of *vara* 'come' in (313a)[13] implies that as the monthly demands kept rising, nothing interfered to check them. While (313b)[14] contains both auxiliary *vara* and auxiliary *irukka* 'be', the latter convey status rather than perfect tense; the speaker has indirect evidence for his statement. In (313c) auxiliary *vara*, when modifying the phrasal verb *katai eẕuta* 'write stories', indicates the story was serialized, representing several instances of the activity over time. In (313d) the speaker reports watching the gradual whitening of the sky; the dawn is presented as a slow, gradual process that occurs regardless of the observer watching it.

(313)a *appuṟam ēkappaṭṭa ṭimāṇṭu mācāmācam ēṟi.k kiṭṭē varatu.*
then increasing demands-NOM monthly rise-CF hold-CF come-PRS-3SN
'Month by month increasing demands kept being made.'

b *avaṉ tāṉiyāka niṟka muṭiyum eṉṟu kāṇpittu.k koṇṭ=ē*
he-NOM self-ADV stand-INF be.able-FUT-3SN say-CF show-CF hold-CF=PCL
tāṉ vantu irukkiṟāṉ.
PCL come-CF be-PRS-3SM
'He has been showing me all along (in different ways) he can stand on his own.'

c *āṉanta vikaṭaṉil katai eẕuti vara.v illai.y=ā?*
Ananda Vigadan-LOC story write-CF come-INF NEG-IND=INT
'Weren't you writing a serialized story in "Ananta Vikatan"?'

13 Janakiraman (1976: 623).
14 Janakiraman (1976: 325).

d *jannal vaẓiyāka.k kīẓvānam veḷuttu varuvatai.p pārttēn.*
window through horizon-NOM whiten-CF come-FUT-VN-ACC see-PST-1S
'Through the window I saw the horizon gradually turning white.'

The newspaper passage in (314)[15] contrasts *vara* and *koṇṭu* + *irukka*. Use of *vara* in the first sentence sets the backdrop for the main action, in which a cult member had performed several child-sacrifices over a period of time. Use of *koṇṭu* + *irukka* sets the stage for the police arrest, which happened while the wizard was reciting spells; here a tactic form relates the event that advances the narrative to its immediate backdrop.

(314) *atika cakti peṟuvataṟkkāka cāmiyar inta pūjaikaḷai*
great power obtain-FUT-VN-DAT wizard-NOM this sacrifice-PL-ACC
$_V[_V$[*naṭatti*] *vantār*]=*ām.* *cāmiyar puttakam oṉṟai*
conduct-CF come-PST-3H=QUOT wizard-NOM book one-ACC
virittu mantiram $_V[_V$[*ōti*] *koṇṭu iruntār*]. *anta nērattil*
open-CF spell recite-CF hold-CF be-PST-3SH that time-LOC
pōlīcār pāyntu ceṉṟu cāmiyarai.k ... kaitu ceytār.
police spring-CF go-CF wizard-ACC arrest do-PST-3P
'It is said that in order to obtain great powers, the wizard was performing these (child) sacrifices. He was reciting spells from an open book at the time when the police rushed in and arrested him.'

The following sentences further illustrate this nontactic, durative auxiliary. The nontactic meaning of *vara* in (315b), for example, implies that no outside influence can restrain the opposition party from its disruptive activities. Further, example (315d) sets the background against which the action of the short story unfolds.

(315)a *māriyai vaṇaṅki vantēṉ.*
Mari-ACC worship-CF come-PST-1S
'I always worshipped Mariyamman.'

b *etirkaṭci kuẓappam tūṇṭi varukiṟatu.*
opposition.party-NOM confusion instigate-CF come-PRES-3SN
'The opposition party is always instigating confusion.'

c *nāyakar maturai talainakarāka koṇṭu āṇṭu vantārkaḷ.*
Nayaks-NOM Madurai capital-ADV with rule-CF come-PST-3P
'The Nayaks ruled with Madurai as their capital city.'

d *civaṉ kōyilai aṭuttirunta tīppeṭṭi.t toẓiṟcālaiyil rācākaṇṇu*
Siva temple adjacent match.box factory-LOC Racakannu-NOM
vēlai ceytu vantāṉ.
work do-CF come-PST-3SM
'Racakannu worked in the match box factory next to the Siva temple.'

15 From the daily newspaper *diṉa tanti*, 6 March 1980, p. 3.

Auxiliary *vara* signals durative aspect, and may be classified as a quantifier of E^n. It is nontactic and compatible with an iterative reading. It combines directly with state and activity predicates, but may combine with accomplishments and achievements only through the use of the imperfective converb. Because it does not encode taxis, it may generate overtones of great duration and irresistability.

AUXILIARY OF SUBSEQUENT ACTION: *vaikka*

The verb *vaikka* 'place' functions as a main verb, a causative verb (Paramasivam 1979) and an indicative auxiliary. As a main verb, it describes the transfer of an object to a specific location or goal, and contrasts with *pōṭa* 'put' which does not specify the goal of the object (Chapter 8).

(316) *avaṉ pustakattai mēcaiyil vaittāṉ.*
he-NOM book-ACC table-LOC place-PST-3SM
'He placed the book on the table.'

Indicative auxiliary verb use

The presence of auxiliary *vaikka* 'place' in an indicative AVC signals that the event denoted by the auxiliate anticipates or precipitates some future action. According to our taxonomy, it marks taxis, E^nE^n, specifically, prospective taxis. Schiffman (1969) labels *vaikka* the auxiliary of "future utility"; Fedson (1981: 263) argues it conveys the notion of "abiding or lasting results," claiming in effect that this auxiliary marks some kind of resultative aspect. Neither characterization addresses the auxiliary's tactic nature; however, Annamalai's (1982: 62) analysis does. He calls *vaikka* "the verb of anticipated consequence," with the meaning of "keep[ing] the performed event in abeyance for some anticipated sequence." Annamalai presents the minimal pair in (317a and b). Although the two strings are homophonous, their bracketings reveal structural differences: the first is a coordinate structure whose verbs belong to two different clauses; the second consists of a single clause in which the two verbs constitute an indicative AVC. The subsequent use mentioned in the gloss in (317b) looks forward to some future event such as reading, selling or even burning the stored newspapers as kindling.

(317)a $[_S[_S$*nāṉ pattirikkaiyai eṭuttu*$]$ *vaittēṉ*$]$.
I-NOM newspaper-ACC take-CF place-PST-1S
'I took the newspaper and read it.'

b *nāṉ pattirikkaiyai* $[_V[_V$*eṭuttu*$]$ *vaittēṉ*$]$.
I-NOM newspaper-ACC take-CF place-PST-1S
'I stored the newspaper (for some future use).'

The subsequent act may have a positive or negative character. In (318) hiding the chocolates prevents the children from eating them right away, preserving them for future consumption. It is that latter action that prompts the use of *vaikka* here.

(318) *ammā cākkalaṭṭai oḷittu vaittāḷ.*
mother-NOM chocolates-ACC hide-CF place-PST-3SF
'Mother hid the chocolates away.'

Note that *vaikka* 'place' does not normally combine with predicates of destruction. When the auxiliate *oẓikka* denotes the destruction of an object, as in (319a), it cannot combine with auxiliary *vaikka* even though the destruction of an army might ultimately lead to peace. But where *oẓikka* denotes the emptying out of cooking vessels in preparation for washing, as in (319b), *vaikka* is permitted. Similarly, the verb *aẓikka* cannot occur with auxiliary *vaikka* when it means 'ruin, spoil' but can do so when it means 'erase (as a blackboard)'.

(319)a ?* *cōẓar anta.c cēṉaiyai oẓittu vaittār.*
Cholas-NOM that army-ACC destroy-CF place-PST-3P
'The Cholas destroyed that army.'

b *pāttirankaḷai oẓittu vai, appuṟam avai kaẓuva.*
pot-PL-ACC empty-CF place-IMP then they-ACC wash-OPT
'Empty out the cooking vessels, then get them washed.'

Annamalai's examples show that the subsequent action anticipated by auxiliary *vaikka* need not ultimately take place. Since the preparatory action in (320) fails in the end, the subsequent action it prepares cannot come about.

(320) *pirittu vaittāl=um atu piriya.v illai.*
separate-AF-CF place-CND=AND it-NOM separate-AF-IN IND-NEG
'Even though he separated it (for future use), it didn't separate.'

Although the auxiliates in such constructions are generally transitive, intransitives may occur in certain settings. By custom, attendance at a wedding may establish a set of reciprocal obligations; when guests sign a register showing the approximate value of their gifts, they may then expect a gift of comparable value when the situation is reversed. Use of *vaikka* in (321) expresses the speaker's cynical commentary on this practice. Alternatively, one might analyze the phrase *kalyāṇattukku.p pōka* as semantically transitive, roughly 'attend a wedding', permitting the use of *vaikka.*

(321) *nām anta.k kalyāṇattukku.p pōy vaikkiṟōm.*
we-NOM that wedding-DAT go-CF place-PRS-1S
'We are going to that wedding for a future use.'

When the predicate is transitive, the referent of the AVC's direct object must persist through the action denoted by the auxiliate, as suggested in the earlier discussion of verbs of destruction. The act of sweeping trash into the street (322a) results in its dispersal; since the trash ceases to exist as a collective entity, use of auxiliary *vaikka* is inappropriate. When, however, the trash is collected into one place for future disposal, as in (322b), *vaikka* is permissible.

(322)a *kuppai teruvil kūṭṭi* {* *vai.* / *taḷḷu.*}
trash street-LOC sweep-CF {place-IMP / push-IMP}
'Sweep the trash out into the street.'
b *kuppai ōlai peṭṭiyil pōṭṭu vai.*
trash leaf basket-LOC put-CF place-IMP
'Collect the trash into the leaf basket (for later disposal).'

Here Schiffman's and Fedson's descriptions of *vaikka* fail because both proposals would apparently permit the auxiliary's presence in (322a).

Sentence (323) is uttered by a grandparent to a granddaughter who had schemed to keep hiding her dolls so others would buy replacement dolls for her. Here the speaker recognizes that the act of "losing" a doll is meant to prompt the purchase of a replacement. The precipitating act thus need not be considered desirable for felicitous use of *vaikka.*

(323) *ippaṭi "tolaittu" vaittāl uṉakku vēṟu bommai vāṅki*
this.way lose-CF place-CND you-DAT other doll buy-CF
koṭukka māṭṭēṉ.
give-INF FUT-NEG-1S
'If you keeping "losing" dolls this way, I'm not going to buy you any others.'

Example (324), from Annamalai (1982), shows that an undesirable event can evoke the use of *vaikka* as long as it requires a subsequent action. The sentences in (325) indicate that the subject of the AVC need not be animate. None of these examples suggests long-lasting results, as Fedson's proposal requires; a subsequent action could readily undo those results.

(324) *nāy cōfāvil mōṇṭu vaittatu.*
dog-NOM sofa-LOC piss-CF place-PST-3SN
'The dog pissed on the sofa (now we'll have to clean it).'

(325)a *maṇṇal pūmpukār turaimukattai.t tūrttu vaittatu.*
sand-NOM Pumpukar harbor-ACC silt.up-CF place-PST-3SN
'Sand silted up the Pumpukar harbor (now it has to be dredged).'
b *pāṟai viḻuntu kukai vācalai mūṭi vaittatu.*
rock-NOM fall-CF cave entrance-ACC close-CF place-PST-3SN
'The rock fell and blocked the cave (requiring its removal).'
c *kāṟṟu aṭittu taṇṭavāḷattai mūṭi vaittatu.*
wind-NOM beat-CF railway.tracks-ACC close-CF place-PST-3SN
'The wind covered the railway tracks (with sand, requiring its removal).'

Annamalai (1982: 66) claims that the subject of the predicate with which *vaikka* combines must be volitional, offering (326) as evidence.

(326) * *patmiṉi azakāka iruntu vaittāḷ.*
Padmini-NOM pretty-ADV be-CF place-PST-3F
'Padmini was pretty (for subsequent use).'

The acceptability of the sentences in (325) argues against volitionality as a necessary criterion for using *vaikka*. Instead, the stativity of the auxilate *irukka* 'be' seems responsible for the unacceptability of (326). Nor do stative dative-subject constructions permit *vaikka*, which expresses a connection between two actions.

(327) * *appāvukku.k kōpam vantu vaittatu.*
father-DAT anger-NOM come-CF place-PST-3SN
'Father was angry (for subsequent use).'

It is always possible, though not necessary, to add an extra clause to make explicit the subsequent action which *vaikka* implies. Though the explanatory clauses in (328a and b) appear to be negative ('so the wind *won't* come in'), they have positive expectations, viz., the desire to remain warm and dry.

(328)a *kuḷinta kāṟṟu varāmal katavai aṭaittu vai.*
cool wind-NOM come-NEGV door-ACC close-CF place-IMP
'Close the door so the cool wind won't come in.'

b *maẓai varum pōla irukkiṟatu. jaṉṉalai mūṭi vai.*
rain-NOM come-FUT-ADN like be-PRS-3SN window-ACC shut-CF place-IMP
'It looks like rain. Shut the window.'

c *ammā eṉakku.c cāppiṭukiṟatukku ellāṟṟaiyum reṭiyāka*
mother-NOM I-DAT eat-VN-DAT all-ACC=AND ready-ADV
eṭuttu vaittu viṭṭu ...[16]
take-CF place-CF leave-CF
'(After) mother made everything ready so I could eat.'

Annamalai adduces the following minimal pair to coax out what *vaikka* contributes to the meaning of the AVC. If the speaker shows concern for the outcome of the action, he uses auxiliary *vaikka* 'place', as in (329b); if he is indifferent, *pōṭa* 'put' is used (Chapter 8).

(329)a *pāṭṭiyai.k koṭṭi.p pōṭu, nāḷaikku vitai* { *pōṭalām.* / ?? *pōṭa vēṇṭum.* }
garden-ACC dig-CF ut-IMP tomorrow seeds { put-PRM / put-INF must }
'Just dig up the garden, then tomorrow we could/?? must plant seeds.'

16 Jeyakantan (1970: 201).

b *pāṭṭiyai.k koṭṭi vai, nāḷaikku vitai* { ** *pōṭalām.* / put-PRM / *pōṭa vēṇṭum.* / put-INF must-FUT-3SN }
garden-ACC dig-CF place-IMP tomorrow seeds
'Prepare the garden, tomorrow we must/??might plant seeds.'

Auxiliary *vaikka* thus marks prospective taxis; its presence in an indicative AVC indicates that a present action, denoted by the AVC's auxiliate, calls forth a subsequent action.

AUXILIARIES OF BENEFACTIVE VOICE: *koṭukka, tara*

Both *koṭukka* 'give' and *tara* 'give to you or me' function as main verbs and indicative auxiliaries. As auxiliaries, they mark the verbal category of benefactive voice: the AVC's action is performed for someone's benefit. In using *koṭukka*, the beneficiary may explicitly appear in a dative-case NP or the postpositional phrase *N-kkāka* 'on behalf of N'. As for *tara*, such expressions are superfluous because the verb itself incorporates reference to a first or second person beneficiary as part of its meaning.[17] Since *koṭukka* can be used with beneficiaries in the first, second or third persons, examples with this auxiliary are generally more plentiful. The AVCs in (330a and b) illustrate the main verb uses of *koṭukka* and *tara*.

(330)a *nāṉ avaṉukku anta.p paṇam koṭuttēṉ.*
I-NOM he-DAT that money give-PST-1S
'I gave him that money.'

b *avaḷ oru rūpāy tantāḷ.*
she-NOM one rupee give.to.you.or.me-PST-3SF
'She gave me/you/us a rupee.'

In forming AVCs, neither auxiliary may combine with intransitive auxiliates, but they may combine with transitives, including affective transitives (333b).

(331)a * *avaṉ pōy koṭuttāṉ.*
he-NOM go-CF give-PST-3SM
'He went (on someone's behalf).'

b * *avaḷ vantu tarukiṟāḷ.*
she-NOM come-CF give.to.you.or.me-PRS-3SF
'She is coming on my/your/our behalf.'

In example (332) the additional participant invoked by use of auxiliary *koṭukka* 'give' is understood not a recipient but a beneficiary: the participant, here one of

17 The person of the beneficiary is disjoint from the person of the subject, so that *tara* cannot be used reflexively.

the professor's students, does not physically receive the petition, but does benefit by its being written.

(332) *āciriyar maṉuvāy eẓuti.k koṭuttār.*
teacher-NOM petition write-CF give-PST-3H
'The teacher wrote a petition (on behalf of a student).'

The direct object of an AVC with *koṭukka* may be concrete (332) or abstract (333a, 337a); yielding right of way in (333a) provides an entitlement, not a physical object. However, as (333a) and (334b) show, the subject of the AVC may be inanimate. The beneficiary should be animate, or capable of interpretation as animate, as in (333b) where *nāṭṭukku* 'for the country' represents a collective polity.

(333)a *āṭṭō vilaki.k koṭuttatu.*
auto-NOM separate-AF-CF give-PST-3SN
'The auto-rickshaw got out of the way for us.'
b *kānti nāṭṭukku.p pukaẓ/cutantiram vāṅki koṭuttār.*
Gandhi-NOM country-DAT praise/independence get-CF give-PST-3H
'Gandhi obtained praise/independence for the country.'

In (334a) the use of *koṭukka* indicates the subject will not submit to his superior's will; in introducing the issue of a 'beneficiary' into the conversation, its use also carries the implication that he is not making life easy for his boss. In (334b) the wind bends a tree branch low so its fruit may be picked. The role of the AVC's subject is thus not crucial to the conditions governing the use of the benefactive auxiliaries; the action, whether deliberate or not, must be viewed as beneficial to someone.

(334)a *avaṉ vaḷaintu koṭukka māṭṭēṉ.*
he-NOM bend-AF-CF give-INF FUT-NEG-3SM
'He will not bend (to his superior's will).'
b *kiḷai kāṟṟil vaḷaintu koṭuttatu.*
branch-NOM wind-LOC bend-AF-CF give-PST-3SN
'The branch bent in the wind (so we could pick its fruit).'

Benefit must be construed broadly enough to include the notion of detriment, as the term "ethical dative" sometimes covers. Example (335), for instance, is appropriate in the following setting. When the speaker's brother tattles on him to their father about some mischief, bringing down parental wrath, the speaker may use auxiliary *koṭukka* even if he is not being sarcastic or does not believe the punishment is beneficial.

(335) *avaṉ appāviṭam eṉakku vācavu vāṅki.k koṭuttāṉ.*
he-NOM father-ABL I-DAT scolding get-CF give-PST-3SM
'He got me a scolding from father.'

Unlike auxiliary *vaikka* 'place', the direct object of an AVC with *koṭukka* need not remain unaltered by the auxiliate's action; (336) may be uttered by someone who wants grain ground into flour.

(336) *atai uṭaittu.k koṭu.*
it-ACC break-CF give-IMP
'Get that broken up/ground for us.'

Further examples from a variety of written sources[18] reinforce our analysis of *koṭukka* and *tara* as benefactive auxiliaries. Because they relate the narrated event

(337)a *attakaiya urimaikaḷai mīṭṭu.t tantatu janatā kaṭci.*
that.kind rights-ACC rescue-CF give-PST-3SN Janata party-NOM
'It is the Janata Party that has rescued those sorts of rights for us.'

b *aṉṟu mutal ettaṉaiyō pērukku avaṉ kaiyāl ettaṉaiyō*
that.day first how.many people-DAT he-GEN hand-INST how.many
vitamāṉa kaliyāṇappattirikaikaḷ accaṭittu.k koṭuttu irukkiṟāṉ.
kinds wedding.invitation-PL print-CF give-CF be-PRS-3SM
'To think of all the different kinds of wedding invitations that he had printed with his own hand for all those different people from the very first day!'

c *veku nēram varai avaṉ kaiyaiyum mutukaiyum*
long time until he-NOM hand-ACC=AND back-ACC=AND
taṭavi.k koṭuttu iruntār.
carress-CF give-CF be-PST-3H
'He was carressing his son's arms and back for a long time.'

d *kuẓantaikaḷai.k koṉṟu rattattai eṭuttu.k koṭukka cāmiyārukku utavi*
child-PL-ACC kill-CF blood-ACC take-CF give-INF wizard-DAT help
āḷāka irunta caṉmukappiṉar kaitu ceyya.p paṭṭār.
man-ADV be-PST-ADN Canmukappinar-NOM arrest make-INF befall-PST-3H
'Canmukappinar who had helped the wizard by killing children and drawing their blood (for him) was arrested.'

e *inta atircciyai avar terintu koḷḷāmal irukka vēṇṭum*
this surprise-ACC he-NOM know-CF hold-NEG-CF be-INF be.necessary-FUT-3SN
eṉṟu añciṉāṉ. āṉāl eṉ mukam eṉṉai.k kāṭṭi.k koṭuttu viṭṭatu.
that fear-PST-1S but my face-NOM I-ACC S how-CF give-CF leave-PST-3SN
'I feared that he might hear of this surprising thing, but my face gave me away.'

to participants in the narrated event, they are symbolically represented as P^nE^n, with the understanding that the category of person, P^s/P^n, can occasionally elaborate P^n, particularly for *tara* 'give to you or me' in specific contexts.

18 In this brace of sentences, example (337a) comes from *diṉa tanti*, 12 December 1979; (337b) from Jeyakantan (1958: 125); (337c) from Janakiraman (1966: 6); (337d) from *diṉa tanti*, 6 March 1980; (337e) from Akilan (1951: 109).

AUXILIARY OF JUDGEMENT: *pārkka*

The verb *pārkka* 'look at, see' serves three functions: as a nonauxiliated verb, a modal auxiliary and an indicative auxiliary. Additionally, the infinitive and conjunctive forms of this verb function as postpositions, governing nouns in the accusative, with the meaning 'toward'. The word's directional component is apparent in (338a and b) where it functions as a verb, and in (338c) where it serves as a postposition.

(338)a *nāṉ avaḷai.p pārttēṉ.*
I-NOM she-ACC look.at-PST-1S
'I looked at her.'

b *pārttu.p pōṅkaḷ.*
look.at-CF go-IMP-H
'Watch where you're going.'

c *nāṉ kōyilai.p pārttu naṭantēṉ.*
I-NOM temple-ACC toward walk-PST-1S
'I walked toward the temple.'

pārkka 'look at' serves as an auxiliary in modal and indicative AVCs; both AVCs broadly indicate the subject is evaluating the auxiliate's action. Consider the minimal pair in (339a and b); while both auxiliaries are implicative predicates, they convey different meanings. (339b) indicates the subject actually engaged in writing to assess its value to him while (339a) indicates merely that he planned to write even if he ultimately failed to do so. In Annamalai (1982) *pārkka*, as an indicative auxiliary, is characterized as the auxiliary of assessment.

(339)a *avaṉ eẓuta.p pārttāṉ.*
he-NOM write-INF look.at-PST-3SM
'He tried to write.'

b *avaṉ eẓuti.p pārttāṉ.*
he-NOM write-CF look.at-PST-3SM
'He tried writing.'

A further characteristic distinguishes the two kinds of AVC: the subject of the indicative AVC must be sentient, resulting in the ungrammaticality of (340b), while the subject of a modal AVC need not be in (340a).

(340)a *rayil narkara.p pārttatu.*
train-NOM move-INF look.at-PST-3SN
'The train tried moving.'

b * *rayil nakarntu pārttatu.*
train-NOM move-CF look.at-PST-3SN
'The train tried moving (to see what it would be like).'

Indicative auxiliary verb use

The presence of *pārkka* 'look at' in an indicative AVC indicates that subject undertakes the auxiliate's activity to assess the value of its outcome. Since it appears to characterize a relation between the narrated event and one of its participants, namely the subject, it belongs to the family of voice distinctions, P^nE^n. And since it involves making judgments, the surface subject must be sentient, capable of such an activity. Auxiliary *pārkka* seems not to be marked for taxis; the judgment arising from the activity need not lead to another event.

In general, auxiliary *pārkka* combines with auxiliates denoting activities, not states. Annamalai (1982: 54) observes that what is assessed varies among sentences and contexts, including different "kinds of qualities of an object, like its merit, appropriateness, effectiveness, physical nature, performance, difficulty level or the ability to perform an event by the subject, the happening of an event." Annamalai's (1982: 54-55) examples use subordinate clauses to make explicit what is being assessed in each case.

(341)a $[_{S0}[_{S1}$ *nāṉ kurutippuṉal naṉṟāka irukiṟat=ā*] *eṉṟu*
I-NOM Kurutippunal good-ADV be-PRS-3SN=INT say-CF
paṭittu.p pārttēṉ]
read-CF look.at-PST-1s
'I read the novel Kurud\tippunal to see if it was any good.'

b $[_{S0}[_{S1}$ *nāṉ cāṭṭai cariyāka irukiṟat=ā*] *eṉṟu*
I-NOM shirt satisfactory-ADV be-PRS-3SN=INT say-CF
pōṭṭu.p pārttēṉ].
put.on-CF look.at-PST-1s
'I tried on a shirt to see whether it was satisfactory.'

c $[_{S0}[_{S1}$ *nāṉ iṅkliṣ marantu kēṭkiṟat=ā*] *eṉṟu*
I-NOM allopathic medicine be.effective-PRS-3SN=INT say-CF
cāppiṭṭu.p pārttēṉ].
eat-CF look.at-PST-1s
'I tried taking allopathic medicines to see whether they were effective.'

d $[_{S0}[_{S1}$ *nāṉ mettai mētuvāka irukkiṟat=ā*] *eṉṟu*
I-NOM bed soft-ADV be-PRS-3SN=INT say-CF
paṭuttu.p pārttēṉ].
lie.down-CF look.at-PST-1s
'I slept on the bed to see if it was soft.'

e $[_{S0}[_{S1}$ *nāṉ muṭikiṟat=ā*] *eṉṟu naṭantu pārttēṉ*]
I-NOM be.able-PRS-3SN=INT say-CF walk-CF look.at-PST-1s
'I tried walking to see if I could.'

f $[_{S0}[_{S1}$ *nāṉ kariyam naṭukkum=ā*] *eṉṟu kiḷārkkukku.p*
I-NOM matter happen-FUT-3SN=INT say-CF clerk-DAT
paṇam koṭuttu.p pārttēṉ].
money give-CF look.at-PST-1s
'I gave the clerk some money to see whether the matter would be taken care of.'

Note that the reason clauses in (341a and b) contain such evaluative expressions as *naṉṟāka* 'good, well', *cariyāka* 'satisfactory'. Felicitous use of *pārkka* requires only that the subject form a judgment, not that he necessarily act on it. Examples (341a and f) show tactic notions do not invariably accompany the use of auxiliary *pārkka*. Thus, *pārkka* marks not taxis, but a species of voice in which the relation between subject and predicate is epistemic. Given our analyses of *irukka* 'be', *viṭa* 'leave', *koḷḷa* 'hold' and *āka* 'become', all of which have epistemic readings, it comes as no surprise that *pārkka* should involve an epistemic relation between a participant and the narrated event.

The following examples from modern literary texts further reinforce these observations. In (342a)[19] it is the examination that leads to the formation of the judgment in the quotation. Note in (342b) that, unlike the most indicative auxiliaries, *pārkka* permits reduplication of its auxiliate.

(342)a *neṟṟiyil kaiyai vaittu.p pārttu viṭṭu uṉakku uṭampu*
forehead-LOC hand-ACC place-CF look.at-CF leave-CF you-DAT body-NOM
cariyāka illai eṉṟēṉ.
well not.be-IND say-PST-1s
'After putting my hand on her forehead (to take her temperature), I said, "You aren't well".'

b *tirumpavum tēyttu.t tēyttu.p pārttu.k koṇṭāḷ.*[20]
turn-INF=AND rub-CF rub-CF look.at-CF hold-PST-3SF
'She turned over and tried rubbing her stomach (to see if it would ease the pain).'

MISCELLANEOUS AUXILIARIES

My fieldwork probably did not uncover all the indicative auxiliaries that might appear in this chapter. Annamalai (1982) analyzes three which did not surface in my own research and, hence, were not submitted to the full battery of tests in Chapters 5 and 6. According to Annamalai's own tests, these three exhibit fewer auxiliary properties than those examined so far but still show enough to prevent the sequences in which they appear from being analyzed as coordinate or compound clauses. These verbs are *kāṭṭa* 'show' and the paired set *muṭiya* 'be finished' and *muṭikka* 'finish'.

Auxiliary kāṭṭa

Annamalai (1982: 59-61) suggests *kāṭṭa* 'show' is the effective counterpart of semantically affective *pārkka* 'look at'. Both involve the formation of a judgment about the AVC's action, but unlike *pārkka*, when *kāṭṭa* is used, the subject under-

19 Akilan (1951: 90).
20 Jeyakantan (1958: 13).

takes the action not to form a judgment himself, but to present the action to another person for judgment. Accordingly, *kāṭṭa* marks voice.

(343)a *nāṉ kumārukku nāvalai.p paṭittu.k kāṭṭiṉēṉ. naṉṟāka*
I-NOM Kumar-DAT novel-ACC read-CF show-PST-1S good
irukkiṟatu eṉṟāṉ.
be-PRS-3SN say-PST-3SM
'I read out the novel for Kumar. He said it was good.'

b *nāṉ kumārukku naṭantu kāṭṭiṉēṉ. avaṉ āccariyappaṭṭāṉ.*
I-NOM Kumar-DAT walk-CF show-PST-1S he-NOM be.surprised-PST-3SM
'I walked for Kumar. He was surprised (to find I could).'

c *kumār annāturai pōla pēci.k kāṭṭiṉāṉ.*
Kumar-NOM Annadurai like speak-CF show-PST-3SM
'Kumar spoke like Annadurai (so we could judge his imitation).'

d *nāṉ avaṉ tavaṟai eṭuttu.k kāṭṭiṉāṉ.*
I-NOM his fault-ACC take-CF show-PST-1S
'I pointed out his mistake (so he could recognize it).'

e *tam tantaiyār iyaṟṟiya kuṟavañciyiliruntu cila*
self-GEN father-NOM composed-PST-ADN Kuravanji-ABL some
pāttukkaḷai.p pāṭi.k kāṭṭiṉārkaḷ.[21]
song-P-ACC sing-CF show-PST-3P
'They sang some songs from the Kuravanji their father had composed (so their audience could judge them).'

If *kāṭṭa* is the effective counterpart of *pārkka* 'look at', the relation between the two would resemble the relation between the effective auxiliary *koṭukka* 'give' and its affective counterpart *koḷḷa* (from **koṭa)* 'hold' in its use as a marker of voice. In the affective versions, the subject directs the activity for his own benefit or judgment; in the effective versions, the subject directs the activity for the benefit or judgment of an other.

Auxiliaries of completion: muṭiya, muṭikka

According to Annamalai (1982), the presence of *muṭiya* 'be finished' or *muṭikka* 'finish' in an indicative AVC signals the completion of an event. They thus convey a kind of punctual aspect; but this does not adequately distinguish them from auxiliaries such as *viṭa* 'leave'. *viṭa* may signal punctual aspect in that the activity simply stops, even before the coda is reached. The difference between *muṭikka* 'finish' and *viṭa* is thus roughly analogous to the distinction in English between 'finish' and 'complete' as against 'stop' and 'cease': in 'he finished reading the book', but not in 'he stopped reading the book', the subject is presented as having read all the way to the end.

21 Caminataiyar (1950: 22).

Recall from Chapter 3 that Tamil verb bases are inherently imperfective, representing processes or activities rather than achievements or accomplishments. If so, this creates frequent opportunities to add an auxiliary to specify how an ongoing activity ends. Use of *muṭiya* 'be finished' or *muṭikka* 'finish' apparently signals that the activity has reached its coda.[22]

(344)a *avaḷ pattu maṇikku.p pāṭi muṭittāḷ.*
she-NOM ten o'clock-DAT sing-CF finish-PST-3SF
'She finished singing at ten o'clock.'

b *avaḷ pattu maṇikku muṭittāḷ.*
she-NOM ten o'clock-DAT finish-PST-3SF
'She finished at ten o'clock.'

Annamalai contends (1982: 47) that (344b) adequately paraphrases (344a), and that the two therefore co-derive from the same underlying structure. Whether we accept this proposal or not, it may be that *muṭikka* 'finish', like *āka* 'become' and *kiẓikka* 'tear', but none of the other indicative auxiliaries, can occur without an overt main verb in surface structure.

If *muṭiya* 'finish' and *muṭikka* focus on a coda, they should apply only to events internally divisible into an onset, body and coda, but not those with a homogenous internal structure, such as stative predicates. This hypothesis is borne out below.

(345) * *patmiṉi aẓakāka iruntu muṭittāḷ.*
Padmini-NOM beauty-ADV be-CF finish-PST-3SF
'Padmini finished being beautiful.'

The effective version of the auxiliary, *muṭikka*, apparently requires an agentive subject and so cannot cooccur with dative-subject verbs.

(346)a * *appāvukku.k kōpam vantu muṭittatu.*
father-DAT anger-NOM come-CF finish-PST-3SN
'Father finished getting angry.'

b * *cāvi katavai.t tiṟantu muṭittatu.*
key-NOM door-ACC open-CF finish-PST-3SN
'The key finished opening the door.'

c * *maycūr kuḷirntu muṭittatu.*
Mysore-NOM be.cool-CF finish-PST-3SN
'Mysore finished being cool.'

On the basis of such sentences, Annamalai states the surface subject must be agentive for auxiliary *muṭikka*, and rules out examples such as (346c) as ungram-

22 I hypothesize that there may be a conversational implicature to the effect that unless otherwise stated, participants in conversation may assume that an activity does pass through all its stages. This would account for the fact that Tamil sentences are not peppered with these two auxiliaries.

matical. However, in the proper context, sentences such as (347) were found acceptable by my informants.

(347) *maycūr kuḷirntu muṭittatu. ippō ūṭṭi kulirntu viṭṭatu.*
Mysore-NOM be.cool-CF finish-PST-3SN now Otthy-NOM be.cool-CF finish-PST-3SN
'Mysore has ceased being cold; now Otthy is cold.'

The sequence of sentences in (347), taken together, expresses the gradual change of seasons with the cool season in one city giving way to the cool season in another. While the main verb *kuḷira* 'be cool' can thus be interpreted as a process here, rather than a state, the subject remains nonagentive. Thus, it is not clear what makes (346a and b) unacceptable. The effectivity of the auxiliary may clash with the dative-subject construction, which has a stative reading.

Further examples from Annamalai's study present both the affective and the effective versions of this auxiliary.

(348)a *nāṉ paẓattai urittu muṭittēṉ.*
I-NOM fruit-ACC peel-CF finish-EF-PST-1S
'I finished peeling the fruit.'

b *cāppiṭṭu muṭintatu.*
eat-CF finish-AF-PST-3SN
'The eating (i.e., the meal) is concluded.'

c *avaḷōṭu pēci muṭiyātu.*
she-SOC speak-CF finish-AF-FUT-NEG-3SN
'Arguing with her will never be concluded (i.e, there's no winning with her).'

The affective version appears to possess more auxiliary characteristics than its effective counterpart. This may be due to that fact that effective *muṭikka* requires the subject NP to direct the action named by the auxiliate, which would appear to be a feature of "main" uses but not auxiliary verb uses. We may provisionally say that these two auxiliaries mark completive aspect, the quantifier of E^n: the action of the AVC is represented as passing through its coda phase.

These three cases suggest that, at least in theory, the set of indicative auxiliary verbs is an open one. Any verb of motion combining with a preceding conjunctive form could come to behave like an indicative auxiliary if over time it became enmeshed in the network of verbal categories that auxiliaries typically express. We have merely concentrated here on that subset which has come conventionally to link certain lexemes with certain grammatical categories in Tamil.

SUMMARY

Ten auxiliaries have been studied here. Auxiliary *āka* 'become' marks the verbal category of status, E^s/E^n: the narrated event occurs in fulfillment of a prior expectation that it would. *kiṭakka* 'lie' marks progressivity and perfectivity in nondiscursive speech. *vara* 'come' marks durative aspect, the quantifier of E^n, and is compatible with iterative interpretations. *vaikka* 'place' marks prospective taxis, E^nE^n: the narrated event anticipates a subsequent event. *koṭukka* 'give' and *tara* 'give to you or me' mark benefactive voice, P^nE^n: the subject performs an action for the benefit of someone else. *pārkka* 'look at' marks a kind of voice, P^nE^n: the subject engages in an activity to judge it. *kāṭṭa* 'show' appears to be the effective counterpart to *pārkka*. *muṭiya* 'be finished' and *muṭikka* 'finish' both mark completive aspect, E^n: the activity of the narrated event is presented as having passed through the coda phase. Distinctions of aspect, voice and taxis are all represented here, making up in part for the relative paucity of these verbal categories in the basic verbal inflections of the language. While future research will doubtless refine various details of these auxiliaries and their lexical properties, we have provided a framework for their analysis in terms of verbal categories.

8 Auxiliaries of attitude and abuse

INTRODUCTION

We now turn our attention to the analysis of those indicative auxiliaries that mark attitude, a verbal category which characterizes the speaker's subjective evaluation of the narrated event. They include *aẓa* 'cry', *aruḷa* 'grace', *oẓiya* 'purge', *kiẓiya* 'be torn', *kiẓikka* 'tear', *tīrkka* 'exhaust', *tolaiya* 'get lost', *tolaikka* 'lose', *taḷḷa* 'push', *pōka* 'go', *pōṭa* 'put' and *vaẓiya* 'drip'.

Linguists familiar with other auxiliary systems might well express surprise at discovering that these lexemes function as auxiliaries; many would probably be hard pressed to find parallels in other languages. And while some studies of Tamil have suggested some of these verbs as possible auxiliaries, solid proof of their extent and systematic nature has heretofore been largely absent. Ours is the first study to present grammatical arguments for the claim that they belong to the same grammatical system as the auxiliaries previously analyzed.

These unusual auxiliaries and their equally unusual semantics naturally raise the question of how we may expand the concept of possible auxiliary verb to encompass them without lapsing into a mere list. The answer lies in establishing the new verbal category of attitude to define them. Parallel to this issue is the question of what kinds of lexemes may serve as auxiliaries of attitude. While applicable to some, e.g., *pōka* 'go', the motive hypothesis, which was invoked for the auxiliaries in Chapters 6 and 7, runs afoul of most attitudinal auxiliaries. The liminal hypothesis is proposed below to explain how such verbs as *kiẓikka* 'tear' or *tolaiya* 'get lost' come to function as auxiliaries.

Verbal category of attitude

The verbal category of attitude is a shifter that characterizes the speaker's subjective evaluation of the narrated event. It must be distinguished from two other categories, status and evidential, with which it might be confused. The formula P^s/E^n, our choice to represent attitude, has been used in Slavic linguistics to represent the verbal category of status (Aronson 1978; Friedman 1977, 1979). In Chapter 6 what we call status in Tamil was treated as the qualifier of E^s/E^n, minimally opposed to tense, the corresponding quantifier. Status characterizes an epistemic relation between the narrated event and the speech event in terms such as evidence, where the evidence is in theory objectively available to all participants.[1] The category of attitude, by contrast, expresses a subjective opinion about the narrated event, attributing sole responsibility for that opinion to the speaker. This contrast is reflected in the differential grammatical behavior of auxiliaries of attitude and status; auxiliaries of attitude, for example, but not status are sensitive to the category of person. This provides one reason for using E^s/E^n to symbolize status, in effect freeing P^s/E^n for attitude. The category that Jakobson (1971: 135) calls evidential and represents by E^nE^{ns}/E^s appears to be nondistinct from status here: nothing in the grammar of Tamil seems to motivate a distinction between the two.

Because it refers to the narrated event, attitude is naturally considered a verbal category. As noted earlier, Schiffman (1969: 26) despaired of including *taḷḷa* 'push' in the same class as *irukka* 'be located', resorting in the end to a redundancy rule, because "in Tamil ... pejorative, clearly a non-aspectual notion, is associated with an aspectual notion as a redundant feature." What unites attitude and aspect, however, is their common reference to the narrated event, in short, to their common status as verbal categories.

Our data reveals a division of attitude into an opposition of admirative versus pejorative. Most Tamil attitudinal auxiliaries convey pejorative attitude in which the speaker negatively evaluates the narrated event; some, such as *taḷḷa* 'push', convey either pejorative or admirative attitude, depending on context. What matters for our purposes is that the presence of an attitudinal auxiliary in an AVC always conveys a nonneutral evaluation. Where an AVC does *not* express the category of attitude, the participants in conversation may conversationally implicate that the speaker holds at least a neutral opinion of the narrated event, for if a pejorative or an admirative opinion were salient, the maxim of relevance (Grice 1967, 1989) would require the speaker to inform his addressee by using conventional linguistic expressions that convey opinions, here attitudinal auxiliaries. Moreover, when one declines to use an attitudinal auxiliary where one might have chosen to do so, one may further Q-implicate (Levinson 2000: 76ff.) a positive evaluation about what is being said. That most of these auxiliaries mark pejorative attitude reflects, I think, a natural presumption that unless the speaker goes out of his way to draw attention to attitude, he takes at least a nominally neutral attitude towards the content of what is said.

No one-to-one correspondence exists between Tamil attitudinal auxiliaries and a set of comparable devices in English; the following examples indicate some ways of glossing the Tamil examples to convey their original flavor. The emphasized portions in (349) represent some of the means English speakers use to express their opinion of the narrated event and its participants, including semi-auxiliaries (349a and b), parentheticals (349c and d) and epithets (349e).

1 Johnson (1981) defines status as the relation between the speech time and event time, using Reichenbach's not Jakobson's system. Nonetheless, her definition comes close to ours. The major difference is that here status describes an epistemic relation, and not a purely temporal one.

(349)a Marge *went and bought* that generic toothpaste.
b Martha *got* her purse *stolen.*
c Millicent went home, *damn it.*
d John *damn near* told Bill everything about my Cayman account.
e Max, *that fool,* dropped in without calling first.

The grammar of attitudinal auxiliaries

Chapters 4 and 5 established that attitudinal auxiliaries pattern with other indicative auxiliaries over against modal auxiliaries, lexical compounds and compound clauses, and that they function as a subset within the set of indicative auxiliaries. For example, with one or two exceptions, no attitudinal auxiliary may be embedded in a causative formation (p. 105); except for *tolaiya* and *tolaika*, no attitudinal auxiliary may appear in indirect discourse (Chapter 5).

The interaction of attitudinal auxiliaries with the category of person also distinguishes them from other indicative auxiliaries. Because person and attitude refer to P^s and because attitudinal auxiliaries generally convey a pejorative opinion, the appearance of attitudinal auxiliaries in the first or second person is marked. In the first person, they sound self-deprecating; in the second, rude or confrontational.[2] Attitudinal auxiliaries are not normally repeated in answers to questions that contain them; such repetition is considered rude. As an answer to (350a), (350b) is cheeky: it mimics and mocks the opinion of the person asking the question. Instead, (350c) is the normal, polite response to (350a).[3]

(350)a *avaṉ colli.t tolaittāṉ=ā?*
he-NOM tell-CF lose-EF-PST-3SM=INT
'Did he go and tell, damn him?'
b ?? *āmām, avaṉ colli.t tolaittāṉ.*
yes he- NOM tell-CF lose-AF-PST-3SM
'Yes, he went and told, damn him.'
c *avaṉ colli.t viṭṭāṉ.*
he-NOM tell-CF leave-PST-3SM
'He did tell.'

However, no auxiliary that marks status, such as *āka* 'become' (Chapter 7) or *irukka* 'be' (Chapter 6), would be exceptional in such exchanges. That attitudinal auxiliaries are sensitive to the interchange of speaker and addressee is evidence that P^s is a crucial element in their definition, but not that of status.

2 This effect is not perceived to be as strong for *pōka* 'go', *pōṭa* 'put', *aruḷa* 'grace', *tīrkka* 'exhaust', and *taḷḷa* 'push'.

3 Disjunctive epistemic taxis, encoded by *viṭa* 'leave', shares in common with pejorative attitude a reference to deviation from a norm; whereas disjunctive taxis signals a deviation from the set of noncontroversial propositions in the context set, attitude marks a deviation from what the speaker believes to be norms of conventional conduct.

Lexicography, localism and liminality

This section speculates on the lexicography of attitudinal auxiliaries. However, nothing in our empirical analysis of the indicative AVC, the category of attitude or the semantics of the individual auxiliaries directly depends on its prior acceptance. It is offered as food for thought for those who wonder why certain lexemes but not others may serve as vehicles for attitude in Tamil. Earlier the motive hypothesis helped us narrow the class of lexemes that might function as auxiliaries. While it clearly applies to such attitudinal auxiliaries as *pōka* 'go' or *tolaiya* 'get lost', it does not capture their distinctive semantics. Typically, attitudinal auxiliaries in Tamil involve verbs of motion that specify neither a determinate manner of execution nor a distinct, positively valued goal. For example, *vaẓiya* 'drip, overflow, ooze' expresses the indeterminate movement of viscous fluids; *pōka* 'go', *pōṭa* 'put', *tolaiya* 'get lost' and *tolaikka* 'lose' express motions with no distinct goal; and *kiẓikka* 'tear' and *oẓiya* 'purge' express transitions into a state of destruction.

I propose the liminal hypothesis (from Latin *limen* 'threshold') to characterize the indeterminate manner and goal of motion that accompanies attitudinal auxiliaries. It assumes that processes are segmented into three stages: (1) separation from an initial stage, (2) passage through a liminal stage and (3) reincorporation into a final stage (see van Gennep 1960). The liminal hypothesis claims that attitudinal auxiliaries focus attention on the liminal stage of a process and, in so doing, bear the opprobrium ascribed to liminality. Further, the tripartite structure of separation, liminal and reincorporation stages may be directly superimposed on the aspectual division of events into onset, body and coda, helping to explain the preponderance of aspectual notions among attitudinal auxiliaries, as well as their underlying unity with nonattitudinal auxiliaries.

Turner (1969) and Douglas (1967, 1975) extend van Gennep's anthropological analysis of rituals to a broader range of social institutions and modes of conduct, concentrating on the properties of liminal stages. Turner (1969) observes that liminal stages are qualitatively different from initial and final stages: whereas the latter two are known positions within the network of social values, a liminal stage is a leap between the two; not firmly anchored to the known values of the endpoints, it slips through the net of determinate social values. This property of in-betweenness colors the liminal stage of a process with shades of awe, uncertainty, power and danger. Douglas (1967) further demonstrates the precariousness and, indeed, impurity associated with liminal stages in animal taxonomies, dietary prohibitions and exchanges such as gift-giving, dowries and sacrifices to divinities. She insightfully argues that liminal stages are negatively evaluated because they lack specific, determinate value.[4] For present purposes, we need show only that liminal stages are negatively valued in contrast to initial and final stages.

4 Social distinctions may be neither fine nor comprehensive enough to include liminal stages. Instead of extending these distinctions, liminal entities and stages are assimilated to the closest determinate value or rejected entirely. Douglas shows that failure to have a determinate value, i.e., to be liminal, is often grounds for rejection from the social network, cognitively or physically.

The rigor and clarity of these studies should not lead us to conclude that the typical response to liminal entities or events is an intellectual one; it is overwhelmingly an emotional one. Given the negative evaluation of such entities and events, liminality typically evokes emotional responses ranging from fear to disgust, from anxiety to awe. An individual's opinions, as well as their emotional expression, are formulated in terms of social norms and channeled through the conventional means available to him, which in the case of the Tamil speech community include attitudinal auxiliaries.

The liminal hypothesis thus predicts that those verbs which focus on the liminal phase of an event are the most suitable candidates to serve as attitudinal auxiliary verbs. While study of individual auxiliaries tends to confirm the liminal quality of most lexemes that serve as attitudinal auxiliaries, not all attitudinal auxiliaries, e.g., *aẓa* 'cry', can be satisfactorily explained by this hypothesis. The most we can suggest at this juncture is a tendency for the verbal category of attitude to correlate with the concept of liminality.

AUXILIARIES OF ANTIPATHY: *tolaiya, tolaikka*

The verb root *tolai-* 'lose' has both an affective stem *tolai.y-a* 'get lost' and an effective stem *tolai.k-ka* 'lose'. Both forms may function as nonauxiliated main verbs and as indicative auxiliaries. As main verbs, they describe a movement with no known destination. In (351a) the subject of affective *tolaiya* gets lost; in (352a) the object of effective *tolaikka* comes to be lost. Corresponding to two parsings, or analyses, (351b) and (352b) each have two readings; the second anticipates the auxiliary uses of these verbs.

(351)a *cītai kāṭṭil tolai-nt-āḷ.*
Sita-NOM forest-LOC lose+AF-PST-3SF
'Sita was/got lost in the forest.'

b *kumār tiruviẓākku.p pōy tolai-ntu viṭṭāṉ.*
Kumar-NOM festival-DAT go-CF lose+AF-CF leave-PST-3SM
'Kumar went to the festival and got lost there.'
or
'Kumar went to the festival, damn it.'

(352)a *paṇattai eṅkē tolaittēṉ?*
money-ACC where lose+EF-PST-1S
'Where did I waste (lit., lose) all that money?'

b *kumār pārkarpēṉā vāṅki tolaittu viṭṭāṉ.*
Kumar-NOM Parker.Pen buy-CF lose+EF-CF leave-PST-3SM
'Kumar bought a Parker Pen and lost it.'
or
'Kumar bought a Parker Pen, damn him.'

Auxiliary verb uses

Schiffman (1969: 174) describes *tolai-* 'lose' as expressing the speaker's disgust or impatience with the content of what is said; he includes affective and effective versions. Fedson (1981: 238) treats affective *tolaiya* as marking a kind of voice that "indicates a general note of exasperation or chagrin which is focused on the actor," while effective *tolaikka* marks "manner of action" and "indicates that the speaker is exasperated with or chagrined by the situation… (Fedson 1981: 282)." Annamalai (1982) argues that they convey the speaker's antipathy towards an undesirable situation. Our analysis agrees substantially with his, although the force of the attitude conveyed appears somewhat milder than he suggests. Both auxiliaries convey the speaker's pejorative attitude toward the narrated event, sometimes targeting the subject, sometimes not.

In Annamalai's terms, *tolaiya* conveys the speaker's antipathy towards the occurrence in the narrated event while *tolaikka* conveys antipathy toward the performance in the narrated event. Affective *tolaiya* expresses the speaker's censure against the occurrence of an event, not necessarily the subject, as Fedson suggests. The occurrence of an event is often sufficient to motivate use of affective *tolaiya,* as in (352a). When effective *tolaikka* is used, the speaker's antipathy may attach either to the performer of the action or to the performance itself (352b). Because effective verbs signal a directed action, *tolaikka* naturally highlights the subject; even so, the subject of *tolaikka* is not invariably the target of the speaker's scorn.

(353)a *avan̠ vantu tolaintān̠.*
he-NOM come-CF lose+AF-PST-3SM
'He came here, damn it.'

b *avan̠ vantu tolaittān̠.*
he-NOM come-CF lose+EF-PST-3SM
'He came here, damn him.'

Both *tolaiya* 'get lost' and *tolaikka* 'lose' combine with a broad range of auxiliates, including stative predicates (354a and b), verbs of location (354c), verbs of action (354d and e), verbs of transaction (354f), verbs of perception (354g) and verbs of propositional attitude (354h). The affective and effective versions may occur with both stative (354a and b) and action verbs (354d and e).

(354)a *inta marattu paẕam eppoẕutum puḷittu.t tolaiyum.*[5]
this tree fruit-NOM always be.sour-CF lose+AF-FUT-3N
'This damn tree's fruit is always sour.'

b *avan̠ contakkāran̠āka vēṟu iruntu tolaikkiṟān̠.*[6]
he-NOM relative-ADV also be-CF lose+EF-PRES-3SM
'He happens to be a relative (I can't avoid helping him).'

5 Fedson (1981: 240).
6 Annamalai (1982: 72).

c *parīṭcaikku nāḷ neruṅkum pōtu paṭuttu.t tolaikkiṟāḷ.*
examination day near-FUT-ADN when sleep-CF lose+EF-PRES-3SF
eṉṉa paṇṇukiṟatu?[7]
what do-PRES-VN
'With examination day approaching, this damned (girl) goes off and sleeps. What's to be done?'

d *nāṉ cirittu.t tolaintēṉ.*
I-NOM laugh-CF lose+AF-PST-1S
'I laughed, damn it (too loudly, nervously).'

e *mēlatikkāri oru jōk coṉṉār. nāṉ cirittu.t tolaittēṉ.*[8]
supervisor-NOM one joke tell-PST-3H I-NOM laugh-CF lose+EF-PST-1S
'The boss told a joke. I damn well had to laugh (for fear of what might happen if I didn't).'

f *avaṉ arittu.k koṇṭ=ē irukkiṟāṉ. paṇattai.k koṭuttu.t tolai!*[9]
he-NOM pester-CF hold-CF=EMP be-PRES-3SM money-ACC give-CF lose-IMP
'He has been pestering me constantly. Just give him the damn money.'

g *vattiyār pārttu.t tolaittu viṭṭār.*
teacher-NOM see-CF lose+EF-CF leave-PST-3H
'The teacher caught them, drat!'

h *ippaṭi.t tāṉ tērtal tōṟum colkiṟāṉ anta ōṭṭu.p poṟukki cuntaraṉ;*
thus EMP election each say-PRES-3SM that vote scavenger Sundaran-NOM
anta.c camayam avaṉ koṭukkum oru rūpāy kācukkāka atai
that time he-NOM give-fut-ADN one rupee cash-ADV it-ACC
nampi tolaikkiṟāṉ inta eccirpoṟukki capāpati.[10]
trust-CF lose+EF-PRES-3SM this rag.picker Sabhabati-NOM
'Every election that vote-scavenger Sundaran would talk just this way. And this time, for the price of a single rupee coin, that ragpicker Sabhapati trusts him, damn fool.'

When auxiliary *tolaiya* and *tolaikka* are negated, the negation does not cancel the speaker's expression of antipathy toward the occurrence or performance of the action in the narrated event. This strongly suggests this facet of meaning should be treated as a presupposition or a conventional implicature (see Levinson 2000). In example (355a) overleaf, the speaker says that the train has not come, and complains that he doesn't like that. The presence of *illai* 'not be' in the sentence does not negate the meaning of *tolaiya*; thus, the phrase cannot mean that the train came (or didn't come) and that the speaker didn't have any antipathy toward the event (or nonevent). Similarly, in example (355b) the negative *māṭṭēṉ* 'I will not' does not negate not the speaker's expression of antipathy, but the activity that is denoted by the auxiliate *kaṟṟu.k koḷḷa* 'learn'.

7 Jeyakantan (1973: 17).
8 Annamalai (1982: 73).
9 Annamalai (1982: 72).
10 Jeyakantan (1958: 109).

(355)a *rayil iṉṉum vantu tolaiya.v illai.*
train-NOM yet come-CF lose+AF-INF IND-NEG
'The train hasn't come yet, damn it all.'

b *nāṉ evvaḷavu connāl=um avaṉ kaṟṟu.k koṇṭu.t tolaikka māṭṭēṉ eṉkiṟāṉ.*
I-NOM how.much say-COND=AND he-NOM learn-CF hold-CF lose+EF-INF FUT-NEG-1s say-PRES-3SM
'No matter how much I tell him, he refuses to learn, damn him.'

In our corpus, unlike Schiffman's (1969: 91), *tolaiya* occurs with the *-atum* 'as soon as' suffix, as in (356). Here *tolaiya* merely conveys antipathy toward the delay, not necessarily toward the subject.

(356) *avaṉ vantu tolaint-atum koṭukkiṟēṉ.*
he-NOM come-CF lose+AF-AS.SOON.AS give-PRES-1s
'I'll give it to him when he damn well gets here.'

Unlike most attitudinal auxiliaries, *tolaiya* 'get lost' occurs freely in the first person without a marked rhetorical effect (357). Note that the auxiliate is the effective (main) verb *tolaikka* 'lose'.

(357) *nāṉ eṉ pāsporṭṭu tolaittu.t tolaintēṉ.*
I-NOM my passport lose+EF-CF lose+AF-PST-1s
'I lost my passport, damn it all.'

Affective *tolaiya* 'get lost' may occur in indirect discourse, embedded by the infinitival complementizer; for example, *pōy.t tolaiya.c coṉṉār* 'he said that someone went damn it'. Conservative speakers find this marginally acceptable. Effective *tolaikka* 'lose' can be embedded under a causative verb when the causer is inanimate, but not when it is inanimate, a constraint which appears to be pragmatic rather than syntactic. Since in (358b) the instrument *avaḷ* 'she' is coerced to speak by the agent *avar* 'he', she cannot be held responsible, and cannot therefore be a target of the speaker's indignation. However, the animate causee *avaṉ* 'he' in (358a) should be able to withstand an inanimate causer such as circumstance; in such a case, the pejorative opinion may attach to the causee.

(358)a *cantarppam avaṉai.c colli.t tolaikka vaittatu.*
occasion-NOM him-ACC say-CF lose+EF-INF place-PST-3N
'Circumstances made him blurt it out.'

b *? *avar avaḷai ellavāṟṟai.y=um colli.t tolaikka.c ceytār.*
he-NOM she-ACC all-ACC=AND say-CF lose+EF-INF do-PST-3H
'He made her blurt everything out, damn her.'

As noted earlier, repetition of an attitudinal auxiliary in an answer to a question that contains that same auxiliary is rhetorically charged. In the response, the auxiliary is either omitted or replaced by *viṭa* 'leave'.

(359)a *colli.t tolaittāy=ā?*
say-CF lose+EF-PST-2S=INT
'Did you go blurt it out?'
b ?? *colli.t tolaittēṉ.*
say-CF lose+EF-PST-1S
'Yeah, I went and blurted it out.'
c *colli viṭṭēṉ.*
say-CF leave-PST-1S
'Yeah, I did say it.'

Annamalai (1982: 75) observes that either the performance or the nonperformance of an event can motivate use of *tolaikka*. In the first gloss of (360), the speaker is impatient to hear what the addressee has to say; in the second, the speaker wants the addressee to remain silent. Both the delay and the eagerness on the part of the subject to speak may evoke use of *tolaikka*.

(360) *colli.t tolai!*
say-CF lose-IMP
'Say it already (I can't wait to hear).'
or
'Go on, say it (I can't stop you anyway).'

tolaiya and *tolaikka* both encode pejorative attitude, P^s/E^n, marking the speaker's antipathy toward the occurrence and the performance of the action in the narrated event, respectively. The antipathy they convey seems to originate from the liminality associated with the verb root which describes a movement whose goal is unknown. The negative connotation of being in a liminal stage is made explicit in the use of these verbs as attitudinal auxiliaries.

AUXILIARY OF RELIEF: *oẓiya*

The *Tamil lexicon* defines the affective verb *oẓiya* variously as 'clean, destroy, die, be at rest', which we amalgamate here as 'purge'. Though paired with effective *oẓikka* 'purge', only affective *oẓiya* functions as an attitudinal auxiliary in our corpus. As a main verb, *oẓiya* 'purge' conveys a basic meaning of cleaning something by removing impurities (361a), which can be extended to dispersal (361b) or tidying up one's affairs (361c).

(361)a *silēṭṭu oẓintatu.*
slate-NOM purge+AF-PST-3N
'The slate is cleaned.'

b *kūṭṭam ozintatu.*
meeting-NOM purge+AF-PST-3N
'The meeting broke up/is over.'

c *vēlai ozinta pōtu varukiṟēṉ.*
work-NOM purge-AF-PST-ADN when come-PRES-1S
'I'll come when the business is out of the way.'

Auxiliary verb uses

Use of *oẓiya* 'purge' signals a catharsis on the part of the speaker that the activity denoted by the AVC is done with.[11] This auxiliary simultaneously combines aspect and attitude. First, it indicates the activity has ceased; second, it attributes to the speaker a release of emotional tension at the cessation of that activity, toward which the speaker had felt some antipathy. The catharsis may be interpreted as relief or dismay. *oẓiya* readily selects auxiliates of action (362) and change of state (363); however, informants found auxiliates of position only marginally acceptable (364), substituting auxiliary *tolaiya* 'get lost' instead. This suggests *oẓiya* selects auxiliates whose aspectual composition is not homogenous but is segmentable into an onset (separation), body (limen) and coda (reincorporation). We may conjecture that the catharsis attaches to the reincorporation stage, when the state of affairs returns to an equilibrium.

(362)a *vīṭu tarakaṉ pōy oẓintāṉ.*
house broker-NOM go-CF purge-PST-3SM
'The real estate broker left (whew, am I ever glad).'

b *cikkireṭṭu viṭṭu oẓintāy=ā?*
cigarette leave-CF purge-PST-2S=INT
'Did you give up those damn cigarettes (come on, do it and give us all a break).'

c *araciyal ulak-il=um, toẓil ulak-il=um, cama urimai, cama antaṣtu,*
political world-LOC=AND labor world-LOC=AND equal right same status
uẓaippukku cama ūtiyam koṭukka.p paṭum pōtu tāṉ niṟapētam
work-DAT same wages give-INF fall-FUT-ANP time indeed discrimination
eṉṉum 'appārttīṭ' inta nāṭṭai viṭṭu oẓiyum.[12]
call-ANP apartheid this country-ACC leave-CF purge-FUT-3N
'It is only when they are given the same political and economic rights, the same status, the same wages for their work, that this country will be rid of this discrimination known as "Apartheid".'

(363)a *atu cettu oẓiyaṭṭum.*[13]
it-NOM die-CF purge-OPT
'Let him die, damn him.'

11 Chapter 3 notes that in Classical Tamil *oẓiya* combined with the negative verbal form and the conjunctive form; however, in Modern Tamil it combines only with the latter.

12 Lakshmi (1983: 37).

13 The two examples that Fedson (1981: 242) provides for this auxiliary have the same auxiliate.

b *tiruṭaṉ cettu oẓintāṉ.*
thief-NOM die-CF purge-PST-3SM
'The thief died (whew, now we can all relax).'

(364) ?? *uṭkārntu oẓintāṉ.*
sit-CF purge-PST-3SM
'He was sitting there (to my dismay).'

oẓiya 'purge' is absent from indirect discourse (365a), but may appear in direct discourse (365b).

(365)a * *pōy oẓiya.c coṉṉār.*
go-CF purge-INF say-PST-3H
'He said to damn it go get lost.'

b *pōy oẓi eṉṟu coṉṉār.*
go-CF purge-IMP that say-PST-3H
'He said, "Go get lost (give us a break, huh?)"'

oẓiya 'purge' appears in the first and second persons only with a marked rhetorical impact. Consider the following examples. When reporting one's thoughts or feelings in Tamil, a speaker obligatorily shifts pronouns and personal endings into the first person inclusive plural (Steever 1981: 81-89). In (366a) the subordinate clause subject *nām* 'we' is coreferential with the dative subject *avaṉukku* 'to him' in the main clause. The most favored reading of this sentence is one in which *nām* and *avaṉukku* are coreferential; on a less favored reading, *nām* refers to a group that includes the speaker and subject. In (366b) the attitude expressed by *oẓiya* is attributed to the speaker of the sentence, but in (366c) it is not. The coreference of *nām* and *avaṉukku* forces us to attribute the pejorative opinion, not to the speaker, but to the referent of *avaṉukku*. This is what gives rise to the oddity of the sentence, which ascribes a strongly self-deprecating attitude to the subject.

(366)a $[_{S0}[_{S1}$ *nām pōṉōm*] *eṉṟu avaṉukku.t teriyum*].
we-NOM go-PST-1P that him-DAT know-FUT-3N
'He knows that he (lit. we) went.'

b $[_{S0}[_{S1}$ *avaṉ pōy oẓintāṉ*] *eṉṟu avaṉukku.t teriyum*].
he-NOM go-CF purge-PST-3SM that him-DAT know-FUT-3N
'He knows that he just upped and left.'

c *? $[_{S0}[_{S1}$ *nām pōy oẓintōm*] *eṉṟu avaṉukku.t teriyum*].
we-NOM go-CF purge-PST-1P that him-DAT know-FUT-3N
'He knows that he upped and went off.'

Several informants report that *oẓiya* 'purge' is used by members of a caste other than their own. A Brahmin speaker claimed he used only *tolaiya* 'get lost', and believed that *oẓiya* occurred only in non-Brahmin dialects. A non-Brahmin speaker, on the other hand, claimed that *oẓiya* was entirely absent from his own speech, occurring among Brahmins. Only intensive dialect study will establish the range of this form; however, the readiness to attribute it to a group other than one's own suggests that *oẓiya* is infrequent relative to *tolaiya*, and that it encodes an attitude strong enough to evoke aversion by polite speakers.

Auxiliary *oẓiya* thus marks pejorative attitude, P^s/E^n: it simultaneously indicates that an action has ceased and expresses the speaker's emotional response toward the cessation of the action. The response is variously interpreted as dismay at the occurrence of the action or relief that it no longer involves the speaker.

oẓiya provides some support for the liminalist hypothesis. Its basic meaning denotes cleaning something by removing its impure elements. A liminal stage may be considered impure or "dirty" in the following sense. Douglas (1967, 1975) recalls Lord Chesterton's famous aphorism, which characterizes dirt as matter out of place, then cogently extends its scope from physical matter to social concepts such as conduct, morality and ontological pollution. The notion of dirt thus applies in abstract as well as concrete domains. Only separation and reincorporation stages have determinate positions in the system of received values (Turner 1969); since the liminal stage lacks a determinate position, it is regarded as "out of place" and, therefore, dirty. Figuratively then, use of auxiliary *oẓiya* in an AVC expresses the speaker's opinion that the associated activity is liminal and dirty, and further indicates that cessation of that activity brings about an emotional catharsis on the part of the speaker.

ANTIPERFECT AUXILIARIES: *kiẓiya, kiẓikka*

The verb root *kiẓi-* 'rip, tear' has affective and effective stems, *kiẓi.y-a* 'get torn' and *kiẓi.k-ka* 'tear', respectively. The *Tamil lexicon* lists several meanings, including 'tear', 'give way', 'burst out', 'lacerate', 'split', 'break' and 'rend', which accompany its nonauxiliated uses. A verb of destruction, it denotes the forcible separation of something whole into many parts. The affective (367a) and effective stems (367b) both serve as main verbs.

(367)a *eṉ caṭṭai kiẓi-nt-atu.*
my shirt-NOM tear+AF-PST-3N
'My shirt was/got torn.'

b *nāṉ eṉ caṭṭaiyai.k kiẓi-tt-ēṉ.*
I-NOM my shirt-ACC tear+EF-PST-1S
'I tore my shirt.'

An additional meaning the *Tamil Lexicon* ascribes to effective *kiẓikka*, one markedly different from the others, is "accomplish, used in contempt." This describes its use as an auxiliary verb of attitude. Annamalai (1982), Fedson (1981: 285) and the *Tamil Lexicon* note *kiẓikka* as an auxiliary; the *Lexicon* gives one example, Fedson, six. Fedson's characterization of it as conveying the speaker's derogatory attitude toward the action of the main verb fails to distinguish this attitudinal auxiliary from others. More important, affective *kiẓiya* also serves as an attitudinal auxiliary.

Both *kiẓiya* and *kiẓikka* convey the speaker's opinion that the auxiliate's activity will fail to reach culmination; that it will cease before reaching its coda, or reincorporation stage. Affective *kiẓiya* signals the speaker's opinion that the occurrence of an activity will not culminate in the normal course of events; effective *kiẓikka*, that the performance of an activity will not culminate. For example, a wife uses the affective auxiliary in (368a) to obliquely criticize her husband for not buying new saris: no matter how many hints she drops, no matter how many promises he makes, he never gets around to buying them. As with other effective verbs, *kiẓikka* draws attention to the subject of the AVC; its use thus promotes subsidiary connotations that the subject is too lazy, indifferent or incompetent to perform the activity in question. In (368b) the speaker criticizes the subject, insinuating that she is too lazy or incompetent to bring the work to fruition.

(368)a *inta vīṭṭil cēlai vāṅki.k kiẓikiṟatu.*
this house-loc sari-NOM buy-CF tear+AF-PRES-3N
'Saris just never seem to get bought in this house.'

b *avaḷ vēlai ceytu kiẓittāḷ.*
she-NOM work do-CF tear+EF-PST-3SF
'She does not/cannot get the work done.'

What is most striking about these auxiliaries, as the careful reader will already have noted, is the discrepancy between their formal tense marking and understood time reference. In (368a) the formal tense is present, but the time reference is habitual, a meaning normally expressed by future tense marking; in (368b) the formal tense is past tense, but the time reference is present. For reasons noted below, auxiliary *kiẓiya* and *kiẓikka* are analyzed as marking tense, specifically what I call the antiperfect tense.

Formal tense marking and time reference

Due to the unusual semantics of these two auxiliaries, many examples below use the complex auxiliate *vēlaiyai.c ceyya* 'do work', allowing us to focus on the auxiliaries. Throughout my corpus, *kiẓiya* and *kiẓikka* show a disparity between auxiliary's formal tense marking and the time reference of the AVC.[14] If the past tense marker signals present time reference, as in (368b), what formal tense marking signals past time reference? Although the common characterization of the past perfect as a "past in the past" might suggest its use to convey past time reference with *kiẓikka*, the result is unacceptable (369a). Auxiliary *kiẓiya* and *kiẓikka* never

14 While Fedson's (1981) glosses make the adjustment between the formal tense of the Tamil auxiliary and the time reference of the nearest corresponding English form, nowhere does her description show any recognition of this discrepancy.

combine directly with auxiliary *irukka* when it expresses perfect tense (*pace* Fedson 1981: 288):[15] the accomplishment reading of the perfect tense is at semantic loggerheads with the meaning of these two auxiliaries. To overcome this difficulty, *koḷḷa* 'hold' combines with the accomplishment predicate *vēlaiyai.c ceyya* 'do the work' to form an imperfective converb which when combined with *irukka* 'be' in (369b), gives rise to a past progressive tense form that has past time reference. In fact, in the antiperfect series, the distinction between past time reference and past-in-past time reference seems to collapse, with both being represented by the past progressive tense form *koṇṭu* + *irukka* 'be V-ing'.

(369)a *? *iraṇṭu varuṣam anta vēlaiyai.c ceytu kiḻittu iruntār.*
two years that work-ACC do-CF tear+EF-CF be-PST-3H
'He "did" that work for two years ("botched" is more like it).'
b *iraṇṭu varuṣam anta vēlaiyai.c ceytu kiḻittu.k koṇṭu iruntār.*
two year that work-ACC do-CF tear-EF-CF hold-CF be-PST-3H
'He "did" that work for two years ("botched" is more like it).'

The antiperfect auxiliaries may combine directly with *irukka*, but in that case *irukka* marks epistemic status, and not perfect tense. This possibility is illustrated both in (370) and in Fedson's example cited in Note 15 below.

(370) *avaḷ vēlaiyai.c ceytu kiḻittu iruntāṟ pōla irukkiṟatu.*
she-NOM work-ACC do-CF tear+EF-CF be-PST-ADN like be-PRES-3N
'It seems like she is incapable of getting any work done (I have indirect evidence for it).'

Both examples (368a) and (371) inflect the auxiliary for the present tense, but the time reference is habitual, a function conventionally reserved for the future tense marker. Neither *kiḻiya* 'get torn' nor *kiḻikka* 'tear' can inflect for the simple

15 Consider Fedson's (1981: 286) example 651, which is reproduced below as (i).

(i) *koḻuntu eṭuttu kiḻittu iruvāy=ō?*
tender.leaf take-CF tear+EF-CF be-FUT-2S=DUB
'So you suppose you could pick tender (tea) leaves, do you?'

The perfect tense reading is simply not available in this instance. Even Fedson avoids it in her gloss, "So you think you'll pick . . . tender (tea) leaves, do you?"

First, the phrase *koḻuntu eṭukka* 'pick tender leaves' is an activity predicate, not an achievement or accomplishment predicate. On the analysis presented in Chapter 6, application of *irukka* to such a predicate gives rise to the progressive, not a perfect, tense reading.

Second, it is most likely that the presence of *irukka* in (i) marks epistemic status; the speaker casts doubt on the subject's suppositions or prespumptions. This, along with the dubitative particle =*ō* 'or, any', is responsible for the presence of verbs of propositional attitude, e.g., *suppose*, *think*, in my gloss of the sentence and in Fedson's original. Her failure to sort out the discrepancy between tense and time reference with these two auxiliaries may also have impacted her ability to appreciate and adequately characterize the perfect with *irukka*.

future tense (372a);[16] instead, one must embed the antiperfect AVC under the present prospective tense form to signal future time reference (372b). The present prospective is a modal AVC in which the modal auxiliary *pōka* 'go' combines with the infinitive of the auxiliate.

(371) *anta vēlaiyai.c ceytu kiẓikkiṟāṉ.*
that work-ACC do-CF tear+EF-PRES-3SM
'He'll always botch that work.'

(372)a *? *anta vēlaiyai.c ceytu kiẓippār.*
that work-ACC do-CF tear+EF-FUT-3SM
'He'll botch that work.'

b *anta vēlaiyai.c [ceytu kiẓikka.p] pōkiṟār.*
that work-ACC do-CF tear+EF-INF go-PRES-3SM
'He is going to botch that work.'

Table 8.1 summarizes the systematic displacement of formal tense marking and time reference in the antiperfect, comparing it with the perfect tense series. To elaborate this comparison, let us assume for the moment that the antiperfect series refers to an interval of time over which the truth of the proposition denoted by the AVC is evaluated. But where the formal tense marking in the perfect series with *irukka* 'be' is assigned on the basis of the temporal interval's endpoint, namely, the reference time, in the antiperfect series it is assigned on the basis of the interval's starting point. It thus appears that *kiẓiya* and *kiẓikka* mark a tense series which is complementary to the perfect tense series in *irukka*. Although aspectual readings

16 Fedson's example 564, reproduced below as (i), shows an apparent instance in which the future tense form directly combines with *kiẓikka* 'tear'.

(i) *ippaṭi paṭṭa arattaikkāraṉ alaṭṭiya vāṟu irukkaiyil*
thus be-PST-ANP chatter.box-NOM pester-PST-ADN manner be-VN-LOC
eṉṉaṟṟai.p paṭittu.k kiẓippatu?
what-ACC study-CF tear+EF-FUT-VN
'What is to be done as long as this chatterbox is pestering us?'

Fedson misidentifies *kiẓippatu* as the third person neuter singular future of *kiẓikka*: but that form is properly *kiẓikkum* 'it will tear'. *kiẓippatu* is a verbal noun where the future tense marker *-pp-* has a modal, not a temporal, function. Moreover, this is a literary rendering of a colloquial phrase that is more naturally expressed with a present tense marker. This is a common literary substitution, as the pair of examples below shows. (iib) is the colloquial phrase; (iia), its literary counterpart. (iia) bears numerous earmarks of the literary variety: use of the noun *vāṟu* 'manner' for the colloquial *paṭi* 'id.', use of the accusative form of *eṉṉa* 'what' *eṉṉaṟṟai* 'what', and the shift of the tense-marker of the verbal noun from present into future.

(ii) a *eṉṉa ceyvatu?*
what do-FUT-VN
'What is to be done.'

b *eṉṉa ceykiṟatu?*
what do-PRES-VN
'What is to be done?'

Table 8.1 Displacement of tense and time reference in the antiperfect series

PERFECT SERIES				
TIME REFERENCE	PAST	PRESENT	HABITUAL	FUTURE
FORMAL TENSE	PAST	PRESENT	FUTURE	FUTURE
ANTIPERFECT SERIES				
TIME REFERENCE	PAST	PRESENT	HABITUAL	FUTURE
FORMAL TENSE	PAST PROGRESSIVE	PAST	PRESENT	PRESENT PROSPECTIVE

may accompany the antiperfect on occasion, its interaction with formal tense marking and time reference indicates that it primarily marks tense.

Comparison with the perfect tense series should help further define the meaning of the antiperfect. Figure 8.1 provides a graphic illustration of what they share in common and how they differ. Both involve temporal intervals over which the truth of the propositions they qualify is to be evaluated. In the perfect series with *irukka* 'be', the last subinterval of the interval that extends from the event time E up to the reference time R contains R; however, in the antiperfect series with *kiẓiya* and *kiẓikka*, the last subinterval does not contain R. The interval that represents the duration of the event named by the auxiliate starts at E, approaches R as a limit but veers off asymptotically before ever reaching R. The aspectual development of the event named by the AVC begins at the onset, passes through the body, but does not culminate in the expected coda; figuratively speaking, it is, "torn" from the time line that traces the natural, orderly progression of events from E to R before reaching the coda, or the reincorporation phase. This helps explain the restrictions on modifying the antiperfect series with the perfect tense marker.

Though the antiperfect auxiliaries combine primarily with auxiliates that denote activities (373d-h), they may combine with other event types. While the auxiliates in (373a-c) commonly have stative readings, they are nonhomogenous states often susceptible of activity readings. Further, verbs of transaction (373i, j) also combine with these two auxiliaries. The auxiliate's aspectual class must thus be segmentable into an onset, body and coda, and should focus on the activity carried out in the body. Use of the antiperfect always conveys a strong emotive undercurrent, as I have tried to reproduce in the glosses. Even in (373d) where two friends are verbally sparring, the use of the antiperfect carries a sharp rhetorical effect.

(373)a *ittaṉai kālam iṅkē [vāẓntu kiẓittu] āki viṭṭatu.*[17]
this.much time here live-CF tear+EF-CF become-CF leave-PST-3SN
'Yeah, we've lived here all this time, for all the good it's done us.'

b *yantiram ōṭi.k kiẓintatu.*
machine-NOM run-CF tear+AF-PST-3N
'The machine runs really well, sure it does.'

17 Fedson (1981: 286).

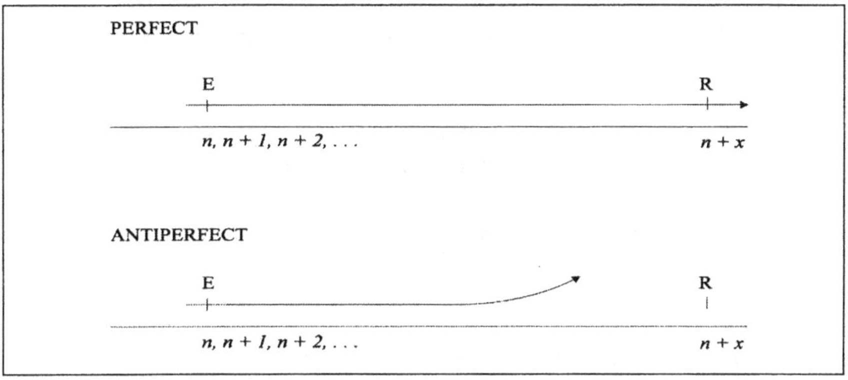

Figure 8.1 Graphic representation of the perfect and antiperfect tense series.

c *pāṟai poṭintu kiḻintatu.*
rock-NOM powder-AF-CF tear+AF-PST-3N
'The rock won't be pulverized (correctly).'

d *tiyāṉam eṉṉa? uṉakku aṟputamāṉa cārīram irukku.*
devotion-NOM what-NOM you-DAT miraculous singing.voice-NOM be-PRES-3N
naṉṉāv=um pāṭarē. nāṉ pāṭi.k kiḻittēṉ.[18]
well=AND sing-PRES-2S=EMP I-NOM sing-CF tear+EF-PST-1S
'Who needs devotion (for music). You have a miraculous singing voice. And how well you sing. What, me sing well? Oh sure.'

e [[*avaḷ pāṭi.k kiḻittu.p*] *pala pēr pārttu irukkiṟārkaḷ*].
she-NOM sing-CF tear+EF-CF many people-NOM see-CF be-PRES-3P
'Sure, everyone's seen her sing soooo well, sure.'

f *inta.p payalkaḷ — eṉṉam=ō ellām tāṅkaḷē muṉṉāṭiyē* [*terintu uṇṭu*
these fellows-NOM what=DUB all self=EMP before know-CF hold-CF
kiḻittu] *viṭa.p pōkiṟār pōla niṉaittu alaiyakiṟārkaḷ.*[19]
tear+EF-CF leave-INF go-PRES-ADN like think-CF wander-PRES-3P
'These fellows delude themselves, thinking that they will learn everything by themselves in advance. Fat chance!'

g *vēlai kiṭaittāl* [*ceytu kiḻittu*] *viṭuvāy=ō? eṉṟu avarkaḷiṭai.y=ē*
work get-CND do-CF tear+EF-CF leave-FUT-2S=INT that they-SOC=EMP
kuṟukkiṭṭāṉ avaṉ.[20]
cut.in-PST-3SM he-NOM
'He cut them short, "So you think you could do it if you got the job? Hah!"'

h *eṉṉa ceytu kiḻikiṟatu?*
what do-CF tear+AF-PRES-3N
'Just what, if anything, is to be done?'

18 Janakiraman (1976: 115).
19 Janakiraman (1966: 34).
20 Jeyakantan (1958: 50).

i *enn=aiyā pericā aṭvāncu koṭuttu kiẕiccāṉ anta reṭṭiyāṉ.*[21]
what=sir big advance give-CF tear+EF-PST-3SM that Reddy man-NOM
'So, is the advance that Reddy guy gave such a big thing?'

kiẕikka tends not to combine with auxiliates which themselves carry negative implications, such as *maṟakka* 'forget, deny' in (374).

(374) ?? *avaṉ maṟantu kiẕittāṉ.*
he-NOM forget-CF tear+EF-PST-3SM
'Oh sure, he's forgotten (he can't even do that well).'

When AVCs with *kiẕiya* and *kiẕikka* are negated, the auxiliary's meaning remained unaffected; it is the activity of the auxiliate that is negated. In uttering (375), the speaker states that the subject does not do anything and, by using *kiẕikka*, injects his opinion that the subject is incapable of performing anything. Thus, the strongly pejorative attitude of the antiperfect should not be confused with grammatical negation.

(375) *nī oṉṟum ceytu kiẕikka.v illai.*
you-NOM one.thing=AND do-CF tear-EF-INF IND-NEG
'You never carry a single thing through to the end.'

In my corpus of elicited and literary examples, *kiẕikka* 'tear' did not occur with the following suffixes: **kiẕitt-atum* 'once one tears', the concessive conditional **kiẕittāl-um* 'even though one tears' or the imperative **kiẕi* 'tear', restrictions which appear to follow from semantic grounds. Felicitous use of the *-atum* 'as soon as' suffix complex in **kiẕitt-atum* requires that the speaker believe that the subject can accomplish the task denoted by the auxiliate, but this contradicts what the speaker purports to believe in using *kiẕikka*, viz., the event cannot be completed. Furthermore, *-atum* is not generally used with nonpunctual auxiliaries, and *kiẕi-* is nonpunctual. The synonymous expression **kiẕitta uṭaṉē* 'as soon as one tears' is also unacceptable, and for the same reason. The concessive conditional form **kiẕittāl-um* 'even though one tore' is also excluded on semantic grounds. The ending for the concessive conditional, *-ālum* 'even though' consists of the conditional suffix *–āl* 'if V' and the clitic particle *=um* 'all, and'; the combination literally means, '*in all cases if V*, (then not V)'. However, use of *kiẕikka* indicates the speaker believes there is at least one case in which the proposition modified by *kiẕittālum* is not true: at the reference time. The inclusive particle *=um* 'all, and' cannot felicitously be used when not all the cases are true. Failure of *kiẕikka* to occur in the imperative may well be due to a pragmatic constraint; one of the preparedness conditions for issuing an order (Searle 1969) is that the speaker should think the addressee capable of carrying out the order; of course, the connotation that *kiẕikka* conventionally carries violates this condition.

21 Fedson (1981: 285).

Example (376) illustrates the use of affective *kiẓiya* to embed a causative construction; in choosing it over its effective counterpart, the speaker obliquely suggests to the addressee (and the subject) that it is circumstance, not personal ineptitude, working against him. (Note incidentally that while the subject is *nīṅkaḷ* 'you', the verb agreement is third person neuter.)

(376) *nīṅkaḷ avaṉai.p paṭikka vaittu.k kiẓikiṟatu.*
you-NOM him-ACC study-INF place-CF tear+AF-PST-3N
'Oh sure, you're able to put your son through school (what with your salary).'

Effective *kiẓikka* can occur without a main verb, when that main verb can be recovered from the immediate linguistic context. While modal auxiliaries freely do this, only two other indicative auxiliaries, *pārkka* 'look at' and *āka* 'become', can do so. Perhaps the modal connotations of inability that often accompany the antiperfect dispose it to behave like a modal auxiliary in this respect. In (377b) the main verb *koṭukka* 'give', which appeared in (377a), has been elided. In (377c and d) the first sentence provides the auxiliate, which is elided in the second sentence in each example (marked by φ). Note in (377c)[22] how the present tense marking of the first sentence is replaced by the past tense marking on auxiliary *kiẓikka.*

(377)a *avaṉ eṉakku.k koṭukkiṟāṉ=ā?*
he-NOM me-DAT give-PRES-3SM=INT
'Is he giving it to me?'

b *āmām, (koṭuttu.k) kiẓittāṉ.*
yes give-CF tear-EF-PST-3SF
'Oh sure, he'll give it to you (but don't hold your breath).'

c *nam kuẓantaikaḷ oẓuṅkāka iruntāl avarkaḷai viraṭṭukiṟāyē?*
our children-NOM properly be-COND them-ACC frighten-PRES-2S=EMP
ām, ām! φ kiẓittārkaḷ.
yes yes tear-PST-3P
'You're going and frightening our children when they are be(hav)ing properly? Sure, like hell they are (behaving properly).'

d *anta.k kālattil utavi ceytu kiẓittār. ippōtu φ kiẓikka.p pōkiṟār.*
that time-LOC help do-CF tear+EF-PST-3H now tear+EF-INF go-PRES-3H
'Oh sure: he's been such a big help in the past, and now he's going to help us?'

Neither *kiẓiya* nor *kiẓikka* occurs in the first person without pronounced rhetorical effect. By repeating *kiẓikka* in reported speech, the speaker registers his indignation at the original speaker and, by that repetition, challenges that opinion. In (378a) the speaker has just been accused of being incompetent to do a job, and retorts by uttering the sentence. The addressee of (378b) has just complained that no one permits him to do any important work, prompting the speaker to reply with (378b) that, in his opinion, he botches the work when others let him.

22 Fedson (1981: 287).

(378)a *nāṉ [ceytu kiẓikkāmal] vēṟu yār [ceytu kiẓittārkaḷ]?*
I-NOM do-CF tear-NEG-CF other who-NOM do-CF tear-EF-PST-3SM
'So, if I can't get the job done, who the hell else can?'

b *nī ceytu kiẓikkaiyil yār vēṇṭām eṉkiṟārkaḷ?*
you-NOM do-CF tear-VN-LOC who-NOM must-NEG-3N say-PRES-3P
'While you were futzing around with the job, who says you shouldn't (have been allowed to) do it?'

Antiperfect and inertia futures

To define the antiperfect more precisely, we elaborate our earlier notion of it as representing a temporal interval that is "torn" from the time line, so the event never reaches its coda, or reincorporation stage. Models of time have been proposed to account for several possible outcomes from a given point of view. Dowty (1979: 148, pass.) and Tedeschi (1981) argue for a unidirectional branching time model in which, from any given point, there are several possible subsequent outcomes, but only one actual past temporal history. This model is supplemented by the concept of *inertia world*, which formalizes the notion of "natural course of events." All temporal histories that fall within the set of inertia worlds are outcomes that would eventuate if things were left to develop naturally. Some temporal histories subsequent to a given time fall within the set of inertia futures, but others fall outside. Consider the diagram in Figure 8.2. There the temporal relation "X is later than Y" is graphically represented by the linear order "X is to the right of Y." All time branches to the right of event time E_1 which pass through the shaded area belong to the set of inertia futures; those that do not constitute the complementary set of noninertia futures. Points with a superscript i, e.g., R^i, are reference points on a temporal history that belongs to the set of inertia futures while those with a superscript -i, e.g., R^{-i}, belong to the set of noninertia futures. Dowty and Tedeschi use this machinery to argue that the semantics of the English progressive tense requires that there be a final subinterval in the set of inertia futures, a condition which closely resembles the semantics for Tamil AVCs with *(koṇṭu)* + *irukka* 'be V-ing'. Note that this model implies—albeit weakly—the possibility of a tense form whose final subinterval is *not* with the set of inertia futures.

Our discussion suggests that in the Tamil antiperfect series, the final subinterval falls outside the set of inertia futures. The temporal history that begins with E_1, when described with the antiperfect, is figuratively deflected or torn away from the set of inertia futures, only to eventuate in the set of noninertia futures. If this is the correct interpretation of the Tamil antiperfect, it will provide some modest empirical support for the concept of inertia future by showing the need to partition future time lines into two sets, inertia and noninertia futures, to reflect the formal linguistic distinction between a perfect and an antiperfect series.

Thus, when a speaker of Tamil uses an AVC with the antiperfect, he expresses the opinion that the event named by the auxiliate will not eventuate in the set of inertia futures (in the shaded portion of Firgure 8.2), but will also fall outside the set of noninertia futures. Use of the antiperfect can convey additional nuances; for

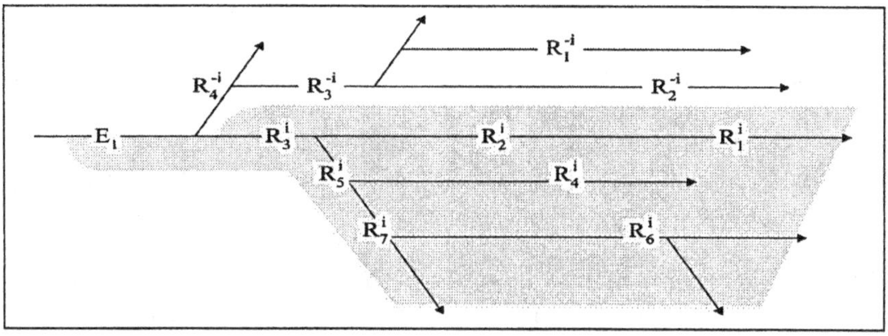

Figure 8.2 Branching futures of perfect and antiperfect tense-forms.

example, the event named by the main verb is useless and without purpose. Sloth, indifference and ineptitude are also often ascribed to the subject of the effective auxiliary *kiẓikka*.

Possible parallels

The antiperfect tense is so striking that it is worthwhile asking whether other languages have anything like it. Some dialects of Kannada, a sister language of Tamil, have what appears to be a cognate. The verb *kisi* 'smile, split, grin' combines with the past conjunctive form of the auxiliate (which is cognate with the Tamil conjunctive) to form an AVC.

(379) *avanu* *māḍi* *kisita.*
he-NOM do-PST-CF smile-PST-3SM
'Sure, he did the work, sure!'

Tempting as it is to see Kannada *kisi* and Tamil *kiẓi-* 'tear' as cognate, it is difficult to relate Kannada *-s-* to Tamil *-ẓ-*. Further empirical work is first needed before pursuing this possible parallel.

The Hopi impotential form broadly resembles the Tamil antiperfect tense series.[23] Whorf (1956) describes the Hopi morph */ʔaṣ/* as the "impotential modalizer." The impotential is described as follows: "It indicates what I might call teleological ineffectiveness (Whorf 1956: 121)." He then elaborates his initial chacterization as follows.

> The criterion that fastens this particular stigma, as it were, of quasireality upon the subject matter of discourse is ineffectiveness in terms of the purpose, goal, drive, need, function, etc., that originally formed the grounds for the action.

23 I am indebted to Caroline Jenkins for bringing the Hopi impotential to my attention.

Elsewhere (Hoijer et al. 1946: 177-78) he continues:

> It indicates insufficient "power" for further actualization of the end or principle of the action or state. Hence, in the reportive or nomic it means that the action or state is in vain ... and to be met with frustration or reversal ... It may denote instability of state ... In the expective it denotes trying without immediate success.

Whorf's description uncannily coincides with the meaning of the Tamil antiperfect. But the Hopi impotential form differs from the Tamil antiperfect in one major respect. As Whorf (1956: 122) notes, "It is a quite unemotional statement; *ˀaṣ* is not an expression of affect but is intellectual, and would be used whether the speaker be unmoved, displeased, or pleased . . ." The Tamil antiperfect, however, is strongly marked for pejorative attitude.

The attitudinal auxiliaries *kiẓiya* and *kiẓikka* thus encode antiperfect tense and pejorative attitude. They signal the speaker's belief that the event named by the main verb of the AVC will fail to occur or be performed. In terms of aspect, the event will not reach its coda. In terms of tense, the event's temporal progress is viewed as being ripped from the natural course of events. In terms of attitude, the speaker's evaluation attributes the lack of the activity's culmination to a lack of critical mass in the situation or incapacity in the performer directing the activity.

Of all indicative auxiliaries, *kiẓiya* and *kiẓikka* seem most like modal auxiliaries in that they appear to involve such concepts as ability, capacity and possibility. This reflects in part the lack of a systematic target structure in English into which the Tamil antiperfect can be translated. The grammar of Tamil allows events to be segmented into their component parts more finely than English; there is consequently a greater formal articulation of the internal composition of events. These two auxiliaries indicate that an event terminates before reaching the coda. There is nothing modal about this any more than there is about an accomplishment verb whose coda is reached. One major remaining problem with these auxiliaries is the range of temporal adverbs that can occur with them; no obvious pattern has emerged so far.

Both *kiẓiya* and *kiẓikka* appear to support the liminalist hypothesis. The temporal history of the event named by the main verb, though anchored in the actual past, is figuratively torn from the set of inertia futures. Though the event named has a separation and a liminal phase, it lacks a reincorporation phase. This lack of resolution and, therefore, persisting liminality contribute to the strong pejorative opinion that accompanies the use of these auxiliaries.

AUXILIARY OF POINTLESS TRANSACTIONS: *aẓa*

The *Tamil Lexicon* defines the intransitive verb *aẓa* as 'cry, weep, lament, whine, waste, spend uselessly'; the first four meanings accompany its main verb use, the last two its indicative auxiliary verb use. As an auxiliary, it combines with auxiliates denoting transactions; its presence in an AVC conveys the speaker's opinion that nobody, particularly the AVC's subject, will benefit by the transaction. *aẓa* corresponds most closely to the benefactive auxiliary *koṭukka* 'give', but additionally conveys the pejorative attitude characteristic of most attitudinal auxiliaries.

Auxiliary *aẓa* 'cry' combines with auxiliates denoting transactions, construed broadly enough to include physical transactions (380a-c), accepting or discharging an obligation (380d-g), making promises (380h) and informing (380i-j). Main verbs as diverse as *koṭukka* 'give', *tara* 'give to you or me', *kaṭṭa* 'tie, pay taxes', *kaṭaṉ tīrkka* 'settle a debt', *eẓuti vaikka* 'bequeath', *nēra* 'vow' and *colla* 'tell, say' appear in our corpus. In (380a) the speaker—who is also the subject—expresses his opinion that a donation to a temple treasury will benefit no one: the money will not reach those it should, the temple has more money than it needs, the speaker is now deprived of its use, etc. Similar readings accompany (380b and c). The speaker in (380h) expresses his discontent with his wife's making a vow to a god, the penance for which may well include abstinence from conjugal relations. In (380i) the speaker reflects that the act of unburdening his mind at the river where he makes his daily prayers does not in fact ease his mind.[24] In the *oppāri* 'lamentation' in (380j) a widow cries that her prayers to the god of death, the 'barren buffalo cow', for her dead husband will neither restore her husband nor comfort her.

(380)a *nāṉ kōyilukku.p paṇam [koṭuttu aẓa] vēṇṭum.*
I-NOM temple-DAT money give-CF cry-INF must-FUT-3N
'I've got to give money to that temple, a lot of good that'll do.'

b *[koṭuttu aẓuta] paṇam vīṇāka pōyiṟṟu.*
give-CF cry-PST-ANP money- NOM waste-ADV go-PST-3N
'The money that I gave up (but didn't want to) has just gone to waste.'

c *tapālkāraṉukku oru rūpāy [koṭuttu aẓutu.t] tolaittēṉ.*
mailman-DAT one rupee give-CF cry-CF lose+EF-PST-1S
'I gave that damn pesky mailman a rupee (it will only encourage other freeloaders to ask for money).'

d *kaṭaṉai.t [tīrttu aẓa] vēṇṭi irukkiṟatu.*
debt-ACC settle-CF cry-INF be.necessary-CF be-PRES-3N
'I have to pay off that debt (he won't let me off the hook).'

e *[kaṭṭi aẓa] vēṇṭum.*
pay.tax-CF cry-INF be.necessary-FUT-3N
'Everyone has got to pay those damn taxes.'

f *māḷikaiyai.y=um āḷai.y=um uṉ talaiyilē [[kaṭṭi koṇṭu] aẓu].*[25]
mansion-ACC=AND man-ACC=AND your head-LOC tie-CF hold-CF cry-IMP
'Go ahead and saddle yourself with (lit., tie yourself to) a mansion and servants, for all the good it will do.'

24 From Janakiraman (1966: 189). In the context of Hinduism and this novel, rivers are personifications of the goddess, so that the speaker is understood to be confiding in the goddess.

25 Fedson (1981: 294).

g *anta vēlaiyai.k* [[[[*kaṭṭi*] *aḻutu*] *koṇṭu*] *iruntār*].
that work-ACC tie-CF cry-CF hold-CF be-PST-3H
'He was tied down to that job, for all the good it did him.'

h *avaḷ cāmikku* [[[*nērntu*] *aḻutu*] *irukkiṟāḷ*].
she-NOM god-DAT vow-CF cry-CF be-PRES-3SF
'She has gone and made a (worthless) vow to the god.'

i *āmām — etu āy iruntāl=um inta iṭattil inta veḷiyil*
yes what become-CF be-COND=AND this place-LOC this field-LOC
inta kāvēriyiṭam vantu tāṉ colli aḻa vēṇṭum.
this Kaveri-SOC come-CF EMP tell-CF cry-INF be.necessary-FUT-3N
'Yes, whatever the matter was, he would have come to this place in this field and confide (his thoughts) to the Kaveri River (but it seemed not to help).'

j *īṉāta erumaikkiṭṭa eṉ kuṟaiyai.c colli aḻutu . . .*[26]
barren buffalo-SOC my grief-ACC tell-CF cry-CF
'Telling in vain my grief to the barren buffalo cow . . .'

The speaker need not feel personally deprived of any benefit from the transaction in order to use *aḻa* felicitously; the transaction may be viewed as wholly unbeneficial. The speaker of (381) may thus commiserate with the addressee, who has to part with something he would like to keep.

(381) *koṭuttu aḻuṅkaḷ!*
give-CF cry-IMP
'Go on, give (some money), what can you do?'

The speaker of (382) may not be venting his wrath toward his servant, whom custom requires he leave some money, as much as toward the social practice that mandates this practise or the irony that his death might bring another some benefit. That is to say, the subject need not be the locus of the speaker's attitude.

(382) *nāṉ avaḷukku āyiram rūpāy uyilil eḻuti vaittu aḻa*
I-NOM her-DAT thousand rupee will-LOC write-CF place-CF cry-INF
vēṇṭi irukkiṟatu.
be.necessary-CF be-PRES-3N
'It seems I have to bequeath her a thousand rupees, for all the good that will do.'

Auxiliary *aḻa* occurs in most grammatical contexts, but not in passive voice (it is intransitive when nonauxiliated); embedded under causative verbs; or following the necessity modal *vēṇṭum* 'be necessary'. It does occur in the imperative (381), the adnominal form and the *-atum* 'as soon as' form. Auxiliary *aḻa* may rarely occur without an overt main verb; in such cases, the 'elided' main verb is always understood to be *koṭukka* 'give', the prototypical verb of transaction.

26 Vanamamalai (1964: 642).

aẓa 'cry' is an auxiliary that marks pejorative attitude[27] and, because it is constrained to combine with verbs of transaction, voice. It conveys the speaker's attitude that the transaction will fail to benefit anyone, a basic meaning that gives rise to circumstantial meanings such as regret or commiseration for the subject of the transaction. It appears in this respect to complement the benefactive auxiliaries *koṭukka* 'give' and *tara* 'give to you or me' (see Chapter 7). The pointlessness of the transactions modified by *aẓa* bears a resemblance to the lack of culmination of activities modified by the antiperfect.

aẓa appears not to support the liminalist hypothesis: it is not a verb of motion. It does, however, denote a physical response to an emotional stimulus, positive or negative, in which the subject temporarily loses control over himself. This loss of control, which is typically viewed with disapproval, may contributed to the pejorative attitude of auxiliary *aẓa*. Nonetheless, the grammar of *aẓa* places it squarely with the other attitudinal auxiliaries.

AUXILIARY OF VISCOSITY: *vaẓiya*

The verb root *vaẓi-* has both affective and effective stems. As a nonauxiliated form, it is glossed as 'overflow, drip, flow'. It typically refers to the uncontrolled oozing of viscous liquids, but is idiomatically extended to certain abstract notions. Accordingly, affective *vaẓiya* 'drip' may select subjects that denote viscous liquids such as oil (383a) or saliva (383b),[28] but not those that denote free-flowing liquids such as water or tears (383c).[29] It is figuratively extended in (383d) to include abstract nouns such as *aṣatu* 'foolishness'. Its effective counterpart appears in (383e) in an extended sense.

(383)a *avaṉ mukattil eṇṇai vaẓikiṟatu.*
his face-LOC oil-NOM drip-AF-PRES-3N
'Oil is dripping from his face.'

b *eccil vaẓikiṟatu.*
saliva-NOM drip-AF-PRES-3N
'Saliva is flowing.

c * *kaṇṇīr vaẓikiṟatu*
tear-NOM drip-PRES-AF-3N
'Tears are oozing.'

27 According to Fedson (1981: 293ff.), "*aẓa* indicates regret or annoyance caused by regret associated with the action denoted by the CP [= conjunctive participle]." Though an apt first approximation, it fails to give substance to the feeling of regret, an emotion which may be provoked by any number of factors. The notion of a pointless, valueless transaction is absent from her description of this auxiliary's meaning.

28 *eccil* 'saliva' is a general term for waste, dirt and pollution.

29 The word *kaṇṇīr* 'tears' is a compound of *kaṇ* 'eye' and *nīr* 'water'.

d *aṣatu* *vaẓikiṟatu.*
foolishness-NOM drip-AF-PRES-3N
'He is hopelessly foolish.'

e *paṇam irukkum pōtu kaṇṭa paṭi celavu vaẓikkiṟāṉ.*
money be-FUT-ANP time see-PST-ANP manner expense drip-EF-PRES-3SM
'Whenever he has money, he spends it on everything he sees.'

Auxiliary verb uses

Only affective *vaẓiya* 'drip' functions as an attitudinal auxiliary in our corpus. It seems to convey the speaker's opinion that the subject of the AVC gives in to his emotions too readily. Under this connotation lies an aspectual core of meaning: *vaẓiya* appears to signal that the activity of the auxiliate is slower than normal during the body of the event. While it might be thought that this auxiliary involves the category of voice due to the involvement of the subject in the speaker's opinion, that nuance may be traced to the affectivity of the auxiliary.

My corpus uncovered only five auxiliates that occur with *vaẓiya*: *aẓa* 'cry', *uruka* 'melt (as the heart)', *uṟaṅka* 'sleep', *kaciya* 'melt, grow tenderhearted' and *tūṅka* 'sleep'. Fedson's sample (1981: 296-97) adds two others: *niṟaiya* 'be full' and *poṅka* 'boil, overflow, be elated'. These auxiliates denote a physical or emotional response to an external stimulus resulting in loss of control and, perhaps, loss of momentum. Example (384a) is apt not only to describe someone who is continually yawning and nodding off, but also to characterize an actor who drawls or slurs his speech. In (384b) *vaẓiya* appears under a causative verb (only when the subject is inanimate); the music is presented as depriving the causee *avaṉai* 'him' of his self-control so that he wanders mentally, and allows his emotions free play, flowing with the current of the music. Example (384d) is said of someone whom the speaker considers too effusive or demonstrative of his emotions so that he always seems caught up in them. A note of lassitude frequently accompanies the use of this auxiliary; in all cases, the subject is presented as having relinquished control over himself and his direction.

(384)a *avaṉ [tūṅki vaẓintāṉ].*
he-NOM sleep-CF drip-PST-3SM
'He was very drowsy/he drawled.'

b *kaccēri avaṉai.t [tūṅki vaẓiya] vaittatu.*
concert-NOM him-ACC sleep-CF drip-INF place-PST-3N
'The concert made him drowsy/nod off/wander.'

c *avaṉ [aẓutu= tāṉ vaẓintāṉ].*
he-NOM cry-CF=EMP drip-PST-3SM
'He really blubbered.'

d *avaṉ [aẓutu vaẓukiṟāṉ].*
he-NOM cry-CF drip-PRS-3SM
'He cries too much/blubbers.'

e *avaṉ avaḷukku mēl [uruki vaẓikiṟāṉ].*
he-NOM she-DAT on melt-CF drip-PRS-3SM
'He gushes all over her/is too mushy with her.'

Not all instances of auxiliary *vaẓiya* convey a strictly pejorative attitude; Fedson (1981) cites two examples in which the speaker comments on the subject's total immersion in the emotion named by the main verb, where the evaluation appears to be mildly positive. She admits these might involve a sequence of two main verbs, but attempts a metaphorical interpretation of the sequence as auxiliate and auxiliary.[30]

(385)a *rājaviṉ mukam malarcciyil poṅki vaẓintatu.*
Raja-GEN face-NOM joy-LOC boil-CF drip-PST-3N
'Raja's face was suffused with joy.'

b *viruntāḷikaḷiṉāl vīṭu niṟaintu vaẓintatu.*
guests-INST house fill-CF drip-PST-3N
'The house fairly overflowed with guests.'

What matters is not whether a particular instance of the auxiliary signals pejorative or admirative attitude, but that the attitude expressed is always nonneutral. In each case, some emotion or physical state is assumed to have overwhelmed the subject, arresting him in the midst of the event. Loss of control may according to context be seen either as a good or a bad thing.[31]

Although it might be objected—with some justice—that an auxiliary dedicated to seven auxiliates hardly constitutes an auxiliary at all, and that one might just as well have seven idioms,[32] these constructions pattern with AVCs over against lexical compounds and other kinds of two-verb constructions in Tamil. For example, the auxiliate cannot be Scrambled away from the auxiliary or Postposed rightwards over it (Chapter 4). Its marking for attitude inhibits it from occurring freely in indirect discourse, which is not an obstacle for lexical compounds. The meaning seems compositional in the way that AVCs are: the main verb on the left is responsible for selection and strict subcategorization while the auxiliary on the right modifies that meaning in a specific way. Below we shall see that in certain respects, *vaẓiya* semantically complements the auxiliary *taḷḷa* 'push'.

vaẓiya exhibits several of the same grammatical characteristics that the antiperfect auxiliaries *kiẓiya* 'get torn' and *kiẓikka* 'tear' do. It does not occur in the imperative, the *-atum* 'as soon as' form, or the *-āl=um* concessive conditional. And like

30 Example (385a) comes from Fedson (1981: 296); (385b) from Fedson (1981: 297).

31 In the context of religious ecstasy, as in the *bhakti* cult, loss of control in favor of the god is positively evaluated, e.g., the phrase *aṉpuḷ uruki aẓuvāṉ* 'he weeps, melting with love (for god)' is common in medieval Saiva bhakti texts.

32 It may be a case of erring on the side of generosity to include this form to illustrate Auxiliary Formation. If further research ultimately proves these seven collocations to be idioms, that would benefit us by having explicit grammatical criteria for idioms in Tamil which are currently lacking.

kiẓiya and *kiẓikka, vaẓiya* cannot directly combine with auxiliary *irukka* 'be located' (386a), but must use the imperfective converb *koṇṭu* + *irukka* 'be V-ing' to do so (386b).

(386)a * *avaṉ* [[*tūṅki vaẓintu*] *iruntāṉ*].
he-NOM sleep-CF drip-CF be-PST-3SM
'He had nodded off.'

b *avaṉ* [[[*tūṅki vaẓintu*] *koṇṭu*] *iruntāṉ*].
he-NOM sleep-CF drip-CF hold-CF be-PST-3SM
'He was dozing off.'

Thus, like *kiẓiya* and *kiẓikka, vaẓiya* appears to be nonpunctual. Figuratively, the progress of the event gets so "bogged down" in the temporal history that it seems never to reach culmination. Failure to reach the coda of the event in a timely fashion accounts for some restrictions noted above. The durativity of this auxiliary disqualifies it from combining with grammatical devices that mark punctual aspect such as the *-atum* 'as soon as' suffix. Provisionally then, *vaẓiya* encodes aspect: the progress of the event is retarded in the body, or liminal stage, of the event. This gives rise to subsidiary connotations that the AVC's subject lacks the requisite control or energy to bring the event to a culmination.

Like most other attitudinals *vaẓiya* does not appear in the first or second person without pronounced rhetorical effect. Use of the auxiliary is self-deprecatory in the first person (387a), insulting in the second (387b).[33]

(387)a *nāṉ* [[*aẓutu*] *vaẓiya*] *māṭṭēṉ*.
I-NOM cry-CF drip-INF fut-NEG-1S
'I will not go and blubber.'

b *nī* [*aẓutu vaẓintatu*] *eṉakku.t teriyāt=ā?*
you-NOM cry-CF drip-PST-VN me-DAT know-NEG-FUT=INT
'Don't I know that you were crying your eyes out?'

Repetition of auxiliary *vaẓiya* in an answer to a question that already contained it is generally viewed as a challenge or a threat. (Such repetition would be unremarkable in the case of a lexical compound verb.) Sentence (388c) with auxiliary *viṭa* 'leave', not (388b) with *vaẓiya*, is the polite way to respond to (388a).

(388)a *nī* *ēṉ* *tūṅki* *vaẓintāy?*
you-NOM why sleep-CF drip-PST-2S
'Why were you dozing off?'

b *nāṉ* *tūṅki* *vaẓiya.v illai.*
I-NOM sleep-CF drip-INF IND-NEG
'I wasn't *dozing* off.'

33 An appropriate gloss of (387b) into English, though not a systematic one, might well be one that overlays the sarcastic labial prosody characteristic of baby-talk on the sentence.

c *nāṉ* *tūṅka.v* *illai.*
I-NOM sleep-INF IND-NEG
'I wasn't sleeping.'

Auxiliary *vaẓiya* 'drip' marks both aspect and pejorative attitude. It indicates that the activity named by the auxiliate has slowed down and is "adrift" in the body of the activity, making no significant progress toward the coda. In this it resembles *kiẓiya* 'get torn' and *kiẓikka* 'tear', where the temporal histories of activites qualified by the antiperfect seem never to reach the coda. The presence of attitude is a conventional signal that the speaker further views this deceleration as a negative, although there may be instances where the evaluation is positive. Several overtones may accompany this meaning on occasion: the subject is weak and has lost control over himself; he can no longer control the direction his actions take.

The liminalist hypothesis helps explain the meaning of auxiliary *vaẓiya*. The deceleration of the rate of the activity named by auxiliate, an aspectual notion, has an attitudinal interpretation. The key to this interpretation lies, I believe, in the fact that as a main verb, *vaẓiya* selects subjects that refer to viscous liquids, not to free-flowing ones. Douglas (1966: 38) annotates a passage near the end of Jean-Paul Sartre's *L'être et le néant*,[34] where he rhapsodizes over the nature of viscosity and its inherent repugnance. It is worthwhile to consider the possibility that his characterization of viscosity aptly describes the slowing down of activity as represented by AVCs with *vaẓiya*.

> Viscosity, (Sartre) says, repels in its own right, as a primary experience … The viscous is a state half-way between solid and liquid. It is like a cross-section in a process in change. It is unstable, but it does not flow. It is soft, yielding, and compressible. There is no gliding on its surface. The stickiness is a trap, it clings like a leech; it attacks the boundary between myself and it. Long columns (of honey) falling off my fingers suggest my own substance flowing into the pool of stickiness. Plunging into water gives a different impression. I remain a solid but to touch stickiness is to risk diluting myself into viscosity. Stickiness is clinging, like a too-possessive dog or mistress … stickiness (is) an aberrant fluid or a melting solid … it makes the point that we can and do reflect on our classifications and experiences which do not fit exactly them … Sartre argues that melting, clinging viscosity is an ignoble form of existence.

Following this lead, we might characterize the liminal phase between solid and liquid as viscous in some sense; in particular, it seems to have no determinate boundaries. It is perhaps this liminality and indeterminacy that invests viscous things with the power to evoke strongly negative reactions.[35]

34 See Sartre (1943: 666-673).

35 The distaste for viscous things is reflected in Tamil epithets for untrustworthy and indecisive people, e.g., *veṇṭikai* 'okra', *viḷakkeṇṇai* lamp oil', as well as the general aversion to *eccil* 'saliva'.

Viscosity thus offers an appropriate trope for auxiliary *vaẓiya*: the activity is suspended in a liminal phase between the separation and reincorporation phases of the process. There is therefore no forward momentum from the subject or anyone else to impel the event toward the coda or, in parallel terms, toward reincorporation.

AUXILIARY OF ACCELERATION: *taḷḷa*

The *Tamil lexicon* glosses *taḷḷa* variously as 'push, be removed, shrink, diminish, expel, neglect, be able'. It functions as a nonauxiliated verb (389a); as an auxiliary, it occurs in indicative AVCs and modal AVCs (389b).

(389)a *avaṉ ennai.t taḷḷināṉ.*
he-NOM me-ACC push-PST-3SM
'He pushed me.'
b *atai.c ceyya.t taḷḷa.v illai.*
it-ACC do-INF push-INF IND-NEG
'He is not able to do/not up to doing that.'

Auxiliary verb uses

As an indicative auxiliary, *taḷḷa* 'push' conveys both aspectual and attitudinal meanings. It signals that the AVC's activity occurs at an accelerated rate, and that the speaker takes a nonneutral opinion about that. The use of *taḷḷa* in (390a) expresses both the speaker's belief that photographs were taken at a greater than normal rate, and his negative evaluation of this accelerated activity. In (390b) the speaker's use of *taḷḷa* indicates his belief that writing ten stories in a one day exceeds the normal output of a writer; here, however, the attitude is admirative. Finally, in (390c) *taḷḷa* indicates that the laborers worked faster than expected; according to context, the attitude can be pejorative, suggesting their work is shoddy, or admirative, suggesting it is efficient. The departure from a normal, expected rate of activity is connected with the speaker's opinion: he may view this favorably or unfavorably; hence, the "good riddance" and "exuberance" readings conventionally ascribed to *taḷḷa* can be viewed as circumstantial readings of the auxiliary's basic aspectual and attitudinal components.

(390)a *fōṭṭō eṭuttu.t taḷḷiṉāḷ.*
photo take-CF push-PST-3SF
'She took too many photographs.'
b *oru nāḷaikku.p pattu katai eẓuti.t taḷḷiṉāṉ.*
one day-DAT ten story write-CF push-PST-3SM
'Wow! He wrote ten stories in one day!'
c *aintu vīṭṭukku oru nāḷil veḷḷaiyaṭittu.t taḷḷiṉāṉ.*
five house-DAT one day-LOC whitewash-CF push-PST-3SM
'He whitewashed five houses in a single day!'

The auxiliates that *taḷḷa* modifies in (390) are semantically transitive; they lend themselves to iterative rather than semelfactive readings; and all are accompanied by the speaker's attitude, pejorative or admirative. Three semantic factors, transitivity, aspectual class and attitude, are investigated below.

Both aspectual class and transitivity figure in determining what kinds of auxiliates *taḷḷa* 'push' may subcategorize. Since the auxiliary was provisionally characterized as marking accelerative aspect, indicating an activity occurs at a rate faster than normal, the auxiliate cannot be a simple stative predicate with no internal aspectual differentiation. It should be an activity predicate capable of segmentation into an onset, body and, perhaps, coda. Further, the meaning of accelerated rate suggests that the auxiliate's activity should be a process with internal repetitions, favoring iterative over semelfactive predicates.

We may stipulate that auxiliary *taḷḷa* combines with transitive main verbs; however, what constitutes transitivity requires further precision. Transitivity may be defined syntactically or semantically; our analysis suggests the semantic characterization is the more important. Example (390c) and others below demonstrate that surface transitivity, such as taking a direct object in the accusative case, is not a necessary condition for *taḷḷa* to combine with an auxiliate. The surface object may be explicit or not; in (391a) the direct object *pattu katai* 'ten stories' is present, but in (392b) the direct object *pukai* 'smoke' is elided. Moreover, the surface object may appear in the accusative (393b), the nominative (391a) or the dative case (390c); it may be "incorporated" or "elided," as in (391b); or it may appear as an adjunct marked by *-āka* (399d and e) or *eṉṟu* (394a).

(391)a *oru nāḷaikku.p pattu katai eẓuti.t taḷḷiṉāṉ.*
one day-DAT ten story write-CF push-PST-3SM
'Wow! He wrote ten stories in one day!'

b *avar φ ūti.t taḷḷiṉār.*
he-NOM blow-CF push-PST-3H
'He chain-smokes (i.e., he blows smoke at an excessive rate).'

Schiffman (1969) notes that *taḷḷa* categorically fails to combine with intransitive verbs, and as the stigmata in (392) show, *taḷḷa* does not combine with main verbs that are syntactically and semantically intransitive.

(392)a * *avaḷ vantu taḷḷiṉāṉ.*
she-NOM come-CF push-PST-3SF
'She came very quickly.'

b * *avaṉ ōṭi.t taḷḷukiṟāṉ.*
he-NOM run-CF push-PRES-3SM
'He runs too excessively.'

Surface transitivity is not a sufficient condition for the use of *taḷḷa* 'push', however. Many transitive affective verbs are stative, denoting the relative positions of two objects; since they are internally homogenous and lack a phase, they are not capable of modification by *taḷḷa* (393a) even when their effective counterparts are (393b). Thus, when a verb root has both affective and effective stems, auxiliary *taḷḷa* combines only with the effective version.[36]

(393)a * *avaṉ maṉaiviyai.p pirintu taḷḷiṉāṉ.*
he-NOM wife-ACC separate+AF-CF push-PST-3SM
'He was separated from his wife excessively.'

b *avaṉ maṉaiviyai.p pirittu.t taḷḷiṉāṉ.*
he-NOM wife-ACC separate+EF-CF push-PST-3SM
'He abruptly separated from his wife.'

Fedson (1981) cites two examples of putatively intransitive verbs that combine with *taḷḷa*:[37] both, however, are semantically transitive. They are factitive, denoting the production of sound. The factitive verb *poriya* 'crackle' in (394a) has a semantic direct object that is realized in surface structure as the onomatopoeic phrase *paṭapaṭa*. This phrase does not mark case, and is introduced into the sentence as an adjunct of the "complementizer" *eṉṟu* 'saying' (see Steever 1988). Similarly, in (394b), the factitive verb *poẓiya* 'overflow (as of sound)' also denotes the activity of creating sound; here the object is understood.

(394)a *avaṉ kōpattil paṭapaṭa.v eṉṟu* $_{AVC}$[*porintu taḷḷi*] *viṭṭāṉ.*
he-NOM anger-LOC ONOM say-CF crackle-CF push-CF leave-PST-3SM
'In his anger, he sputtered, making the sound "patapata".'

b *taṟceyalāka avaḷai.p pārttāl=um* $_{AVC}$[*poẓintu taḷḷuvāḷ*].
by.chance her-ACC see-COND=AND overflow-CF push-PST-3SF
'Even if she saw her by chance, she would break into a flood of speech.'

While several auxiliates considered thus far are factitive, *taḷḷa* also combines with other transitives. To claim, for example that *pustakam vāṅka* 'buy books' in (395) is factitive because it represents, say, the creation of a personal library would distort the use of this term.

(395) *avaṉ pustakam vāṅki taḷḷukiṟāṉ.*
he-NOM book buy-CF push-PRES-3SM
'He is buying books like there's no tomorrow.'

Although our data is fragmentary, the presence of certain determiners with the object appears to reduce the acceptability of AVCs with *taḷḷa* 'push'. My principal informant found (396b) to be specific in a way that (396a) was not, even though

36 While Fedson (1981: 254) claims that *taḷḷa* may combine with both intransitive and transitive verbs, her use of these terms is misleading in this context. She uses them to describe what Paramasivam (1979) describes as affective and effective, respectively. As noted in Chapter 3, affective verbs may be transitive or intransitive, depending as they take a direct object or not.

37 Fedson (1981: 255).

both refer to the writing of a book. The determiner *oru* 'one, a' in (396b) seems to impose an achievement reading, representing the creation of a single book, not an activity reading with a rate that can be accelerated. As such, a semelfactive reading would discourage use of *taḷḷa*. By contrast, (396a) could be viewed as an activity in which the writing of numerous individual chapters results in the creation of a masterpiece.

(396)a *jānakirāmaṉ "mōka muḷḷai" oru mātattil eẓuti.t taḷḷiṉār.*
Janakiraman-NOM Moka Mul-ACC one month-LOC write-CF push-pst-3h
'Janakiraman wrote (the novel) "Moka Mul" in just one month!'
b ?? *oru pustakattai eẓuti.t taḷḷiṉār.*
one book-ACC write-CF push-PST-3H
'He dashed off a book.'

taḷḷa 'push' fares better with auxiliates whose objects are concrete (397a) not abstract (397b). The difference between (397a) and (397b) may be ascribed to the distinction between concrete or abstract or, perhaps, to the distinction between specific and nonspecific noted above.

(397)a *oru nāḷil vākkaḷar paṭṭiyalai accaṭittu.t taḷḷiṉārkaḷ!*
one day-LOC voter ballots-ACC print-CF push-PST-3P
'They printed up the voters' ballots is just one day!'
b *? *tērtal oru nāḷil naṭatti.t taḷḷiṉārkaḷ!*
election one day-LOC conduct-CF push-PST-3P
'They held the election in just one day!'

Both restrictions may well follow from the requirement that *taḷḷa* should combine with an auxiliate that has internal phases which can be accelerated. The use of a determiner or a mass noun would tend to impose a semelfactive reading on the AVC, rather than an iterative reading. Iterative activities, having internal phases, may better lend themselves to occurring with *taḷḷa*. Further, *taḷḷa* does not modify the causative auxiliaries *ceyya* 'do, make' or *vaikka* 'place': both are accomplishment verbs and semelfactive, two factors that tend to lower the acceptability on an AVC with *taḷḷa.*

Semantics

Previous analyses do not recognize the various facets of *taḷḷa*'s meaning. Schiffman (1969) focuses on attitude, characterizing its meaning as "good riddance": the speaker is glad that the action is over and done with. However, this might better characterize *oẓiya* 'purge' than *taḷḷa*. Schiffman's (1969: 169) further claim that *taḷḷa* involves "the notion of getting rid of something," an interpretation controverted below by (398b) and (399e), among others, appears to be an artefact of his corpus of just three examples. Fedson (1981: 254) argues that negative notions such as "good riddance" do not invariably accompany auxiliary *taḷḷa*; the admirative use of the auxiliary supports her conclusion.[38] However, our evidence does not support her further conclusion that *taḷḷa* is devoid of evaluative meaning. As with certain other auxiliaries, the speaker's evaluation may be admirative or pejorative: what matters is that both are nonneutral attitudes.

Schiffman's limited corpus might lead us to believe that *taḷḷa* is exclusively associated with pejorative attitude; but the examples in (398) below clearly show that it can express the speaker's admiration. Suppose that the telegraph receiver in (398a) has printed 200,000 telegrams whereas the usual receiver usually fails from metal fatigue after 100,000 uses: in operating at twice its expected output, it evokes use of *taḷḷa*. Without excessive personification, it would be farfetched to apply the term exuberance to the inanimate subjects in (398a and b), as Fedson's treatment seems to require. So exuberance is at best a circumstantial meaning accompanying animate subjects.

(398)a *ettaṉai.t tanti inta ricīvar aṭittu.t taḷḷiṉatu!*
how.many wires this receiver-nom beat-CF push-PST-3N
'(Just think) how many telegrams this receiver has printed!'

b *inta.p pēṉā ettaṉai.k katai eẓuti.t taḷḷi irukkiṟatu!*
this pen how.many story write-CF push-CF be-PRES-3N
'(Just think) how many stories this pen has written!'

A wider variety of auxiliates in AVCs with *taḷḷa* 'push' is illustrated opposite, allowing us to appreciate its semantics more fully. Example (399a) conveys the speaker's opinion that the matter may be carried out quickly; use of the auxiliary commits the participants to having an evaluation, positive or negative, according to context. Sentence (399b) expresses the speaker's amazement that the subject performs so quickly and effortlessly.[39] Example (399c) expresses the speaker's disgust that someone would have so rapidly smoked up all his cigarettes. Example (399d) is a humorous comment on the subject's voracious appetite and fondness for this kind of rice cake. Sentence (399e) expresses the speaker's wonder at the singer's rapid succession of songs. Example (399f)[40] registers profound dismay that the subject, a notorious criminal, has killed so many people. Finally, sentence (399g) expresses the speaker's disapproval that the subject should pander to the baser instincts of youngsters All have emotive overtones which, depending on context, may be pejorative or admirative.

38 Fedson uses the term "exuberance" to describe part of the auxiliary's meaning; the other part the "speedy execution" of an event. Both parts of this characterization are in need of clarification: it is not clear, for example, how the term exuberance may felicitously apply to actions with inanimate subjects. Nor does she explain how the execution of the event may be speedy in terms of the aspectual class of the auxiliate.

39 Here the auxiliate is an idiom that describes an effortless action.

40 Tamizvanan (1976: 94).

41 I note that in (399h), auxiliary *taḷḷa* occurs with an indirect object, *pace* Schiffman (1969) who claims this is not possible. The indirect object is usually understood as a *for*-dative, a beneficiary, rather than as a *to*-dative, a recipient.

(399)a *atu* [*viṭṭu.t* *taḷḷukiṟa*] *oru kāriyam.*
that-NOM leave-CF push-PRES-ANP one matter-NOM
'That is a matter to be disposed of quickly.'

b *avaṉ* *parīṭcai* [*ūti.t* *taḷḷiṉāṉ*].
he- NOM exam-ACC blow-CF push-PST-3SM
'He just breezed through the exam like it was nothing.'

c *yār* *cikkireṭṭu* [*ūti.t* *taḷḷiṉārkaḷ*]?
who- NOM cigarette blow-CF push-PST-3P
'Who smoked up all my cigarettes?'

d *jāṉ* *iṭliyāka* [*tiṉṟu* *taḷḷukiṟāṉ*].
John-NOM idly-ADV gobble-CF push-PRES-3SM
'John really packs those idlies away.'

e *maturai cōmu* *tiyākarāja kīrttaṉaikaḷāka.p* [*pāṭi.t* *taḷḷuvār*].
Madurai Somu-NOM Tyagaraga hymn-PL-ADV sing-CF push-FUT-3H
'Madurai Somu always reels off the hymns of Tyagaraja one right after the other (i.e., in rapid succession).'

f *ettaṉai.y=ō* *pērkaḷai* *avaṉ* *īvu irakkam iṉṟi* [[[*koṉṟu*]
how.many-DUB people-ACC he-NOM without.mercy kill-CF
taḷḷi] *irukkiṟāṉ*].
push-CF be-PRES-3SM
'He has killed ("bumped off") countless people with no mercy.'

g *avaṉ* *iḷaiñarukku* *ippaṭi* *paccai* *kataikaḷai* *eḻuti.t* *taḷḷiṉāṉ.*
he-NOM youth-DAT this.way fresh story-PL-ACC write-CF push-PST-3SM
'He ground out many such explicit stories for youngsters.'

Auxiliary *taḷḷa* 'push' thus encodes aspect and attitude. Its presence in an AVC indicates that the phase or rate of the activity named by the auxiliate is accelerated. The speaker views this acceleration with a nonneutral attitude, pejorative or admirative: examination of the context of utterance determines which is intended. Included among the possible circumstantial meanings are surprise, admiration, shock, disdain and bewilderment. *taḷḷa* does not combine with stative verbs, seems uncomfortable with semelfactive verbs and is best suited to activity verbs with an internal rhythm that can be accelerated.

Auxiliary *taḷḷa* lends support to the liminalist hypothesis; its use signals a deviation from a norm, viz., an expected rate or pace of activity. Further, this deviation, aspectual in nature, occurs within the body, or liminal stage, of the activity.[42] In one sense, *taḷḷa* 'push' is aspectually opposed to *vaḻiya* 'drip': both auxiliaries comment on the rate at which an activity occurs with *taḷḷa* exceeding the norm and *vaḻiya* falling short of it. And while the subject of an AVC with *taḷḷa* is often viewed as having an excess of energy, the subject of *vaḻiya* is conversely viewed as having little or none.

42 As the lowered acceptability with accomplishment verbs indicates, reaching the reincorporation stage may not be salient in defining *taḷḷa*.

AUXILIARY OF ABRUPTNESS: *pōṭa*

The *Tamil Lexicon* glosses *pōṭa* as 'cast down, put, draw, set in position, drop'. It functions as a main verb and indicative auxiliary. In certain dialects, e.g., that of Tirunelvelli, there appears to be no contrast between *viṭa* 'leave' and *pōṭa* 'put'; a single form, pronounced *piṭa*, does duty for both. As a main verb, *pōṭa* describes the transfer of an object to an unspecified position or location: the final goal or destination is not of interest in (400a). In this respect, *pōṭa* contrasts directly with *vaikka* 'place'. *pōṭa* seems to incorporate an implicit locative expression "away from the subject," rather than "toward a goal." In (400b) the addressee is commanded to serve rice on banana leaves, the exact placement of the rice being unimportant (or, perhaps, understood), probably because the rice is about to be eaten.

(400)a *avaṉ atai.k kīḻē pōṭṭāṉ.*
he-nom it-ACC down put-PST-3SM
'He put it down (somewhere).'

b *cōṟu pōṭu!*
rice put-IMP
'Serve the rice.'

Auxiliary verb uses

Annamalai (1982) characterizes auxiliary *pōṭa* 'put' as the "verb of casualness," and Fedson (1981: 274) concurs. When *pōṭa* modifies a directed action, it conveys the speaker's opinion that the subject performs the action without anticipating its outcome or consequences. As the discussion of the minimal pairs (329a and b) in Chapter 7 has already suggested, auxiliary *pōṭa* is an attitudinal counterpart to *vaikka* 'place'. *pōṭa* 'put' combines only with transitive verbs, not intransitives (401). Further, when a root has affective and effective transitive stems, *pōṭa* combines only with the effective stem (402b), not the affective stem (402a). *pōṭa* thus modifies directed actions.

(401) * *maḻai peytu pōṭṭatu.*
rain-NOM rain-CF put-PST-3N
'It rained casually.'

(402)a * *avaṉ maṉaiviyai.p pirintu pōṭṭāṉ.*
he-NOM wife-ACC separate+AF-CF put-PST-3SM
'He got casually separated from his wife.'

b *avaṉ maṉaiviyai.p pirittu.p pōṭṭāṉ.*
he-NOM wife-ACC separate+EF-CF put-PST-3SM
'He forceably separated his wife (from someone else).'

The presence of auxiliary *pōṭa* in a verbal threat adds an extra note of menace. The presence of *pōṭa* 'put' in (403), for example, conveys the speaker's attitude that he cares about neither the consequences of his threat nor the possibility of reprisal, both of which make for a more compelling threat.

(403)a *tōlai urittu.p pōṭuvēṉ.*
skin peel-CF put-FUT-1S
'I'll skin you alive.'

b *talaiyai.c cīvi.p pōṭuvēṉ.*
head-ACC shave-CF put-FUT-1S
'I'll shave your head right off.'

The action of the auxiliate must be viewed as directed, not accidental (404).

(404) *? *kai tavaṟi kaṇṇāṭiyai uṭaittu.p pōṭṭēṉ.*
hand slip-CF glass-ACC break-EF-CF put-PST-1S
'My hand slipped and I broke the glass.'

pōṭa selects main verbs denoting actions, not occurrences: *naṭakka* 'happen' in (405a) denotes an occurrence while *ceyya* 'do, make' in (405b) denotes a directed action.

(405)a * *eṉṉa naṭakka.k kūṭāt=ō atu naṭantu pōṭṭatu.*
what-NOM happen-INF should.not=OR it-NOM happen-CF put-PST-3N
?? 'What should not have happened, casually happened.'

b *eṉṉa ceyya.k kūṭāt=ō atai.c ceytu pōṭṭāṉ.*
what-NOM do-ACC should.not=OR it-ACC do-CF put-PST-3SM
'What should not have been done, he deliberately did it.'

Auxiliary *pōṭa* 'put' is sensitive to semantic transitivity: it may combine with intransitive verbs, and even dative-subject verbs, if in context they permit a transitive, directed action reading. A bus conductor barks out (406a) at a passenger trying to board without a ticket; use of *pōṭa* conveys his opinion that the rider was trying to deceive him. Though sneezing is not usually viewed as a voluntary act, it can be modified by *pōṭa* in the following situation. A thief utters (406b) to his accomplice to chastise him for doing something that might give them away; by using *pōṭa*, he accuses the accomplice for failing to consider the consequences of an otherwise innocuous act. The presence of *pōṭa* in the dative-subject construction in (406c), where the subject *avaṉukku* 'to him' is considered an experiencer rather than an agent, conveys the speaker's belief that the subject did nothing to counteract his increasingly insolent behavior.

(406)a *bassil [ēṟi.p pōṭṭu] ṭikkeṭṭu vāṅkāmal irukka muṭiyum=ā?*
bus-LOC rise-CF put-CF ticket buy-NEG-VF be-INF be.able-FUT-3N=INT
'Do you think you can simply board the bus without first buying a ticket?'

b *tummi.p pōṭṭāy!*
sneeze-CF put-PST-2S
'You sneezed (on purpose, heedless of the consequences).'

c *avaṉukku.k koẓuppu ēṟi.p pōṭṭatu.*
he-DAT insolence-NOM rise-CF put-PST-3N
'He's gone and gotten insolent.'

Several circumstantial readings may accompany *pōṭa*, including carelessness, casualness, callousness and force. All emanate from the basic meaning in which the action is performed without regard for future consequences.

Additional examples display the range of auxiliary *pōṭa* 'put'. Its presence in (407a) conveys the speaker's attitude that the cooking was abruptly set aside to

(407)a *camaiyal muṭittu.p pōṭṭu avaḷ vīṭṭai.k kūṭṭiṉāḷ.*
cooking finish-CF put-CF she-NOM house-ACC sweep-PST-3SF
'After the cooking was done and out of the way, she swept the house.'

b *oru kaṭṭurai vantu irukkiṟatu. ataṟku oru maṟappu eẓuti.p pōṭṭaṭṭum=ā?*[43]
one editorial come-CF be-PRES-3N it-DAT one rebuttal write-CF put-OPT=INT
'An editorial has appeared (in the competing newspaper). Should I write off a rebuttal to it?'

c *anta.c ceyti eṉṉai.t tūkki.p pōṭa vaittatu.*
that news-NOM me-ACC hang-CF put-INF place-PST-3N
'That news (i.e., a death) gave me a jolt.'

d *atai.t tolaittu.p pōṭṭēṉ.*
it-ACC lose+EF-CF put-PST-1S
'Yeah, I lost it (want to make something of it?).'

e *kalyāṇa.t tētiyai muṭinta varai nāṉ taḷḷi.p pōṭa virumpukiṟēṉ.*[44]
wedding date-ACC as.far.as.possible I-NOM push-CF put-INF wish-PRES-1S
'I want to put off the wedding date as far as possible.'

f *pēy maẓai anta.p pantalai.c cāyttu.p pōṭṭatu.*
ghost rain-NOM that shed-ACC lean-EF-CF put-PST-3n
'A gale knocked that shed down.'

g *kaṭavuḷ (*vīpatttiṉāl) eṅkaḷai ippaṭi kaṣṭappaṭa vaittu.p pōṭṭāṉ.*
god-NOM disaster-INSTR us-ACC this.way suffer-INF place-CF put-PST-3SM
'God makes us suffer this way (*with disasters) (we can't fathom it).'

h *iṅkē eṉṉa aviẓttu.p pōṭṭu āṭukiṟārkaḷ=ā?*[45]
here what untie-CF put-CF dance-PRES-3P=INT
'Is there anyone here dancing, having thrown off his dhoti?'
i.e.,
'Is there anyone dancing naked here?'

tackle another chore. In (407b) it indicates that a rebuttal should be published, no matter the consequences; in this, (407b) resembles the threats in (403). The phrase *taḷḷi.p pōṭa* 'put off' in (407e) contrasts with the phrase *taḷḷi vaikka* 'postpone': in

43 Akilan (1951: 34).
44 Akilan (1951: 46).
45 Patmanapan (1977).

the former, the speaker does not care whether a new date is set, while the latter indicates the speaker wants to reschedule the event. When auxiliary *pōṭa* modifies a causative verb such as *vaikka* 'place' in (407g), it disallows any intermediate agent; felicitous use of *pōṭa* thus requires the subject be seen as the immediate agent of the action. In using *pōṭa* in the rhetorical question in (407i), the speaker scolds his audience for thinking he would be so thoughtless as to dance naked in the street, simultaneously indicating by its rudeness that the speaker has little concern for what they think.

The indicative auxiliary *pōṭa* marks both pejorative attitude and punctual aspect. Its presence in an AVC indicates that the direct action is over and done with, much like the disjunctive taxis reading of *viṭa* 'leave'. But the action does not prepare for, lead up to or connect with any other action as with *vaikka*, and this gives rise to the circumstantial readings that the subject performs the action casually, carelessly, without regard for consequences.

Auxiliary *pōṭa* supports the liminalist hypothesis. As a main verb, it describes the movement of an object away from the speaker without specifying a destination; as an auxiliary, the completion of an event without concern for its consequences. The object and action, respectively, therefore pass through a separation phase and into a liminal phase without prospect of reincorporation; neither is directed toward a definite goal. This liminality may be largely responsible for the negative attitude.

AUXILIARY OF EXHAUSTION: *tīrkka*

The meanings attributed to the root *tīr-* include 'end, exhaust, vanish, complete, leave, solve, divide, destroy, remove'. It has affective and effective stems, *tīra* and *tīrkka*, respectively. Both serve as main verbs but in my corpus only *tīrkka* functions as an indicative auxiliary.

Consider *tīra* 'be exhausted' (408) and *tīrkka* 'exhaust' (409) as main verbs. They convey a nuance of removing or completing a thing by exhausting it or reducing it to nothing; in the process, a quantity is depleted.

(408)a	*maṉṉeṇṇai*	*tīrntu*	*pōyiṟṟu.*	
	kerosene-NOM	exhaust-AF-CF	go-PST-3N	
	'The (supply of) kerosene is exhausted.'			
b	*eṉṉuṭaiya.k*	*kuḻappam*	*tīra.v*	*illai.*[46]
	my	confusion-NOM	exhaust-AF-INF	IND-NEG
	'My confusion did not settle down.'			
(409)a	*kaṭaṉai.t*	*tīrttu*	*viṭṭatu.*	
	debt-ACC	exhaust-EF-CF	leave-PST-3N	
	'The debt was settled.'			

46 Akilan (1951: 20).

b *vīcī arai maṇi nēram āki.y=um anta viṣayattai.t*
V.C.-NOM half hour time become-CF=AND that matter-ACC
tīrkka.v illai.
exhaust-EF-INF IND-NEG
'Even though he had half an hour, the Vice-Chancellor did not settle the matter.'

c *camūkattiṉ nōyai.t tīrukkum vaittiyaṉ alla nāṉ.*[47]
society-GEN ills-ACC exhaust-FUT-ANP physician-NOM become-NEG I-NOM
'I am not a physician who removes society's ills.'

Auxiliary verb uses

In my corpus of both elicited and literary material, only the effective form *tīrkka* 'exhaust' serves as an indicative auxiliary verb. However, Fedson (1981: 231-33) presents several examples of affective *tīra* 'be exhausted' as an indicative auxiliary. My informants generally rejected them as auxiliaries in speech; however, since I was unable to submit them to the full battery of grammatical tests in Chapters 4 and 5, no final decision concerning its auxiliaryhood can be made here.

The presence of auxiliary *tīrkka* 'exhaust' in an AVC conveys the speaker's attitude that the subject has expended all he is going to on the action denoted by the auxiliate. He has exhausted all strength, desire or will power to continue; hence, the activity comes to a halt. In one sense, it appears to be the attitudinal counterpart of *muṭikka* 'finish' (Chapter 7). How then does it contrast with *pōṭa* 'put'? Utilizing the distinction made in Chapter 6 between subject-oriented (p. 194) and object-oriented verbs (p. 204), *tīrkka* seems subject-oriented while *pōṭa* 'seems object-oriented, roughly corresponding to the difference in English between *stop reading* and *finish reading*. In uttering (410a) the speaker conveys his opinion that the subject has spoken and, due to exhaustion, exasperation or indifference, stops speaking. Similarly, (410b) conveys the opinion that the subject stopped drinking due to satiety, boredom or the like. The activity ceases because the subject has withdrawn from participation in it.

(410)a *avaṉ colli.t tīrttāṉ.*
he-NOM say-CF exhaust-PST-3SM
'He stopped speaking (i.e., he has said it and gotten it off his chest).'

b *kuṭittu.t tīrttāṉ.*
drink-CF exhaust-PST-3SM
'He has done with/had his fill of drinking.'

tīrkka 'exhaust' categorically fails to combine with affective main verbs, as the ungrammaticality of the examples in (411) show.

47 Akilan (1951: 11).

(411)a * *pōy.t tīrttāṉ.*
go-CF exhaust-PST-3SM
'He's done going.'
b * *ōṭi.t tīrttāṉ.*
run-CF exhaust-PST-3SM
'His running finished.'
c * *tūṅki.t tīrttāṉ.*
sleep-CF exhaust-PST-3SM
'His sleeping stopped.'

The auxiliary selects effective verbs that represent a dynamic action. The type of event must be one that is not homogenous throughout its duration and one that is perceived to require a supply of energy to sustain it. *tīrkka* 'exhaust' thus does not select states or occurrences, but directed actions, achievements and accomplishments. Even though *tīrkka* need not select an animate subject, the subject should be capable of interpretation as an agent. The failing rain in (412a), for example, is personified as an agent capable of damaging crops or helping them grow. The crying fits in (412b and c) are activities which the subjects are seen to prolong, and which finally abate once the subject's strength wanes.

(412)a *maḻai koṭṭi.t tīrkkum.*
rain-NOM pour-CF exhaust-FUT-3N
'The rain will blow itself out.'
b *avaḷ aḻutu.t tīrttāḷ.*
she-NOM cry-CF exhaust-PST-3SF
'She cried herself out/dry.'
c *kuḻantai [aḻutu.t tīrttu] viṭṭu ippōtu tāṉ tūṅkukiṟāṉ.*
child-NOM cry-CF exhaust-CF leave-CF now EMP sleep-PRES-3SM
'After crying his eyes out, the child is sleeping now.'
d *avaṉ colli.t tīrttatum avaḷ vantāḷ.*
he-NOM say-CF exhaust-AS.SOON.AS she-NOM come-PST-3SF
'As soon as he had stopped speaking, she came in.'

Auxiliary *irukka* 'be located', *viṭa* 'leave', and *āka* 'become' may modify an AVC with auxiliary *tīrkka*; however, in general, auxiliary *koḷḷa* 'hold' and *vaikka* 'place' may not (but see below). These latter two are marked for taxis, *koḷḷa* marking conjunctive and *vaikka* subsequent taxis. Both characterize one narrated event as being related to some other narrated event, current or later. *tīrkka* is not merely nontactic; it appears to preclude a reading of taxis which connects one narrated event with another. The action of the auxiliate modified by this auxiliary is over and done with; since it will not likely be resumed, it can have no bearing on another event.

Like other attitudinals, *tīrkka* 'exhaust' occurs in direct discourse (413a), but not indirect discourse (413b).

(413)a *atai viṭṭu.t tīr eṉṟu coṉṉāṉ.*
it-ACC leave-CF exhaust-IMP say-CF say-PST-3SM
'He said, "Let it go/drop at that."'

b * *atai viṭṭu.t tīrkka.c coṉṉāṉ.*
it-ACC leave-CF exhaust-INF say-PST-3SM
'He said to drop it at that.'

In the imperative, *tīrkka* 'exhaust' is generally followed by auxiliary *koḷḷa* 'hold', as (414a) shows. This need not contradict the earlier observation that *tīrkka* is not ordinarily modified by *koḷḷa*. Chapter 6 introduced a circumstantial meaning of auxiliary *koḷḷa* which marks voice rather than taxis; in this setting it marks a suggestion. Here the subject-orientation of *tīrkka* and the self-oriented voice of *koḷḷa* seem to reinforce one other.

(414) *colli.t tīrttu.k *?(koḷḷuṅkaḷ).*
say-CF exhaust-CF hold-IMP
'Say it and get it off your chest.'

Fedson's (1981: 280) view of affective *tīrkka* leads her to a different position. She says that "the situation denoted by the CP [=conjunctive participle] is viewed as performed totally, as fulfilled to its capacity." The event named by the main verb is "consummated." It is unclear how one can apply the notion of consummation or fulfillment to examples (412a-c).[48] How does the subject of (412b) consummate the activity of crying? Consummation is a notion more properly applied to achievements and accomplishments than to activities; our examples make it clear that *tīrkka* combines with auxiliates that denote activities, as well. More to the point here is the fact that some of her examples allow an admirative as well as a pejorative attitude. While (415a) readily allows an admirative interpretation, the remaining two examples are more consistent with a pejorative interpretation. In (415b) the speaker comments on foreigners' lack of respect for marriage: it is taken so lightly abroad that they can do it in a very short time. Similarly, in (415c) the speaker has gotten bored with talking and decides simply to stop. In the event, this auxiliary is accompanied by a nonneutral attitude.

(415)a *avar anta vīṭ=ē atirum paṭi cirittu.t tīrttār.*
he-NOM that house=EMP resound-FUT-ANP manner laugh-CF exhaust-PST-3H
'He laughed so loud that the whole house boomed.'

b *cīmaiyil vivakam arai maṇiyil [ceytu tīrttu] viṭa]*
abroad marriage half hour-LOC do-CF exhaust-CF leave-INF
caukariyaṅkaḷ uṇṭu.
facility-PL-NOM exist-3N
'There exist in foreign countries facilities to conduct marriages in half an hour.'

48 Fedson (1981: 280-81).

c *pēcuvatu ellām [pēci.t tīrttu] āki viṭṭatu].*
speaking all speak-CF exhaust-CF become-CF leave-pst-3N
'All there was to be said, is said and over.'

Semantics—Liminality

Auxiliary *tīrkka* 'exhaust' supports the liminalist hypothesis. By withdrawing his sustaining energy, the subject abandons an action midway before it comes to its natural conclusion. It has stopped, but not necessarily finished. The action fails to reach its coda and floats in limbo without subsequent effect. Without the energy or effort to sustain the activity named by the auxiliate, the subject abandons that activity in a liminal phase before it reaches its natural conclusion in the coda.

Auxiliary *tīrkka* 'exhaust' thus marks aspect and attitude. It indicates that the auxiliate's activity has ceased during the body, or liminal stage, rather than passing to the coda, or reincorporation stage. Its nontactic nature suggests that the energy which might propel an activity or series of activities along a time line is spent, and can therefore lead to no subsequent event. Additionally, it conveys the speaker's attitude that the subject ceased the activity because it had expended its strength or desire to see the activity through to the coda. This generally carries a negative evaluation; however, at least in the literary example in (415a), it seems capable of an admirative reading.

A TURN FOR THE WORSE: *pōka*

Perhaps the most common motion verb in Tamil, *pōka* means 'go, depart, extend, leave, spread, lapse, change'. It is an affective verb paired with effective *pōkka* 'make go, spend', not *pōṭa* 'put' as Pope (1895) and others thought. It may serve as a main verb, indicative auxiliary or modal auxiliary (marking prospective tense).

As a main verb *pōka* 'go' describes the movement of the subject without specifying direction or ultimate destination. When it occurs in contexts where it contrasts with *vara* 'come', it signals movement away from a deictic center, usually anchored by and identified with the speaker, by means of a conversational implicature (see Steever 1979). It is unmarked with respect to *vara* and therefore occurs in contexts of neutralization (e.g., "wherever he goes/*comes'). By itself *pōka* indicates movement, only implying a goal; another expression, usually a dative such as *ūrukku* 'to town' in (416a), may be used to make the goal explicit.

(416)a *avaṉ ūrukku.p pōṉāṉ.*
he-NOM town-DAT go-PST-3SM
'He went to his town.'

b *avaḷ ammā vīṭṭukku.t tirumpi pōvāḷ.*
she-NOM mother house-DAT turn-CF go-FUT-3SF
'She will go back to her mother's house.'

Indicative auxiliary uses

Auxiliary *pōka* 'go' combines with nonagentive verbs which denote a change of state and may be either gradual or abrupt. It marks attitude, signaling the speaker's opinion that the change is one for the worse or, at the very least, without immediate benefit or consequence. Though paired with effective *pōkka* 'make go', only the affective form may function as an indicative auxiliary. In its most frequent form, it occurs in the third person neuter singular, viz. *pōyiṟṟu* 'went', *pōkiṟatu* 'goes' and *pōkum* 'will go'. Other forms do occur, but less frequently.

Consider example (417a), which may be uttered in the following context. A man asks his wife to prepare a special dish for dinner; she replies that the cooking preparations are over for the day. Here use of *pōka* serves to indicate her regret. A street vendor recommends his bangles to a customer, claiming that nothing bad would happen to them. *pōka* indicates a transition into an undesirable state, a possibility denied in (417b). The auxiliate need not be semelfactive: (417c) describes a key being lost many times. In this respect, it contrasts with *viṭa* 'leave', which prefers semelfactive main verbs.

(417)a *camaiyal muṭintu pōyiṟṟu.*
cooking-NOM finish-CF go-PST-3N
'The cooking is finished.'

b *vaḷaiyal karuttu.p pōka.v illai.*
bangles-NOM tarnish-CF go-INF IND-NEG
'The bangles will not tarnish.'

c *ippōtu aṭikkaṭi cāvi tolaintu pōkiṟatu. eṉṉa maṟati!*
now often key lose+AF-CF go-pres-3N what forgetfulness-NOM
'Your key is getting lost a lot these days. What forgetfulness!'

d *inta.p pustakam maṭṭum tolaintu pōka vēṇṭum eṉṟāl*
this book only lose+AF-CF go-INF must-FUT-3N say-COND
nāṉ uṉṉai.c cummāka viṭa māṭṭēṉ.
I-NOM you-ACC alone leave-INF fut-NEG-1s
'If this book gets lost, I will not leave you alone.'

pōka and *viṭa* 'leave' contrast in the following pairs. A woman who has applied a cosmetic mark to her forehead, might utter (418a) to express her dismay that it smeared. A dispassionate report of the same situation would likely use (418b) to signal a change of situation. *pōka* in the first sentence signals the speaker's opinion that the change was bad. (419a) describes a slow crop failure, due to long neglect or drought: *pōka* is consistent with a gradual change, but *viṭa* is not. (419b) describes a sudden crop failure, due, say, to rapid flooding.

(418)a *poṭṭu aẓintu pōyiṟṟu.*
tilak-NOM smear-CF go-PST-3N
'The tilak got smeared.'

b *poṭṭu aẓintu viṭṭatu.*
tilak-NOM smear-CF leave-PST-3N
'The tilak was smeared.'

(419)a *payiṟu aẓintu pōkum.*
crops-NOM destroy-CF go-FUT-3N
'The crops will get destroyed.'

b *payiṟu aẓintu viṭum.*
crops-NOM destroy-CF leave-FUT-3N
'The crops will be destroyed.'

The surface subject of the AVC cannot be agentive; in general, *pōka* 'go' does not combine with effective main verbs because they represent actions directed by the subject. In (420a), for example, it is a policeman's blow that makes the man recoil; in (420b) a gardener's negligence lets the weeds grow wild.

(420)a *pōlīcār aṭitta maṉitaṉ curuṇṭu pōṉāṉ.*
police-NOM beat-PST-ADN man-NOM curl-CF go-PST-3SM
'The man who was hit by the police crumpled (under the impact).'

b *kāḷai vaḷarntu pōyiṟṟu.*
weeds-NOM grow-AF-CF go-PST-3SM
'The weeds have grown up.'

c *avaṉ vayiṟu kāyntu pōyiṟṟu.*
his stomach-NOM dry+AF-CF go-PST-3N
'His stomach dried up (i.e., he was so hungry he would eat anything).'

There is no external force that could account for the event in (421a), but in (421b) tooth decay or old age could account for tooth loss.

(421)a ?* *avaṉ viẓuntu pōṉāṉ.*
he-NOM fall-CF go-PST-3SM
'He went falling.'

b *pal viẓuntu pōyiṟṟu.*
tooth-NOM fall-CF go-PST-3N
'The tooth fell out.'

The aspectual class of the verbs with which *pōka* 'go' combines should be a process, which may or may not induce a change of state. A number of Tamil verbs exhibit different meanings, and for each meaning a different aspectual class: *pōka* combines only with those that are processes or change of state. *pāya*, when it means 'flow' (422a) may combine with *pōka*, but not when it means 'spring, leap' (422b). When it means 'twitch' (423a), *āṭa* combines with *pōka*, but not when it means 'dance' (423b). Further, *piṭikka* may combine with *pōka* when, as a dative-subject verb, it means 'like', but not when it means 'grab' and takes a nominative subject.

(422)a *vayilukku.t taṇṇīr pāyntu pōyiṟṟu.*
field-DAT water-NOM flow-CF go-PST-3N
'The water kept flowing into the field.'

b * *peṇpuli pāyntu pōyiṟṟu.*
tigress-NOM spring-CF go-PST-3N
'A tigress lept out.'

(423)a *kai āṭi.p pōkum.*
hand-NOM dance-CF go-FUT-3N
'His hand will twitch.'

b * *avaḷ āṭi.p pōvāḷ.*
she-NOM dance-CF go-FUT-3N
'She will go and dance.'

Besides attitude, auxiliary *pōka* also marks aspect, which is suggested by the fact that it favors verbs denoting a gradual change or verbs with iterative readings. Although it seems the attitudinal counterpart of auxiliary *vara* 'come', *vara* may combine with agentive actions while *pōka* may not. Like *vara*, *pōka* does not mark taxis; but unlike *vara*, it marks pejorative attitude.

To combine achievement or accomplishment verbs with *pōka*, they must use imperfective converb with *koḷḷa*. The following examples (Fedson 1981: 125) contrast *vara* and *pōka* in this usage. The latter, but not the former, marks pejorative attitude. In (424b) the speaker conveys his negative evaluation of the event named by the auxiliate, finding the voice discordant or whiny. Such overtones do not accompany (424a). The phrase *kural uyara* 'voice rises' may be an accomplishment in the sense, '(the) voice became loud', in which case *koḷḷa* is added to form its imperfective converb.

(424)a *kōpuviṉ kural uyarntu koṇṭ=ē vantatu.*
Gopu-GEN voice-NOM rise-CF hold-CF=EMP come-PST-3SN
'Gopu's voice kept rising.'

b *kōpuviṉ kural uyarntu koṇṭ=ē pōyiṟṟu.*
Gopu-GEN voice-NOM rise-CF hold-CF=EMP go-PST-3SN
'Gopu's voice went right on going up.'

Fedson (1981) characterizes *pōka* as contributing the meaning that the event continues on without being checked or interfered with. This, however, does not wholly distinguish it from her treatment of *vara*. The nontactic nature of *vara* may incidentally convey the nuance that there is no interference. The difference follows from the fact that *pōka*, but not *vara*, encodes attitude, viz., the speaker's belief that the persistence of the activity, or the state it would result in, is undesirable. It is not always easy to discern the pejorative attitude in every example. Along with *pōṭa* 'put' and *tolaiya* 'get lost', *pōka* seems in some instances to have undergone semantic attrition, making its attitudinal content harder to detect.

pōka is consistent with the liminalist hypothesis: it describes a movement that has separation and liminal phases, but no reincorporation phase. The movement is away from the deictic center, and figuratively, away from the center of control. But its pejorative attitude is relatively weak.

AUXILIARY OF BENEDICTIVE VOICE: *aruḷa*

Most of the attitudinal auxiliaries analyzed so far exhibit two tendencies: first, they mark pejorative attitude. Only *taḷḷa* 'push' and, perhaps, *vaẓiya* 'drip' and *tīrkka* 'exhaust' may occasionally convey admirative attitude; even so, pejorative attitude dominates. This likely reflects a general presumption that while being polite tends to exact a minimal linguistic cost, one must go out of one's way to express rudeness or a negative attitude. Thus, in the absence of any explicit marking for pejorative attitude, one may conclude that the speaker holds a neutral attitude about the narrated event and conversationally implicate that he holds a positive one. Second, many of the attitudinal auxiliaries seem to involve some aspectual modification of the narrated event.

The verb *aruḷa* 'grace, deign, bestow' departs from these tendencies in two ways. First, it functions predominantly as an attitudinal auxiliary conveying the speaker's positive attitude; second, it appears to involve the category of voice. It seldom occurs in modern colloquial Tamil, being restricted primarily to religious ceremonies and to formal occasions when it is apparently borrowed from the diglossic high register (*centamiẓ*). It appears frequently in classical literature, particularly in the medieval devotional literature of the poet-saints, nor is it unknown in the ancient language.

Main verb uses of this form are therefore rare in the modern language; example (93), from the *caṅkam* anthology *puṟanāṉūṟu* 393.14, shows that as a main verb it once meant 'bestow, give graciously'.

(425)	*veṇṇina*	*mūri*	*aruḷa . . .*
	white flesh	piece.of.meat	bestow-INF
	'As you bestowed some white meat . . .'		

But it now occurs, for the most part, as the component of a lexical compound verb, e.g., *aruḷi ceyya* 'to give graciously', or in indicative AVCs. Since no independent main verb use is synchronically available, it is among the most idiomatic—and marginal—of the Tamil indicative auxiliaries.

In an AVC *aruḷa* 'grace' conveys the speaker's attitude (P^s) that the subject's performance (P^n) of the action denoted by the main verb (E^n) is a gracious act. Specifically, *aruḷa* marks attitude (P^s/E^n) and voice (P^n/E^n), specifically what I call *benedictive voice. aruḷa* is not simply an honorific marker. Honorification is essentially a variety of person, P^s/P^n, which characterizes the relation between the speaker and other participants in terms of social status, and not a verbal category. Honorification generally requires that each time the revered person is mentioned, an honorific form be used, e.g., a personal ending, an address term. One cannot, for instance, alternate between the honorific plural and the intimate singular verb endings when referring to the same person in a discourse. *aruḷa* marks instead a kind of voice; it behaves differently from honorification in that it does not accompany each reference to the subject, but only the subject's role in certain key actions. That is, it correlates what the speaker (P^s) considers to be an important action (E^n) with the subject of that action (P^n). The correlation of P^n with E^n thus gives rise to voice, P^nE^n. It is the subject's involvement in the event that invests it with what the speaker views as noteworthy.

The actions that *aruḷa* qualifies tend to mark key actions or turning points in a narrative, those that advance the plot, punctuate it or mark its climax. In uttering (426a), the speaker indicates that the subject, the goddess Meenakshi, has acted in such a way as to open a new, positive development in the myth. In (427b) Siva curses a would-be usurper whom he has finally subdued in a series of battles; this action terminates the episode. In (427c) *aruḷa* qualifies both the entrance and exit of the deity who played a role in the intervening events, framing the entire episode.

(426)a *mīṉāṭci colli aruḷiṉāḷ.*
Meenakshi-NOM say-CF grace-PST-3SF
'Meenakshi spoke/deigned to speak.'

b *nī curamīṉ vaṭivaṅ koṇṭu kaṭalil uẓaḷa.k kaṭavāy*
you- NOM shark-GEN form take-CF sea-LOC whirl-INF cross-FUT-2S
eṉa.c cāpittu aruḷiṉār.
say-INF curse-CF grace-PST-3H
'He (= Siva) cursed him saying, "You will wander the seas as a shark."'

c *pulavar vaṭivam koṇṭu vantu aruḷiya cōmacuntarāka kaṭavuḷ*
poet form with come-CF grace-PST-ADN Somasundaran god-NOM
tiṭīreṉṟu aṅkiruntu maṟaintu aruḷiṉār.
suddenly there-ABL disappear-CF grace-PST-3H
'The God Somasundaran, who had come in the guise of a poet, suddenly disappeared from there.'

aruḷa may also cooccur with a human subject. Examples such as (427a, b) do occur in certain settings in modern spoken Tamil. (427a) describes a priest officiating at an annual death ceremony; these kinds of locutions are used to address elders on such days. Example (427b) may be a request from a disciple (*ciṣayaṉ*) to his preceptor (*kuru*) to explain an esoteric point of philosophy, music or grammar. There are strong religious overtones in such cases, and social status is rigorously observed. Outside religious or formal settings, especially when there is little disparity in the social status of the participants, use of *aruḷa* may be very sarcastic, and even pejorative. Example (427c), from Fedson (1981: 235), illustrates just such a tongue-in-cheek use of *aruḷa.*

(427)a *eẓuntu aruḷiṉār.*
rise-CF grace-PST-3H
'He got up.'

b *vivaram colli aruḷuṅkaḷ.*
details say-CF grace-IMP-H
'Please give some details.'

c *paricōtaṉaikku varukiṟavarkaḷ ivarkaḷ pēcum tamiẓai.y=um*
examination-DAT come-PRES-VN-3P these-NOM speak-FUT-ANP Tamil-ACC=AND
poruṭṭu aruḷvārkaḷ eṉṟu nampukiṟēṉ.
bear-CF grace-FUT-3P say-CF trust-PRES-1S
'And I trust that those who have come for the examination will bear with the Tamil that these people speak.'

In such instances, the speaker conveys his evaluation that the subject is behaving haughtily, holding himself above those around him. Example (428a) might have been uttered by the opposition leader to the then Chief Minister, MG Ramachandran, familiarly known as MGR; use of *aruḷa* would suggest that the Chief Minister was putting on airs. Use of this auxiliary in (428b) is both sarcastic and humorous. The writer makes the oblique comment that the subject, the Tamil counterpart of Inspector Clouseau, has done the principal a real favor in revealing his true identity. In both cases the speaker considers the subject to be behaving in a haughty manner. This ironic trope may well be the most common use of *aruḷa* in everyday modern spoken Tamil.

(428)a *em ji ār tiruvāy malarntu pēci aruḷiṉār.*
MGR-NOM blessed.mouth bloom-CF speak-CF grace-PST-3H
'MGR deigned to speak, opening his blessed mouth.'

b *nāṉ tāṉ vittal rav, ci ai ṭi eṉṟu pirincipalukku.t taṉatu cuya*
I- NOM EMP Vittal Rao-NOM CID say-CF principal-DAT self true
uruvai.k kaṭākṣittu aruḷiṉāṉ.
form-ACC condescend-CF grace-PST-3SM
'He condescended (to reveal) his true form: "I am Vittal Rao, of the C.I.D.".'

Fedson (1981) distinguishes sharply between what she calls *aruḷa*'s "serious" use (427a) and its "parody" use (428b). Both appear, however, to be circumstantial readings of *aruḷa* 'grace', to be ascribed to factors of different contexts not the invariant meaning of the auxiliary. Attitude is present in both extremes, as confirmed by the various grammatical tests for attitudinal auxiliaries. Admirative attitude tends to occur when the auxiliary qualifies the act of a superior, such as an elder, a guru, or a god; pejorative attitude when the subject has roughly the same social status as the speaker or other participants.

It is difficult to recruit *aruḷa* 'grace, bestow' to the defense of the liminalist hypothesis.[49] As an auxiliary of voice, it does not appeal to the aspectual triad of onset, body and coda of an event on which the liminalist triad of separation, limen and reincorporation is superposed. However, auxiliary *aruḷa* is used at crucial junc-

49 Historically, of course, the verb meant 'bestow' and, as a verb of transaction, could be analyzed with reference to the motive hypothesis as the benefactive auxiliaries were in Chapter 7.

tures in a narrative to resolve some aspect of the plot; it is at the level of the narrative, rather than the single sentence, that an event modified by *aruḷa* may be said to point to the coda, or reincorporation stage. The admirative attitude that accompanies this auxiliary may well derive from the positive evaluation ascribed to the coda phase of an event in contrast to those auxiliaries which convey pejorative attitude by focusing on the body, or liminal stage. The pejorative interpretation may follow as an ironic interpretation of the admirative.

aruḷa thus marks benedictive voice and attitude. It marks crucial actions by the subject that advance the narrative. The speaker evaluates this action with admirative or pejorative attitude, depending on context.

SUMMARY

The verbal category of attitude was introduced to analyze these twelve auxiliaries; this shifter, represented by P^s/E^n, characterizes the speaker's subjective evaluation of the narrated event. It helps explain the syntactic and semantic peculiarities of these auxiliaries, and has been shown to perform work in the grammar of Tamil, notably in predicting the interaction of these auxiliaries with direct and indirect discourse, as well as with causation. As a grammatical category, attitude supports our treatment of these twelve verbs as auxiliaries because it endows them with a verbal category, expression of which is necessary if a verb form is to be considered an auxiliary at all. At the same time, their virtually identical behavior with respect to the auxiliaries in Chapters 6 and 7 over against lexical compounds, modal auxiliaries and compound clauses helps validate attitude as a verbal category. Our analysis of attitude as a verbal category suggests the necessity of revising the category of status, as well.

The semantic properties of the attitudinal auxiliary have been analyzed here more thoroughly than heretofore, both for the entire class and for its individual members. Their cooccurrence restrictions, for example, have been explored more closely than before. In addition to attitude, many of these attitudinals encode perfectly ordinary verbal categories such as aspect (*taḷḷa* 'push'), tense (*kiẓiya* 'tear'), or voice (*aẓa* 'cry'). The role of the auxiliate's aspectual class seems to be particularly important in the analysis of the aspect and tense.

Independent of the semantic and syntactic arguments for auxiliaryhood, the liminal hypothesis was proposed to account for the choice of several lexemes that serve as attitudinal auxiliaries. Verbs that signal movement in an indeterminate manner or to an unknown destination, verbs that lack a reincorporation phase, predominate in this set. The negative evaluation associated with liminality seems to foster the pejorative attitude that accompanies most of these auxiliaries. This hypothesis, however, it is not entirely waterproof; in particular, there is difficulty in explaining attitudinal auxiliaries of voice, e.g., *aẓa* 'cry', *aruḷa* 'bestow', just by referring it to the liminalist hypothesis.

The arguments and evidence provided in Chapters 4 and 5 should remove any doubt that attitidunal auxiliaries pattern grammatically with the remaining, nonattitudinal auxiliaries over against modal auxiliaries, lexical compound verbs and compound clauses. The observed differences between attitudinal and nonattitudinal auxiliaries, which partitions them into two subsets of indicative AVCs, may be traced for the most part to their semantics.

Our analysis tends to dispel the apparent idiomaticity of the attitudinal auxiliaries; they are not quaint and exotic figures of speech, but components of an elaborate, well-articulated grammatical subsystem. Their analysis, as well as the analysis of other grammatical forms and processes that conventionally encode attitude, affect or emotion, has suffered from a methodological prejudice that ignores such forms and processes as peripheral to grammar. This study demonstrates that the study of such phenomena is as conducive to grammatical analysis as other, more prosaic linguistic phenomena.

9 Conclusion

After traversing several hundred pages and nearly one thousand examples, we have reached the end of this lengthy project. While not everything of interest that could be said about the Tamil auxiliary verb system has been said here, our analysis provides a comprehensive picture of this facet of Tamil grammar, and may serve as a foundation for further study of auxiliary phenomena in Tamil and elsewhere. We take this opportunity to point up some of the topics that naturally grow out of our analysis of the Tamil indicative auxiliary verb system and to offer some closing remarks on the usefulness of Auxiliary Formation as a model for analyzing auxiliary verb phenomena. It is my hope that, having come this far, this analysis will have provided readers with a gentle validation of this model's usefulness in linguistic description.

OPPORTUNITIES FOR FURTHER STUDY

The open-ended nature of our inquiry has raised the possibility for a variety of projects worthy of further study, ranging in size from squibs to M.A. theses, from articles to books. Further analysis of Tamil morphology, syntax and pragmatics will almost certainly lead to amendments to a number of the specific analyses that were made here, as well as to discoveries that do not directly involve auxiliary verb phenomena. To take but one example, the interaction of tense and temporal adverbials, touched on lightly in Chapters 6 and 8, will clearly benefit from more focused research. The continued lexicography of Tamil auxiliaries should also yield novel and rich results; some of the major auxiliaries such as *irukka* 'be' and *viṭa* 'leave' (is there just one?), not to mention the more exotic ones such as *tolaikka* 'lose' and *kiẓikka* 'tear', deserve monographs of their own.

Miscellaneous attitudinal auxiliaries

Quite conceivably, the twelve verbs analyzed in the previous chapter may not exhaust the set of attitudinal auxiliaries in Tamil. A quick survey of the specialist literature reveals further potential candidates, e.g., *aṭikka* 'strike', *alaiya* 'wander, waiver', *kaṭṭa* 'tie', *koṭṭa* 'pour', *eṭukka* 'take', *tiriya* 'wander, *niṟka* 'stand', and *viẓa* 'fall'. Fedson (1981), for example, makes the claim that *eṭukka, kaṭṭa, koṭṭa,* and *viẓa* are auxiliaries; however, that claim rests on pretheoretical intuitions, not explicit grammatical criteria. A subsequent year of fieldwork in India in 1984–85 allowed me to weigh these putative indicative auxiliaries against the various tests developed in Chapters 4 and 5 with respondents. Ultimately, these putative auxiliaries failed to pass muster, demonstrating gross syntactic behavior more characteristic of lexical compounds than auxiliary compound verbs.[1] Nonetheless, for reasons given below, it is instructive to review some of them.

Before grammatical tests showed it not to be an auxiliary, the verb *tiriya* 'wander' in (429) was hypothesized to convey pejorative attitude, aspectually characterizing an event as wandering and pointless, stuck, as it were, in a liminal phase. The verbs *alaiya* 'waiver, billow' and *alaipāya* 'billow, surge', in (430)[2] and (431)[3] respectively, seemed to convey meanings similar to *tiriya* 'wander', but did not focus on the subject's control or responsibility. In (432) *aṭikka* 'strike' seemed to convey the notion that the action was abrupt and uncontrolled,[4] much like the established attitudinal auxiliary *pōṭa* 'put'.

(429)a *avaṉ pēci.t tiritāṉ.*
he-NOM speak-CF wander-PST-3SM
'He speaks aimlessly.'

b *kaṅkāvai.p paṟṟi avatūṟu pēci.t tirikiṟa kaṉēcaṉiṭam avaḷ*
Ganga-ACC about slander speak-CF wander-PRES-ANP Ganesan-LOC she-NOM
ōyāmal canṭaikku niṟkiṟāḷ.[5]
ceaselessly fight-DAT stand-PRES-3SF
'She ceaselessly fight with Ganesan, who goes around speaking slander about Ganga.'

c *anta.p paiyaṉ ōttu.t tirikiṟāṉ.*
that boy-NOM screw-CF wander-PRES-3SM
'That boy just screws around.'

(430) *inta.p payalkaḷ – eṉṉamō ellām tāṅkaḷē muṉṉāṭiyē terintu uṇṭu*
this fellows-NOM what-DUB all self-EMP before know-CF hold-CF
kiẓittu viṭa.p pōkiṟār pōla niṉaittu alaiyakiṟārkaḷ.
tear-CF leave-INF go-PRES-3P like think-CF wander-PRES-3P
'These fellows delude themselves, thinking that they could learn everything by themselves. Fat chance!'

1 This underscores the need to provide grammatical criteria and tests, rather than to rely solely on lexical resemblances or intuitions. It is a particular lexeme's interaction with the grammatical structures of Tamil that determines whether or not it is an indicative auxiliary verb.

2 Janakiraman (1976: 115).

3 Janakiraman (1966: 71).

4 The *kriyāviṉ taṟkālat tamiẓ akarāti*, a dictionary of Modern Tamil, claims (1992: 15) that *aṭi* 'strike' functions as both a modal and an indicative auxiliary. Although it did not pass our tests for auxiliaryhood with our respondents, it may serve as an indicative auxiliary in other dialects.

5 Jeyakantan (1978: 11).

(431) *patiṉāyira.k kaṇakkilē ūrellām ṭeṇṭar koṭuttu viṭṭu alaipāyaṟār=ē*
10,000 count-LOC town.all tender give-CF leave-CF wander-PRES-3N=EMP
eṅkaḷ mutalāḷi, avar eppaṭi iruppār?
our rich.man he-NOM how be-FUT-3H
'And how would our friend, the rich man, be if he frittered away tenders worth tens of thousands of rupees all over town?'

(432) *avaḷ alaṟi aṭittāḷ.*
she-NOM shriek-CF beat-PST-3SF
'She shrieked out.'

Further, in (433a),[6] *koṭṭa* 'pour' appeared to convey a negative evaluation and, like *taḷḷa* 'push', accelerative aspect. But whereas *taḷḷa* was susceptible of both pejorative and admirative readings, *koṭṭa* admitted only a pejorative reading. The verb *kaṭṭa* 'tie' in (433b)[7] appeared to convey a sense of force and single-mindedness that the subject brings to accomplish the event named by the main verb. *eṭukka* 'take' in (433c)[8] appeared to contribute the nuance, according to Fedson (1981), that the action was viewed as an ordeal. It resembles *vaẓiya* 'drip' in meaning, except that some external force holds the subject suspended in the liminal phase, the ordeal. In (433d and e),[9] the verb *viẓa* 'fall' seems the opposite of *vaẓiya*: it signals a movement into a personal state that can be violent. Finally, *niṟka* 'stand' seemed to be an attitudinal counterpart to *kiṭakka* 'lie' (434).[10]

(433)a *iṅklīṣil nāṅku pustakattai.p paṭittu viṭṭu ulaṟi koṭṭukiṟāṉ.*
English-LOC all book-ACC read-CF leave-CF babble-CF pour-PRES-3SM
'He reads a bunch of English books, then babbles on about them.'

b *anta nīṇṭa muṉṉuraikku oru muḷai aṟaintu kaṭṭiṉār.*
that long preface-DAT one point strike-CF tie-PST-3SF
'He drove home the point of that long preface.'

c *inta.k kēḷvi toṇṭaraiĪ. ampāka tuḷaittu eṭuttu viṭṭatu.*
this question-NOM devotee-ACC arrow-ADV pierce-CF take-CF leave-PST-3N
'This question pierced (and festered in) the devotee like an arrow.'

d *viciṟiyāl viciṟi koṇṭē tūṅki viẓukiṉṟaṉar.*
fan-INSTR fan-CF hold-CF=EMP sleep-CF fall-PRES-3P
'They are nodding off to sleep as they keep fanning with the fan.'

e *erintu viẓintāḷ muṉiyammāḷ.*
burn-CF fall-PST-3SF Muniyammal)-NOM
'Muniyammal fell/burst into a rage.'

6 Fedson (1981: 289).
7 Fedson (1981: 289).
8 Fedson (1981: 251).
9 Fedson (1981: 291), Jeyakantan (1958: 110).
10 In Middle Tamil, this verb served as a (nonattitudinal) auxiliary in the perfect tense series (see Steever 1993). It is conceivable that in certain dialects it acquired a new value as auxiliary *irukka* 'be' consolidated its position as the auxiliary of the perfect tense series in Modern Tamil.

(434) *kaṭaiciyil avar pēccu maṟupaṭiyum anta vaẓakkamāṉa viṣayattukk=ē*
finally his talk-NOM again that usual matter-DAT=EMP
vantu nikkaṟatu.
come-CF stand-PRES-3N
'Finally, his talk returned to the usual topic.'

Tempting as it was to regard these candidates as instances of attitudinal auxiliaries and therefore to discover, in contrast to general expectations, a potentially open-ended class of auxiliaries, they all failed our tests for auxiliaryhood with respondents. A discursive characterization of the candidates' apparent lexical properties, however plausible or elegant, is insufficient to add them to the class of auxiliary phenomena. Indeed, their superficial resemblance to indicative AVCs demonstrates just how crucial the application of those tests is in determining which sequences contain auxiliaries and which do not. Such constructions might have continued to masquerade as AVCs, and such verbs as auxiliaries, had not our model compelled us to look at linguistic data and behavior that others had ignored.

Nonetheless, these examples suggest how some indicative auxiliaries may arise within the context of Tamil syntax. As stated above, these collocations behave more like what we have been calling lexical compound verbs with one important exception: they reverse the usual order of modifier-modified that is characteristic of lexical compounds. Recall that Chapter 3 presented examples of some lexical compounds allow the permutation of the two constituent verbs. The first verb in a lexical compound typically modifies the second, specifying manner or direction. If the unmarked order in (435a) is reversed so that the second verb comes to qualify the first, as in (435b), the resulting collocation then resembles the surface word order characteristic of the auxiliate and auxiliary in a Tamil AVC.

(435)a *avaḷ puruṇṭu uraṇṭāḷ.*
she-NOM turn-CF roll-PST-3SF
'She writhed.'

b *avaḷ uraṇṭu puruṇṭāḷ.*
she-NOM roll-CF turn-PST-3SF
'She writhed.'

All things being equal, it is plausible that an auxiliary such as *vaẓiya* 'drip' (Chapter 8) could have followed this developmental path, originating as part of a lexical compound, undergoing transposition and subsequently being reanalyzed as an auxiliary. Unfortunately, the dearth of attestations of attitudinal auxiliaries in earlier texts, the majority of which are in compact verse, may make philological confirmation of this proposal difficult. Nevertheless, this situation suggests a variety of studies that may be pursued for Modern Tamil, such as dialect comparison and language acquisition studies. Nor should we despair of discovering further attitudinal or, indeed, nonattituduinal auxiliaries in Tamil. During the history of Tamil, normative pressure appears to have been exerted primarily on the diglossic "high" variety, *centamiẓ*, but not the various regional and social dialects that cover the "low" variety, *koṭuntamiẓ*. Additionally, with literacy traditionally at low levels (only recently has it reached about 55%), there have not been strong media channels through which such normative influence might flow. Thus, with no brake on the centripetal forces that encourage dialect differentiation, auxiliary systems in each dialect might easily diverge from those in the other dialects. That being the case, it is very likely that the study of various dialects will reveal lexical and other variations that were not encountered in our corpus.

Verbal categories

Another potentially rich topic for study are the verbal categories of Tamil. Their analysis, still very much in its infancy, will benefit from intensive research of the basic verb forms in Chapter 3, as well as an analysis of the modal auxiliaries. This is the first time the category of status has been proposed for Tamil; further research will elaborate its form, meaning and use. Another first, the category of attitude, should prove useful in describing certain auxiliary phenomena in languages other than Tamil. Care must be taken at the very start, however, not to confuse these various terms with the ways in which they have been used in other linguistic studies. For example, our definition of status differs from that used in Slavic linguistics, but so long as we take heed of their different underlying definitions, we can avoid the needless confusion that might arise from equivocation over terminology.

Other Dravidian languages, many of which appear to have robust auxiliary verb systems, provide strong indications of attitudinal auxiliaries. The examples noted here concentrate mainly on attitudinals since the nonattitudinal auxiliaries are more easily found in grammars and the specialist literature.[11] Potential attitudinal auxiliaries in Kannada include *hāku* 'throw' (similar to Tamil *pōṭa* 'put') *esu* 'cast', *tīr* 'exhaust' (cognate with Tamil *tīrkka* 'id.'), *kisi* 'grin' and *hōgu* 'go', the last two of which are exemplified here.[12]

(436)a *avanu* *māḍi* *kisita.*
he-NOM do-PST-CF grin-PST-3SM
'He doesn't work well.'

b *māḍi* *koṇḍu* *hōguvavaru* *hōguttāre.*
do-CF hold- PST-CF go-FUT-VN-3P go-PRES-3P
'People who are accustomed to do such things will continue to do them.'

Kannada also has a slew of nonattitudinal auxiliary verbs such as *iru* 'be', *biḍu* 'leave', *koḍu* 'give', *baru* 'come', and *nōḍu* 'look at', whose functions resemble their Tamil counterparts—and save for the last, cognates—*irukka* 'be', *viṭa* 'leave',

11 Here the grammatical labels in the interlinear glosses are merely aids to the reader, and do not reflect the kind of morphological analysis undertaken for Tamil in Chapter 3.

12 Note that unlike its apparent Tamil counterpart, the auxiliary *pōka* 'go', the Kannada auxiliary *hōgu* 'go' may occur without an auxiliate. The auxiliary *hōguttāre* 'they go' occurs without the (complex) auxiliate *māḍi koṇḍu* 'doing', although it is directly recoverable from context.

koṭukka, 'give', *vara* 'come' and *pārkka* 'look at', respectively. See Bhat (1979), Sridhar (1990) and, especially, Brown (1997) for further examples and analysis of the Kannada auxiliary system.

Telugu (Subbarao 1979), the Dravidian language with the greatest number of speakers, has its share of apparent auxiliaries, some of which may be considered attitudinal in nature.

(437)a *āme ilāṭi vedhava pani cēsi kūrcondi.*
she-NOM such bad work do-CF sit-PST-3SN
'She really did a bad job.'

b *rāma sītāni aḍigi cāwaḍu.*
Rama-NOM Sita-ACC ask-CF die-FUT-NEG-3SM
'Rama (stubbornly) won't ask her.'

c *rāmayya ī pani iṣṭaw̃ waccinaṭlu cēsi pārēsāḍu.*
Ramayya-NOM this work like come-PST-ANP-AS do-CF throw-PST-3SM
'Ramayya did this work as he please (carelessly).'

d *nēnu ī pani cēsi wēstānu.*
I-NOM this work do-CF toss-FUT-1S
'I will certainly do this work.'

There are also nonattitudinal auxiliary verbs such as *kon* 'hold' (cognate with Tamil *koḷḷa* 'hold'). See Krishnamurti and Gwynn (1985) for further details.

Malayalam (Nayar 1979) seems to have its share of attitudinal auxiliary verbs, as well. The Malayalam auxiliaries *pōka* in (438b) and *tulayuka* in (438c) are lexical cognates of their Tamil counterparts *pōka* 'go' and *tolaiya* 'get lost', respectively.

(438)a *bābu pāl nilattu oẓiccu kaḷannu.*
Babu milk floor-LOC pour-CF cast-PST
'Babu intentionally poured milk on the floor.'

b *balūṇ poṭṭi.p pōkum.*
balloon burst-CF go-FUT
'The balloon will get burst.'

c *avan ellām eẓuti.t tulaccu.*
he all write-CF destroy-PST
'He wrote and spoiled everything.'

d *naṭe tuṛannu kaẓinnu.*
door open-CF be.finished-PST
'The door has opened.'

Malayalam has other auxiliaries, as well: *vay* 'place' (cf. Tamil *vaikka* 'place'), *var* 'come' (cf. Tamil *vara* 'come'), *koḷ* 'contain' (cf. Tamil *koḷḷa* 'hold'), *koṭu* 'give' (cf. Tamil *koṭukka* 'id.'), and *nōkkuka* 'look at' (cf. Kannada *nōḍu* 'id'.). See Asher and Kumari (1997) for further analysis. Since Malayalam and Tamil are closely related languages, several tests for auxiliaryhood, but not all, may ultimately carry over from Tamil into Malayalam. Readers are forewarned, however, that since Malayalam lacks personal endings for finite verbs, arguments from Subject-Verb Agreement will have to be radically altered or abandoned altogether.

Ekka (1979) gives examples in Kurux, a North Dravidian language, of what seem to be attitudinal auxiliaries; they are often glossed as intensives with a nuance of unexpectedness.

(439)a *tammbas keppas xane sukri kirrim biccia.*
father scold-PST-3M because Sukri go-PST-EMP cook-PST-3F
'Because her father scolded her, Sukri ran away.'

b *jõxas eRpāti boṅṅgas keras.*
servant house-abl run-pst-3m go-pst-3m
'The servant suddenly ran off from the house.'

Auxiliary *biccia* 'cook' in (439a) denotes a completed action which was not expected. It may behave like Tamil *viṭa* 'leave', or like *pōṭa* 'put'. Example (439b) contains an example of a genuine serial verb formation functioning as an AVC: both the auxiliary and main verbs are inflected for congruent tense and personal endings. Auxiliary *keras* 'go' is completive and also expresses a nuance that the action was not expected.

Our analysis of the auxiliary verb system of Tamil raises several additional questions which have not been specifically addressed here. Is there an upper limit on the number and variety of grammatical categories a language can exhibit? Can the grammar of Tamil sustain the diversity of verbal categories it currently exhibits? Will historical change elaborate these various distinctions or whittle them down? All things being equal, it would appear that those auxiliaries with the most specific meanings and therefore lower frequency, such as *vaẓiya* 'ooze', would tend to be the most unstable and, therefore, liable to idiomaticization or loss. In effect, those auxiliaries that are least "locked in" to the network of grammatical oppositions would be most vulnerable to change. While these questions have been framed in diachronic terms, they may also be stated in terms of dialect variation.

Compound verbs

For this book truly to live up to its name requires a companion volume on the modal auxiliary verb system of Tamil. Since on our analysis modal auxiliaries minimally contrast with indicative auxiliaries, their analysis would naturally help us to refine our analysis of the indicative auxiliary system proposed here. Another class of phenomena that contrasts with indicative auxiliaries, what I have called lexical compounds, also deserves a separate study. It would open up a vast, unexplored area of Tamil grammar and, I hope, provide us with good grounds for abandoning the term lexical compound verb, which has been applied to them in this book as something of a makeshift, for something more apposite. Either one of these two topics would very likely result in a work as large at the present one.

Variation

How the Tamil auxiliary system varies across space, society and time calls for the appropriate geographical, sociolinguistic and historical studies. A study of indicative auxiliaries in Sri Lankan Tamil, for example, would provide us with an index of the extent to which that variety and the continental dialect described here have diverged. Some social dialect differences, reflecting primarily traditional caste distinctions, were preliminarily noted under the auxiliaries *koḷḷa* 'hold' (pp. 197-98) and *oẓiya* 'purge' (pp. 249-50), but hardly amount to a systematic treatment. It would be worthwhile in this context to revisit Dale's (1975) project of collecting systematic data from many different communities, armed this time with the results presented here.

Chapter 2 raised the possibility of historical linguistic studies of auxiliaries throughout the various stages of Tamil. This is in fact one topic in this section where we can point to established studies of the history of the Dravidian verb rather than having to issue what are, in effect, promissory notes to be redeemed by future study. Since we lack access to speakers of Old Tamil, alternative methods, including internal reconstruction, comparative methodology and philology, are needed to firmly establish the existence of AVCs in Old Tamil. For certain AVCs, such as the negative periphrastic conjugation, e.g., *celvēm allēm* 'we will not go', the demonstration of their auxiliaryhood is made easier by the fact that certain sister languages, such as Muria Gondi (Steever 1998: 290-91), preserve this construction morpheme for morpheme as an AVC to the present (Steever 1993: 114).

Historical studies of the Tamil auxiliary system naturally dovetail with comparative studies in the Dravidian languages, which would in turn promote areal studies for South Asia, as well as general typological studies. Comparison with other languages in the South Asian *Sprachbund*, most notably Indo-Aryan, might cast additional light on the mutual influence of Dravidian and Indo-Aryan. While superficially similar to the Dravidian auxiliary verb, Indo-Aryan compound verbs (Vale 1948, Hook 1974) appear to be substantially different, resembling more than anything else the lexical compounds of Tamil. Hindi compound verbs, for example, are negated only rarely and then with reservation while Tamil auxiliary compound verbs are easily negated. The elaborate Dravidian system could well be the model on which the Indo-Aryan system is calqued. Masica (1976) had conjectured that the opposite might be true because, given the data available to him at the time, the Hindi compound verbs seemed to outnumber their Tamil counterparts; however, a revised tally based on work such as this one might now suggest a different direction. Future study will help us determine the extent of mutual influence between the two groups, or whether each one developed its systems of compound verbs individually. The collection of papers in Verma (1993) plots some of the directions that areal research on compound verbs in the South Asian linguistic area, including auxiliaries, has taken.

On a parallel course, studies such as Heine (1993) and Kuteva (2001) have indicated how typological studies of auxiliaries have developed in roughly the same time frame. Also of interest to general linguistics is the role that auxiliary phenomena have played in the study of grammaticalization. For example, in proposing their model of grammaticalization, Hopper and Traugott (1993) have showcased the historical tendency of lexical verbs to develop into auxiliaries, then clitics, then affixes. In a simplified—perhaps oversimplified—reading, they appear to define an auxiliary as that which diachronically follows a lexical verb and precedes an affix. What is obviously lacking from this characterization is an independent synchronic definition of auxiliary that need not refer to the historical trajectory they propose. Our discussion of Auxiliary Formation appears to have more in common with Bybee, Perkins and Pagliuca's (1994) approach, which they call grammaticization. It is to be preferred because they view the typological and, perhaps, historical development of auxiliaries as a mapping of one construction into another, instead of the evolution of one lexical item into another linguistic element such as a clitic or affix.[13] Auxiliary Formation, as introduced here, thus holds the potential to enrich existing treatments of grammaticalization.

The very act of raising questions and proposing topics for further study creates in some sense a responsibility to provide solutions for them. While numerous questions about auxiliary verb phenomena and related topics both in Tamil and in other languages have been raised in this section and elsewhere in this book, the answers to many of them have not been provided here and are unlikely to be provided in the near future. The material resources needed to properly research and satisfactorily answer these issues, chief among them time, are simply not within the grasp of any one person. Nevertheless, I hope that I have discharged at least part of the responsibility this analysis has created by offering the model of Auxiliary Formation as a new means of framing and answering questions that arise in the study of auxiliary verb phenomena.

AUXILIARY FORMATION AS A GUIDE

Since its introduction in Chapter 1, Auxiliary Formation has maintained a relatively low profile throughout the exposition, taking on the role of an unobtrusive guide in our analysis of Tamil auxiliary verb phenomena. No attempt was made, as is commonly done, to promote its virtues over those of other models through a blow-by-blow comparison and tally of their relative merits and deficiencies. Not only would such an exercise inordinately lengthen this book, but it strikes me as premature and, from one perspective, it flatly misses the mark. Auxiliary Formation's worth lies not so much in what it can tell us about different linguistic theories, but what it can tell us about language and languages. Indeed, its primary value may be considered even more basic: it resides in how this model gets linguists to observe

13 In particular, Bybee et al. (1994: 11) indicate that they view the grammaticization of auxiliary phenomena as involving not merely independent words or affixes, but structures: "... in tracing the origin of grammatical meaning, we must attend to the syntax and morphology of the source construction and not simply to the referential meaning of its lexical items."

phenomena they might not have noticed under different circumstances; how it raises questions that they might not otherwise have asked; and how it suggests unfamiliar places to look for the answers to those questions. Here, Auxiliary Formation is offered as a cumulative and composite answer to these basic issues as they are raised and applied in the study of auxiliary verb phenomena, particularly those in Tamil.

First and foremost, the model of Auxiliary Formation asks us to treat auxiliary verb phenomena as objects of synchronic study, not merely as historical residue from earlier stages of a language or a source for new affixes. Without this model, auxiliaries are explained by reference to earlier stages of the language with the consequence that they are viewed synchronically as idioms and their analysis is effectively reduced to tracing how the meaning of certain verbs came to expand over time while their privileges of occurrence correspondingly shrank. With Auxiliary Formation as their guide, researchers are now compelled to look for connections and explanations within the synchronic grammar of the language.

Second, and no less important, Auxiliary Formation holds that the analysis of auxiliary phenomena transcends lexicography and necessarily involves morphology and syntax. Perhaps the turning point in Benveniste's treatment of Auxiliation was his realization that traditional treatments of auxiliaries did not provide a proper morphological segmentation of auxiliary constructions, thereby concentrating all auxiliary functions in the auxiliary verb and ignoring the potential contributions of the auxiliate and its form, as well as the AVC. Without Auxiliary Formation, the analysis of auxiliaries begins and ends in the lexicon so that all linguistic generalizations focus on individual words; with Auxiliary Formation, the analysis of auxiliaries is now referred to a designated construction, the AVC, and so necessarily involves the morphological and syntactic dimensions of language structure.

Without Auxiliary Formation and its insistence on proper morphological analysis, all auxiliary functions are ascribed to the lexical entry of individual auxiliary verbs. As a result, the choice between infinitive and conjunctive as the auxiliate's form is treated as largely random and devoid of grammatical consequence, a position taken by Lindolm (1975) and Fedson (1981). With Auxiliary Formation, however, analysis of the AVC follows proper procedures of morphological segmentation so that its functions are distributed over both the auxiliary and the auxiliate. In short, the structure and meaning of the AVC are both viewed as compositional, so that the structure and meaning of the whole is presumed to be a function of the structure and meaning of its component parts. This places the linguist in a position to ask which forms may, and which forms may not, serve as the form of an auxiliate, a question routinely bypassed in studies of the auxiliary. Analysis of the Tamil forms that may serve in this capacity led to the discovery of the invariant meanings of the infinitive and conjunctive form, expressed in terms of an opposition of mood between an unmarked modal and a marked indicative form. Beyond this specific result, the category of mood has proved useful elsewhere in the grammar of the language, receiving independent confirmation from its interaction with such diverse grammatical phenomena as modal polarity items (Chapter 3) and *ki*-echo Formation (Chapter 4).

With Auxiliary Formation's characterization of the AVC as a construction, it may be compared and contrasted with other, apparently similar constructions in the language. In one stroke, this enables us to distinguish the AVC from complex clauses and lexical compounds, on one hand, and to make more precise its intrinsic defining characteristics, on the other. Comparison with complex clauses indicates that each AVC, no matter how internally complex, has but one denotational function; comparison with lexical compounds, that the AVC's characteristic meaning elaborates the construction's grammatical, not its lexical, meaning.

Without Auxiliary Formation, an auxiliary's relation to the set of verb forms would be fortuitous; with Auxiliary Formation, the AVC is treated as a periphrastic verb, namely a construction that *ex hypothesi* has the properties of a verb. And if the AVC is a species of verb, we are then compelled to ask in what ways it differs from simple, nonauxiliated verbs. The answer, as has been urged here, is that the two constitute an opposition of unmarked simple verbs and marked periphrastic verbs. This aided us, for example, in our search for grammatical contexts in which such an opposition might be neutralized; confirmation of this hypothesis appears in Chapters 4, 5 and 6.

Further, without Auxiliary Formation, the interaction of auxiliaries with other syntactic phenomena in the language is viewed, again, as random and arbitrary. With Auxiliary Formation, however, the AVC is identified with a family of structures or derivations from which its interaction with other syntactic phenomena can be shown to follow. This model compels us to look for structures old and new that verify the structural analysis of the AVC. On the premise that the AVC functions as a single verb in its grammatical frame, as proposed in our model, we can now predict how it will interact with such rules as Clefting and Right Dislocation. On the premise that the auxiliate bears the AVC's denotational function, we can also predict much of its interaction with S-deletion, Negation, Causation and *ki*-echo Formation. Prior to this analysis, no one had provided empirical arguments for a derivation of the AVC; indeed, after Schiffman (1969) concluded that the underlying structures of auxiliary phenomena in Tamil must differ radically from their English counterparts, researchers largely abandoned attempts to provide an explicit analysis of the syntactic structure of Tamil auxiliary verbs, generally retreating into protracted and dilatory lexical analysis.

In first separating, then correlating, the lexical, morphological, syntactic and semantic dimensions of auxiliary phenomena, Auxiliary Formation opens the possibility of studying the various facets of the AVC independently, in particular without constant reference to the particular auxiliaries that appear in it. Accordingly, this model prompts us to ask which contexts require, and which prohibit, AVCs, leading in turn to the discovery in Chapter 5 of how both discursive speech and reported speech may influence the distribution of AVCs and the verbal categories they convey in Tamil utterances, something no previous analysis had proposed.

Because meaning is the primary criterion for establishing morphological units, structures and boundaries, it comes as no surprise that compositionality applies in semantics as well. Without Auxiliary Formation, the meaning conveyed by an AVC need not bear any consistent relation to the meanings of its constituent parts, a position advanced in one case by Herring (1991); as a result, the meaning of any particular auxiliary could be viewed as an obscure idiom resistent to analysis. With Auxiliary Formation and its robust presumption of compositionality, the AVC's denotational and inflectional functions are associated with both the auxiliary and the auxiliate in a well-defined manner. From this it follows that the study of verbal categories is central to the analysis of AVCs, a position not systematically considered before. It also supported the discovery of the verbal categories of status and attitude in Tamil, as well as their characteristic grammatical behavior, leading in turn to led to more specific semantic analyses of individual auxiliaries than had hitherto appeared in the literature. And as the "new" categories of mood, status and attitude came into sharper focus, the corresponding definitions of aspect, tense and voice were clarified; in particular, freed from the burden of describing all indicative auxiliaries, the category of aspect could be applied with greater rigor to a subset of verbal phenomena in Tamil.

Since on this model individual auxiliaries do not carry the entire burden of auxiliary-related properties, more attention could be paid to the analysis of the twenty-five individual auxiliaries without encumbering their descriptions with extraneous, indeed misleading, material. Without the requirement of compositionality, for example, the mismatch between formal tense and time reference of the auxiliaries *kiẓiya* 'get torn' and *kiẓikka* 'tear' in Chapter 8 might have been treated as a mere idiom, and their unique semantics overlooked. In the same vein, the correlation between formal tense marking and status in auxiliary *irukka* 'be located' in Chapter 6 would most likely not have been recognized. By relieving individual auxiliaries of the sole responsibility of encapsulating all the morphosyntactic and semantic properties of auxiliary phenomena, Auxiliary Formation has somewhat paradoxically helped to promote a more focused and concerted lexicographic analysis of auxiliary verbs. This led us to conclude, for example, that verbs of motion dominate the set of potential auxiliaries and that verbs of indeterminate motion and goal are favored for attitudinal auxiliaries.

The morphosyntactic opposition between unmarked simple verb forms and marked AVCs is also reflected in their respective semantics. In general, the characteristic meanings of AVCs prove to be more specific than the meanings of the basic verb forms of the language. This opposition also prompted us to ask, for example, what semantically distinguishes simple tense-forms from their periphrastic counterparts. This led us to conclude in Chapters 3, 6 and 8, for example, that while periphrastic tense-forms are positively marked for reference to temporal intervals, simple tense-forms are unmarked.

Without Auxiliary Formation, auxiliary verb phenomena might be viewed as decorative, even annoying, grammatical idiosyncrasies of a language, a reaction not unknown to students of Tamil. With Auxiliary Formation, we are obliged to ask what functions AVCs serve within the grammar of the language. We come to see that AVCs are means of encoding verbal categories that are not expressed in the simple verb forms of the language. In the case of Tamil at least, AVCs are generated in part to compensate for the paucity of the major parts of speech in the language. The verbal categories of taxis, status and attitude, in particular, make up for the lack of basic conjunctions, adverbs and other sentential connectives in the language as well as the syntactic and communicative functions that are popularly associated with them. Perhaps it is because basic verb forms such as the infinitive and conjunctive already serve to express primitive interclausal relations in Tamil that the process Auxiliary Formation elaborates them, in the shape of AVCs, to amplify and extend their primal function. It is this property of AVCs, which Annamalai (1982) calls verbal extension, that makes Tamil such a good proving ground for the model of Auxiliary Formation, where many of its consequences may be followed and amply illustrated.

Auxiliary Formation is in any event a guide, not a master; a linguist must still exercise judgment in its use, and not rely on it as a discovery procedure. Whether there are one or two auxiliaries *viṭa* 'leave', for example, must still be decided on the basis of further empirical study. As advertised in Chapter 1, however, the model of Auxiliary Formation is robust enough to embrace this kind of variation. And although the model's methodology requires that we seek compositionality in our analysis of AVCs, the study of individual AVCs has revealed that this formal and semantic transparency may be lost over time, often as a prelude to a historical linguistic change (Steever 1993).

The foremost goal of this book has been to enhance our understanding and appreciation of the Tamil auxiliary verb system by bringing Auxiliary Formation to bear on its analysis. To that end, I believe the model of Auxiliary Formation has proved its usefulness in leading to a more systematic and insightful analysis of the Tamil auxiliary verb system than has hitherto appeared. Clearly, however, this model also has implications both for the study of auxiliary verb phenomena in other langugages, and for how such phenomena may eventually be incorporated into a model of universal grammar. But even in that lofty realm, the substantive legacy of our analysis will reside less in the formalisms or the programs of linguistic analysis it has employed and more in the way it gets linguists to look at the structure, meaning and use of auxiliary verb phenomena. If the model of Auxiliary Formation can suggest new kinds of questions for linguists to ask about auxiliary verb phenomena, unusal places to look for answers to those questions and untried connections with other dimensions of linguistic structure that they might not have considered before, it will have fulfilled much of its promise for enhancing our study of language.

Bibliography

Agesthialingom, S. 1967. *A generative grammar of Tamil (a fragment of Tamil syntax)*. Department of linguistics publication no. 11. Annamalainagar: Annamalai University.

Akilan. 1951. *ciṉēkiti*. Madras: *pāri puttakap paṇṇai*.

āṉanta vikaṭaṉ. (A weekly magazine.) Madras: *vācaṉ papḷikēṣaṉs*.

Anderson, J. 1973. *An essay concerning aspect*. Janua Linguarum, Series Minor, 167. The Hague: Mouton.

Andronov, M. 1969. *A standard grammar of modern and classical Tamil*. Madras: New Century Book House.

Annamalai, E. 1997. *Adjectival clauses in Tamil*. Tokyo: Institute for the Study of Languages and Cultures of Asia and Africa, Tokyo University of Foreign Studies. (Publication of 1969 Ph.D. dissertation, University of Chicago.)

———. 1979. Aspects of aspect in Tamil. *International journal of Dravidian linguistics*, 8.260-67.

———. 1982. Dynamics of verbal extension in Tamil. *International journal of Dravidian linguistics*, 11.22-166.

——— and S.B. Steever. 1988. Modern Tamil. In S.B. Steever (ed.), *The Dravidian languages*.

Arden, A.H. 1891. *A progressive grammar of the Tamil language*. Madras: The Christian Literature Society.

Aronoff, M. 1975. *Word formation in generative grammar*. Cambridge: MIT Press.

Aronson, H. 1978. The interrelationship of mood and aspect in Bulgarian. *Folia slavica* 1.

Asher, R.E. 1966. The verb in spoken Tamil. In C.E. Bazell, J.C. Catford, M.A.K. Halliday and R.H. Robins (eds.), *In memory of J.R. Firth*, pp. 15-29. London: Longmans.

———. 1985. *Tamil*. London: Routledge.

——— and T.C. Kumari. 1997. *Malayalam*. London: Routledge.

Bennett, D. 1975. *Spatial and temporal uses of English prepositions: an essay in stratificational semantics*. London: Longman.

Bennett, M. 1981. Of tense and aspect: one analysis. In P. Tedeschi and A. Zaenen (eds.), 1981.13-30.

Benveniste, E. 1946. Structure des relations de personne dans le verbe. *Bulletin de Société Linguistique* 43.

———. 1948. *Noms d'agent et noms d'action en indo-europeen*. Paris: Adrien Maisonneuve.

———. 1959. Les relations de temps dans le verbe. *Bulletin de Societe Linguistique*, 54.69-82.

———. 1965. Structure des relations d'auxiliarité. *Acta Linguistica Hafniensia* 9.1-15.

———. 1966. *Problèmes de linguistique générale* 1. Paris: Gallimard.
———. 1968. Mutations of linguistic categories. In W.P. Lehaman and Y. Malkiel (eds.), *Directions for historical linguistics*, pp. 83-94. Austin: University of Texas Press.
———. 1974. *Problèmes de linguistique générale* 2. Paris: Gallimard.
Bhat, D.N.S. 1979. Vectors in Kannada. *International journal of Dravidian linguistics* 8.300-309.
Bharattiyar, S. 1962. *pāratiyar kavitaikaḷ*. Madras: *paẕaṉiyappa pirantars*.
Bloch, J. 1946. *Structure grammaticale des langues dravidiennes*. Paris: Adrien-Maisonneuve.
Bolinger, D. 1971. *The phrasal verb in English*. Cambridge: Harvard University Press.
Bright, W. and J. Lindenfeld. 1968. Complex forms in colloquial Tamil. In Bh. Krishnamurti (ed.), *Studies in Indian linguistics*, pp. 30-45. Annamalainagar: Centre for Advanced Studies in Linguistics.
Britto, F. 1986. *Diglossia: a study of the theory, with application to Tamil*. Foreword by C. Ferguson. Washingto, DC: Georgetown University Press.
Brown, P.J. 1997. Explicator compound verbs in Kannada. Unpublished Ph.D. dissertation, La Trobe University.
Bybee, J., R. Perkins and W. Pagliuca. 1994. *The evolution of grammar: tense, aspect, and modality in the languages of the world*. Chicago: The University of Chicago Press.
Caldwell, R. 1856. *A comparative grammar of the Dravidian or South-Indian family of languages*. Reprinted in 1976 by The University of Madras Press, Chennai.
Cāminātaiyar, U. Vē. 1982. *eṉ catittiram*. Chennai: *cāminātaiyar nūl nilaiyam*.
Carden, G. and D. Pesetsky. 1977. Double-verb constructions, markedness, and a fake co-ordination. *Papers from the Thirteenth Regional Meeting*, pp. 82-92. Chicago: Department of Linguistics, University of Chicago.
Chevillard, J-L. 1998. *Le commentaire de Cēṉāvaraiyar sur le Collatikāram du Tolkāppiyam*. Pondicherry: Institut Français de Pondichéry.
Christdas, P. 1988. The phonology and morphology of Tamil. Ph.D. dissertation, Department of Linguistics, Cornell Universirty.
Chomsky, N. 1957. *Syntactic structures*. Janua Linguarum, Series Minor, 4. The Hague: Mouton.
———. 1965. *Aspects of the theory of syntax*. Cambridge: MIT Press.
Clackson, J.P.T. 2004. Latin. In R. Woodard (ed.), *The Cambridge encyclopedia of the world's ancient languages*, pp. 789-811. Cambridge: Cambridge University Press.
Comrie, B. 1976. *Aspect*. Cambridge: Cambridge University Press.
———. 1981. On Reichenbach's approach to tense. *Papers from the Seventeenth Regional Meeting*, pp. 24-30. Chicago: Department of Linguistics, University of Chicago.
Corre, A.D. 1962. The structure of Tamil. Unpublished Ph.D. dissertation, University of Pennsylvania.
Croft, W. 2003. *Typology and universals*. Cambridge: Cambridge University Press.
Dale, I. 1975. Tamil auxiliary verbs. Unpublished Ph.D. dissertation, School of Oriental and African Studies, University of London.
Davidson, D. 1980. *Essays on actions and events*. Oxford: Clarendon Press.
Deigner, J. 2000. *Syntaktische analyse von Verbalpartizip und Infinitiv in modernen Tamil* (Beiträge zur Kenntnis südasiaticher Sprchen und Literaturen, 5). Wiesbaden: Harrassowitx Verlag.
diṉa maṇi. (Daily newspaper.) Chennai.
diṉa tanti. (Daily newspaper.) Chennai and Madurai.

Dixon, R.M.W. 1976. Syntactic orientation as a semantic property. In J. McCawley (ed.) 1976: 347-362.

Douglas, M. 1966. *Purity and danger*. London: Routledge and Kegan Paul.

———. 1975. *Implicit meanings*. London: Routledge and Kegan Paul.

Dowty, D. 1979. *Word meaning and Montague grammar*. Dordrect: D. Reidel Publishing Company.

Dupuis, J. 1863. *Grammaire française-tamoule, où les régles du tamoul vulgaire, celles de la langue rélevée, et celles de la poésie se trouvent exposés*. Pondicherry: Imprimerie des Missionaires Apostaliques.

Ekka, F. 1979. Some apsects of Kūṛux aspect. *International Journal of Dravidian Linguistics*, 8.277-284.

Emeneau, M. 1938. Echo-words in Toda. *New Indian Antiquary*, 1.98-112.

———. 1939. Another example of the echo-word motif in Dravidian folktales. *Journal of the American Oriental Society*, 59.503-05.

———. 1965. *Collected papers: Dravidian linguistics, ethnology, and folklore*. Berkeley: University of California Press.

Fabricius, J. 1972. *Tamil and English dictionary*. Tranquebar: Evanhelical Lutheran Mission Publishing House.

Fabricius, J. and C. Breithaupt. 1789. *A grammar for learning the principles of the Malabar language, properly called Tamul of the Tamulian language*. Reprinted by the Scholar Press, Menton.

Fedson, V. 1981. The Tamil serial or compound verb. Unpublished Ph.D. dissertation, University of Chicago.

———. 1993. Complex verb-verb predicates in Tamil. In M.K. Verma (ed.), *Complex predicates in South Asian languages*, pp. 63-76. New Delhi: Manohar.

Freed, A. 1976. The semantics of English aspectual complementation. Ph.D. dissertation, Department of Linguistics, University of Pennsylvania.

Frieden, R. 1975. The analysis of passives. *Language* 51.384-405.

Friedman, V. 1977. *The grammatical categories of the Macedonian indicative*. Columbus: Slavica Publishers, Inc.

———. 1979. Toward a typology of status: Georgian and other non-slavic languages of the Soviet Union. In Clyne et. al. (eds.), *The elements: A parasession on linguistic units and levels*, pp. 339-350. Chicago: Department of Linguistics, University of Chicago.

Friedrich, P. 1974. On aspect theory and Homeric aspect. *International Journal of American Linguistics* (Memoirs 28), 40, 2. Pt. 2.

Grice, H. P. 1975. Logic and conversation. In Cole and Morgan (eds.), *Syntax and semantics 3: Speech acts*, pp. 41-58. New York: Academic Press.

———. 1989. *Studies in the way of words*. Cambridge: Harvard University Press.

Gruber. J. 1976. *Lexical structures in syntax and semantics*. Amsterdam: North-Holland Publishing Company.

Halliday, M.A.K. and R. Hasan.1976. *Cohesion in English*. London: Longmans.

Haugen, E. 1987. Danish, Norwegian and Swedish. In B. Comrie (ed.), *The world's major languages*, pp. 157-179. London: Croom Helm.

Heine, B. 1993. *Auxiliaries*. New York: Oxford University Press.

Herring, S. 1991. Functions of the verb in Tamil narration. Ph.D. dissertation, Department of Linguistics, University of California, Berkeley.

Hoffman, T.R. 1966. Past tense replacement and the modal system. Harvard University report NSF-20. Reprinted in J. McCawley (ed.) 1976b, pp. 85-100.

Holisky, D. 1981. Aspect theory and Georgian aspect. In Tedeschi and Zaenen (eds.) 1981, pp. 127-144.

Hook, P. 1974. *The compound verb in Hindi.* Ann Arbor: Center for South and Southeast Asian Studies, University of Michigan.

Hopper, P. and E. C. Traugott. 1993. *Grammaticalization.* Cambridge: Cambridge University Press.

Jakobson, R. 1971. Shifters, verbal categories and the Russian verb. In *Selected writings II: word and language*, pp. 130-147. The Hauge: Mouton.

Janakiraman, Ti. 1966. *ammā vantāḷ.* Madurai: *mīṉāṭci puttaka nilaiyam.*

———. 1976. *mōka muḷ.* Madurai: *mīṉāṭci puttaka nilaiyam.*

———. 1980. *koṭṭu mēḷam.* Madurai: Vayal Publishers.

Jesperson, O. 1965. *The philosophy of grammar.* New York: W.W. Norton and Company.

Jeyakantan, Ta. 1958. *oru piṭi cōṟu.* Madurai: *mīṉāṭci puttaka nilaiyam.*

———. 1970. *cila nēraṅkaḷil cila maṉitarkaḷ.* Madurai: *mīṉāṭci puttaka nilaiyam.*

———. 1973. *jeyakāntaṉ ciṟukataikaḷ.* New Delhi: National Book Trust.

———. 1978. *kaṅkai eṅkē pōkiṟāḷ?* Madurai: *mīṉāṭci puttaka nilaiyam.*

Johnson, M. 1981. A unified temporal theory of tense and aspect. In Tedeschi and Zaenen (eds.), 1981, pp.145-176.

Jottimuttu, P. 1956. *A guide to Tamil.* Madras: The Christian Literature Society.

Kachru, Y. 1993. Verb serialization in syntax, typology and historical change. In Verma (ed.) 1993, pp. 115-134.

Kandaih, T. 1967. The syntax of the verb in Ceylon Tamil. Unpublished Ph.D. dissertation, University of London.

Karttunen, L. 1974. Presupposition and linguistic context. *Theoretical Linguistics*, 1.181-194.

———. 1976. Discourse referents. In McCawley (ed.) 1976, pp.363-386.

Keane, E. 2001. Echo words in Tamil. Unpublished Ph.D. dissertation, Oxford University.

Keay, J. 2000. *The great arc.* New York: Harper Collin Publishers.

Kothandaraman, Pon. 1977. *The verb in modern Tamil.* Chennai: Pulamai Press.

kriyāviṉ taṟtālat tamiḻ akarāti. 1992. Chennai: Cre-A.

Krishnamurti, Bh. 2003. *The Dravidian languages.* Cambridge University Press.

——— and J.P.L. Gwynn. 1985 *A grammar of modern Telugu.* Delhi: Oxford University Press.

Kurylowicz, J. 1973. *Esquisses linguistics I.* Munich: Wilhelm Fink Verlag.

Kuteva, T. 2001. *Auxiliation: an enquiry into the nature of grammaticalization.* Oxford: Oxford University Press.

Laksmi. 1983. *oru kāviriyaip pōla...* Chennai: *pūṅkoṭi patippakam.*

Lees, R. 1960. The grammar of English nominalizations. *International Journal of American Linguistics*, 26.3.

Lehmann, T. 1989. *A grammar of modern Tamil.* Pondicherry: Pondicherry Institute of Linguistics and Culture.

———. 1994. *Grammatik des Alttamil.* Stuttgart: Steiner Verlag.

———. 1998. Old Tamil. In S. Steever (ed.), *The Dravidian languages*, pp. 75-99.

Levinson, S. 2000. *Presumptive meanings.* Cambridge: MIT Press.

Lindholm, J. 1969. The role of *iru* 'be' in a grammar of Tamil. Unpublished M.A. thesis, University of Chicago.

———. 1971. Cleft sentences in Tamil and Malayalam. In V.I. Subramonian (ed.), *Proceedings of the first conference on Dravidian linguists*, pp. 296-306. Trivandrum: Dravidian Linguistics Association.

———. 1975. The conceptual basis of the Tamil adverbial participle. Unpublished Ph.D. dissertation, University of Chicago.

Lyons, J. 1977. *Semantics 2.* Cambridge: Cambridge University Press.

Masica, C. 1976. *Defining a linguistic area: South Asia.* Chicago: University of Chicago Press.

McCawley, J.D. 1975. Morphological indeterminacy in underlying syntactic structure. In F. Ingeman (ed.), *1975 Mid-America linguistics conference.* Lawrence: University of Kansas.

———. 1976a. Remarks on what can cause what. In M. Shibatani (ed.), *Syntax and semantics 6: The grammar of causative constructions.* New York: Academic Press.

———. 1976b. *Syntax and semantics 7: Notes from the linguistic underground.* New York: Academic Press.

———. 1979a. *Adverbs, vowels and other objects of wonder.* Chicago: University of Chicago Press.

———. 1979b. Presupposition and discourse structure. In C. Oh and D. Dinnen (eds.), *Syntax an semantics 9: Presupposition.* New York: Academic Press.

———. 1982. *Thirty million theories of grammar.* Chicago: University of Chicago Press.

———. 1988. *The syntactic phenomena of English, vols. I and II.* Chicago: University of Chicago Press.

———. 1993. *Everything that linguists have always wanted to know about logic (but were ashamed to ask).* Chicago: University of Chicago Press.

McCoard, R. 1978. *The English perfect: Tense-choice and pragmatic inferences.* Amsterdam: North-Holland Publishing Company.

Morgan, J. 1972. Verb agreement as a rule of English. *Papers from the eighth regional meeting*, pp. 278-286. Chicago: Department of Linguistics, University of Chicago.

Nayar, V.R. 1979. Aspectual system in Malayalam. *International Journal of Dravidian Linguistics*, 8.289-299.

Paramasivam, K. 1971. Verbal nouns in literary Tamil. In V.I. Subramonian (ed.), *Proceedings of the first conference of Dravidian linguists*, pp. 240-46. Trivandrum: Dravidian Linguistics Association.

———. 1979. *Effectivity and causativity in Tamil.* Trivandrum: Dravidian Linguistics Association.

———. 1983. *ikkāla.t tamiẓ marapu.* Sivagangai.

Patmanapan, Ni. 1977. *yāttirai, aṉupavaṅkaḷ, camar.* Madurai: Muttu Patippakam.

Pope, G. 1855. *A handbook of the Tamil language.* Chennai.

Pullam, G. and D. Wilson. 1977. Autonomous syntax and the analysis of auxiliaries. In *Language* 53.741-788.

puṟanāṉūṟu. 1958. Madras: *pāri nilaiyam.*

Ramanujan, A.K. and E. Annamalai. 1968. Materials for a reference grammar of Tamil. Unpublished manuscript, University of Chicago.

Ramaswamy, K. 1978. Correlative clauses in Tamil. Unpublished paper read at the Twentieth Seminar on Dravidian Syntax. Annamalainagar: Centre for Advanced Studies in Linguistics.

Reichenbach, H. 1947. *Elements of symbolic logic.* New York: Free Press.

Renou, L. 1938. Le suffix védique *-tṛ-* et les origines du futur périphrastique. *Bullétin de la société linguistique* 39.101-132.

Ross, J.R. 1972. The category squish: endstation haputwort. In *Proceedings from the eighth regional meeting*, pp. 316-328. Chicago: Department of Linguistics, University of Chicago.

Sartre, J.P. 1943. *L'être et le néant: essai d'ontologie phénoménologique*. Paris: Gallimard.

Schiffman, H. 1969. A transformational grammar of the Tamil aspectual system. Ph.D. dissertation, University of Chicago. Published as volume 7 of *Studies in linguistics and language teaching*, Seattle.

———. 1999a. *A reference grammar of Spoken Tamil*. Cambridge: Cambridge University Press.

———. 1999b. The role of metaphor in the grammaticalization of aspect in Tamil. Paper presented in panel on spatial metaphors in language, American Anthropological Association. Chicago, November 1999.

Scholten, C.G.M. 1988. Principles of universal grammar and the auxiliary verb phenomenon. Ph.D. dissertation, Department of Linguistics, University of Maryland.

Searle, J. 1969. *Speech acts: an essay in the philosophy of language*. Cambridge: Cambridge University Press.

Shopen, T. 1971. Caught in the act. *Proceedings of the seventh regional meeting*, pp. 254-263. Chicago: Department of Linguistics, University of Chicago.

Spear, A. 1982. The Black English semi-auxiliary *come*. *Language*, 58.850-872.

Sridhar, S.N. 1990. *Kannada*. London: Routledge.

Stankiewicz, E. 1962. The interdependence of paradigmatic and derivational patterns. *Word*, 18.1-23.

Steever, S.B. 1979. Conversation and lexical structure. *Journal of Madurai Kamaragj University*, 8.1-12.

———. 1981. *Selected papers in Tamil and Dravidian linguistics*. Madurai: Muttu patippakam.

———. 1983. A study in auxiliation: the grammar of the indicative auxiliary verb system of Tamil. Ph.D. dissertation, Department of Linguistics, University of Chicago.

———. 1987. Tamil and the Dravidian languages. In B. Comrie (ed.), *The world's major languages*, pp. 725-746. London: Croom Helm.

———. 1988. *The serial verb formation in the Dravidian languages*. New Delhi: Motilal Banarsidass.

———. 1993. *Analysis to synthesis: The development of complex verb morphology in the Dravidian languages*. New York and Oxford: Oxford University Press.

———. 1996. Tamil writing. In Peter T. Daniels and William Bright (eds.), *The world's writing systems*, pp. 426-30. New York: Oxford University Press.

———. 1998. *The Dravidian languages*. London and New York: Routledge.

———. 2000. Review of J. Deigner. *Syntaktische analyse von Verbalpartizip und Infinitiv in modernen Tamil*. *JAOS* 120.

———. 2002a. Review of Harold Schiffman. *A reference grammar of spoken Tamil*. *Language* 78.314-316.

———. 2002b. Direct and Indirect Discourse in Tamil. In M. von Roncador and T. Gueldemann (eds.), *Reported Discourse: A Meeting Ground for Different Linguistic Domains*, pp. 91-108. Amsterdam: John Benjamins Publishing Co.

———. 2004. "Old Tamil," in R. Woodard (ed.), *The Cambridge encyclopedia of the world's ancient languages*, pp. 1015-1040. Cambridge: Cambridge University Press.

Subbraro, K. 1979. Secondary verbs in Telugu. *International Journal of Dravidian Linguistics*, 8.268-276.

Tamil lexicon. 1924-1939. Madras: University of Madras Press. (Reprinted 1982.)

Tamizvanan. 1962. *niyūyārkkil caṅkarlal*. Madras: *maṇmēkalai piracuram*.

Tedeschi, P. 1981. Some evidence for a branching-futures semantic model. In P. Tedeschi and A. Zaenen (eds.), 1981, pp. 239-270.

Tedeschi, P. and A. Zaenen. 1981. *Syntax and semantics 14: tense and aspect*. New York: Academic Press.

tirumantiram. 1962. Madras: Saiva Siddhanta Society.

tiruviḷaiyāṭal purāṇam: maturaikkāṇṭam. 1972. Madurai: *mīṉāṭci cuntarēcuvar tirukkōyil*.

tolkāppiyam collatikāram. 1974. Madras: Saiva Siddhanta Society.

Turner, V. *The ritual process*. Ithaca: Cornell University Press.

Vale, R.N. 1948. *Verbal composition in Indo-aryan*. Poona: Deccan College Post-graduate and Research Institute.

van Gennep, A. 1960. *The rites of passage*. Chicago: University of Chicago Press.

Vanamamalai, Na. 1964. *tamiẓār nāṭṭup pāṭalkaḷ*. Madras: New Century Book Book House.

Vendler, Z. 1957. Verbs and times. *Philosophical Review* 66.143-160.

———. 1967. *Linguistics in philosophy*. Ithaca: Cornell University Press.

Verma, M.K. (ed.). 1993. *Complex predicates in South Asian languages*. New Delhi: Manohar.

Vinson, J. 1943. *Manuel de la langue tamoule*. Paris: Imprimerie Nationale.

Whorf, B.L. 1938. Some verbal categories of Hopi. *Language* 14.275-286.

———. 1946. The Hopi language, Toreva dialect. In H. Hoijer (ed.), *Linguistic structures of native America*. New York: Viking Find.

———. 1956. *Language, thought, and reality*. Cambridge: MIT Press.

Zwicky, A. 1978. Arguing for constituents. *Proceedings from the forteenth regional meeting*, pp. 503-512. Chicago: Department of Linguistics, University of Chicago.

Index

accomplishment
57, 102, 172, 176, 236, 250, 280
achievement 57, 172, 236, 280
activity 57, 172, 175-176, 222, 248, 254 254, 264, 268; activity predicates 202
adjectival participle 67. *See also* adnominal verb form
adnominal verb form **67-68**
adverbial participle 78. *See* conjunctive form
affective lengthening (of vowels) 156
affective voice **57–59**, 278
affirmative paradigm 61
Affix-Hopping 9
agglutinating morphology 33, 55
āka 18, 36, 48, 93, 123, 170, **209–216**; agentivity 213; as marker of status 210, 214; as transitive verb 210; defective paradigm 170, 211; finite forms 170; selectional restrictions 211; with verbal noun auxiliate 212
Aktionsart 49
al 39. *See also āka*
alaipāya, as potential auxiliary 291
alaiya, as potential auxiliary 290
anaphor 124. *See* S-Deletion
Anderson, J. 26
Andronov, M. 54, 63
Annamalai, E. 31, 42, 49-51, 54, 68, 72, 111, 121, 169, 178, 179, 211, 233, 244, 250, 274, 302
antecedent 124
anterior interval 168, 179
anterior taxis 79
antipathy 243
antiperfect tense 65, **250–260**; displacement of tense and time reference 254; formal tense marking 251; Hopi impotential 259; imperfective converb 252; inertia future 258; liminalist hypothesis 260; possible forms 256; possible parallels 259; selectional restrictions 256; time reference 251; vs. perfect tense 254
apodosis 25, 71
Arden, A.H. 204
Aronoff, M. 208
Aronson, H. 24, 86, 179, 239
article 170
aruḷa 19, **285–288**; extended use 286; voice marking 285
Asher, R. 31, 54, 55, 60-62, 86, 295
aspect 24, 44; as a metonym 87; as a verbal category 24; distributive 196; punctual 187
aspectual class 57, 82, 254, 283. *See also* event type
aspectual division of events 242
aspectual strengthening 175
aṭikka, as potential auxiliary 290
attitude 7, 23, 159, **239–241,** 294; admirative 240, 272, 288; and person 241; causative formation 241; grammar 241; indirect discourse 241; pejorative 240, 268, 272; shifter 23; verbal category 23
AUX 2, 42, 161
auxiliaries (behavior of): in questions and answers 140, 241; lexicography 26; major 167; minor 167; relative order 160; sources for 25-28, 168
auxiliary (in Modern Tamil) 10, 16; abruptness 274-277; acceleration 268–273; anterior interval 168-185; antipathy 243-247; benedictive voice 285-288; benefactive voice 99, 229–231; completive 235–238; conjunctive

connector 195-208; definition 10; disjunctive connector 185-195; ditransitive 19; durative 220-225; exhaustion 277–281; fulfillment 209–216; intransitive 18; invariant meaning 167; judgment 232–234; perfect of nondiscursive speech 216-220; pointless transaction 260–263; relief 247-250; rules of thumb 3; subsequent action 225–229; transitive 18; turn for the worse 281-285; viscosity 263–268; vs. auxiliate 10
auxiliary balance 1, 44
auxiliary compound verb 5; attitudinal 6; conjunctive form 81; denotational function 6; infinitive 77; inflectional function 6
Auxiliary Formation 2, **9-12**, 20, 53, 72, 86, 142, 144, 160, 298-302; applied to AVC 134; conjunction strategy 21; cyclicity 20, 135; expressive function 13; external functions 13, 28–30; internal functions 13; semantic function 13, 22–25, 168; synchronic process 2; syntactic functions 13, 14–18
auxiliary verb construction: definition 9
auxiliary verbs 3; criteria for 45, 50
auxiliate 10, 16, 54, 60; denotational function 10, 68; vs. auxiliary 10
auxiliation **9–12**, 10; in grammaticalization 298. *See also* Auxiliary Formation
AVC 9; adverbial adjunct 96–97; complement clause 99; derivation 18, 91, 300; direct object 97; indirect object 99–101; multiple nesting 135, 161, 201; satellites 96–101; segmentation 12; skewed distribution 145; subject of 91–96; transitivity 12; underlying structure 91, 92; vs. simple verb 144. *See* auxiliary verb construction
aẓa 19, **260–263**; antibenefactive voice 164; vs. *koṭukka* 261; without overt auxiliate 262

backwards pronominalization 4
bare verb base 39
benedictive voice 285, **285–288**; vs. honorification 286
benefactive 99, 100
benefactive auxiliary: voice marking 231
beneficiary 100, 229; vs. indirect object 100
Bennett, M. 26, 177
Benveniste, E. 9, 16, 104, 110, 123, 143, 146, 177, 299
Bhat, D.N.S. 295
Bloch, J. 28, 41
body (of event) 57, 242
Bolinger, D. 20
bounded movement rules 111–120
Bright, W. 42, 161
Britto, F. 31
Brown, P. 295
Bybee, J. 298

c-command 36, 94
Caldwell, R. 41
Carden, G. 22
case 33; case marking 100
categorial grammar 93
causative: entailment 58; morphological 58, 60, 102, 106–108; operator 102; periphrastic 58, 102, 103–106; suffix 55; verb: *ceyya* 60, *paṇṇa* 60, *vaikka* 60; vs. effectivity 58
Causative Formation **102–107**, 241
centamiẓ 31, 285, 293
ceyya-emphatic 6, 77, 85, 87, 182-183
CF-Postposing **118–120**; formulation 118
Chomsky, N. 9, 43, 161
Chomsky-adjunction 18, 142
Christdas, P. 33
Clackson, J.P.T. 13
Clefting 17, 114, **114–116**; formulation 114
clitic 8, 33, 35, 61, 71, 86, 103, 108, 121, 128, 132-133, 159-160, 216, 298
coda (of event) 24, 57, 236, 242, 254
cohesion 168
collatikāram 37, 38, 46
comparative philology 40
complex clause 13, 88
complex sentence 35, 210; coordinate 35; subordinate 35
compositionality 13, 51, 54, 87, 299, 300
compound clause 4
compound verb 5, 48, 89, 90
conditional verb form 25, 48, 70, **71–74**; as hypercorrection of adnominal 72; concessive 71, 256; tense marking 72
conjugational patterns 55

Conjunction 22, 127–140
conjunctive connector 197–208
conjunctive form 70, **78–85**; use of 145
CF-Postposing. *See* Conjunctive Form Postposing
Conjunctive Form Postposing **118-120**; formulation 118
connector 23, 49
constituent structure combinatorics: gross 15; petty 16
context set 180, 184, 186, 189, 190, 191, 208, 216, 241
contexts of neutralization 6, 14, 87, 281
conventional implicature 110, 188, 245. *See also* presupposition
conversational implicature 65, 176, 190, 199, 218, 240, 245, 285
coordinate sentence 90, 225
Coordinate Structure Constraint 22, 89, 115, 117, 121
Corre, D. 127
cross-categorial derivation 21
cryptotype: aspect 54; event type 54; mood 54
CSC. *See* Coordinate Structure Constraint

Dale, I. 1, 38, 41, 42, 44-47, 127, 163, 206
Danish 21
Davidson, D. 102
dative subject 35, 100, 228, 237, 275
De Morgan Law (quantificational analog) 174
deep structure 15, 43; formation rules 14; morphological indeterminacy 16
deictic center 220; assimilation of 154
Deigner, J. 74
deletion site 124
delicacy of implication 44
denotational function (of auxiliate) 6, 10, 13, 21, 60
derivation 18, 53
designator 22
determiners 15, 28
deverbal noun 20, 68; as potential auxiliate 69
diglossia 31, 285, 293; high 31; low 31
direct discourse 36, **153–160**, 183; affective vowel lengthening 159; exclamations 159; vocative phrases 159
directed action 274
discours. *See* discursive speech
discursive speech **146–153**, 159
disjunctive connector 185–195
disjunctive taxis; epistemic 241
distributive pronoun 213
Dixon, R.M.W. 196
Douglas, M. 242, 250, 267
Dowty, D. 57, 102, 175, 258
Dravidian 21, 29, 40, 136, 294
Dupuis, J. 41
durative: auxiliary 220–238; durative contexts 139; stative predicate 175; vs. progressive 175

eccam 67
éffectif 147. *See* temporal organization
effective voice **57–59**
effectivity 55; vs. causativity 58; vs. transitivity 58
Ekka, F. 296
Emeneau, M.B. 136
emphatic verb form 132
eṉa 'say' 36
English 12, 13, 20; perfect 177, 210
epistemic interval 179
epistemic perfect 179, 252. *See* status
equational sentence 114
Equi-NP Deletion 19
ethical dative 230
eṭukka, as potential auxiliary 291
European structuralism 14
event: event time 254; event type 54. vs. action 211. *See also* achievement, accomplishment, activity, aspectual class, state
evidential 239, 240. *See also* status
evidentiality 159
existential quantifier 170
explicator compound verb 5
external syntax 88, 144-166

Fabricius, J. 40, 55
factitive verb 270
fake coordinate structures 22
Fedson, V. 1, 39, 41, 42, 47-49, 73, 79, 132, 169, 244, 250, 251, 264, 270, 299
finite verb 34-35, 54, 60, **61-66;** negative 66; paradigm 35
finiteness: as a syntactic property 60
Firth, J.R. 44
formation rules: deep structure 14; surface structure 15
frames: that prohibit AVCs **149–151**; that require AVCs **151-153**

free form: vs. bound form 33
Freed, A. 57, 76
French 11, 13, 147; aorist 147; imperfect 147; perfect tense series 11; pluperfect 147; present of definition 147; prospective future 147;
Friedin, R. 20
Friedman, V. 25, 239
Friedrich, P. 56
fusional morphology 55, 57, 65
future tense 64
future-oriented complement 126

gender 23, 33, 65
generalized connector 23, 167, 198, 195, 208
generative grammar 14, 37, 42, 161
German 20; addressee passive 27
grammatical categories 22
grammatical formatives (of Tamil) 60–66
grammatical pun 129
grammatical relations 100
grammaticalization 8, 298
grammaticization 298
Greek 40
Grice, H.P. 240
Gricean pragmatics 14
gross combinatoric restrictions 15
Gruber, J. 18
Gwynn, J.P.L. 295

Halliday, M.A.K. 168
Hasan, R. 168
Haugen, E. 172, 179
hearsay clitic 159
Hebrew 40
Heine, B. 12, 14, 297
Heroic NP Postposing 116
Herring, S. 14, 42, 51–52, 64, 135, 159, 301
Hindi 108, 297
Hoffman 43
Holisky, D. 24, 56
honorification 65, 285, 286
Hook, P. 108, 297
Hopi 259; impotential 259
Hopper, P. 298
hortative 61
hypercorrection (of conditional for adnominal form) 72
hypernym 26
hyponym 5, 26, 76, 80

idioms 155, 265, 299, 301
illocutionary force: nondeclarative 61
imperative 61
imperfective converb 162, 197-199, **202–204**, 208, 218, 221, 284
indefinite quantifiers: as modal polarity items 86
independence: strong 25; weak 25
indicative: auxiliary 168; AVC 88; mood 85, negative 174
indicative compound verb 6; diagnostic test 7
indirect discourse **153–166**, 241
Indo-Aryan 40, 297
inertia future 258
inertia world 258
infinitival relative 74
infinitive 34, 70, **74–78**; as citation form 69; as finite verb 74-75, 82; as least marked verb form 78; vs. emphatic verb form 127
INFL 2
inflection 53
inflectional function (of auxiliary) 6, 10, 13, 21
internal syntax **88**, 88-143
interval 62, 65; epistemic 172; temporal 65, 172, 301
irukka 18, 27, 51, 65, 167, **168–185**, 290; anterior temporal interval 177; circumstantial meanings 171; durative reading 175; durative tense 171; epistemic status 252; evidential perfect 172, 178; existential quantifier 170; indicative auxiliary 168, 171; interval 171; main verb 168; main verb use 169–171; marker of status 172; modal auxiliary 168; morphological prop for tense 170; negation 173; perfect tense 168, 172; perfect tense reading 176; progressive reading 175; progressive tense 172; prospective tense 168; temporal interval 172; vs. *viṭa* 177
Irula 31
island constraints 117, 122
iyalpu 62

Jakboson, R. 22, 24, 44, 49, 61, 78, 146, 153, 172, 184, 240
Jenkins, C 259
Jespersen, O 44, 154, 159
Johnson, M. 240
Jottimuttu, P 49

kālamayakkam 62
kālavaẓuvamaiti 62, 179
Kachru, Y. 43
Kandiah, T. 172, 184, 202
Kannada 294; antiperfect parallel 259
Karttunen, L. 180
kaṭṭa, as potential auxiliary 291
kāṭṭa **234–235**; vs. *pārkk*a 234
Keane, E. 33, 136, 139
Keay, J. 153
ki-echo Formation 84, 86, **136–140**; and modality 137
kiṭakka 18, 27, **216–220**; circumstantial readings 216; indicative auxiliary 218; main verb 217; verb class 217
kiẓikka 19, 32, 65, 106, 250–260, 290; without overt auxiliate 257
kiẓiya 19, 32, 65, 250–260
koḷḷa 19, 23, 51, 151, 167, **197–208**; and imperfective converb 202; as main verb 197; as modal auxiliary 197; as class I verb 199; as class IV verb 199; Brahmin dialect 181; consequence 201; from Old Tamil *koṭa* 199; indicative auxiliary use 198; instrumentality 201; progressive tense 198; properties of indicative 199; reflexive voice 198; reflexivity 207; self-benefactive voice 198; subject-orientation 206; tactic uses 200
Kothandaraman, P. 54
koṭṭa, as potential auxiliary 291
koṭukka 99, **229–231**, 261; benefactive voice 164
koṭuntamiẓ 31, 291
Krishnamurti, Bh. 2, 295
Kui 97
Kumari, T.C. 295
Kurux 296
Kurylowicz, J. 66
Kuteva, T. 21, 27, 297
Kuvi 97

Latin 13, 40, 74
Lees, R. 44
Lehmann, T. 31, 32, 40, 54, 61, 71
Levinson, S. 65, 199, 240, 245
lexical compound verb 5, 48, 81, 114, 130, 138, 265, 285, 291, 296; conjunctive 80; definition 5; idiomatic 80, 119, 131; infinitive 76; surface structure 90, 114
lexical decomposition 15
Lexical Insertion 15, 18, 43, 142
liminal phase 242, 247
liminalist hypothesis 27, **239-243**; *tīrkka* 281; *taḷḷa* 273; *vaẓiya* 267; liminality 242–243, 281; *oẓiya* 250
limitation: on parts of speech 28; on verbal categories 28
Lindenfeld, J. 161
Lindholm, J. 54, 74, 79, 114, 169, 170, 299
localism **25–28**
locative case 169
logical category 127
Lyons, J. 26

M-implicature 87
Macedonian 25
macro-durative aspect 203
main verb 26; vs. auxiliary verb in traditional grammar 3
major parts of speech 33
Malayalam 31, 295
malivuppatippu 173
Manda 97
markedness 14
markedness relation 14; simple vs. periphrastic verb 12, 14
Masica, C. 5, 297
matrix-complement construction 4, 76, 89, 102, 113, 115, 117; conjunctive 78; infinitive 76
maxim of relevance 240
McCawley, J.D. 14, 15, 74, 88, 100, 102, 163, 170, 174, 180
McCoard, R. 177
metaphor 1
micro-durative aspect 203
Middle Tamil 60, 70, 216, 221, 292; causative 106
mikuti 62
minor parts of speech 33; adverb 33; conjunction 33; determiner 33
missionary grammatical tradition 37, 40
modal auxiliary, *koḷḷa* 85
modal compound verb 6
modal polarity item 87
Modern Tamil 31
modes d'énonciation 146
mood 24, 62, 78, **86–87**, 149, 299
Morgan, J. 22
morphology: agglutinating 55; derivational 53; fusional 55, 57, 65; inflectional 53
motive hypothesis 26, 239, 242
movement rules 111-120

multiple auxiliaries, order of 165
Muria Gondi 39, **297**
muṟṟeccam 39. *See also* serial verb construction
muṟṟu viṉai 60, **78**
muṭikka **235–237**, 274
muṭiya **235–238**

naṉṉūl 37
narrated event 22; temporal organization of 147
narrative genre 14, 51, 221, 288
natural relevance **80**
Nayar, V.R. 295
negation **107–111**; modal AVC 108; morphological 107
negative data 32, 42, 51
Negative Raising 174
negative verb: combining form 70; conditional 70; conjugation 29, 77; paradigm 61; perfect in modal contexts 174
nested AVCs: derivation 135; multiple nestings 144, **160-166**, 201
neutralization 123; attitude vs. mood 159; AVCs vs. simple verbs 173; direct and indirect evidence 181; tense distinctions 182
niṟka 27, as potential auxiliary (in Modern Tamil) 291
nominalized verb 69
nonce formation 55
nondiscursive speech **146–153**, 151, 218; instructions 151; *kiṭakka* 216; laws 151; natural processes 151; prescriptions 151; threats 151
nonfinite verb, negative 72
noninertia futures 258
Norwegian 21
noun classifier systems 23
noun-verb compound 55
nuance 1, 48
number 23, 33, 65

object-orientation 194, 278
object-verb agreement 97
Old Tamil 21, 31, 37, 66, 116, 297; *aruḷa* 38; benedictive voice 38; benefactive voice 39; conjunctive form 38; disjunctive taxis 38; durative 38, 39; *irukka* 38; *iṭa* 38; negative auxiliary 38, 39; *oẓiya* 38; *paṭa* 38; passive voice 38; pejorative attitude 38; progressive tense 38; *tara* 39; *vara* 38, 39
onomatopoeia 57, 192, 270
onset (of event) 24, 57, 242
ontological commitment: epistemic perfect 179; mood; 62; tense-forms 65, 184
opposition: affective vs. effective voice 39; direct vs. indirect discourse 153; discursive vs. nondiscursive speech 146; infinitive vs. conjunctive 74, 83; modal vs. indicative 86; privative 86; simple vs. periphrastic verb 2, 12, 14, 65, 300; temporal interval vs. temporal point 65
optative 61
oẓiya 18, **247–250**; vs. *tolaiya* 249

Pagliuca, W. 298
pāl 23
Paramasivam, K. 40, 48, 54, 56, 179, 199, 206, 270
pārkka 19, **232–238**; derived postpositions 232; modal auxiliary 232; voice marker 233
participants: in the narrated event 22; in the speech event 22
particle 20
particle insertion **132–134**
passive 6, 38, 87, 262
past tense **62–63**; future time reference 46; primary use 62; secondary uses 63
paṭa 6
patch 22
Pengo 97
perfect tense: inferential 172; periphrastic verb 9; with *kiṭakka* 216
periphrastic verb form 53
Perkins, R. 298
permissive 61
Persian 66
person 23, 33, 65, 146; as metonym 146
personal ending (of Tamil verbs) 65, 66, 285, 296
Pesetsky, D. 22
petty combinatoric restrictions 15, 54
peyareccam 67, 67–68
phonological word 18
phonology 32; borrowed periphery 32; native core 32
plural: exclusive 65; inclusive 65, 249
pōka 19, **281–285**; change of state 282
pōkka 281

polycategorial attachment 18
Pope, G.U. 41
portmanteau morph 57
postposition 34
pōṭa 19, **274–277**, 291; auxiliary of abruptness 274; circumstantial readings 276; effective stems 274; vs. *vaikka* 274
pragmatic constraints 214; on AVCs 145; on syntactic structure 145
predicate nominal 35, 36, 78, 114, 115
Predicate Raising 18, 22, 213
preparedness condition 256
present tense **63–64**; primary use 63; secondary use 64; past time reference 64
presupposition 110, 245
progressive; activity predicate 175
projection: auxiliate 87; auxiliate to AVC 53
prospective tense 6, 65, 253, 281
protasis 25, 71
Proto-Dravidian 210
Pullum, G. 50
punctual contexts 139

Q-implicature 240
qualifier (verbal category) 23, 239
quantifier (verbal category) 23, 240
quantifier indefinite 170

Raising to Subject Position 22
Ramanujan, A.K. 42, 178
Ramasamy, K. 121
redundancy rule 43
Reduplication **130–132**, 140, 145; iterative 130; lexical compound verb 80, 130-131; modal AVC 132
reference time 254
reflexive 205
Reichenbach, H. 61, 177, 240
reincorporation (phase) 242
relative clause 68
RCF. *See* Relative Clause Formation
Relative Clause Formation 115, **120–123**, 144; adnominal strategy 121; correlative strategy 121; equi-strategy 121
relative tense. *See* taxis
Renou, L. 21
reported speech 153
Right Dislocation 17, **116–118**; formulation 116
Right-Node Raising 128

Romance languages 9
Ross, J.R. 50

S-deletion 17, **123–127**; formulation 124
same-subject condition (on conjunctive form) 79
Sanskrit 32, 55
periphrastic future 21
Sartre, J.P. 267
satellites (of AVC) 10, 16, 54, 81, 89, 124, 142
Scandinavian languages 172, 179
Schiffman, H. 1, 42, 43-44, 169, 178, 244, 269
Scholten, C.G.M. 14
scope: modal vs. indicative 163
Scrambling 18, 89, **111–114**, 112, 265; and AVC 114
Searle, J. 256
selection restrictions 15, **101–102**
self-affective auxiliary 206
semantic primes 18
semi-direct discourse 155
separation (phase of event) 242
serial verb construction 21, 39, 61
shifter 23, 61, 154
Shopen, T, 22
simple verb 10, 53
Sinhala 15
Slavic 239, 294
South Asian *Sprachbund* 297
Spear, A. 7
speech event 22
squish 50
Sridhar, S.N. 295
Stankiewicz, E. 53
state 57, 102, 176, 228, 254; predicates 202
stative participle 203
status 23, 167, 179, 239, 240, 294; *āka* 214; prospective status 167
Steever, S.B. 31, 37, 41, 42, 54, 74, 116, 159, 249
strict subcategorization **91–94**; rules 15
style 1, 44
Subbarao, K. 295
Subject-Auxiliary Inversion 7, 8, 50
Subject-Object-Verb (word order) 34
subject-orientation 204, 280
Subject-Verb Agreement 39, 34, 61, **94–96**
subjectivity 148
supine 61
suppletion 13, 198

surface structure: surface structure formation rules 15
SVA 94. *See* Subject-Verb Agreement
Swedish 21
syntactic categories 20, 127

taḷḷa 19, 42, **268–273**; aspect 268, 273; aspectual class 269; attitude 268, 269; iterative predicates 269; transitivity 269, 270; vs. *vaẓiya* 273
Tamil lexicon 34
Tamil traditional grammar 37, 38
Tamil verb classification 55
tara **229–231**
taxis 19, 23, 24, 69, 80, 178, 185, 213, 200; prospective 225; subsequent 279
teḷivu 62
Tedeschi, P. 258
Telugu 295
temporal history 258
temporal interval 65, 172, 253, 254, 301
temporal organization 147; *See* éffectif.
tense 23, 34, 44, 61; correlation with status 179
tense-forms 62; periphrastic 65; primary use of 62; secondary use 62; simple 65
threats 150
tīra, as potential auxiliary 278
tiriya, as potential auxiliary 291
tīrkka 19, **277–281**
Toda 27, 137
tolaikka 19, 42, **243–247**, 290
tolaiya 18, 110, **243–247**
tolkāppiyam 37, 38, 46
transformation 7, 15, 22
transitivity: semantic 223, 269; syntactic 269; vs. effectivity 58
Traugott, E. 298
Tree Pruning 18, 142
tree structure: wellformedness 17
Turner, V. 242, 250

vaikka 19, **225–229**; anticipated consequence 225; causative verb 225; future utility 225; indicative auxiliary 225; intransitive auxiliate 226; main verb 225; subsequent taxis 225
Vale, R.N. 297
van Gennep, A. 242
vara 18, **220–225**; durative aspect 225; imperfective converb 221; nontactic use 220; past perfect 221; vs. *koṇṭu+irukka* 222
vaẓiya 19, 93, **263–268**; admirative attitude 265; as an idiom 265; iterative use 223; liminalist hypothesis 267; nonpunctual aspect 266, 267; pejorative attitude 265
Vendler, Z. 57, 175
verb base 55–60; imperfectivity 56-57, 236
verb form 54-55; finite 60-66; morphophonemic class 56; nonfinite 67-82
verb kinds: change of state 282; motion 26; transaction 254, 260, 262
Verb Raising 22
verb root 55, 56–57; durativity 56–57; event type 57
verbal categories 24, 44, 240, 294
verbal extension 392
verbal noun 67; verbal noun in *-al* 40
Verma, M.K. 297
viṉaippeyar 67-70. *See also* deverbal noun
viṉaiyeccam 48, 67, **70–74**, 168
Vinson, J. 41, 72
viracōẓiyam 37
viraivu 62, 63
viṭa 19, 23, 45, 51, 151, 167, **185–195**, 290; auxiliary verb uses 185; disjunctive anterior taxis 186; epistemic use 190; in indirect commands 193; in questions and answers 194; object-orientation 195; phonological reduction 196; status 186; taxis 185; temporal uses 189; verb of change of situation 190; voice 186
viẓa, as potential auxiliary 291
voice 23; voice suffix 55
vowel, overlong 156
VP-deletion 140

Western grammatical tradition: diachronic bias 8; lexical bias 8
Western traditional grammar 37
Wilson, D. 50
Whorf, B. 54, 179, 259
word order 20; SOV 34
word-formation rules 13, 22, 25, 28, 53;
word-order rule 20

Zwicky, A. 16

For Product Safety Concerns and Information please contact our EU representative GPSR@taylorandfrancis.com
Taylor & Francis Verlag GmbH, Kaufingerstraße 24, 80331 München, Germany

www.ingramcontent.com/pod-product-compliance
Lightning Source LLC
Chambersburg PA
CBHW071234290426
44108CB00013B/1411
* 9 7 8 1 1 3 8 9 9 6 7 3 1 *